Ibrahim Babangida

The Military, Politics and Power in Nigeria

Published by:
Adonis & Abbey Publishers Ltd
P. O. Box 43418
London, United Kingdom
SE11 4XZ

Nigeria
Adonis & Abbey Publishing Co
P.O. Box 10546
Abuja, Nigeria
Tel: +234 (0)8165970458

http://www.adonis-abbey.com
Email: editor@adonis-abbey.com

First Edition, May 2012

Copyright 2012 © Dan Agbese

British Library Cataloguing-in-Publication Data
A catalogue record for this book is available from the British Library

ISBN: 9781906704964 (paperback)
        9781906704971 (dust jacket)

The moral right of the authors has been asserted

All rights reserved. No part of this book may be reproduced, stored in a retrieval system or transmitted at any time or by any means without the prior permission of the publisher

Layout Artist, Jan B. Mwesigwa

Printed and bound in Great Britain

Ibrahim Babangida

The Military, Politics and Power in Nigeria

Dan Agbese

Contents

Contents v

Acknowledgements ix

Introduction xiv

Prologue
Stepping out of the Shadow 1

Chapter One
The Orphan 9

Chapter Two
Setting Out 19

Chapter Three
Good Bye, Set Square 41

Chapter Four
A Crack in the Wall 71

Chapter Five
The Rise of Yakubu Gowon 89

Chapter Six
The Baton Changes Again 109

Chapter Seven
The Dimka Coup 127

Chapter Eight
The Second Republic 157

Chapter Nine
The Augean Stable 173

Chapter Ten
In the Saddle 193

Chapter Eleven
The Parting of Ways 213

Chapter Twelve
Rocking the Boat 221

Chapter Thirteen
A New Political Order 263

Chapter Fourteen
The Shuffle 285

Chapter Fifteen
Hands across the Heart 301

Chapter Sixteen
Bridges across Nations 323

Chapter Seventeen
Crises of Power...349

Chapter Eighteen
June 12 377

Epilogue 403

References...409

Index 425

Dedication

For the Agbese Royal Family
Thank you all for being there for me.

Other Books by Dan Agbese

- Style, The Newswatch Style Book
- Fellow Nigerians: Turning Points in the Political History of Nigeria
- Nigeria, their Nigeria
- Style, A Guide to Good Writing
- The Reporter's Companion
- The Columnist's Companion: The Art and Craft of Column Writing

Books Edited

- Newswatch Conversation with IBB
- In the Service of My Country, Selected Speeches of Abdulahi Adamu, 1999-2007
- The Energy Crisis in Nigeria

Acknowledgements

A book begins its life as a mass of data gathered and sorted into meaningful heaps by researchers. My luck here came in the shape of my cousin, Steve Attah Esa. Steve is one of the most meticulous men in the tough and intricate business of research. His capacity for ferreting information, no matter how minor, was truly impressive. Within the first few weeks of his settling down into the research and despite the crying inadequacies of office and logistical support, he gathered almost everything written about President Ibrahim Babangida in the local and foreign news media in almost no time at all. No exaggeration.

I understood where his energy and enthusiasm came from. He had just picked up a master's degree in international law and diplomacy from the University of Jos when he joined me in researching this book. His lessons on research methodology and all that were still fresh in his mind. He put them to good use for me. Either he alone or both of us together conducted the more than fifty interviews with the members of the president's family, his primary and secondary school mates and classmates, some of his surviving primary and secondary school teachers, his colleagues in the armed forces, his civilian friends and political associates and a host of others.

The recollections of Babangida's childhood and his formative years make this a different biography from several books that came before it. Steve flawlessly transcribed all these interviews – and the files piled up in my study and, to be honest, gave me what was obviously the writer's equivalent of stage fright.

Steve has since moved on to better things in the presidency, thank goodness. I still regard him as my 'co-conspirator' in writing this book. I fully indemnify him against its inadequacies but share with him whatever commendations it may earn. For fear of saying much less than I intended in expressing my gratitude to him, permit me to settle for just this: thanks, Steve.

Anyone writing a biography is certain to confront tough challenges and frustrations. I had my fair share of those. Babangida was the main source of my frustrations. He gave me several appointments but failed to keep them after he left office. I was truly anxious to do more than fill in the gaps. I wanted the full story of what has passed into our political history as the June 12 debacle. He promised me documents but failed to give them to me. I should have known that June 12 remains a sensitive subject to him and the country.

Professor Isawa J. Elaigwu, professor emeritus and president of Inter-Government and Social Research, IGSR, Jos, read the first eight draft chapters of the book. And he became my needler, as in he needled me without let. He urged me to go ahead and finish the book even if I did not hear another word from Babangida on June 12. He put me in touch with a reputable publishing company in the United Kingdom, Adonis & Abbey.

I have very high regards for Elaigwu's opinions. Elaigwu is a renowned scholar and a prolific author. He wrote the very well regarded biography of former head of state, General Yakubu Gowon. His favourable opinion on my first attempt at writing a biography encouraged me to return to the trenches.

It should be obvious that I owe Elaigwu much more than I can say. Without his constant needling, this book would still be gathering dust on my library shelf as an unfinished manuscript. He offered me very valuable suggestions that helped to improve the book. I know I owe him a debt of gratitude that is more than I can repay. Thank you, *Degedege*.

I also did something rather daring. I pressed an officer and a gentleman into my service in the course of this work. I was anxious to ensure that all the facts in the book checked out. I reached out to a tough officer but a kindly soul, Brigadier-General Haliru Akilu, former director of Military Intelligence. He is one of the few younger elements in the armed forces that are very close to Babangida. Akilu offered me every assistance in my research into the life and times of Babangida. He granted me interviews and even helped me meet some other people who knew Babangida well and who were willing to talk about those things the public never knew about him.

I feared I might be pushing it by asking him to read the manuscript. But he put me at ease. He was happy to read it. He read it with a fine toothcomb. I am truly amazed by the intellectual rigour and meticulousness he brought to bear on the manuscript. He has a head full of all the facts and dates. He crosschecked information for me and helped in filling up gaps in the narrative. He saved me, in some cases, from the embarrassment of repeating popular but false stories of roles played by some individuals in the coup that brought Babangida to power.

General Akilu knows how I much value his help. If I cannot proclaim my gratitude loudly enough from this podium, he knows I will always remain grateful to him. Thanks again, general.

Let me now turn to my well-known foot soldiers, who have always been there for me and helped me struggle through one book after the other in the last few years. Here they are: Mohammed Haruna, the erudite newspaper columnist, Yakubu Mohammed, another well-known newspaper and magazine columnist and my younger brother and political scientist, Professor Pita Ogaba Agbese of the University of Northern Iowa in the United States of America. Each of them read the manuscript. Each of them balanced his tough views with kind words. The combined effect of these forced me to spend lonely days and nights in the trenches polishing the manuscript. The book, as usual, benefited immensely from their suggestions on its improvement. I am grateful to all of you, guys.

A new foot soldier made his debut here: my son, Okibe. He is a voracious reader. I was glad I pressed him into service too. He was so thorough that not even one misplaced comma or semi-colon escaped his eagle eyes. He picked out facts that either contradicted themselves or did not quite check out. He pointed out omissions and gaps in the narrative. As you would imagine, all these meant more work but think of the alternative – a book with gaping holes in it. I am grateful, son.

The man who made the book possible was, of course, General Ibrahim Badamasi Babangida himself. He was willing to let me tell his story. I sometimes wondered if he knew the risk he was taking with a rookie biographer. I should not have worried. At what I believed would be my last interview with him, I thanked him most sincerely for his time and his willingness to let me try my hands at telling his story. He surprised me by paying me what I came away with as the ultimate compliment from him. He said: "Dan, I have been told that you have credibility. I want to be part of that credibility." I felt humbled. I was glad he knew I was not going to write a hagiography – all the saccharine stuff that would make him sweet but a creature of the imagination without faults and without even a stray pimple on his face.

Babangida gave me all the help I needed to make this a complete story of his life and his times in office. He granted me four interviews – three before he left office and one after he left. Our first interview was at his new office in Aso Rock, Abuja, not long after he moved into the new federal capital; our second was in Harare, Zimbabwe, where he was attending a summit of heads of state of OAU, the third, which I thought was the final one, was in his office in Abuja. The fourth was in his Minna hilltop home in Niger State.

At each of these interviews, he was candid but never let down his guard. He is the real master of incomplete sentences but he is always charming about it. He does get away with a lot because he does not engage in combative interviews. He treats an interview like a friendly chat – and handles it ever so charmingly. I extend to him my profound gratitude.

Authors can never fully express the depth of their gratitude to the many guardian angels that they press into service in the course of their writing a book. I am in good company. I cannot even possibly remember everyone who assisted me along the way in diverse ways with research, information and encouragement and suggestions in the course of writing this book. There were big players and bit part players. I acknowledge everyone's help. I am grateful to every one of them. Not every one of them has been named here but all of them have my tonnes of gratitude.

Many people granted Steve Attah Esa and me interviews for this book. They ranged from Babangida's family members, his former teachers, his former school and classmates, military colleagues, both junior and senior, and the young public servants whose friendship he cultivated on the way to the top.

Some of them necessarily stood out by the quality of information they shared with us. It is only fair that I single them out for their invaluable contributions to the enrichment of this book. They were the former Chief of Staff, Army, the late Major-General Hassan Usman Katsina, former head of state, General Abdulsalami Abubakar, former Chief of Naval Staff and later Deputy Chief of Defence Staff, Vice-Admiral Murtala Nyako, Lt-General Garba Duba, Lt-General Joshua Dogonyaro, Major-General Gado Nasko, Major-General Sani Sami, Major-General Mohammed Magoro, Col Sani Bello, the late Major-General John Mark Inienger, Major-General Chris Abutu Garuba, Brigadier-General John Shagaya, Col Abubakar Dangiwa Umar, Brigadier-General Tony Ukpo, the late Col Yohanna Madaki, Hajia Hanatu Gambo, the late Alhaji Kere Ahmed, Alhaji Aliyu Wushishi, the late Alhaji Aliyu Mohammed, the late Yahuza Makongiji, Alhaji Musa Izom, Professor J. Ndagi, the late Jerome Idoko, Mr. Leslie Akande, Malam Dauda Gulu Yunusa and Alhaji Buba Ahmed.

Babangida's ADC at the time, the late Col (and later Major-General) Nuhu Bamali, deserves to be remembered here for facilitating some of the interviews I had with the former president. He once told me: "Dan, the president is relying on this book." It is a pity he did not live to see its publication. Thanks, general, for being there for me.

I acknowledge with gratitude the support of my publishers, Adonis & Abbey. Dr. Jideofor Adibe, an executive director of the company, deserves my special thanks for superb editing and libel reading of the manuscript.

Readers are kindly invited to note two important points. The first is that the military men who played key roles in this narrative did so at various times and with various lower ranks. In almost all cases, by the time the story ended, they had risen through much higher ranks in the armed forces as one, two, three or four star generals. However, I chose to use the rank of each man, including Babangida, as it was at the time such a person played the particular role that formed part of the Babangida story. I believe it would be wrong, for instance, to call Babangida a general when the first coup took place in 1966. He was a lieutenant.

The second point worth noting is the use of quotations in the book. All quotations not referenced were taken from interviews granted my research assistant and me. I refrained from prefacing all such quotations with their source, as is the tradition in newspapers. It would make poor reading.

When the writer's work is done he remembers his family and friends who endured his absence when he was physically present. For the writer, those lonely moments with the computer screen and the keyboard usually permit no third party. It is a hallowed ritual that makes the frustrations barely bearable. The good thing is that you can always turn to your family and friends later and say: 'Pardon me for appearing to neglect you. It was not for the love of the computer. Duty called. But thanks for your understanding and support.'

Introduction

This book too was a victim of June 12. I started researching it long before June 12 chanced along. But it affected its planned date of publication in two significant ways. Firstly, June 12 was a messy epitaph to Babangida's eight years in office. A rush to publish the book at the time became clearly inadvisable. It risked being dismissed off hand as a condemnable attempt to launder the image of the man on whom almost everyone was anxious to bury in a mountain of unsightly opprobrium.

Secondly, Babangida was the principal actor in that political drama of the absurd. I felt that this book would be incomplete without the full story of June 12 – how it happened and why it happened. It is also part, and perhaps, the most important part of his story. Despite several servings from other observers, close or distant to the annulment of 'the freest and fairest election' in the country, the leading actors kept mum. I thought I could break through the mist of June 12 and expose the lies and the half-truths and the outright duplicity of some of its protagonists busy parading themselves as the champions of the debacle.

The only man who could tell the authentic story of June 12 was Babangida. The only man not willing to tell it was Babangida. At my first interview with him after he left office, he threw teasers at me. He appeared almost eager to tell the story. He gave me snippets. These appetisers whetted my palate for the main course. He promised me documents and tapes of the Armed Forces Ruling Council meetings in which the annulment of the election was the only subject of discussion. The documents, he assured me, would clearly show me that the latter day champions of June 12 were really its sworn enemies. Twice he agreed to see me again on it and twice he did not feel obliged to keep his promise to me. The reporter in me was looking for an exclusive from the former president. I guess his instinct told him he was walking into a reporter's trap. He turned back from the path. I felt frustrated, to put it mildly.

I approached this biographical undertaking with the ingrained curiosity of the reporter - and an old one at that. But it is an intellectual rather than a reportorial enquiry. I wanted to explore the Babangida mystique, his indefinable stamp on his style of governance. To borrow from the Americans, I wanted to see if the man was real. He came on the scene on August 27, 1985, waving the banner of human rights and offered himself almost merely as the servant of the people – he and his colleagues laid no claims on monopoly of wisdom – and thus invited the people to lead him where they wished to be led. This was unusual in a military dictator. His policies and programmes recognised no sacred boundaries. He wanted to bring everything into the Babangida orbit with his indelible stamp on it. What was pushing him and where was it pushing him and the country?

I suspected the answers to the making of the country's future president might be buried somewhere in his background. I hunted and mined that background – his parentage and early life in primary and secondary schools and his military career. The key to the Babangida mystique is in his character. He is a complex character, as complex and as complicated as they come. His towering contradictions that came to be the hallmark of his style of governance should arouse the curiosity of psychoanalysts. You can be sure no one will take it up.

We, Nigerians act quite strangely in certain respects. We are perhaps the most verbally aggressive people on earth yet we are generally and inexplicably uncurious about our leaders. We hardly know our leaders. We never try to know them so that we can put their decisions and actions in perspective. We simply accept each one of them thrown or thrust on our political stage as the leader we had been waiting. We accept him instantly as a God send. And our leaders crowned with this halo felt obliged to act to type – as God send. Smart men and women give us lollypop offerings as biographies that tell us nothing we need to know about our leaders. These hagiographies are intended to consolidate the halo and the persona.

My ambition, of course, was to write a definitive biography of the most controversial political figure in the country today. Babangida, love him or hate him, remains an issue in our national politics. Yes, as the years distance him from his days in power and as new events shape and reshape the direction of the politics of Nigeria his era begins the inexorable process of becoming a distant memory. The echoes fade into the distance, the memory fades but time does not obliterate it. Babangida more than other ruler, military or civilian before or after him, was the architect of the new political shape of the country. He did it by default – and it came by accident. He cannot take credit for it because June 12 was a political accident he did not expect to happen. It was an unintended consequence of his transition to civil rule programme that he dribbled past one goal post after the other. Is life unfair?

The Babangida era is now firmly locked up in our national history. It remains a very important part of our national story. This book is an intellectual excursion into that era and the role of the military in the politics and power struggle in Nigeria. The story cannot be told in one book. This book does not pretend to *the* definitive story. It is only a modest contribution to the story of Nigeria. As a biography, it is not even the exclusive story of one man and his place and role on the political stage. It is the story of several other actors on the stage and how they too contributed to events that shaped the Babangida era, and, naturally, the *post* Babangida era.

The Babangida era did not begin on August 27, 1985. The events that shaped it did not begin on that day either. Nor did they end on August 27, 1993 – the day he stepped aside from the presidency and became just another private Nigerian again. He was part of the story but it was not his story from the beginning. His decision to go into the army, for instance, may be seen as the beginning of his story. But it was not his decision. The decision was made for him and eight of his former classmates in the Provincial Secondary School, Bida, by the dynamics of the Nigerian political story.

We are all subject to the fate decreed by the ubiquitous 'what if?' question. What if the northern establishment allowed the young Babangida to pursue his initial ambition of becoming a civil engineer? What if Nzeogwu and his fellow four majors had not dragged the army into our national politics on January 15, 1966? No prize for the right answers. Life would have taken Babangida through a different path. If he had become an engineer, he most probably would have joined the civil service as a pupil engineer and risen through the ranks and retired.

Had the army stayed off politics, Babangida, like all the military rulers before and after him, might have ended his military career as an unknown face and name even on the streets of his home Minna, Niger State. Had the coup been a genuine revolutionary intervention by the army for national salvation and the soldiers did not turn the guns on themselves, the story of Nigeria would have been different too. And Babangida and the other khaki men might have played their different roles differently.

Several books were written on the unfolding era when Babangida was in power. Perhaps several more have been written since then. And many more may still be written from other perspectives. It is no longer possible to tell our national story without Babangida's part in it. He was the leading actor on our political stage for eight years. In that time, he affected the course of our national events, for better, for worse, in a way that few, if any, before him did. As we say in Agila about the alligator, Babangida has since left the stream but his tail is still in the water. Those who want to dismiss him as an irrelevant quantity in national politics have problems doing that. Anyone who thought the former president was a superannuated political actor must have been surprised by the kind of following he garnered when he teased the nation into believing he wanted to contest the presidential election in 2011.

Babangida has unwittingly spurned a cottage industry. That industry relentlessly churns out only one product: criticism, more uninformed than informed. His good deeds have been more or less buried by his wrongs.

Of these, of course, June 12 is it. June 12 is his albatross, his cross. He will carry it, for better or worse, for the rest of his life. And because of June 12, some lesser men after Babangida strut the stage, savouring local and international accolades. Yet, interestingly, Babangida made June 12 possible – by default. And by default, he consecrated June 12 as the defining moment and the definitive factor in our national politics. It does not matter that he takes no credit for it. It matters that in June 12, he created what consumed him but saved Nigeria.

Prologue

Stepping out of the Shadow

At the close of work on Thursday, February 12, 1976, Lt-Colonel Ibrahim Babangida, inspector of recce, Nigerian Army, went to Mayong Barracks, Yaba, Lagos, to visit some of his friends. One of them was Colonel Abdul Wya; the other was Colonel Ayuba Tense. The three officers, joined by a few others, had some drinks in the officers' mess. They chatted generally about nothing in particular.

Col. Babangida is a gregarious man. He loves the company of his friends. He has always conducted his social life in obedience to a Hausa proverb, *zumunta a kafa take*. Its rough translation: you build love and friendship with the feet. This time, however, there was something more to his gregarious nature. As a lieutenant colonel, he was the most junior member of the Supreme Military Council in the Murtala Muhammed administration. He played a key role in bringing that government to power in the overthrow of General Yakubu Gowon on July 29, 1975. His regular visits to army barracks and such middle-ranking and senior officers like Col Wya provided a good link between such level of officers and the government. The government felt it needed to keep its fingers on the pulse of the soldiers, to monitor their feelings and thus avoid the mistake the Gowon administration made of keeping its distance from its main constituency.

Babangida fitted the role. A relaxed, witty and genial officer with a gift for remembering names and faces, the colonel was popular with the officers and men. And he is a generous man - generous with his time and his resources. He almost always invites other people's confidence. People trust him partly because he is a disarmingly simple man and partly because he always stood on the side of junior officers and other ranks.

Babangida returned to his official residence at No. 19, Ikoyi Crescent, Ikoyi, Lagos, later that evening. Shortly after dinner, his phone rang. It was Wya calling to invite Babangida to a party that night. As a young officer, Babangida loved parties and the good life. He thought about the invitation. He was tempted to go but somehow, his reply was no. He had been out most of the day after work. He was now tired. He had an early day ahead of him. Col. Babangida was chairman of the re-organising committee of the Nigerian Army. Government was planning a massive demobilisation of the army. The plan had been in the works since the end of the Nigerian civil war in January 1970, when the country found itself saddled with an army too large and unnecessary for peacetime duties. The Gowon administration had been tardy over the issue. The Murtala administration saw it as one of its immediate national assignments. Lt-General Theophilus Yakubu Danjuma, the Chief of Army Staff, appointed Babangida as head of a committee to work out the demobilisation plan. It was the colonel's first major professional assignment in the new military administration.

After weeks of painstaking work, he was now ready to brief his superiors. The briefing was scheduled for 9 o'clock the following morning, Friday, February 13. He needed to have a clear head for the assignment ahead. He, therefore, declined Wya's invitation to the party. He retired to bed early.

Babangida is an early riser. He has a habit of getting to his office either at the same time with the cleaners or shortly after them. The next day, as usual, he was up early. He was in the bath at 6 o'clock when he heard the phone ringing. His young wife, Maryam, answered it. It was Wya at the other end. It was rather early and Mrs Babangida wondered why. Wya put her at ease. He told her he had an important message for her husband because he was travelling out of Lagos that morning. He neither gave Mrs Babangida the message to pass on to her husband nor did he request the colonel to return his call. Babangida himself was slightly puzzled over what the colonel had said. He was not aware that Wya was travelling out of Lagos. They were together most of the previous day but he did not mention the trip. But the colonel knew such things were not unusual in the army. When duty calls, officers must obey.

Babangida shrugged it off and went on to prepare for his work with his eye on the wall clock. He did not want to be late for that important meeting. All the general officers commanding the three divisions of the army were already in town for it. With a good-bye wave to his wife, Babangida jumped into his official car. As his driver drove out of his residence, he noticed the traffic indicator indicating a right turn. He ordered his driver to turn left. It was instinctive. He thought the traffic would be heavy on the right route. He did not want to be delayed. His driver took the new route and entered Kingsway Road. They drove on to the colonel's office at Army Headquarters, Ministry of Defence, on the Marina.

There was a slight air of subdued confusion at the army headquarters. Groups of soldiers and civilians were talking rather excitedly among themselves. Babangida took in the scene but thought nothing of it. It was a typical daily scene at the ministry of defence. Maybe, he thought to himself, by the time he was through with the re-organisation and the demobilisation of the army, there won't be much room for idle soldiers spending their early morning in idle gossip among themselves and with civilians.

Then Babangida saw Major-General Alani Akinrinade, GOC, 1 Division of the Nigerian Army, based in Kaduna.

General Akinrinade: "My friend, where have you been? We have been looking for you."

The colonel was surprised. Why would anyone be looking for him? He was still very early for the 9 o'clock meeting. All he could mutter was: "But sir, I am not late."

The general puckered his brows in genuine surprise. "Haven't you heard what happened?" he asked the colonel, some irritation creeping into his voice.

"No Sir," the colonel replied. The general wasted no further time. "There is a coup," he told Col Babangida. He ordered him to go and see the Chief of Army Staff immediately.

Babangida bounded upstairs towards the office of the chief of army staff. His heart was pounding. Who, he wondered was behind this latest madness? The Murtala administration had come to power six months earlier on a wave of popular support. The policies of the administration were winning it friends almost daily throughout the country. People, once thought to be untouchables, had been reduced to jobless people as the administration moved into the public service, getting rid of "dead woods" and those with conspicuously declining productivity. Who must have interrupted this? How come he, the contact man with the junior officers, had no inkling of the dangerous plan afoot? As the questions crowded him, Babangida noticed that the news of the coup had begun to spread. Most of the senior officers at defence headquarters had their radio sets tuned to the Nigerian Broadcasting Corporation and were listening to Lt-Col Bukar Suka Dimka broadcasting the *overthrow* of the Murtala administration.

This was a national tragedy. Babangida knew it. Babangida and Dimka were friends. At Babangida's wedding in 1969, Dimka played a major role as a member of the organising committee. What, the colonel still wondered, must have driven him to this reckless military adventure? Dimka was not the sort of man who would organise something as delicate as a coup d'état successfully. Dimka demonstrated that with his coup announcement. He imposed *a dawn to dusk* curfew throughout the country and warned that anyone who tried to oppose him would be shot. His curfew meant that everyone must be indoors from morning until night and then free to be out all night. That a lieutenant colonel in the Nigerian Army did not know the difference between *dusk* and *dawn* did strike everyone as amusing in the dangerous business of toppling a government.

Gen. Danjuma had anxiously waited for Col Babangida. As soon as the colonel arrived, the general, an austere professional soldier with little time for pleasantries, ordered him to "go and flush out" Dimka from the radio station. There was no time to waste.

Babangida dashed downstairs. The subdued air of confusion he noticed a few minutes earlier had thawed into a free-flowing river of confusion. Everyone had now heard the news. The reaction was typical of a confused situation. Subdued bedlam among the various small groups of discussants.

Babangida picked his way through the milling, confused crowd in a hurry. He had no illusions about the enormity of his new assignment. Flushing out the coup plotters would certainly lead to loss of lives. What was more, he was going to take on his own friend in the possibly bloody battle ahead. Duty, he knew, called. And duty comes before friendship and the sentiments attached thereto.

As he pushed his way through the crowd, Babangida began to work out in his mind a plan to "flush out" Dimka. He decided that he was going to use minimum force for a maximum result. His immediate problem now was how to get out of the ministry of defence to where he could mobilise loyal troops. He was not even sure where he could find such troops. He did not know yet who was in it and who wasn't. As he thought about this, his dilemma deepened.

The traffic congestion that morning was typical of Lagos. A gridlock. There was almost no movement. Babangida's driver had gone to park his car at the official parking lot. As the colonel puzzled over what to do, a military policeman, Cpl Ochodugbo Ogiri, arrived on his army motorcycle. For the second time that morning, Babangida's instinct made the decision for him. He jumped on the pillion of the machine and ordered the bewildered corporal to take him to Bonny Camp, Victoria Island, on the double. On the way, the colonel changed his mind and ordered the soldier to head for Ikeja cantonment instead. A colonel on the pillion of a motorcycle being ferried across town by a corporal was an unusual sight. The time on February 13, 1976, was unusual.

One of Babangida's most daring military exploits, "the flushing out of Dimka" had begun. It was to bring him to public attention as a brave soldier. When the coup was put down, Babangida became almost a living legend. His name went before him.

Mohammed Haruna, a veteran journalist, former managing director of New Nigerian Newspapers Limited as well as former editor-in-chief of *Citizen* weekly newsmagazine, is one of Babangida's younger friends. He recalls that by the time he met the colonel for the first time sometime in 1976, "there was already this aura of an invincible person, somebody who went out there and confronted Dimka unarmed. I mean, you saw him there at the airport and you could see that he was the star of the crowd, sitting there and everybody surrounding him. You could see that everybody was revolving around him."

In a confidential report dated April 12, 1976, the army recommended Babangida for the military award of River Niger Star for the role he and four other officers played in crushing the attempted coup .The military secretary, Col Gado Nasko, wrote of Col Babangida:

> This officer at the greatest risk to his personal safety and the nation in particular, confronted the leader of the attempted coup and when appeal to reason failed, directed troops to finally crush the attempted coup.

It took almost eight years before the rest of the civilian population heard of Babangida again. On December 31, 1983, the armed forces overthrew the Shehu Shagari administration in the Second Republic. On January 1, 1984, Babangida, a major general, was named Chief of Army Staff in the new military administration headed by Major-General Muhammadu Buhari. He had made it to the top of his profession, which is the ultimate ambition of all military officers. As Chief of Army Staff, Babangida was also a member of the highest ruling body in the country, the Supreme Military Council, SMC. He served in that body in the Murtala/Obasanjo administration as well. It was, therefore, a return to a familiar turf after the civilian interregnum of four years and three months.

Babangida kept to the background, more or less for twenty months. He granted only one major media interview and that was to *The Guardian* newspaper, in which his most memorable quote was that the administration would *not tolerate undue radicalism.* It was seen as a veiled warning to the young and radical elements in the armed forces who might have felt that their older and senior colleagues were short of the radical transformation they had envisaged in effecting the change of government.

On August 27, 1985, the general was in the news again. A few hours earlier, Nigerians woke up to the rather unsettling martial music on their radio sets. The military had struck again - against themselves. Brigadier Joshua Dogonyaro, the man who broadcast the change of government early that morning, told the nation that the Buhari administration, accused of a multitude of sins of omission and commission, had been toppled. Major-General Ibrahim Badamasi Babangida emerged as the new military leader, taking on the title of president.

At long last, he had arrived at the pinnacle of power. The general took part in all the successful coups in the country since July 1966. He was always one of the kingmakers. Now he was the king. Looking rather casual in his army fatigue, he greeted the nation with what became his trademark - a toothy smile. But he was greeted with a cautious applause occasioned by a certain degree of public cynicism. What difference would he make? What was more worrying to the generality of the people was that the change meant that there would most probably be another long winter of military rule in the country before the civilian politicians would be allowed back on the political turf.

In his maiden broadcast to the nation, Babangida promised to make a difference. He tried to re-assure the people that it was not for himself that he took on the mantle of leadership of the country but for the country itself. This was how he memorably put it:

> This country has had since independence a history mixed with turbulence and fortune. We have witnessed our rise to greatness, followed with a decline to the state of a bewildered nation. Our human potentials have been neglected, our natural resources put to waste. A phenomenon of constant insecurity and overbearing uncertainty has become characteristic of our national existence. My colleagues and I are determined to change this course of history.

The cloud of cynicism still hovered over Babangida's sunny disposition. His honesty in offering the country a new kind of leadership with a sense of direction clearly mapped out, had yet to pierce that cloud. Still, there was something fresh from a military dictator who was anxious right from the beginning not to be seen as a dictator. In the months following his assumption of office, Babangida opened his doors to all comers and all shades of political opinions. He threw his arms around the nation in a warm bear hug. The nation saw a new man, a new military leader and a new style of political leadership. Sure-footed but casual, he had told the nation in his first broadcast that he and his colleagues did not claim monopoly of knowledge or wisdom in the task he and his colleagues had set for themselves. He needed everyone's advice and he was prepared to listen to anyone or groups of persons who had anything worthwhile to offer him. The nation, naturally, responded to his friendship and his humaneness and began to call him by his initials: **IBB**.

This is the story of **IBB**, the little orphan from Minna, Niger State, who became his own man at the age of fourteen. It is the story of his life and his meticulous plan for a steady rise to the top of his profession and the leadership of his country. It is the story of his leadership of the most populous black nation in the world. It is the story of his promise to his country and its people on the morning of August 27, 1985. It is the story of power and politics in Nigeria. It is the story of his daring moves. And it is the story of the promise of a revolution that took him and the nation that far and yet not that far.

Babangida was an astute and calculating officer. Imaginative and pragmatic, bold but flexible, generous but tough, Gen Babangida touched the lives of all Nigerians for good or ill, redrew the political and administrative map of the country and shook up virtually all its institutions. He is many things to many people. Like the elephant described by the blind men, everyone has his own definition of the real Babangida, depending on how he feels him. This, then, is the story of Nigeria, Babangida's Nigeria. It is also the story of its politics and the power game with two sets of opposing actors – civilian politicians and military politicians.

Chapter One

The Orphan

He wasn't from a rich family
–Kere Ahmed

Seventy-four kilometres west of Minna, capital of Niger State, lies Wushishi, headquarters of the local government that bears its name. It is a fairly developed local government headquarters with modern amenities. The roads in the inner sections of the town are well laid out and tarred. They bear the names of important Nigerian citizens. Near the hub of the town where the main motor park is located, two roads join the Zungeru-Bida thoroughfare. The road to the left from the Zungeru end approach is called Maryam Babangida Drive, named after the First Lady, Mrs Maryam. The road to the right from the same end is M.T. Kontagora Road, named after the minister of works and housing in the Babangida administration, Major-General Mamman Kontagora. The main road in the town is Ibrahim Babangida Road, named after the nation's former number one citizen, President Ibrahim Babangida.

It is, naturally, the most important road in the local government headquarters and, therefore, the busiest. The Water Board, the Electricity Board and People's Bank are located on this road. But the most important landmark on that road is the town's only hospital, Innawuro Aishatu Babangida Hospital, named after the president's mother. The president himself on a state visit to Niger, his home state, commissioned the People's Bank in 1991. Wushishi is President Babangida's ancestral home. It is a home he has not forgotten.

The town now has pipe-borne water, telephone and electricity. Television antennae sprout from the top of private homes in most parts of the town. There are a few palatial buildings there too. One of them belongs to Lt-General Muhammadu Inuwa Wushishi, Chief of Army Staff in the Second Republic. Garba Wushishi, minister of information in the Shagari administration, owns another prominent house there. The third such house is owned by Alhaji Mustapha Aliyu. These palatial buildings more or less welcome visitors entering the town from the Zungeru end to the north. But most of the town has not shed the rural look typical of northern Nigerian towns - thatched mud houses and mud houses with weather-beaten corrugated iron roofs. Wushishi has two secondary and two primary schools.

In the early part of this century, Wushishi was a small, rural settlement, said to have been founded by the Nupe who still predominate there. Like a magnet, Wushishi attracted people from various parts of Nigeria - Igbos from the Eastern Region, Yoruba from the Western Region and Hausa/Fulani from the Northern Region and minority ethnic groups from almost every part of the country. The rainbow collection of big and small ethnic groups made Wushishi something of a cosmopolitan town in an interesting rural setting. Hundreds of the early Igbo and Yoruba settlers chose to "naturalise" in Wushishi. Today, their descendants know no other homes in the country but Wushishi.

One of the early Hausa settlers in Wushishi was Malam Ibrahim, a young man from Sokoto. He and his parents left Sokoto several years earlier and settled in Kano. Ibrahim was an adventurous young man. He did not like the settled life of his parents. He wandered off in search of adventure and excitement. No one knew what was driving him but he was always on the move. He stopped over in several villages long enough to rest and earn enough money to take him to another town or village. He travelled by foot and sometimes he rode a horse or a donkey. He had no prior idea of where he was going. He just went where his instinct told him. He settled down briefly in Kontagora. Something told him to move on. He did.

Ibrahim's next stop was Wushishi. He had no plans to settle down there either although he liked the village. He decided to remain there for a while, do some farming and then get on with his adventures. Love changed his plans. Ibrahim met Halima, a beautiful, young Hausa girl, and fell in love with her. Something told him he had found a wife. Like all young men smitten with the bug of love, Ibrahim wasted little time in making his intentions known to the girl and her parents. Ibrahim was a good-looking young man. Halima loved him. Her parents accepted him but on one condition. If he wanted to marry their daughter, he must settle down in Wushishi. They did not want their married daughter to be taken out of the village to where they might possibly never see her again. Malam Ibrahim was confronted with a dilemma. But love will always conquer. He accepted the condition. His wandering days had come to an end.

Ibrahim was popularly called Malam because he became a well-known koranic teacher in the town. He made his home near a tall tree called rimi. His nickname, Malam na Rimi, came from that tree. The tall tree 'died' and was felled only in 1990. The place where it stood remains undeveloped, perhaps in honour of the late Malam. Malam Umaru Yaro, one of the oldest men in Wushishi, remembers Malam Ibrahim as a very prominent and popular man in the town. He was revered as a learned man, a man of wisdom by all the villagers. He took young boys and girls under his protective wings and taught them about Islam and the mysteries of Allah and the works of the prophet. He gave his time to the affairs of Wushishi and was always ready to assist all those who needed his help.

Malam Ibrahim's marriage was blessed with six children - four boys and two girls. They were, in order of birth, Fatima, Muhammadu Badamasi, Aliyu Wushishi, Hassan, Mohammed Danladi and Hauwa'u. They all grew up in Wushishi.

Around 1936, Muhammadu Badamasi, the second oldest child and the first son, was employed as a messenger to the colonial district officer in Minna. His new job kept him shuttling between Minna and a village called Tah. In 1938, he decided to settle down in Minna partly to make his job easier and partly because Minna, headquarters of Niger Province, was developing fast as the biggest town in the area. He wanted to be part of that development.

He was already married to Aishatu, a very beautiful and fair-complexioned girl. Malam Yaro, her only surviving brother, says his sister was a very beautiful girl. He still lives in their old house where he and his late sister grew up in Wushishi. The building now has a red brick fence around it.

When Muhammadu Badamasi moved to Minna, his brothers, Aliyu, Hassan, Mohammed Danladi and his sister, Hauwa'u, the youngest, all decided to go and live there too. There was no particular reason for this. The most probable reason was that all of them wanted to continue to live in one locality as one big, happy family.

Malam Muhammadu Badamasi's job made him a very important man in Minna. As a messenger, he had access to those in authority, the most important people, the clerks and other administrative staff of the provincial administration in Minna. His position attracted friends to him. He married two more wives. His first wife, Aishatu, had five children for him. But most of them died in infancy. Their first child was a girl, Halimatu, who died. The second child, a boy, named Ibrahim, was born on August 17, 1941. He was variously known as Ibrahim Maigari, Ibrahim Maigari Wushishi and later as Ibrahim Muhammadu. After Ibrahim, Aishatu had another girl, Nana, and then a set of female twins, Hasanna and Husaina, all of whom died in infancy. Their last child was Hannatu Gambo.

Only Ibrahim and Hannatu Gambo are still alive. Ibrahim is General Ibrahim Badamasi Babangida, former president of the Federal Republic of Nigeria and Commander-in-Chief of the Armed Forces. Hannatu Gambo is a housewife and lives with her second husband in Minna. Their father had four other wives, none of whom had a surviving child.

When Ibrahim was about five, his father took him back to Wushishi where he lived with his relations for sometime before returning to Minna to begin his education in the primary school in the town.

Aishatu did not quite bring up her two children. She divorced Malam Muhammadu and married an emir of Wushishi when Ibrahim and his sister Hannatu were very young. But two years later, she took ill and died. Muhammadu did not live much longer after that. He too took ill. He had jaundice. When his illness became serious and the local herbal treatment could not help him, Malam Muhammadu was taken to the family home of his close friend, Ahmadu Bawa, Madaki Kontagora, in Kontagora to attend the only hospital in the area, a missionary hospital known as Tungan Magajiya; not to be confused with a village that bears the same name. Malam Muhammadu retired from his job as a messenger in 1948. He never recovered from his illness. He died at Kontagora. He was only 45 years old.

His good friend, Malam Ahmadu, was the headmaster of the Minna primary school. One of his former pupils, former head of state, General Abdulsalami Abubakar, remembers him as "a bloody good teacher, kind-hearted but a very strict disciplinarian."

On the death of his good friend, Malam Ahmadu took Ibrahim under his protective wings in the school. He had an obligation to his late friend to help bring up his only son. He was one of the earliest people to make an impression on the young Ibrahim. He was strict but fair. He was kind but he did not let anyone take advantage of that, least of all, his late friend's only son, Ibrahim.

Ibrahim and Hannatu, now orphans, were taken to live with their grandmother, Halima, popularly known in Minna as Maigari, at Plot S.E. 55A, Bosso Road, Minna. The old woman was very close to her late son. She transferred that affection to his first and only surviving son, making sure he lacked nothing. She was fiercely protective of the boy and showered him with a combination of the maternal and paternal love fate had denied him from his natural parents. She took such good care of her grandchildren that Hannatu did not even know she was not her mother until she grew up and married. "It took me so long because my grandmother treated me like her own daughter," she says.

Like all young Muslim boys and girls, Ibrahim went to a Koranic school in Minna. But from his close association with the colonial authorities, his father knew then that Western education would become an important thing in the near future in the country. He sent Ibrahim to the Gwari Native Authority primary school in Minna in 1950. He went to the primary school on the same day with his childhood friend, Abdulsalami Abubakar. They have walked the same path ever since. Both of them joined the army and each became a four star general. And interestingly, both of them also ruled Nigeria: Babangida as president for eight years and Abubakar as a head of state for only eleven months. Malam Mohammed Bako, a close friend of both families, took the two future generals to school. Their first teacher in the primary school was Yakubu Paiko, who has since retired from the public service. He is now a member of the Niger State Education Board.

Ibrahim's father, despite his generous heart and a willingness to give to others, was not a rich man. His salary as a messenger was not enough to comfortably maintain his polygamous home. In those days, if a father could not afford to pay the meagre school fees, the school authorities allowed him to pay in kind with farm produce. Malam Muhammadu cultivated dawa (guinea corn) and he paid his son's school fees with it.

Ibrahim was the greatest beneficiary of his late father's generosity. His late father's closest friends took care of him. One of those friends was the late Emir of Minna, Alhaji Ahmadu Bahago. He was very kind and generous to Ibrahim. His uncles also made sure he did not lack the basic things he needed to continue his education. One of them, Malam Abdullahi Mai Kano, was fairly well to do. He worked in the local dispensary at the time. He retired from service many years later as a nursing superintendent.

Young Ibrahim was a very popular boy in the primary school. He earned this kind of attention by default. He was the son of a well-known father. Nigerians who worked with the colonial administration in those days were very well known and respected in their localities. As an orphan, Ibrahim attracted a great deal of unsolicited sympathy. The older boys in the school were fiercely protective of him. The younger boys admired him and boys of his age showed an uncommon understanding of his situation in life. But most importantly, Ibrahim was a generous boy. He inherited the habit of sharing from his father. It is a habit he has maintained and it is a habit that has served him well in life too.

Recalls Babangida:

> My father was very well known. He wasn't rich but he was prepared to give all he had to somebody who needed it much more than he. Eventually, he developed this strong belief that whatever he had was God-given and he had to share it with others less privileged.

A father's creed, a son's belief. Babangida's generosity is legendary. All those who are close to him speak of his willingness to share whatever he has with others. As a student, he gave food and money to those who asked for them. Sometimes he deprived himself to help other boys. He explains:

> I have always felt that whatever I get, I should share it with others who don't have and this I did quite a lot to a certain extent. Sometimes, even school uniform. I gave it to others whose clothes were bad and my uncle would ask me what I had done with it and I would say I gave it to somebody whose parents could not afford to buy for him.

In the secondary school, this created the impression that he was from a well-to-do family. The late Alhaji Yahuza Makongiji, former director of information, Plateau State, as well as former director of culture, Nasarawa State, who was Babangida's classmate in the Provincial Secondary School, Bida, recalled: "We tended to believe at that time that he came from a wealthy family (because) any time we were broke, we would ask him for something like one shilling and he would give us. He was very generous at that time."

The late Alhaji Kere Ahmed, former director of administration, Nigerian Television Authority, was Babangida's mate in secondary school. Ahmed was one year his senior. Said Ahmed: "Babangida did not come from a rich home but he was never really in need. He never was one of those students that you saw poverty all over them."

Lieutenant-General Garba Duba was his classmate in secondary school. He said of Babangida's kindness to others: "Well, right from the beginning, he had this quality of being very friendly, very easy-going and above all, extremely generous. So, if you missed an exercise book or a pencil and you asked Ibrahim Babangida, he would surrender his own and go and buy or get another one. So, he became generous and this attracted people to him."

Ibrahim Babangida rather liked the impression that he was from a rich family and encouraged it. His generosity may have come to him as a family trait but as he grew up, Babangida carefully cultivated and nurtured that habit because he appreciated its value in social relations. It is one habit that has always served him well, as we shall see, in his various situations in later life, even as president of the Federal Republic of Nigeria.

Babangida cultivated another habit in school, which he has carried along with him all his life. This is loyalty to his friends. As a primary school pupil and as a secondary school student, Babangida was very protective of his close friends. He defended them against others and sometimes he took punishments for them too. Major-General Abdulsalami Abubakar recalls: "I can say right from his childhood, he is somebody who cared for other people. At least, I know that he got into trouble because of me because he was always taking my fights off me."

Said Babangida: "Loyalty is very important to me. None of my friends will ever say that I forget them in their times of need. I protect those close to me because I believe I have an obligation as a friend to do so."

Generally, however, Babangida was not a troublesome boy although he always looked like he was built to fight. He was stocky or, in his own words, "compact and sturdy." He has more or less retained the same physique. This earned him the nickname, *Kulele* in secondary school. He always found the name amusing. He was a boy with a lot of compassion. He learnt early in life to say sorry when he was wrong. He once pushed a boy his age into ashes that he did not know were still hot. The boy was injured. Babangida felt truly sorry.

It would also be correct to say that as a boy he fancied himself in a position of leadership. He, therefore, tended to treat his friends with a certain air of superiority. An elder brother, perhaps. Or perhaps, he relished the role of the father figure. What death deprived him of early in life, he appeared to want to give to others: the care and protection of a father. Both in secondary school and in the army, Babangida tended to make friends with the younger ones, always playing the role of a father to the hilt. It was partly because of this that he always gave to those who asked him and even some who didn't and went to the rescue of those who had problems.

Among his mates, he led and they followed. They accepted him as *primus inter pares.* His grandmother's house became the meeting point for him and his friends. Even when he went to secondary school, his friends from other parts of Niger Province went to spend holidays with him in Minna. Kere Ahmed was a member of Ibrahim Babangida's circle of childhood friends. Both of them grew up in Minna. He said of Babangida at that period:

> It is incredible but even at that time, he just happened to be that kind of person that things revolved around him. He wasn't from a rich family. His was not the richest family amongst those of us that were students in Minna in those days. And somehow, religiously every morning, we would assemble in front of their house any time we were on holidays, sit around and talk from about 9.00 am until it got too hot for us to sit in front of the little cement decking in their house. I think the primary reason was that somehow, even though you would have little differences between different parties in our group, Babangida was the one person none of us disagreed with. He was the most agreeable person for all of us to converge around. And we could leave there to continue our little quarrel somewhere else, but somehow, while we were there, things just centred around him.

Major-General Abubakar also remembers those early days and the influence Babangida exerted on other boys in Minna:

> Their house was sort of central in Minna town, very close to the night market, very close to the mosque, very close to our playground. So, naturally, the whole children gathered around that area and naturally, his house became a meeting point and naturally, he drew attention from quite a number of people; quite a number of children took to him.

The seed of the Babangida mystique was thus sown early. He nurtured it over the years. His method might have varied according to the circumstances but the essentials have remained more or less the same. He learnt early to listen to other people. He learnt early to control himself. He positioned himself always as the leader of his group and everyone accepted him. Kere Ahmed recalled that "others looked up to him for guidance." But looking back, the general now says what drew people to him as a boy was not only his generosity but "my ability to relate to people quite easily."

Ibrahim Babangida was a very neat pupil and student. Two of his teachers played a major role in this. The first was his father's friend, Malam Ahmadu Bawa, father of Alhaji Ibrahim Ahmed Kontagora, formerly of FRCN, in the primary school. The old teacher became Babangida's role model for neatness and a high taste in good clothes. The Malam was usually very neat and very well dressed and he insisted that all his pupils must always be neat. He inspected them in the school parade every morning, paying particular attention to their teeth, uniform, fingernails and toenails. "God help anybody he found either with long nails or unpolished teeth. If he found ink on your uniform," the general recalls, "you will get the beating of that day."

In the secondary school, Babangida met another young teacher, Leslie Akande, who looked like a younger version of Malam Ahmadu Bawa. He was always very neat and well dressed. He became Babangida's second role model. Akande, says the general, "dressed fairly decently and casually. His dresses were very good. Whatever he put on, he made sure it was something attractive."

One other man who played a major role in shaping Babangida's life in the primary school was the late Malam Awesu Kuta, a tough disciplinarian who was very fond of the English language. It was his best subject. He was a good-looking young man with a very sweet voice. From the way he spoke English, many of his pupils thought he grew up in England. He was a very good teacher and he worked hard to make sure his pupils developed similar interest in the subject he loved so much. He made them write little essays known in primary schools in those days as composition. What the pupils looked forward to mostly were the oral English sessions at which they read out their work or recited passages given to them to cram. Babangida particularly welcomed those sessions.

Kuta had won over the young boy to his own love of the English language.

In 1956, Kuta organised a reading competition for the senior pupils. Babangida and Abdulsalami Abubakar jointly won it. The prize was a princely six pence. Each pupil received three pence. Their joy knew no bounds. It boosted their morale. But Babangida was rather casual about it as if he expected to win any way. No big deal, no big celebration. He did not take his prize money home. He spent it on sugar and groundnuts for his friends. It was his final year in the senior primary school also known as *remove* school. He ended it in style.

Chapter Two

Setting Out

I was confused, bewildered
–Ibrahim Badamasi Babangida

Bida is only 84 kilometres from Minna. Ibrahim Babangida had never been there, although he had heard so much about the town. There was something mysterious, something mythical about Bida. Grown-ups told children like Babangida frightening stories of witches and wizards in Bida. People did not go out at night in Bida, they said. They told the boys that witches ate children who went out at night. And those who peeped through the keyhole at night saw snakes and fire.

Such stories made Babangida afraid of Bida. When therefore his letter of admission into the Provincial Secondary School, Bida, came, he thought he had been sentenced to the equivalent of death. How could he go to the town where witches and wizards reigned and people were not allowed out at night? He told his grandmother about it. The old woman laughed. She too had heard those stories but knew them to be fairy tales. She told her grandson not to worry. He would be in safe hands. She told him that the Etsu Nupe would protect him and he would come to no harm in Bida. The Etsu was his late father's friend. Thus reassured of safety, Babangida prepared for a new life beyond Minna.

In January 1957, Babangida, his friend, Abdulsalami Abubakar, and Samuel Bala Kuta were put on the Baro-Badegi train from Minna on their way to the Provincial Secondary School, Bida. It was the second time Babangida was leaving the familiar surroundings of Minna, his home. The first was almost a year earlier in 1956 when he and Abubakar went to Kaduna to represent their school during Queen Elizabeth II's visit to Nigeria. Babangida enrolled in the school as Ibrahim Badamasi. He changed his surname to Babangida on his return from India after his commissioning into the Nigerian Army as a second lieutenant. Babangida was the name by which his father was popularly known. He was Muhammadu Badamasi Babangida, MBB. Ibrahim was named after his grandfather. His decision to use his father's last name rather than his middle name has a ring of vanity of the young. The only reason was that he liked the initial, IBB. His school registration number was 211. He was 16 years old.

Despite the stories of witches and wizards, Babangida had looked forward to the school for one good reason. His friend, Kere Ahmed, was a year ahead of him there. From Ahmed, he learnt that most of the teachers were Englishmen. For Babangida, this was a particularly good piece of news. It meant he would be taught English by English men.

The Provincial Secondary School, Bida, was the only secondary school in Niger Province at the time. Although the students were drawn mostly from that province, there were boys from other parts of Nigeria too. For instance, Shehu Malami came from Sokoto Province. Isaac Umar, Tanko Obe, Yahuza Makongiji and Buba Ahmed came from Benue Province.

Babangida and Abubakar were well received by boys from other parts of the province, notably, Kontagora, Zuru and Abuja. But the two boys faced an unexpected problem. Some of the boys from the rural areas of the province regarded them as city boys. Rural boys did not trust city boys. The latter, out of jealousy, perhaps, tended to see city boys as a show off. The belief and suspicion bred unnecessary animosity between them. The animosity was somewhat complicated by the determination of the rural boys to show the world that they were as enlightened as the city boys.

One of such boys in Babangida's class was Sani Bello, who also went into the army and retired with the rank of colonel. Bello was the aide-de-camp to the late Major-General J.T.U. Aguiyi-Ironsi. He comes from Kontagora in the then Niger Province. He was the smallest boy in the class but he was the most outspoken and about the most rebellious. He frequently took on the city boys in contests of will and learning. He could afford it because he was a very brilliant boy. He was known among his classmates as *the little boy with big ideas*. Most of his big ideas had to do with contests between the rural and city boys to prove who was superior. He was the one most likely to disagree on many issues.

Babangida and Bello were in the same dormitory, Sudan House. Both boys liked each other. But it was Babangida who broke down the wall of hostility that Bello had erected around himself. They became friends. Bello's hostility towards the city boys ceased and he entered the new circle of Babangida's close friends, among whom were Abdulsalami Abubakar, Gado Nasko and Mohammed Magoro. Nasko and Magoro also were in the army and retired as major generals. Nasko was minister of Federal Capital Territory in the Babangida administration. Magoro was minister of internal affairs in the Buhari administration. Two other boys in the group were Buba Ahmed and Samaila Ahmed. They did not go into the army but they too moved up in life. Buba was minister of sports in the Shehu Shagari administration in the Second Republic and Samaila retired as assistant director of prisons.

A special bond of friendship separated five of these boys from the others. The five came to be known as Group of Five or the Gang of Five. The members were Ibrahim Babangida, Buba Ahmed, Samaila Ahmed, Mohammed Magoro and Abdulsalami Abubakar. Bello did not make the gang.

The members of the group shared some common interests, endowments and abilities. Samaila Ahmed said that they had identical interests in most things. They wore the same type of clothes. They really stood out in the school. Academically, they were among the top ten in the class. All of them were also very good in sports. Babangida was an all-rounder. He played hockey, cricket and football. In the school's football team, the first eleven, he played in both the centre-half and the full back positions. Defence was really his best position. His opponents always found his defence virtually impenetrable. He was nicknamed *Block Buster*. Babangida was in the school's first eleven from form three and that, said Col Bello, "was not a mean achievement in the school that had some of the best footballers in northern schools."

Bello played table tennis and lawn tennis. The other four members of the Gang of Five were in the school's first eleven too. Samaila Ahmed was the captain. Magoro was a striker, Abubakar was the goalkeeper and Buba Ahmed played in the centre forward. Samaila Ahmed and Magoro were also in the hockey eleven. Magoro, a tall, athletic boy, became the sports captain.

Babangida also met and became friends with some other boys who were to feature prominently in his life in later years. Nearly all of them went into and rose to become big shots in the armed forces. Among them were Major-General Sani Sami, the Emir of Zuru, Kebbi State, Lt-General Garba Duba and the late Major-General Mamman Vatsa, who was executed in January, 1986, allegedly for plotting the overthrow of President Babangida.

Nasko first met Babangida in Kaduna during the Queen's visit in 1956. He had gone there to represent his school, Kontagora senior primary school. This is how he remembers their first meeting:

> He created so much impression that in no time we became very close. I liked his jovial attitude, his generosity and he was eloquent and sociable. He interacted freely with everybody around and this tended to have attracted me to him. We became playmates, we joked and by the time we were going away, one could feel the spellbound around.

The two boys exchanged addresses. Nasko did not think much about it. He had met a boy he liked and who had promised to remain his friend. To him, that was only typical of boys their age. But one Sunday afternoon, he was given a letter. Surprise! It was from "this new friend that I found," Ibrahim Babangida. He had kept his promise to write to Nasko. In his letter, Babangida told Nasko of his safe journey back home to Minna and expressed the hope they would meet again. Less than a year later, they did. They became classmates in form one in the provincial secondary school. Their paths and destiny have hardly separated since January 1957.

The Gang of Five was a close-knit group. They protected their individual and collective interests. They settled all their quarrels among themselves. Buba Ahmed recalls that if they had a problem they could not solve among themselves, they consulted some other close friends. Bello was one of those "outsiders" whose views were respected by the group. Vatsa was another.

There was another less cohesive but radical group in the school known as NEPU (Northern Elements Progressive Union) named after the radical political party led by the late champion of the *talakawa,* Malam Aminu Kano. Sani Sami, known in the school as Sani Dabai, was one of the leading members of this radical group. He and Babangida remain close friends. Sami also went into the army and retired with the rank of major general. He is the current Emir of Zuru in Kebbi State.

Members of this group behaved like politicians on the stump. They harangued the "conservatives" in the school. In prep, Duba recalls, "they would make noise and would not allow other students to face their studies." In Babangida's class, this group once staged what was then a rebellion. The school tradition was that the class monitor did not sweep the classroom. This group objected to this practice, insisting that all students were equal and therefore, everyone, monitor or no monitor, must sweep the classroom when it was their turn. Their campaign for the need to change the practice was so strong that the school authorities gave in and the policy was changed. Sami recalls that the head boy and the prefects frequently *bribed* members of his group with groundnuts, biscuits, sweets and bananas so they would not make trouble.

Only Babangida could pacify the members of NEPU when they were in their worst behaviour, tearing the school down with the ire of their radical rhetoric. He could count on close friends like Sami. Although they regarded Babangida as a conservative, they respected him because he was the only one who made genuine attempts to understand them. He mixed freely with them, listened to their radical views on any and everything and helped those who had personal problems. He was often amused by the solutions the radicals proffered for mankind's hydra-headed problems but if he was contemptuous of those views, he did not let anyone know it.

Babangida's ability to keep this radical group more or less in check did not go unnoticed by the school authorities. When the time came to pick a head boy who commanded the respect of both the radical and conservative student groups, Block Buster was the natural choice. Two members of his own group, the Gang of Five, Mohammed Magoro and Buba Ahmed, were house captains or prefects.

There is no watershed in the development of innate abilities but it would seem that by this time, Babangida had two things going for him. The first is that he had become a good listener. He was prepared to give his time to hear out arguments and the outpouring of personal grievances. In arguments, he had learnt to play the devil's advocate.

Secondly, Babangida had learnt the importance of the middle course in human relations. You could not find him in either extreme of the political spectrum - the right or the left. This assured him of some trust from both the right and the left. His ability to steer a middle course combined with his ability to listen to all shades of political opinions were to become, after Bida, the unique materials in the meticulous construction of his road to the top of his profession and ultimate political power as president of the federal republic.

Babangida charmed his way into the heart of his teachers in Bida. His geography teacher in form three, the late Jerome Idoko, former Benue State chairman of the Code of Conduct Bureau, said the future general was a very good student - "humble, good in sports and very neat in appearance."

Professor Jonathan Ndagi, former vice-chancellor, Federal University of Technology, Minna, and former Nigerian High Commissioner to Australia, taught Babangida mathematics. He said Babangida was good in class, sports and was "quite likeable, never bullish."

One teacher who was very close to Babangida was Alhaji Hamidu Ladan Zuru, former general manager of the Northern Regional conglomerate, the New Nigerian Development Company Ltd., Kaduna. He taught English and mathematics. He was Babangida's housemaster as well as the school's sports master. Teacher and pupil met on several fronts and on all the fronts, the former found the latter a remarkable boy - neat, punctual, serious with his studies and his games and very friendly. Alhaji Ladan Zuru is now a private businessman living in Kaduna.

Col Bello, one of the radical boys, agreed that Babangida had considerable charm. No teacher could fail to notice the boy with the lilting voice with a large fellow student followership. But some of his classmates believed that Babangida ingratiated himself with the teachers for purposes of personal reward. He respected the school authorities and the school regulations. He did not ruffle feathers.

Said Bello: "Babangida avoided any acts of confrontation with any of us and that made him exceedingly popular to a fault with the teachers. All the teachers liked him."

Alhaji Abdulmumuni Manga, one of his classmates and former controller of prisons, shares the same opinion. He says Babangida was very likeable and full of jokes and was in very good terms with most of his teachers. Another former classmate, Malam Dauda Gulu Yunusa of the National Transport and Technology Institute, Zaria, says Babangida's cheerful and smiling face made it easy for him to win friends among students and teachers alike.

II

Babangida's first big problem as a head boy came rather unexpectedly. But it gave him an opportunity quite early in his new position to test his leadership. There was a Pakistani in the school who taught science. He did not get on well with the school authorities. But he was fond of the students. Quite suddenly, the Pakistani was asked to go on transfer to another school. The boys felt the school authorities were unjustly punishing the teacher and they insisted he must be allowed to remain in the school. When the school authorities ignored their demand, the boys went on strike. They refused to attend classes. Tension was high in the school. The principal appeared helpless. The members of staff were scared. The action was led by the radical NEPU group. The principal, Mr S.A. Skillbeck, turned to Babangida for help. Babangida recalls:

> The principal called me and said I had to find a way of defusing this tension. I was able to get together all the monitors of the various classes. I talked to them about how foolish it would be to do this thing. I told them it was not the best way and they all agreed. Tension was reduced and we all in the school got together with the Pakistani and took a group photograph.

The crisis ended. But the Pakistani left the school.

One teacher charmed the charmer: Mr Leslie Akande. He was educated in England on a three year Northern Nigerian scholarship and returned to Nigeria in 1961. He was appointed an education officer and posted to the Provincial Secondary School, Bida. He taught geography in the lower forms and took the upper forms in metal/wood work classes. Ibrahim Babangida was in form five.

Akande was a good-looking, well-dressed young man. Buba Ahmed, remembers him as a "flamboyant and excellent teacher." His appearance was what Babangida loved. He was always neat and very well dressed. Being neat was something Babangida had learnt from the primary school.

Akande set himself apart from the other Nigerians on the school staff. The other Nigerians treated the white teachers with deference bordering on the obsequious but Akande treated them with no more respect than was due to them. He was only 26 and was only five or six years older than most of the boys in the school. He still felt like one of them. And because he was not married, he spent most of his free time after school hours with the boys, playing football and other games with them.

There were four senior Nigerian members of the staff in the school. Two of them, the bursar, Alhaji Saidu Bida, *Madaki Bida,* and Dr Onimole, popularly called 'Papa," a science teacher, were in their early fifties; the other two, Akande and Yaya Abubakar, were bright young men in their middle twenties.

Abubakar was newly graduated from the University of Ibadan. He taught biology. There were 26 white men on the staff. Both the principal and the vice-principal were, of course, white. The senior Nigerian members of staff had their own separate staff common room. They were not allowed in the staff common room for the whites.

Akande had quite a bit of youthful fire burning in him still. He decided to challenge this segregation by pretending he did not know there was a 'whites only' staff common room. He went there to drink tea during tea break. He found himself barred from entering the room. He was shocked. As a student in England, Akande had been subjected to racial discrimination. He was not going to allow himself to suffer the indignities of racial discrimination in his own country, now independent of British colonial rule. He blew up.

He stormed into the principal's office without knocking. A startled Skillbeck looked up to find the young man glowering at him. Akande accused him of practising apartheid in the school. "I am made to understand that I cannot drink my tea or coffee where these blinking English boys are drinking their own in the staff common room because I am black!" he thundered. He told the principal he would not accept to be treated as a second-class citizen in his own country. He stormed out again, banging the door.

The stewards in the common room and the principal's clerical staff must have watched the storm in both places with quiet amusement. Soon, the words were out: Akande had stood up to the white teachers and told them off. This was an incredible feat because white people in Nigeria in those days generally enjoyed an elevated status just below the gods. Akande became a hero to the young boys, particularly, the senior boys.

The other boys respected him for standing up to the authority but Babangida saw him as someone who had fought an unjust system. This increased his admiration for the young teacher. Akande admired Babangida too because he saw Babangida as one student who was "always sure of himself."

Evidence of how much Akande truly admired Babangida must be his remark on the future president's second term's report in form five. Babangida scored 45 per cent in woodwork. Akande noted that the *"exam report does not justify his ability in this subject"* but went on to praise Babangida as *"a real gentleman."* Teacher and student formed a bond of mutual admiration, a bond that was to benefit Babangida not too long after.

III

The head boy and the prefects of the school were usually chosen just before the end of the school year in October/November from among form five boys. In October/November of 1961, the principal convened a staff meeting to choose the next set of prefects and the head boy. Each possible candidate was individually assessed and scored by each teacher.

Babangida had been a very popular student. He was level-headed and one of the few senior boys who enjoyed the friendship of senior and junior boys. He was nominated for the post of head boy. A couple of other boys were also nominated for the same post. You would think there would be no dissenting voice over Babangida's nomination, considering his popularity among his teachers. There was. When the votes were counted, Ibrahim Babangida did not score the highest mark. Another boy did. But Akande believed that despite his lower mark, Babangida was the most suitable boy to head the school. He spoke at length in his favour, pointing out what he saw as his leadership qualities. In the end, he convinced the rest of the staff and Babangida was appointed the head boy.

Babangida's choice came as a surprise to some of his own classmates. Although Nasko said they were not surprised that he made it because of his active participation in all the school activities, they had expected either Yahaya Eboh, the oldest boy or Samuel Bala Kuta, the monitor, to be made the head boy.

Why did Akande prefer Babangida? Babangida was not his favourite boy in his class. The honour went to Sani Bello, because, according to Akande, "I thought he was extremely handsome like me and very good in my subject. The second was a boy called Umoru Gbate who was next to Sani Bello as my favourite and Ibrahim then would come close third."

But he fought to make Babangida the head boy in preference to his own favourite boys because he saw him as a boy who was always sure of himself, very sure of himself. I like people who are sure of themselves like me, with all sense of humility. I have always thought that this is a young man who is most calculating and who will surprise anybody. And those surprise packages I think Nigerians have really got a dose of them. Unpredictability, that is. Can you predict him too much because of the way he wants to come out? For you to do the sort of thing he is doing now, you must be very alert at all times. He was a student who, if teachers too are allowed to have respect for their students, was one of those I had respect for.

Babangida has never been an easy person to predict. Some of his friends and classmates in secondary school thought this was a major weakness, not strength in his character. It irritated some of them that they never knew where he stood on certain issues. Alhaji Samaila Ahmed has never liked this trait in him

because when you give somebody hope and eventually that hope is dashed, you know, it is not fair. He will tell you yes, even when that yes is no. Even in the school, things which he should normally say no to, he would say yes because he didn't want to displease people.

Alhaji Ladan also thinks this is one weakness he noticed in General Babangida early in his life. He thought he would act differently as president because

any ruler who feels that he has to please everybody is in trouble. You cannot please everybody. One can consider this a weak point: if you can't say no to some but say yes to everybody, then it is a very big problem.

As we shall see, this did, indeed, create problems for him as president. Some of his close aides and friends complained that his problem was that he and his administration had "too many friends."

Babangida's unpredictable trait and the tendency to please everyone blossomed into full, flowery splendour and earned him his most enduring, national nickname, Maradona, after the Argentine footballer, Diego Maradona, who dazzled the world with nimble footwork in the 1986 World Cup. He enjoyed watching the public guess his actions and decisions. August 27, the anniversary of his assumption of power, became the favourite season for the guessing game in the news media. Babangida took some of his major political decisions on that day every year. It was not for nothing, therefore, that August became the most important month of his presidency. The daily human traffic to Dodan Barracks, Lagos, was heaviest in August. The traffic shifted to Aso Rock Villa, Abuja, after the nation's capital was formally shifted to Abuja on December 12, 1991.

Everyone went there to lobby for one favour or the other, the most important subjects being the creation of states and local governments and the appointment of new military governors and ministers. As August 27 approached each year, those who regarded themselves as informed Babangida watchers took a keen delight in predicting which way the president would be moving. His close aides said that he read the daily newspapers and weekly newsmagazines to see how much Nigerians really knew him. He would point out some particularly funny predictions and laugh until the tears came down.

Perhaps, what he enjoyed even more was showing Nigerians and those who had taken it upon themselves to predict him that he and he only knew his own mind and where he would be going at any point in time. Sometimes when the prediction of the presidential watchers proved accurate, Babangida either deferred his decision on the particular subject matter or changed it entirely. It is amazing that a man who is so gregarious could also be so secretive.

There was something else Akande saw in Babangida in Bida. His "innate ability to remember names. Ibrahim will remember the first name of virtually anybody that he has met. I don't know many people who have that rare gift."

It is a gift that Babangida has always put to good use. According to Sami, Babangida used to call "everybody, including the junior boys, by name. It is one of the things he has carried on till today. He is one of the senior officers I know who can call any officer by his name in the armed forces, not only in the army. And that earns him a lot of respect because when you see an officer going and you think maybe the president doesn't know him, the president will call him by his first name and the officer will be surprised and very happy. I think it is a very good quality."

Vice-Admiral Murtala Nyako, Chief of Naval Staff, says Babangida once embarrassed him when he called "one of my lieutenant commanders by his first name. I had to shake my head, wondering who he was referring to. I don't have to tell you that he is gifted in that direction. He remembers names very, very well."

Babangida may have seemed sweet and meek but he has always had a rebellious, stubborn streak in him. He describes himself as "reasonably stubborn." His choice of words in talking about himself always provides some clues to his character traits. He likes to listen to other people's views but quite often he flows with his own decision. Nyako describes him as "adamant." Stubborn and adamant point to his tendency to flow with his instinct even if it means his courting unpopularity. Despite his friendly disposition, when duty called, he could be quite tough even on his friends. In the primary school, he once punished his own friend, a boy whose name he now remembers only as Jibrin. He ordered the boy to put his head and hands between his legs and remain there until he, Ibrahim, was satisfied that he was sorry for whatever he did.

In school, when Babangida tweaked the whiskers of the authorities, he did so for two reasons - either to fight for what he believed was a just cause or to take the Mickey out of them. He showed that side of him twice in Bida.

Bida was, and is, a very hot and humid town. The school regulation stipulated that after lights out, all students must go to bed. The senior boys enforced that regulation on the junior boys but exempted themselves. When the senior boys were sure that the junior boys had gone to bed, they brought out their mats or beds to enjoy the luxury of fresh air in the open.

This particular night, the heat was unbearable. The junior boys were sweating and squirming on their beds. They knew the senior boys were out in the open, enjoying a privilege to which they were not entitled to under the school regulation. Babangida felt this was unfair. The school regulation did not give the senior boys the right to sleep in the open while the junior boys steamed in their own sweat in the room. He decided to do something about it, if only to let the senior boys know that the junior boys too were human beings.

He organised the junior boys and all of them took their mats and went outside to sleep. The head boy, Garba Dada (known then as Garba Adamu Paiko), was furious. He was even more shocked to know that Babangida was behind it. Dada decided to do nothing about it because his relationship with Babangida went a few years back. Dada recalled that when Babangida entered the senior primary school, his father called him and told him: "This boy is your younger brother. I have entrusted him into your hands in the school. Whatever he does, make sure you put him on the right track."

This night of rebellion, the words of the old man came back to Dada. Should he punish his *own brother?* He swallowed his fury and merely cautioned the boys. Babangida was in form four.

Sometimes, Babangida used other boys to test the waters with the school authorities. According to Musa Hassan Izom, Babangida would sometimes push other boys to do what he clearly knew would put them into trouble. When such boys got into trouble, however, Babangida did not abandon them. He came to their rescue. In this way, he achieved two things. He remained, in the eyes of the school authorities, an obedient boy; and among the junior boys, he was seen as a dependable boy. Some of his classmates resented this because they believed, according to Izom, that he was sacrificing them for his own ends.

Members of the Gang of Five were not blatantly lawless but occasionally, they tended to see themselves, as a special group of students who were entitled to certain privileges that other students might as well accept were theirs as of right. They broke school regulations occasionally when they were in form five. They would break out of the school and go to town and return late.

Babangida recalls:

> We were senior enough not to be intimidated. We were a bit independent of others from form five. I remember one day we went out and the head boy was a chap called Abubakar Rimi (Abubakar Usman in those days) and we came back fairly late. He was there waiting for us. We just didn't bother. We just rushed him and went back the other way. We were seniors, a rebellious group at the time.

Babangida believes that part of the reason why he was made the head boy was because the school authorities realised that if there must be peace in the school, then "the most sensible thing to do was to make one of us a head boy."

Babangida was a good student. Or, in the words of Duba, "an all-round student." He did very well in English, history, geography, science, Hausa, Arabic and mathematics. His term reports showed that he scored consistently high marks in all those subjects and was always in the top five in the class. But he was not a swot. He refused to bury himself in his textbooks. He preferred interacting with people most of the time. As Nasko put it: "You will never fix him in one place. If you leave him here, any point you go, you will find him. Always moving, wanting to interact with other people; maybe that's how he became the best, learning from other people."

By the time he was in form five, Babangida had convinced himself that he could learn more from people than "spending my time with my books." This change of attitude did affect his grades in the school even though he put the interaction into effective use. He and his friends organised themselves into small study groups for discussions. This way, he had the best of both worlds. He saved himself the rigours of swotting but kept abreast of his lessons. Still, his grades were no longer up to par.

His teachers began to worry about his ultimate result in the school certificate examination. His first term test results averaged a C. His principal, Skillbeck, remarked of that performance: *"Commendable work out of class - not so good in class, however. I hope he will retain his ambition for a good certificate."*

In form five, Babangida settled his mind on a career. Engineering. There was no particular reason why he chose engineering. He did not have personal contacts with engineers. Somehow, the word sounded right to him. To be an engineer, you must be good in mathematics, a subject

Babangida was not particularly good at. To remedy this, he decided he needed extra lessons. Zuru gave those extra lessons in his house, proof, said his old teacher, that Babangida took his studies seriously.

Babangida's best subject was English language. Nasko believes his proficiency in English was simply God's gift. "Nobody could beat him in that subject. So, that's why we nicknamed him Mr Bill" he recalled.

Mr Leonard George Bill was the English master who, according to Buba Ahmed, was "meticulous and extremely good in English." He came to Bida from Government College, Keffi. Bill, like most teachers in the school, liked Babangida and encouraged him in the subject he loved so much. This created some problems for the future president with some of his classmates. They became both jealous and suspicious of his consistently high marks in English language. Okay, he was good but was he truly so good that no other student came within a mile of him? they wondered.

One of the students who answered that question in the negative was Izom who now works with the Abuja Agricultural Development Programme. He believed Babangida was not the best student in English language. Bill had simply anointed him as the best because, according to Izom, the English master had allowed his liking for Babangida to becloud his judgement. Izom was convinced that as long as Bill remained the English master, it would be folly for any students to entertain the hopes of beating Babangida in that subject.

Izom felt frustrated by this because he genuinely believed he was as good as, if not better than, Babangida in that subject. He felt Bill was deliberately discouraging and frustrating him by consistently awarding him poor marks in English language. Bill himself did not care who knew whom he liked and whom he did not. He hated students who were not good in the English language - written or spoken. He had an undiplomatic way of letting such students know what he felt about them.

Izom, totally dissatisfied with Bill's opinion of his own performance in English language, decided to test the teacher's honesty about Babangida's rating in that subject. He spoke to some of the boys who also resented Babangida's favoured status with Bill. In their final year in form five, these students hatched a plot to trap the teacher and his favoured student. One day, the students were given an essay to write. It was to be submitted to Bill the next day after breakfast.

When the students went for breakfast, Izom finished his food quickly and ran back to the classroom to carry out the plot. He took Babangida's exercise book and copied the essay into his own exercise book. When the essays were passed, the "conspirators," one of whom was Sani Bello, ensured that Izom's exercise book was on top and Babangida's at the bottom so that Bill would see Izom's first. The next day, the pranksters waited with quiet amusement to see what the result would be. Babangida scored nine points out of ten. Izom five!

Babangida knew about the prank much later. He is still amused by it. He also recalls that in elementary school, another boy had done the same thing. He copied and passed off Babangida's work. "I think our headmaster was able to compare the two and concluded that the boy could not do that sort of work and that he must have copied it because everybody knew the boy was not capable of coming up with work like that. It was instant justice." The boy was punished. Izom was not.

Izom did not let the matter rest there because he was convinced Bill hated him. He took his case to the principal. His action did not improve his marks in the English language either. Izom believed that the best student in English language was Yamusa Keffi.

His school reports, however, showed that Babangida rightly earned the nickname of Mr Bill. He consistently maintained an excellent result in English. He placed first most of the time. He disappointed his teachers twice only in that subject. The first time was the first term in form II. He scored 51 per cent in English and placed 15th in it. The second time was his first term result in form IV in 1960. He scored only 45 per cent in English and placed 14th. Indeed, all his results for that term were generally disappointing. He did so poorly that his form master remarked: *"This is a disappointing result for a boy who can reach the top of his class."*

Babangida returned to form in the second term with good results in all the subjects. Well, not quite all the subjects. He did poorly in woodwork, prompting the woodwork master to remark, with a certain measure of personal disappointment: *"There is no necessity for a boy of his calibre to be doing so poorly."*

One could understand the wood master's disappointment. Babangida managed a princely score of 16 per cent and placed 12th out of 13 in the subject. The woodwork master (not Akande by this time) was not the only teacher who was not quite happy with Babangida that term although he scored above 60 per cent in all the other subjects. His history master said he performed *"slightly below maximum."* His mathematics teacher said he *"expected a better result"* and warned him to *"take more care."* He obtained 65 per cent in mathematics. Even with a 65 per cent score in English, which placed him first in that subject, his English master warned him *"to be more careful if he wishes to retain this position next term."*

The most important observation on Babangida that term came from his form master. His report is worth quoting in full because it said something about the essential Babangida, his inclination in later life to push so far but not that far. He wrote:

> Ibrahim is blessed with natural capabilities for all fields of endeavour. Every-

thing comes easy to him. He takes advantage of his innate capabilities and does fairly well. I suspect that because studies, athletics, etc., come easy to him he does not always work at 100 per cent effort. A fine boy.

Whatever his performances in class were, no one could take away from Babangida the fact that he remained, in the view of his teachers, one of the best boys the school ever had. Right from form one until he left the school five years later, one principal after the other and one house master after the other rated him as *well-behaved; very intelligent; hardworking; the neatest in class; has very good conduct.*

Bill, a former officer in the British army, was the school career guidance counsellor. It is not certain what role he played in Babangida's ambition to become an engineer. But it is certain that the army was not something Bill recommended for his star pupil. Duba also wanted to become an engineer or a doctor. Neither he nor Babangida achieved what they initially set their eyes on.

IV

In 1962, Nigeria was two years old as an independent nation. Many of the colonial administrators and professionals were still in government, helping the newly indigenised public service adjust to the changes in the country's circumstances. The Northern Region was particularly short of trained indigenous manpower. It was a major problem the premier of the region, the late Sir Ahmadu Bello, the Sardaunan Sokoto, an astute politician and administrator, knew he must tackle if independence was to bring its full benefits to the people.

The northerners had a crucial place and role to play in shaping the new nation's destiny. The premier knew that the next few years would be crucial for the region. If it did not produce the required manpower, it must continue to depend either on expatriates or the other regions, the East and the West, each of which had more trained indigenous manpower than the Northern Region. The Eastern and the Western regions had introduced a policy to indigenise their public services. The north would have to do the same. It was the new political game by the regions.

The objective was to ensure that the civil service of each region was controlled by its indigenes. In desperation, the north was forced to turn to other countries, particularly Pakistan and Egypt, for professionals such as doctors, pharmacists and teachers. That was a stop gap. No one knew that better than the Sardauna himself. The pressure on the premier was not only in finding enough administrative and professional personnel of

Northern Nigerian origin for the regional civil service but also in ensuring that in the letter and spirit of federalism, the north must be represented in the federal public service as well. It was a Herculean task.

In early 1962, therefore, the premier toured various secondary schools in the region to give the students pep talks. He spoke of career opportunities in the public services of the Northern Region and the federal public service. He spoke of career opportunities in the armed forces, particularly the army, and what part they, the boys from the north, must play if they expected to share in the opportunities in the federation. The premier was particularly worried that time was running out for the north. If the remaining colonial administrators and professionals left, the north would be in trouble. Given their comparative advantage in Western education, the Eastern and the Western regions were assuming commanding heights in the federal public service.

In addition to his visits to schools and colleges, therefore, the Sardauna also sent his ministers to their home provinces to give career talks to the young boys and girls, particularly those in their final years in secondary schools. The message was: prepare to play your role on the stage in the unfolding national drama.

Sir Ahmadu Bello visited the Provincial Secondary School, Bida, twice in 1962 alone. Each time, he spoke to the senior boys who were on the verge of choosing their careers. Magoro said that the premier was always "hammering on nothing other than that we should be serious with our studies because we were coming out at the time the colonial masters were leaving the country. He told us that whether we liked it or not, the burden of responsibility was going to fall on some of us and we had to be ready. And he emphasised the military."

According to Bello, the late premier told the students: "My children, the future of this country will be determined by who owns the army; therefore, I call upon you to join the army."

The army was the biggest armed force in the country. The Nigerian Navy and the Nigerian Air Force were fledgling armed forces at the time. Nigeria's defence capability was very dear to the Northern Peoples Congress, the NPC, which controlled both the northern region and the federal government. In its manifesto before independence, the party had drawn attention to the vulnerability of the country. Its skies were undefended because it had no air force. The navy could not guarantee its maritime interests and security because a local training school for the navy was set up in Apapa, Lagos, only in 1958 - two years before Nigeria became independent.

The navy, known then as the Royal Nigerian Navy, did not even own a warship until 1959. Sometime in 1960, parliament passed the Royal Nigerian Military Force bill. Its purpose was to confer the title of "royal" on the army and the navy on the country's attainment of independence in October 1960.

An equally intense one by the ministry of defence complemented the campaign waged by the premier. That campaign had won the hearts of a few other boys before Babangida's set in Bida. Muhammadu Inuwa Wushishi, Ibrahim Adetunji Taiwo, Garba Dada and Haruna Auna were some of the former students of the school who had chosen a military career. They were all young army officers by the time Babangida and his classmates were being wooed to choose the army.

Not long after the premier's visit, a military team led by Alhaji Ibrahim Tako, *Galadima Bida*, minister of state for defence in charge of the army, visited the school to lecture the fifth form boys on the great career opportunities in the armed forces. Alhaji Mohammed Ribadu was the minister of defence. He too knew the role the military would play in post independence Nigeria. He was also worried that the north lagged behind the other two regions in the officer corps of the armed forces - the army and the navy. Ribadu was anxious to redress this as quickly as possible. He, therefore, worked out those tours to recruit young northern secondary school leavers into the armed forces. He assigned his minister of state the task.

Some military personnel accompanied the minister of state on the tour of the few secondary schools in the north. One of them was a young army officer from the north, Captain Yakubu Gowon, who became the second military ruler in the country only four years later. He also became the first four-star general in the Nigerian Army. Captain Gowon was a handsome officer with delicate features. His uniform fitted him like a second skin. Sani Sami still remembers how the future general turned out - "dressed up nicely with his Sam Browne belt." Gowon made quite an impression on the young boys.

Captain Gowon was Dr Onimole's student in Barewa College, Zaria. When he saw his former student resplendent in his military uniform, the old teacher could not control his joy. He showed the captain round the school as one of his successful former students, an example worthy of emulation by the other boys.

As part of the process of wooing the boys, a sergeant major demonstrated weapon handling. He stripped down a light machine gun and reassembled it quickly - to the rhythm of his own internal military command. The boys watched, fascinated. At the end of the lecture and the impressive demonstration, the minister asked for volunteers for recruitment into the army. Fourteen hands went up. Some of those hands belonged to Ibrahim Babangida, Gado Nasko, Buba Ahmed, Mohammed Magoro, Sani Sami, Sani Bello, Abdulsalami Abubakar, Mamman Vatsa and Ibrahim Umar Sauda.

Vatsa and Sauda did not need to be persuaded. They had always been attracted to the army. Sauda often talked about the army to his classmates. Such was his interest in it that by the time he was in form three, he began to call himself "general." In form five, he *promoted* himself "marshal" and *promoted* Vatsa, a very intelligent boy, who lived a rather regimented life, a "general." The nicknames stuck to both boys throughout their school career. Vatsa did become a major general but Sauda, a striking boy with the natural build for the military, did not make it beyond the rank of a lieutenant. He was one of the first military casualties of the Nigerian civil war on the federal side. He was crushed against a tree by a military vehicle whose driver he was directing on how to properly park. Sauda loved orderliness. It killed him.

One boy who strongly needed to be persuaded to join the army was Garba Duba. When Babangida found his friend did not put up his hand as a volunteer, he nudged him in the ribs and whispered to him to do so. Duba was reluctant. He was not interested in the army because he had seen something of soldiers and he did not like what he saw. He comes from Kontagora whose neighbours are Zuru, well-known warriors. Duba used to see "them with their bows and arrows (and he) used to get frightened and run away as a child."

A large number of Zuru people were in the army and every time they came home on leave, the mere sight of them frightened some of the boys, including Duba. "So, that fear," he now recalls, "was there in my mind. To take up a gun and shoot people scared me." He wanted to have nothing to do with the army. He was nursing his quiet ambition of becoming either a doctor or an engineer, safe from gun and violence.

On the other hand, Babangida and the other boys tried to persuade Nasko not to join the army. They advised him to go to an Arabic or Islamic school because he took his religion rather seriously. He still does. But he liked the army and felt that his classmates were merely teasing him. He ignored their advice. Nasko thinks it was fate that led all of them into the army. In form five, he was not thinking of a particular career yet. Like his other classmates, he had taken the HSC entrance examination and looked forward to further studies. All that changed, thanks partly to Ibrahim Umar Sauda.

Late in February 1962, Tako kept his promise and sent the boys the necessary application forms for the army entrance examination into the military college. The minister did not have the luxury of forgetting his promise because Sauda pestered him. Babangida's application form was dated May 7, 1962. His examination number was 2912.

All the fourteen boys filled and returned their forms to the ministry of defence. But when they were invited for the entrance examination in Kaduna, thirteen of them went. The fourteenth boy, Buba Ahmed, did not go for the examination because his mother did not want to hear of her son joining the army. And that was that.

The school was on a three-month holiday and a trip to Kaduna was an adventure many of the boys did not want to miss. By this time, however, the enthusiasm to join the army had largely worn off and many of the boys were now reluctant to go. They felt they were being forced into something they did not particularly like. To show their resentment, some of them decided they would fail the examination. They discussed this plan among themselves. Bello and Nasko talked it over. They consulted Babangida who had held a similar discussion with some of their classmates.

Babangida took over command of the situation. He had thought about it carefully and come to the conclusion that failing the examination would be a disgrace to their school. They did not have to let the school down. A better and more honourable course of action, he reasoned, would be to pass the examination but refuse to enlist in the army. He gathered his classmates together and spoke to them at length about this. He argued that if they failed, no one in the school would believe that they failed deliberately. The boys were persuaded and agreed to pass the examination. But that was where their army career would begin and end, they thought. They had already taken the qualifying examination into the higher school certificate, HSC, with the prospects of higher education and other careers. Several of them had now decided on their future careers, the army not included.

Something rather strange, in their view, struck the boys from Bida. In the examination hall, they found undergraduates, graduates and some young men who were already working, taking the examination with them. That could only mean one thing: it was a serious matter. "We began to think," said Nasko, "this must be important. We began to think that if this thing was good enough for graduates and under-graduates, then it must be something worth being taken seriously. So, we decided to do more than pass the examination. We decided to do our best." Both the entrance examination and the interview were conducted in Kaduna on July 3, 1962.

After the examination and the interview, many of the boys thought no more of the army. Back in school, they went on to prepare for and write their school certificate examination. If they thought that taking the entrance examination was a healthy prank they could get away with, the Northern Nigerian Government did not think so. The government had no illusions about the effectiveness of its campaign. It suspected that despite the valid case it might have made before the boys, some boys did not particularly look forward to joining the army. They preferred what they considered to be more glamorous careers such as medicine, engineering and law. The army, the intelligent boys among them sincerely believed, was for school dropouts and average students who would not be admitted into the HSC.

The Northern Nigerian government fully understood the situation. It came up with a solution, which gave the boys little room to manoeuvre. The government decided that those who passed the entrance examination into the NMTC but refused to go into the army would not be given HSC scholarship. The 'waverers' were cornered.

Late September 1962, Babangida received a letter through their family Post Office Box 6 in Minna. In the letter dated September 24, the assistant adjutant-general, Royal Nigerian Army, informed him that he had been successful in the entrance examination into the Nigerian Military Training College, Kaduna. He was told to report at the Depot Royal Nigerian Army, Zaria, on Monday, October 15, "for enlistment and preliminary training" unless he had reasons to defer his call up to a later date in the year. Before he could act on it, however, army headquarters sent him a telegram, advising him to choose to either report in Zaria, on October 29 or NMTC, Kaduna, on December 16. But the army headquarters made the decision for him. In another telegram, the assistant adjutant-general cancelled his earlier telegram and advised Babangida to report to NMTC on December 10.

Eight of his classmates received a similar letter and similar telegrams. They were Sani Sami, Garba Duba, Mohammed Magoro, Sani Bello, Mamman Vatsa, Gado Nasko, Ibrahim Sauda and Muhammed Ndakotsu. They had all been selected for Course Six in the NMTC.

On December 9, 1962, Ibrahim Babangida was on the train from Minna on his way to Kaduna for his rendezvous with destiny. It was a path recommended by one of his referees when Babangida took the entrance examination into the military college. Alhaji Abubakar Bale, *Madawaki Bida*, a school manager and senator in the N.A. Central Office, Bida, wrote a referee's report to the brigade commander, Kaduna, dated May 31, 1962. In it, he said of Babangida: *"I think that the army offers his best choice of career and that he would do very well."*

Alhaji Abubakar said he had known Babangida since he entered the secondary school in 1957 and that as a school captain, Babangida "shows a remarkably well-developed sense of responsibility and is a good organiser capable of using his initiative sensibly."

Babangida's principal, Skillbeck, shared the view with Bale. In his own confidential report in support of Babangida's application, Skillbeck wrote: *"He has had a very good academic career and has usually been top of his class. He is proving himself an efficient and co-operative school captain and he would be a very good army material."*

Babangida proved both men right.

V

Babangida left Bida in 1962 with glowing laurels. He won the school honours as a head boy as well as in academics, football, hockey, cricket and athletics. He did not collect his school certificate from the school until May 23, 1991, when, as part of his official visit to Niger State, he visited his old school. He had visited the school on one previous occasion. On November 17, 1973, Babangida, then a lieutenant colonel serving with the 4 Recce Regiment, Ikeja, was among a group of old boys led by Col Inuwa Wushishi, who visited the college. Lt-Cols Sani Bello and Mohammed Magoro were also in the team.

As with Wushishi, the home of his parents and where he spent part of his formative years, Babangida continues to show that he does not forget his roots - ever. On May 21, 1993, he paid his third visit to the school and commissioned the school's IBB Library. The occasion was the glittering gathering of the old boys of the school under the aegis of the Bida Old Students Association, BOSA, which, like Barewa Old Boys Association, BOBA, boasts of leading Nigerians in the military, politics, academics and industry. The library project, to which Niger State contributed N300,000.00, was financed principally by members of BOSA and named after one of the most distinguished old boys of the school.

Babangida was to personally finance four important projects in the school on the recommendation of BOSA. One was the Etsu Nupe Endowment Fund for the benefit of students from poor homes. The late Etsu, Muhammadu Ndayako, father of the late Etsu, Umaru Sanda Ndayako, took particular interest in the welfare of teachers and students of the school. He sent a ram to every teacher whose wife had a baby.

The second project was the Ndakotsu Computer Centre in the IBB Library. This project was named after the late Lt-Col Mohammed Ndakotsu Dokotigi, Babangida's classmate, a maths buff and the first army engineer. He served in the same unit with Babangida during the Nigerian civil war.

The third project, the U.K. Bello Villa, the new residence for the college teachers, was named after the late Lt-Col U.K. Bello, Babangida's aide de camp, who was killed in the abortive coup against the president on April 20, 1990. He too was an old boy, who, according to Babangida, was "an embodiment of loyalty, dedication and hard work in the service of his country."

The man who whetted Babangida's appetite for mathematics and sport, Alhaji Ladan Zuru, national president of BOSA, an old student and an old teacher of the school to boot, had the fourth project, a new sports complex, Ladan Zuru Sports Complex, named after him for his contributions to the development of all facets of sports and his dedication to the growth of the school. Alhaji Ladan introduced the Gymnastics Club, of which Babangida was a member.

On December 8, 1962, Ibrahim Babangida took one final look at his school and walked out into the uncertainties of the larger world to begin a career and a new life. On May 21, 1993, nearly 31 years later, he returned to the school in pomp and glory as president. The timid, lonely orphan who was "confused and bewildered" about Bida was paying homage to his roots where it all began.

Chapter Three

Good Bye, Set Square

Look, whatever he wants to do, just let him do it
–Abdullahi Lajoji

The Nigerian Army has had a coat of many colours. It is an offshoot of a small private army set up to protect the administrative and commercial interests of the British colonialists in the latter half of the 19th century. There may have been several of such armies but the Nigerian Army can, quite legitimately, trace its ancestry to the Hausa Constabulary set up in 1863 and commanded by Captain John Glover. It became the Royal Niger Constabulary in 1866 with the added responsibility to maintain law and order and administer justice in the areas controlled by the Royal Niger Company under the royal charter granted to the company.

The first regular army, really, was the West African Frontier Force raised by Captain Lugard in 1899. In 1901, all private armies maintained by commercial interests were fused into this new military body. But a unified army emerged only in 1914 after the amalgamation of the Northern and Southern Protectorates into one country, Nigeria. The Northern Regiment and the Southern Cadets Regiment merged and became the Nigeria Regiment. The new Nigeria Regiment remained part of the West African Frontier Force and fought World War I under that larger, unified command.

The West African Frontier Force was renamed the Royal West African Frontier Force in 1928. The Nigeria Regiment remained part of this larger army until the 1950s when the British colonial authorities granted each of the national regiments constituting the RWAFF autonomy as the national armies of those countries. Queen Elizabeth II visited Nigeria early in 1956 and bestowed on the Nigeria Regiment the honour of being known as the Queen's Own Nigeria Regiment.

One major development took place around this time. The British authorities recognised the need to train indigenous officer corps of the army in its West African territories. The nationalist struggle was already in ferment in virtually all the British colonies in West Africa. In 1953, therefore, the British set up a military training institution known as the Regular Officers' Special Training School, in Teshie in the Gold Coast

(Ghana) to provide a basic, six-month military training for all RWAFF officer cadets. Successful cadets went on from there for a formal military training in British military institutions, notably Sandhurst and Mons, and were commissioned into the army as second lieutenants.

By 1953, the first indigenous Nigerian army officers emerged. There were four of them. Lt Ugboma, the first Nigerian to earn a royal commission, was commissioned in 1948. The others were Lt Wellington Bassey, Lt J.T.U. Aguiyi-Ironsi and Lt Samuel Ademulegun. The last two played some major roles in the post independence army of Nigeria. Aguiyi-Ironsi became the first indigenous General Officer Commanding the Nigerian Army and later, the first military ruler with the title of Head of State and Supreme Commander of the Armed Forces. He ruled for seven months and was killed in the revenge coup of July 29, 1966. Ademulegun was the GOC, First Division of the Nigerian Army, Kaduna. He was killed in the coup of January 15, 1966.

Teshie served its own purpose in its own time. But as the wind of independence became a gale in each country, the need for each country to look inward and take a greater control of its own military affairs became stronger. The British authorities recognised this nationalistic sentiment and encouraged each country to make its own internal arrangements for the training of its indigenous officer corps. Teshie, consequently, broke up in early 1960.

For the Nigerian government, the challenge of producing sufficient numbers of officers to take over from the British army officers after independence was enormous. In 1959, a year before independence, there were only 30 indigenous Nigerian army officers. Their regional distribution was a pointer to future political problems. Of the 30 officers, six were from the north, fourteen from the east and 10 from the west. The bulk of the other ranks came from the Northern Region.

With the break up of Teshie, the Nigerian government set up a similar military institution, the Royal Nigerian Military Forces Training College, better known by its later acronym, NMTC, in Kaduna, capital of the Northern Region. The Prime Minister, Alhaji Sir Abubakar Tafawa Balewa, formally commissioned the college in April 1960. Sir Abubakar said Nigeria's independence that was only six months away would be meaningless unless there was a strong army to protect that independence. The only way to produce that kind of army, he reasoned, was to train the men, beginning with the basic military training at home. He said the college was to primarily prepare potential infantry officers for further formal military training abroad.

The first set of officer cadet corps was admitted into the college in March 1960. Some of the cadets in the set were Theophilus Yakubu Danjuma, Ben Gbulie, Chiabi, Ayo Ariyo, Samuel Ogbemudia, Simon

Uwakwe, Pius Eromobor, Emmanuel Abisoye, Ignatius Obeya, Alabi Isama, Sule Apollo, Ihedigbo, Julius Alani Akinrinade, David Bamigboye and Martin Adamu.

On December 10, 1962, Course Six opened at the NMTC. Sixty young men reported to the commandant of the NMTC to begin their basic military training. One of them was Ibrahim Badamasi Babangida. When he received the second and final letter dated November 16, 1962, from army headquarters in Lagos, offering him admission into the NMTC he restrained himself from jumping for joy. He seemed to have been ambivalent towards a military career. One part of him wanted it but the other part did not. The part that wanted it pushed him to take the entrance examination into the Boys Company, Zaria, in 1954. He was successful.

The Boys Company was set up that year to give secondary and military education to Nigerian boys for four years from the age of fourteen. It was primarily for boys who intended to make their career in the army. Babangida wanted to go to the school but his uncles refused. His family did not seem to think highly of the army at the time. Babangida accepted their decision. But the decision by his uncles did something to him that no one who was close to him suspected. It hurt his pride. His uncles had no reasons to believe that Babangida and the army had not heard the last of each other.

As his close friends were to learn in later life, if Babangida feels that his pride has been hurt over something, it engenders in him a resolve to do or get it. He felt his uncles had challenged his decision to do what he would with his own life. Although he accepted their decision without further argument, Babangida knew, as General Douglas McArthur once said, that he would be back.

Meanwhile in secondary school, he began to develop some interest in another career – engineering. He dropped hints about this among some of his close friends. He poured his energy into mathematics and began to show evidence of the analytical mind of the engineer. Interestingly, however, some of his teachers, including the principal, Skillbeck, believed Babangida was a good material for the army. Skillbeck said so in his recommendation in support of Babangida's application.

When the telegram came informing him of his admission into the NMTC, Babangida acted the confused innocent. Clutching the piece of paper, he went in search of his other classmates who took the entrance into the NMTC with him. He found that Gado Nasko, Sani Sami, Sani Bello, Mohammed Magoro and Abdulsalami Abubakar had also been admitted into NMTC. That was a good sign. He and his friends were going to the same school. That alone, he thought, would erase any doubts or objections his uncles might have against his military career.

Fate dissolved his worst fears. None of the boys admitted into NMTC had a choice. The Northern Nigerian government wanted all of them in the army. And that was that. The government decision made things relatively easy for Babangida. If his uncles objected to his going into the army, he could argue that the decision was not his but the government's. He could do nothing about it.

Babangida went home with the telegram and told his uncles he had been admitted into the NMTC. To his surprise, his uncles had not changed their mind about the army. They still refused. They did not like the army but they did not tell Babangida why. The only member of the family who wore a uniform was a warder in the prisons service. He was Babangida's paternal uncle, Aliyu Wushishi.

This time, however, their opposition met a more determined Babangida. He was no longer prepared to let them have their way. Joining the army had become a settled matter in his mind. Two things, at least, informed his decision. Firstly, he had learnt everything he could about a military career from two former old boys of his school, 2Lt Inuwa Wushishi and 2Lt Garba Dada. Babangida had consulted them and sought their advice even before the telegram offering him admission into NMTC came.

They told Babangida fascinating stories about life in the army as officers. They advised him to join the army. If he wanted to be an engineer, the army had that opportunity. He would miss nothing he ever wanted to do, they told him. Moreover, they replayed in his ears the campaign of the premier and the minister of defence. Government would not waste its money and time recruiting boys into the army if it was not convinced of the role it would play in the new nation, they argued. He too should be part of whatever role the army would play. Whatever lingering doubts Babangida melted away.

Secondly, nine of his former classmates had also been admitted into the college. That was important to him. He was going to remain in the good company of his close friends and together, they would make a career in the army.

The *imam* of Minna, Alhaji Abdullahi Lajoji, was Babangida's maternal uncle. He was so close to the *imam* that he was nicknamed *Jinkan Imam* (grandson of the *imam*). Babangida took his problem to the old man and sought his support in the choice he had made for his life. He acknowledges that it was the *imam* who "really saved me from my uncles." The *imam* called a family meeting to resolve the matter. When everyone had had their say, he ruled: "Look, whatever he wants to do, just let him go and do it. What you need to do is for all of us to pray for him," he ruled. Case closed.

II

December 10, 1962, was a new day in more senses than one in the life of Ibrahim Babangida. On that day, he said a long good bye to the setsquare and his ambition to become an engineer. On that day, he and eight of his former class-mates from Bida joined 51 other boys from various parts of the country who reported to the commandant of the Nigerian Military Training College, Kaduna, to begin their basic military training as cadet officers.

What was his first day of his new life like? Babangida recalls:

> It was hell because here we were, bushmen in *kaftan* or big gown. The moment we stepped in they started shouting at us. That is the normal thing - to break you. Some sergeant majors started shouting at us. They doubled us, booed us and called us names. That is always the first thing in the army. They psychologically make you look a bloody fool. And that was what they did to us. They asked us to lie down and kicked us. Oh, it was hell. In fact, after the first experience, there were some of us who thought we were going to run away.

Officer cadet Garba Duba could not take it anymore. He ran away from the college. His parents lived in Kaduna. When the young cadet got home and told his father he had had it with the army, the old man suspected some of his son's other friends might be feeling the same way. He immediately stepped in to abort whatever alternative plans the other boys might have had in mind. He called the boys from Bida and sat them down to a long pep talk on their future responsibilities as army officers. Then he came down hard on them. He told them others had been through the same training. They too were human beings. If those other boys could take it, so could the confused boys before him. They had no alternative, he emphasised. He told them he would make sure they remained in the college and did their best. He cooled down again, patted them on the back and told them to return to the college. They all went back, dragging Duba with them. The boys soon settled down to business.

But it certainly was not an easy life. Nasko recalls:

> You know, when you get there, they will bash you for the first two months. It was nothing other than drilling. We weren't allowed to go anywhere. We had to polish our boots until we could see our faces in them. Then we had to run and do obstacle races. They had to make sure all of us were physically fit and mentally alert. We were given weapons training - stripping weapons and assembling them and then we went on practice firing. In addition to all these, we had our academic subjects such as general knowledge, current affairs, map

reading, history, military history and other subjects to cover. Life was tough.

Babangida did not find the course easy either. In the final confidential report shortly before he passed out of the college in April, 1963, the chief instructor in the officer cadet wing of the NMTC, Captain Cruickshank, noted that although Babangida

> "received a good all-round report from his platoon instructor, who described him as lively and conscientious, I have found him to be an average cadet with a pleasant manner but an unimpressive classroom performance, being 41st in the order of merit. There were 60 cadets in his class."

Babangida remembers two men in NMTC who made impressions on him and his subsequent military career. One was Captain Martin Cokshine, an English man, who was the future general's company commander. "He impressed me a lot," said Babangida. The other officer was a young Nigerian, Captain Christian C. Ude, his platoon commander. He retired from the army with the rank of major during the Nigerian crisis of 1966 - 1970. He and Babangida became "very, very close."

One other cadet who was also very close to Ude was Sani Abacha, who, like Babangida, had a rewarding career in the army. He was a four star general, Chief of Army Staff, minister of defence as well as Chief of Defence Staff in the Babangida administration. He staged a coup against the Interim National Government in November 1993 and became head of state. He died in 1998.

Babangida and Abacha were Ude's favourite cadets. When Babangida was in the Indian Military Academy, he and Ude wrote each other quite frequently. Ude always ended his letter to his protégé with this admonition: *Work hard. Play hard. Pray hard.*

NMTC provided a six-month basic military course. Students were taught the rudiments of their profession such as field-craft and weapon training and a little bit of the organisational set up of the army. At the end of the course, cadets who passed the final examinations were sent to military institutions in some Commonwealth and other countries, which offered assistance in the training and development of Nigeria's military manpower. Britain, the United States, India, Pakistan, Ethiopia, Canada and Australia were some of the countries that offered this aid to the country.

NMTC students did not choose the countries or military institutions themselves. The commandant of the college, in consultation with army headquarters, did so. In 1962, however, the minister of defence, the late Alhaji Muhammadu Ribadu, decided it would be more helpful to Nigeria if specific countries were responsible for specific military needs of the nation. India was chosen for the army (which was why it helped to set up the Nigerian Defence Academy, Kaduna); Britain was chosen for the navy and West Germany for the air force.

In 1963, India offered eight places to Nigeria in the Indian Military Academy, Dehra Dun in the state of Uttar Pradesh. Babangida, Magoro, Sauda and Duba were among those selected for the course in India. All of them could not go at once because the academy did not have enough room. India was at war with China over a border dispute between the two countries at the time. India, therefore, needed more room to train its own manpower needs. The academy was virtually packed full. One class alone had between 200 and 300 students. It was all India could do to offer only a few places to Nigerian students. The eight boys from NMTC were, therefore, broken into two groups of four. Cadets Babangida and Magoro were in the first group that left for India in April 1963. It was Babangida's first trip outside Nigeria.

Babangida and his colleagues were not the first Nigerians in the Indian Academy. Some other cadets had trained there before them. They even met some of them, one of whom was Umaru Salihu, who died during the Nigerian civil war. India was something of a culture shock for the young men from Nigeria. The people were not out rightly hostile to foreigners but they made them feel like the strangers that they were. Babangida recalls his first experience nearly 30 years later with some awkward amusement:

> I found that our hair became an object of attraction. People wondered if it was natural or artificial. Children ran after us wherever we went, laughing because of the colour and nature of our hair. You noticed that people were always looking at you. I had occasion when some children, even some grown-ups, were touching my hair to see if it was natural.

If the Indians wondered about his hair, Babangida was equally surprised at what he saw of the Indian society. He had never heard of vegetarians. Babangida found it both amusing and curious that there were people who did not eat meat. More curious still was the mode of the dressing of some of the men he saw – the Sikhs and their turbans.

Nothing prepared him for a society divided strictly on class lines. "It was my first time of coming into contact with class distinction," the general said. The caste system in India was and remains strong. It is not something foreigners understand easily. It is at the root of their complex social, religious, economic and political system.

Life in the academy was tough for the young Nigerians. India's war with China made the normally demanding military training at the academy even tougher. The student population was unusually large - about

1,000. The entire training was geared towards responding to the war. It exposed the Nigerians to a war situation although they did not engage in combat. Magoro recalls that life in the academy "was very rough. Very rough! Virtually for twenty-four hours, nothing but training. We hardly had the time to even sleep."

The training was rigorous. Officer cadets who could not measure up were either relegated in class or kicked out of the academy. The academy tolerated no laggards. No one could be sure of commissioning until they were commissioned. A cadet could lose his commissioning even five minutes before the ceremony if he was found to be wanting in any aspects of the course.

The formal training in the academy lasted from April to September 1963. The young Nigerians made it. When their big day arrived for the commissioning on September 26, the young Nigerians felt greatly relieved. They had gone through the crucible. Their career in the army was now a reality. Babangida was a sector commander in the academy with the rank of corporal. He recalls:

> It was a big sigh of relief that we had virtually gone through the most difficult aspect of our formative life in the military. It was a very big relief and I was convinced then what I went through in the academy prepared me sufficiently for whatever other difficulties may lie ahead in my professional career. It was a big sigh of relief for me.

After his commissioning as a regular combatant officer in the Royal Nigerian Army (a month before it became the Nigerian Army) with a personal army number N/438, 2Lt Babangida was attached to an Indian army regiment known as 17 Horse Poona Regiment before returning to Nigeria. He had chosen the armoured corps. That was a bit of a surprise. In secondary school, he had prepared his mind for a career in engineering. It would seem natural to expect him to seize the first available opportunity to realise that ambition. It is difficult to say if engineering was on his mind at this point in time in his life.

At the academy, there was a great deal of competition among the instructors to win over students to their various areas of specialisation - the infantry, artillery, armour and engineering. Each instructor played up his specialisation as the superior arm of the army. Babangida fell in love with armour because the armour officers had "a peculiar way of dressing" which attracted him. The armour officers had an aristocrat, soldierly bearing; their swagger stick was different and their uniform and lanyard were "very, very attractive." They seemed to walk more smartly than the other officers too. Their apparent feeling of superiority was unmistakable. It was the kind of company Babangida liked to keep. He elected to keep that company although at the time the Nigerian Army did not have an armoured corps. That was why he became a recce officer on his return home from the Indian Academy. Babangida's choice of the armoured corps turned out, like most of his decisions early in his life, to be a choice informed by foresight, as we shall see later in this book.

Officer cadet Garba Duba was in the second batch that went to India four months after the Babangida group. It was the first time the two friends had been separated for so long since they entered secondary school together. Duba became one of Babangida's early converts to the armoured corps. Duba too was aware that the Royal Nigerian Army did not have an armoured corps but he had enough faith in his friend's judgement to accept to become an armour officer.

2LT IBRAHIM BABANGIDA returned to Nigeria in January 1964. The Indian Academy was through with him. He was posted to the reconnaissance squadron, First Brigade, Nigerian Army, Kaduna. A tall man with the bearing of a typical, legendary soldier, Brigadier Samuel Adesujo Ademulegun, commanded the brigade. He had an overwhelming presence that cast a shadow over his subordinates. He was a much-respected officer. Babangida soon found out why. The brigadier was fiercely intolerant of incompetence. In Ademulegun's military philosophy, you were either a good soldier or not a soldier at all. There was nothing in between. Only the best officers and men were good enough for the brigadier. Babangida remembers him as "a bloody good soldier. We always shivered when we knew he was around. He was very dominating."

Babangida stood before this dominating presence shortly after he was posted to the brigade. He was attending the brigade commander's interview. The brigadier had received Babangida's report from the Indian Military Academy from Army Headquarters in Lagos. He did not like what he saw. The academy had rated Babangida's performances as average. An average officer in his brigade? He promptly sent for Babangida. Ademulegun looked up at the young man before him and in a barely restrained voice, he read the young second lieutenant the riot act. He told him:

> Look here, my young man. I am supposed to be writing about you once in a year but I am going to put you on probation and there will be a report about you every three months until we see that you improve.

He curtly dismissed Babangida. He did not say what would happen if Babangida did not improve. Babangida knew the consequences of his failure to improve. If he failed to improve, Ademulegun would be as good as his words. He would kick him out. Babangida's ego and pride were hurt but he admitted to himself that the brigadier was fair in placing him on probation. In latter years, he would admit that that singular action challenged him more than anything else in his life. It helped to shape in him the resolve to prove his professional worth. He set to work to prove himself; to show that whatever happened in India was now behind him. He did not know how far his military career would carry him at this point but he knew one thing for sure: he would not be kicked out of the army for incompetence.

Actually, the decision to place Babangida on probation for a year was taken by army headquarters in Lagos and not by Ademulegun. Nearly three months before Babangida and his course mates returned from India, the Indian Military Academy had sent their confidential reports ahead of them. Babangida and Ibrahim Sauda were rated below average in the final assessment of their performance. Babangida received C- (low average).

He and Sauda were posted to the Recce Squadron in Kaduna. In a memo dated January 11, 1964 signed for the acting adjutant-general, Captain Yakubu Gowon, conveyed the GOC's order to Ademulegun that both men "be put on probation for a year and reported on quarterly till they have improved." As if that was not enough, the acting adjutant-general wrote another letter on February 24, 1964, directing the brigade commander to interview Babangida and Sauda and to warn them that "...they will be on special probation for one year. The future of the officers," the memo added rather ominously, "will depend on the progress they make during the period they are under probation." The first report on them was due August 20.

Interestingly, despite his poor final result, the Indians still believed Babangida would do well in his chosen career. His battalion commander, Lt-Col J.V. Pinto, wrote of the young second lieutenant:

> A smart gentleman cadet with a soldierly bearing whose turn out is good. He can express himself well. He is reserved and does not mix easily. His manners are pleasant. He has a fair sense of duty and has the necessary dash, determination, initiative and self-confidence. He exercises command effectively. He is tough and can stand up to sustained mental and physical effort.

Babangida played soccer and represented his battalion in the academy. A bit strange though that Babangida could be said to be reserved and not mix easily, considering his circle of friends in secondary school. But the report did tell the truth about him. Even back home in Nigeria, he felt more comfortable in the company of his childhood friends such as Duba and Nasko. The main reason is that Babangida is essentially a very shy man. He has worked hard, particularly as a public officer, to conquer his shyness but in his early days in the army he was a lot more cautious with new friends. In only a few cases did he ever hit it off with strangers. This partly explains why he tends to remain loyal to old friends. He does not open up to strangers easily, if you discount his certain air of bonhomie.

In Kaduna, Babangida set to work to save himself from the professional equivalent of the death sentence. He had a year to prove that he could make it in the army. Luck was on his side. His immediate boss, the squadron leader of the recce squadron, Captain Ofong U. Isong, liked him. It was Isong's duty to write periodic reports on him to the brigade commander. Babangida got on "very, very well with him. He was," the general admits, "very fond of me."

Isong regarded Babangida as his ward. He felt a responsibility to make a good officer and a good soldier out of the young man. He helped him in any way he could. Babangida responded to his tutelage like a good pupil.

Six months after his first interview with the brigade commander, Babangida was again summoned to Ademulegun's office. His heart was in his mouth as he walked briskly towards the brigadier's office. In the outer office, he tried to make some jokes with the military assistant. Babangida was trying to gauge his mood to alert him to what awaited him on the other side of the brigadier's door. He went in trembling but came out a happy man. He was off the hook. After only two reports from Babangida's immediate boss in the recce squadron, Ademulegun was quite satisfied that the lieutenant was of the professional calibre he wanted in his brigade.

In a report dated August 7, 1964, Isong wrote:

> This officer looks shy and one would tend to think he is not mature. He is naturally quiet and does not take part in conversation easily.
> He is keen and eager to learn. When confronted with problems, he asks questions and always seeks the advice of those who can be of help to him.
> His sense of responsibility is rapidly growing and he accepts responsibility without fear. His activities so far with the squadron have been satisfactory.
> This officer will no doubt, prove a success and will certainly be up to the required standard. At present he still requires supervision to certain extent over his work. He is young and doubtless to say, he has the will to learn and the understanding necessary.

Ademulegun forwarded this report to army headquarters with the following remarks: "Babangida appears to have decided to settle down to work. I recommend that there is no further need for special reports on him."

The General Officer Commanding the Nigerian Army, Major-General C.E. Welby-Everard, simply noted: "I concur." And that was it.

Babangida lived in the unmarried officers' quarters near the officers' mess along Kanta Road, Kaduna. He shared a room with his close friend, 2Lt Garba Duba. They turned the second room into a living room. They ate together and as young men, hit town together. Duba was more or less Babangida's banker. He kept most of his money with him. That suited Duba just fine. It meant any time he needed money, he simply took whatever he needed from his friend's "deposit" with him. Babangida was, as usual, casual about this although he did not have other sources of income. He was carefully nurturing the image he cultivated in secondary school – the image of a generous man willing to suffer that others might not; the image of a young man to whom money meant a lot less than true friendship. He never asked Duba to give account of the money he kept with him. Sometimes, he acted as if he even forgot he kept money with his friend. And because of Babangida's complete trust in him, Duba himself learnt to be a good "banker."

Babangida was a young officer about town. His favourite drink was whiskey with water. He gave up alcohol after his holy pilgrimage to Mecca in 1976 in fulfilment of his promise to himself that he would do just that. He loved parties and did not find female company an unnecessary distraction. But he never smoked. For him and his friends in Kaduna, the good times simply rolled. At weekends, they went out to parties, which, in their parlance, were known as cock crawling. They went out early and came back in the small hours of the next morning. Duba did not drink alcohol.

The cock crawlers were birds of the same feather. One of them was Sunday Ifere, now late, who, like Babangida, was a second lieutenant. Ifere received his military training in Ethiopia. He too chose the armour corps because, according to him,

> in any army, the armour officers are special. Not that they are special because they have two heads but that they are the best trained. By the time an armour officer is promoted a captain, he must have been trained in the UK, the United States, India or Pakistan while some of his colleagues may not even know Murtala Muhammed International Airport.

Ifere returned to Nigeria in 1965 and was posted to the recce squadron in Kaduna. He came with a Volkswagen car. It did not take him long to know that he and Lts Babangida, Duba, Mayaki and Anifowoshe "were of the same stock in behaviour and so on." They became a close-knit circle of friends and would pile into Ifere's car in some of their outings. When Babangida bought his own car, he became more or less the driver for the group.

One of Babangida's closest friends who did not exactly belong to the group of cock crawlers was the ascetic 2Lt Gado Nasko, an artillery officer. He trained at Mons Officer Cadet School of Artillery, Larkhill, in the United Kingdom. He shared a room with Ifere in the same block with Babangida in the unmarried officers' quarters. As childhood friends and former classmates in Bida, Nasko, despite his rather serious attitude to life, kept Babangida's company. They went out together occasionally on Nasko's bicycle.

They went to the Palace Hotel, Kaduna, one night to watch a live band. They left the hotel about 11.00 pm. Nasko's bicycle had no light but it was their only means of transport. They got on it. A policeman stopped them on the way and arrested them for riding a bicycle without light at night. They told him the streetlights were enough. The policeman said the law did not say so. He would take them to the police station, he said. Nasko and Babangida pleaded with him but the policeman insisted on doing his duty. He would take them to the police station and let them explain themselves to his superior officers there.

Perhaps, if he had known that he was dealing with army officers, he would have acted differently. Nasko and Babangida refused to tell him who or what they were because if the matter became much more serious, a superior police officer would report them to their superiors in the army too. They could be in trouble.

Babangida suggested they take a short cut to the police station. The policeman agreed. Nasko was dragging the bicycle in front, followed by the policeman with Babangida in the rear. Suddenly, Babangida slapped the policeman hard across the face from behind. Nasko, startled by the sudden sound of the slap, turned and saw the policeman running for dear life but vowing to get the "offenders" the next day.

Nasko rebuked Babangida. "How could you do a thing like that?"

Babangida simply grinned and told him, "Let's ride our bicycle." They laughed and rode back to their quarters.

Ifere was Babangida's senior in the army but because his training in Ethiopia lasted longer than Babangida's in India, the latter was already in the unit by the time Ifere returned home. Their friendship brought Ifere under Babangida's tremendous professional influence. Ifere was a rather zealous young officer. Babangida helped to cool that zeal early in their military career. On one occasion, some officers placed under Ifere failed to perform their duty. The choice before Ifere was simple. The officers had failed to do their duty and they must be punished in accordance with military regulations. The lessons he was taught in the military academy were still fresh in his mind.

For no apparent reason, he thought he should discuss what form of punishment he would give the erring officers with Babangida. Babangida advised Ifere to warn the officers and let them know, in no uncertain terms, that if it happened again, they would be severely punished. That was not the typical reaction of young officers. Ifere expected anything but that but he took the advice, somehow convinced that because they were such good and warm friends, Babangida could not have advised him to take action he knew could ruin his military career. Ifere, who retired with the rank of major general, recalled:

> He told me that in putting into practice what one learnt in the academy, one should at least put into consideration, the environment and the character and behaviour of the people. And I found out he never misled me and the friendship actually developed. He wasn't the type of person that would say "go ahead" and eventually I would find myself in trouble with my superiors because if I continued with the style I wanted, there would come a time when I would find two or three officers under me having extra duties and my boss would begin to wonder what happened to my man management which I learnt in the academy. I found that by following him, I would be able to learn more and improve in my handling of the unit entrusted to me.

The bond of friendship between the two young officers became tighter. Ifere admired Babangida's cool, almost detached professional judgement. He found him incredibly unruffled when all around him were losing their heads. "He was very calm," said Ifere. He went on:

> Nothing moved him. If you saw him any time and he was not smiling, he must be thinking. And as soon as he found the solution to what he was looking for, he came back to his normal, calm, laughing self."
>
> Babangida was great fun to be with. If he sensed tension in any gathering, he cracked a joke, everybody laughed and the tension melted. Said Ifere of the president's jokes: "He was very good at that." It rubbed off on his close friends. Those of us who have been close to him developed the same attitude. In those days, we would sit around, order cow leg pepper soup and tell all sorts of jokes. And we learnt to keep calm, not to panic. This won for us the loyalty of soldiers who felt confident in the hands of officers who they knew would not panic under any situation.

This must be seen as part of the rather complex nature of Babangida. A shy man who does not mix easily and yet was the life of any gathering? His confidential reports from India to Nigeria spoke of his shyness. Rather difficult to fathom? Hardly. Although what had become clear at this point in his career was that Babangida had become more sure-footed and, therefore, more relaxed about life, he took his time to warm up in a new environment. He admits that as a young man, "I was quiet in an environment that I was not familiar with."

Babangida liked to study his environment and the people he met. His policy was not to rush into making friends because once he made them he kept them. And because he had trained himself to be a good listener, he always appeared to detach himself from the crowd so he could listen more attentively to everyone's points of view. This gave, and still gives, him command of his environment and situations.

Babangida's most important education was acquired from the enduring institution known as human beings. He treasures the company of people. His ability to win friends and influence people has been his greatest asset in his professional life as a soldier and in his socio-political engineering as president of the Federal Republic of Nigeria. As a young officer, Babangida encouraged his fellow officers to mix freely with the rank and file in the army. "We could mix freely with all the soldiers," Ifere recalled.

John Shagaya testifies to that. After completing his studies at the Nigerian Military School (formerly Boys Company), Zaria, Shagaya was posted, along with six of his classmates from NMS, to the 1 Recce Squadron, Kaduna, in 1964. He was what the army calls an other rank – a non-commissioned officer. Some of the officers in the squadron at the time, all second lieutenants, were Babangida, Duba, Chris Ugokwe, Alhassan Yakubu, Yakubu Anifowoshe and J.C. Ojukwu. Shagaya recalls:

> The impression one had of these young officers at the time and particularly Babangida was that whereas our colleagues, ex-military school chaps, met with hostility and intimidation in other units of the Nigerian Army, we had a fantastic, humane relationship with these young officers. What drew Lt Babangida very close to some of us was the fact that he was a sportsman. He used to play soccer very well, both for his unit and his brigade. He also used to play hockey and being NMS boys, sporting activities were one of the major activities we used to do. We found ourselves interacting with the officers, not like soldiers and officers.

What particularly impressed the young soldiers was that Babangida took more than a professional interest in them. He was interested in their welfare as well. He encouraged the ex-NMS boys to register and study for the GCE. Shagaya said Babangida "went out of his way sometimes to pay for our course fees to ensure that we developed educationally. He also ensured that we did our regimental courses to the extent that within one and half years, we had become highly-trained soldiers."

Shagaya and Babangida's professional paths were to cross so many times, cementing their private and professional relationship. Shagaya later received his commission and rose to the rank of a brigadier-general and was one of the 23 officers who staged the coup against Buhari that brought Babangida into power in 1985. He was Babangida's first minister of internal affairs.

Something else developed from the close interaction with the officers and men which Babangida, Ifere and Duba had fostered. At first Babangida and Ifere took it as a hobby challenging each other as to who would remember the names of officers and other ranks in their units more. When they found this was useful, the two men went one step further. They compiled the personal details - marital status, number of children, hometowns, etc - of all the officers and men in the regiment. They called this the *Unit Bible*.

The main lesson of the *Unit Bible*, according to Ifere, was that an officer must ask after the welfare of his men and troops. He explained:

> The two of us kept strictly to the teaching of the Unit Bible. There is nothing that gives a soldier more confidence than when you ask about his wife or child. He will go home and tell his wife: 'Do you know that *Oga* even remembers the name of our child? If anything happens to the child, *oga* will be angry.' That kind of thing inspired the soldiers to work harder. If a soldier misbehaved, we checked his personal details in the *Unit Bible* and we said no wonder because he has 13 children, may be due to pressure at home that was why he behaved like that. We used to compensate for this burden of family problems.

Such was Babangida's influence on his close friends that they nicknamed him **The Boss.** It also became a mutual nickname with Babangida, Ifere and Duba.

Remembering names and recognising faces is at the heart of the Babangida mystique. Nearly six years after he became president, he went on a state visit to his home state, Niger. At the civic reception in Minna, he decided to move around, greeting people and acknowledging their greetings. He saw a man in the crowd straining his neck, apparently to have a better view of the nation's number one citizen. Babangida recognised him immediately. He called the man by his nick name. The poor man froze in surprise. He and Babangida were classmates in the primary school and had not seen each other for about 35 years.

IV

In the mid-sixties, Kaduna, capital of Northern Region, was a sleepy town. Its most important residents were mainly civil servants. There were not many indigenous bureaucrats in the high echelons of the civil service. But there were newly minted young administrative officers, some of whom were educated in the United Kingdom. These young men were the cream of the society, the rising stars in the firmament of the Northern Regional government.

The young army officers were part of this cream. Nearly all of them were unmarried. Their pay was good. And like all young men, with money to burn, the young army officers hit the high road to good living. Their influence on the town did not go unnoticed. Many civilians longed to cultivate the friendship of these young officers: some for the immediate benefits of drinks in the local hotels; others for loftier reasons. Two hotels, The Greens and Spring Hotel were the favourite haunts of the young officers and their new civilian friends.

Babangida felt the need to encourage the growing interaction between the young officers and the young bureaucrats in the civil service. He did not think it was enough for them to meet in hotels for a few drinks or attend all night parties. Something more constructive could be made from this growing bond of friendship. Babangida appeared to have seen further ahead than his friends. He saw the young officers and the young bureaucrats as lucky actors cast in certain leading but different roles in the immediate post-independent Nigerian nation.

The young bureaucrats would be taking on more responsibilities in response to the exigencies of the political development in the country. The young officers would also be assuming greater responsibilities in the security of the nation. There was need for such different groups playing almost identical roles, to get to know and understand one another. As mess secretary, Babangida devised a plan for the military to officially sanction and effect this interaction. His proposal was simple. He called for the admission of selected young bureaucrats and young professionals in the private sector as honorary members of the officers' mess. The army authorities accepted his proposal.

This innovation, according to Ifere, had a salutary effect on both sides. For the officers, he said, it helped in building up their sense of maturity: "how to talk, who to talk to and so on." Perhaps for the civilians, it lessened the fear of the military. They could relate to the young officers as friends and "mess mates."

Two such civilians have remained close friends of the president. One was Haruna Kolo, who was an assistant secretary in the federal public service; the other was the late Adamu Augie, who was a producer and ace newscaster with the Broadcasting Corporation of Northern Nigeria, BCNN, and later NTA.

Babangida had helped to construct a vital bridge between the two worlds. He has not always directed traffic on that bridge but as we shall see later in this book, he has always taken more than a casual interest in the traffic on it. The civilians became the main source of Babangida's political education, which came in most useful for him as events shot the military into the nation's political leadership and progressively moved the future general towards the top of the political totem pole.

In India, Babangida saw a nation at war and what war entailed - at least from the safe distance of his classroom. He did not have a field experience. It took only a few months and then a little over two years for him to face the grim realities of war back home.

His first experience was the Tiv riot in the mid-sixties. The riot was a festering political sore in the Northern Region. Long before Nigeria gained independence in October, 1960, there were agitations for the creation of more regions out of the Northern, Western and Eastern regions. The agitation was particularly strong in the minority areas of those regions. Various pressure groups were set up in these areas to force the colonial authorities to create new regions. Her Majesty's government, appointed the Sir Willink Commission to look into those agitations and advise on how to respond to them. The commission acknowledged that the minorities had genuine reasons for their fear but ruled the creation of states out of the question because it believed that those fears could best be taken care of administratively. Her Majesty's government heeded the advice and left well alone.

The Middle Belt Congress, UMBC, led by the late Joseph Sarwuan Tarka, championed the agitation for a Middle Belt Region. UMBC, a leftist party, found a political soul mate in the Action Group, AG, led by Chief Obafemi Awolowo in the Western Region. AG supported the creation of more states. The Northern Peoples Congress, NPC, that controlled the government of Northern Nigeria, was stoutly opposed to the balkanisation of the region into states. Leaders of the UMBC and other state movements in the region were often victimised by the government.

Tiv Division in the then Benue Province became a hot bed of political clashes between rival political supporters. These clashes degenerated into a series of serious crises soon after independence in 1960. The police were unable to contain the violence. Government had to bring in the army as a last desperate resort.

The army launched a containment operation code-named *Operation Adam*. Babangida took part in *Operation Adam Three*. There had been *Operation Adam One* and *Operation Adam Two*. Some of the others who took part in *Operation Adam Three* with Babangida were Duba, Captain Remawa, Lt M.B. Mayaki, Lt-Col Pam and Major Abba Kyari. Pam was the boss of the recce regiment in the operation. Remawa headed the recce squadron in the Wukari sector of the operation. Babangida served under him there. The squadron took charge of all the areas north of Wukari including Ibi and Gidan Ayu riverine village to the northeast of Ibi. The areas also included Takum, Donga, Zaki-Biam and all the areas southeast of Wukari.

The 3 battalion was responsible for all the other areas south of the recce sector - Katsina Ala, Gboko and Makurdi. Babangida was a troop leader. Shagaya, a non-commissioned officer at the time, served under him. A recce platoon is usually smaller than an infantry platoon. This makes for closer contacts between recce officers and men in the same platoon. It was easy, therefore, for Shagaya and the other soldiers to come in close contact with Babangida. Shagaya recalls that Babangida displayed a capacity for hard and extra work. He carried out all assignments given to his platoon personally. His testimony:

> He never delegated the responsibility to his second in command, his platoon sergeant or sergeant major. He took personal charge and ensured the success of every operation. He was mindful of the fact that it was an internal operation. He also ensured that justice was not miscarried by troops under his command. You could see in him courage and determination to succeed. He was also very concerned about the welfare of his troops.

Babangida received a commendation from that operation.

Major Hassan Usman Katsina, a recce officer, returned from the Staff College, Camberley, England, in December 1964. He was posted to the recce squadron in Abeokuta. He was given only a few days to move. But before he did, he was ordered to proceed to Makurdi to take over the recce regiment from Pam who was leaving for Tanzania on a military assignment. Major Abba Kyari was Pam's second in command and should have taken over the regiment from him but he had been nominated for an overseas course.

A month after Katsina took over, Kyari left for an artillery course in the United States. Katsina found Babangida to be "a brilliant officer" and made him his staff officer. He was in charge of planning in the headquarters of the recce regiment in Makurdi. It was here that Babangida met briefly with one of the legendary Nigerian army officers, Brigadier Zakari Maimalari, who was passing through Makurdi. He stayed the night with Katsina. The brigadier and the major stayed up late at night playing scrabble. Babangida stayed up with them. It was the closest he came to knowing the brigadier. He never saw him again. He was killed a little over one year later in the first military coup of January 15, 1966.

It did not take too long for Babangida to charm his way into Katsina's heart. Both men soon became quite close. The major found the lieutenant to be "a very jovial officer." He made a joke of serious matters and had his fellow officers frequently wiping off tears of laughter from their faces. Katsina has a rather casual disposition but poor responses to his orders frequently angered him. He said he often found himself "shouting and fuming when something went wrong."

Babangida would play the nurse over his frayed nerves. Katsina, now late, retired as a major general. He was military governor of the Northern Group of Provinces during the Ironsi military administration. He was also Chief of Staff, Army and later Chief of Staff, Supreme Headquarters in the Gowon administration. He said Babangida "would try to cool me down jovially and within minutes, we would be laughing together."

In a confidential report from the theatre of *Operation Adam Three*, Katsina said of Babangida:

> A very cheerful officer who is always smart and alert. Though young, he has shown himself very capable of shouldering high responsibilities. He is disciplined, confident and popular. He is very keen at his duties and has tremendously helped his unit commander in running the efficiency of TAC HQ (OP ADAM III) at Makurdi. He is trying very hard to improve his military knowledge. 2Lt Babangida has a bright future in the Nigerian Army.

How truly prophetic Katsina's last sentence!

Katsina drew his officers close to himself. He too was young and loved those things young men love. Like most soldiers, he was pretty comfortable with the bottle and the stick (cigarettes). This made it easy for him to freely socialise with the junior officers under him. They often played scrabble and listened to the BBC far into the night. "We were always together; living together, joking together. They were all my friends rather than just working colleagues," Gen Katsina recalled.

Babangida was the closest man to the major in the group. Katsina's living room served as his office. Babangida had a room on the other side of the living room and he never went to bed until the major retired every night. From that vantage position, Babangida was much more than a night nurse to the major. He was learning from the major and the major was learning a great deal from this young officer too.

What particularly impressed Katsina was Babangida's humaneness. As far as Katsina could see, Babangida did not see his duty in the Tiv riot as a military assignment to crush the rioters. He saw it as an opportunity to save and rehabilitate the victims of the political violence. Katsina supported his every suggestion along this line. The men and officers of the recce regiment soon found themselves playing the role of humanitarian aid workers - distributing clothes to the victims of the riot. The clothes came from the army divisional headquarters in Kaduna because Katsina had succeeded in convincing his commanding officer, Ademulegun, who in turn had convinced the premier of the Northern Region, the late Sir Ahmadu Bello, of the need to assist those who had lost all their personal belongings in the riot. "That is why my name is very well known in Tiv land," Katsina said of the role he and his staff officer played.

Back from that theatre of violence, Katsina and Babangida returned to their unit now commanded by the former, in Kaduna. But in May 1965, they went off again on a routine military exercise in Gaidam near the Nigeria-Cameroun border in the then Borno Province. Gaidam is a fairly big town with its own district head. It had some things that were of interest to officers and men of the recce regiment. Katsina allowed the officers and men to go to the town "to enjoy it." But they must return at a designated time. More often when the time came, most of the officers and men did not return. Yet the officers punished the other ranks that failed to return on time.

Babangida felt this was unfair. The officers were, he felt, trying to live above the law. What to do? His answer came one day when Katsina noticed that none of the officers had returned to camp on time. Only Babangida was in the camp. Katsina ordered him to "go back into the town and bring me any officer who had passed this time." Babangida told him that even "some of my seniors like Ray were out." How was he to bring such people to the commander?

Katsina decided both of them should do the job together but Babangida said he could handle it. He mounted a one-man checkpoint and all the officers returning late were caught. It was an opportunity Babangida had been waiting for to tell the officers they were not above military regulations. If the troops must observe the time out regulation, so must the officers. Little did he know that the biggest "culprit" would be Katsina himself. Babangida was surprised to see the major returning late from the town that night. And he too was found on the other side of the roadblock. How come? No sweat, Katsina said. He had not violated his own orders. He had merely decided to go and look for Babangida in the town himself! "We had a big laugh," said Katsina.

Late in 1965, Babangida was off again to a flash point - the Western Region - torn by political violence, the violence that was to lead to major political developments for the entire country. In Operation Cockscrow, the army assisted the police in various parts of the region to restore peace, law and order. Political differences between Chief Obafemi Awolowo, national leader of the Action Group and former premier of the

Western Region and his former deputy and premier of the region, Chief Samuel Ladoke Akintola, had boiled over. It was political violence on an unprecedented scale in the country.

In what came to be known as Operation Wetie, (wet him with petrol) political opponents and their property were routinely doused with petrol and set on fire. Arson was rampant. The violence was beyond the competence of the police. The army had to be called in. Four recce units were sent from Kaduna to the West to assist the 4 Battalion, which led the operation. Babangida led one of the recce units. Duba, Alhassan Yakubu and Ugokwe led the others. The recce squadron headquarters was at Top Camp in Ibadan. Babangida's troops operated in Ikare and Akure areas in Ondo Province. The operation was suddenly terminated on January 11, 1966. Babangida and his colleagues returned to Kaduna on January 12.

In less than one year, Babangida had been at two different political boiling points in the country. He had played a role in both of them. As a young officer, truly apolitical in the best British military tradition, Babangida believed he had done no more than his duty in obedience to the orders of his commander-in-chief. Unknown to him and millions of other Nigerians, he had begun what was to become a long trek to the destiny that fate had decreed for him.

The shadow of the Nigerian political crises had begun to lengthen, drawing the new nation inexorably under it. In desperation, the political leadership had, perhaps, inadvertently, involved the military in their resolution - to suppress the mayhem and restore some sanity, law, order and peace to the troubled spots in the federation. It is debatable if the decision of the political leadership influenced the thinking of the five young majors who planned and executed the overthrow of the Balewa administration in January 1966. But the involvement of the military in the resolution of the bloody civil crises must have contributed in creating the impression that the civil authority had completely lost the will and the ability to contain them. Something was bound to give. It did.

Welcome to a brave new world. Babangida as a young boy

Babangida's father, Malam Muhammed Babangida, with his daughter, Hanatu

Babangida's only sister, Hajiya Hanatu Gambo

Babangida (middle) with Abdulsalami Abubakar (1st left) and Mohammed Magoro (2nd right) and a friend

The two future generals and heads of state: Babangida (r) and Abdulsalami Abubakar

The young man about town: Babangida in suit and sunshade

Young love birds: Babangida and Maryam

Till death them part. Babangida and Maryam at their wedding

Aisha   *Muhammed*

Babangida's children

Aminu   *Halima*

Chapter Four

A Crack in the Wall

Coups succeed coups. This won't be the end of it
–Major Hassan Usman Katsina

At 3 am, January 15, 1966, Lt Ibrahim Babangida returned from cock-crawling to his bachelor pad on Kanta Road, Kaduna. He did not have to wait for sleep. It came almost immediately he hit the bed. At about 4.30 - 5.00 am, there was a repeated banging on his door. The sleepy lieutenant suspected that one of his close friends, who knew he came in late, was being mischievous. He refused to answer the door. He rolled over on his side and tried to go back to sleep.

His caller refused to give up. He went round to his window and repeatedly rapped on it. Babangida jumped out of bed and drew away the window blind. He recognised the 'intruder,' Lt Christopher Ugokwe. He gestured frantically to Babangida to open the door. Both men, good friends were in the recce squadron. They went to work together in the same Land Rover every morning.

Ugokwe was virtually out of breath as he rushed into Babangida's room. He did not give Babangida the chance to ask questions. He told him: "Come on, dress up, let's go to the office." Babangida thought his friend must be out of his mind. He smiled and told Ugokwe he was tired. All he wanted was to be left alone to enjoy his sleep. Why would he be going to the office so early any way? It was a Saturday. Ugokwe suspected that Babangida was unaware of what was happening.

Ugokwe: Don't you know what's happening? There is trouble.

Babangida knew better than to ask further questions. He quickly put on his uniform. He and Ugokwe jumped into the Land Rover and drove and headed for the headquarters of the recce squadron at Ribadu Cantonment located at the present site of the Nigerian Defence Academy, NDA. On their way, they passed by the ministers' quarters at Ungwar Shanu. There, indeed, the two young officers saw the fiery face of trouble. The official residence of the premier of the Northern Region, Sir Ahmadu Bello, Sardaunan Sokoto, was on fire. The first thought that came to Babangida's mind was that the political violence in the country might have spread to the regional capital. Arsonists must have set the premier's house on fire.

It was not unthinkable. Powerful as he was, the late premier lived a simple, private and official life. He lived among his ministers. He did not have a battery of security men around him in the office or at his official residence. A devout Muslim, Bello left his personal safety severely in the trusted hands of Allah. Daring arsonists would not have found it impossible to assault his house. But Babangida could not convince himself what he saw that night was the handwork of arsonists.

He and Ugokwe hardly spoke to each other on their way to the office. They drove in silence, each man pre-occupied with his own thoughts. They met their squadron leader, Major Hassan Usman Katsina, in the office. The major had gone to the office as soon as he got wind of the trouble. He was trying to reach some senior officers when Babangida and Ugokwe came in. One of those Katsina tried to reach but failed was Colonel Okoro. Katsina, lighting one stick of cigarette after another, tried to remain calm. His subordinates knew he was as troubled as they too were. They watched him with mounting apprehension.

Within minutes of Babangida's arrival in the office with Ugokwe, more and more officers and men of the recce squadron rushed into the office. The sound of small arms fire in various parts of the town sent them racing to the office. None of them quite knew what was going on.

Katsina knew. He decided to tell the officers what he knew. He told them that the army had staged a coup against the civilian regime. He told them of his brief meeting with Major Chukwuma Kaduna Nzeogwu, chief instructor at the Nigerian Military Training College, NMTC, in the office earlier that night. Nzeogwu was armed with a sub-machine gun and was attended by well-armed soldiers. Nzeogwu asked Katsina which side he was on. Was he with him or with them?

Katsina and Nzeogwu were classmates at Sandhurst. Although they were not close friends, they were on quite good terms. Katsina did not know what his friend was talking about but he appreciated the choice he had to make. He could not argue with an armed man, heavily guarded by equally well-armed soldiers. He told Nzeogwu they had always known each other and that he certainly would be where his friend was. Katsina then told the officers it was their duty to "defend your environment." Their environment was the regional capital, Kaduna. Babangida and other officers later organised patrol of the town "to make sure that calm was maintained throughout Kaduna."

The Nigerian armed forces had broken with their ingrained British military tradition of leaving politics to politicians. They had stepped on the hallowed but messy grounds of politics. Katsina *saw* where this would lead. Nzeogwu and his co-plotters had opened the Pandora's Box. Katsina told Babangida and the other young officers close to him: "I know coups succeed coups. This will not be the end of it. This country will continue to witness coups d'état."

II

Lt Nasko lived in the officers' mess at Kalapanzi barracks, Kakuri, Kaduna South. At about one o'clock that morning, Major Alex Madiebo, the battery commander, woke him up. He was surprised to see the major in a loincloth, popularly known as *wrapper*. Madiebo told Nasko one mad man had killed the Premier and many other people. According to Nasko, "he told me I should immediately get dressed to mobilize the troops and get ready to defend the barracks and that we should be prepared to defend it to the last of our troops. So, I immediately dressed up, went innocently. I didn't even realise there was a lot of danger but I began to mobilize and deploy the troops."

Actually, Nasko narrowly escaped from being used in the coup. Nzeogwu ordered him that night to command the battery which went to support what Nzeogwu had said was a routine night military exercise, code-named *Operation Damisa*. Nasko protested. He did not want to command somebody else's troops with whom he had not been training. He knew the risk of refusing to take orders from his superior. To protect himself, Nasko took his case to the battery captain, Captain Abdul Wya. Wya agreed with him and took up the matter with Nzeogwu. He dropped Nasko and picked Lt Olafenha to command the support battery troop. Nasko was the only one left in the officers' mess. His colleagues who did not go for the exercise melted into the town "for one thing or the other."

At about 7.00 am, Captains Domkat Bali and Wya went to the barracks and asked Nasko what was happening. He told them what he knew which was no more than what Madiebo had told him. The three officers were discussing the confused situation when Madiebo came back, now in uniform. He gathered all the other officers together and told them what was happening. There had been a mutiny led by Nzeogwu. He told them the premier, the brigade commander and some other people had been killed. He had been in touch with Nzeogwu on the phone. He said he was going to meet him at the brigade headquarters. Nasko and the other officers, who believed that Madiebo was "a very loyal officer" and not part of what was happening, tried to persuade him not to go. He could be in danger. Madiebo told them not to worry. He said he knew Nzeogwu and that he would persuade him to give up his so-called revolution. "So," said Nasko, "we agreed but we told him we were going to zero our guns on the brigade headquarters and if anything should happen to him, we were going to demolish the place."

Madiebo returned two or three hours later and told them everything was under control. He said that the GOC, Major-General Johnson Thomas Umunnakwe Aguiyi-Ironsi, had escaped death and in control with the support of loyal officers and men. The picture was still unclear in Kaduna. Nzeogwu reached Lt-Col Chukwuemeka Odumegwu-Ojukwu, commander of the 5th Battalion in Kano, on phone and, according to Ojukwu, asked him for "a whole lot of things - vehicles, money, etc." Ojukwu refused to take orders from him. Nzeogwu was his junior. It was still unclear to Ojukwu what was going on in Lagos. He was the only one holding out against Nzeogwu in the north. Lt-Col W.U. Bassey, commander of the Depot, Nigerian Army, Zaria, had "left his command and fled."[1]

Nzeogwu ordered all the officers in Kaduna to report at brigade headquarters where he briefed them. With a heavy bandage around his neck and his left arm, he relished his new status of a hero. He told them the military had taken over the government of the Federation and that his task was to secure the Northern Region in the name of the Supreme Council of the Revolution of the Nigerian Armed Forces. He called for their co-operation in the big task of solving Nigeria's political and social problems. He told them local military commanders so empowered, in accordance with the extra-ordinary decree he had just issued would appropriately punish those who were not with him.

But despite Nzeogwu's bravado, the 'revolution' was not going well. He waited for word from his co-conspirators assigned to Lagos, Ibadan and Enugu. There was no broadcast from Lagos announcing the military take over as was planned. What went wrong?

Nzeogwu later drafted a speech that he broadcast on the NBC, Kaduna. "In the name of the Supreme Council for the Revolution of the Nigerian Armed Forces," Nzeogwu declared, "martial law over the Northern Provinces" and suspended the constitution of "the regional government (and) the elected assembly." He went on to justify their action:

> The aim of the Revolutionary Council is to establish a strong, united, and prosperous nation, free from corruption and internal strife. Our major aim of achieving this is strictly military, but we have no doubt that every Nigerian will give us maximum co-operation by assisting the regime and not, repeat not, disturbing the peace during the slight changes that are taking place.

The enemies of his revolution were

> the political profiteers, swindlers, the men in the high and low places that seek

bribes and demand ten per cent, those that seek to keep the country divided permanently so that they can remain in office as ministers and VIPs of waste, the tribalists, the nepotists, those that make the country look big for nothing before international circles, those that have corrupted our society and put the Nigerian political calendar back by their words and deeds.

In his capacity as the leader of the Revolutionary Council, Nzeogwu summoned all senior civil servants in Kaduna to the brigade headquarters. He spoke to them about what he and his co-conspirators had done and asked for their co-operation with the Revolutionary Council. The business of government, he said, must go on. The regional ministers had been relieved of their duties. The permanent secretaries were now in charge of the ministries until further notice. The police were similarly given instructions on what to do.

Nzeogwu did not even order the arrest of the politicians. Perhaps, he did not quite know what to do with them, the most obvious enemies of the revolution. Alhaji Isa Kaita, minister of education, went to see Nzeogwu at his headquarters to find out what he wanted to do with them (the ministers). Nzeogwu received him politely and reportedly told him that although the operation he carried out had to be bloody, he did not mean any harm to them. They were free to stay in Kaduna or anywhere else in the country for that matter. It was enough that they were no longer ministers.[2]

He addressed a press conference on Sunday, January 16, at which he announced that he had appointed an 18-man cabinet made up of civil servants for Northern Nigeria "to stamp out tribalism, nepotism and regionalism." He said his regime intended to stay in office just long enough to normalise government machinery. "We only moved out the trouble-makers in our midst and we hope things will be all right," he said, raising more questions than answers.

Something else was unclear, indicating the rather unsettled situation in which the major now found himself. In what capacity did he speak for the Revolutionary Council of the Nigerian Armed Forces? Although he said he was in charge of the Northern Provinces, he took no leadership title either. Still, his broadcast made him the hero of the 'revolution.'

The bottom fell out. Army headquarters in Lagos distanced itself from the coup. Nzeogwu's broadcast in Kaduna the afternoon of January 15 was followed almost immediately by a short official statement broadcast on NBC, Lagos, dismissing the coup d'état as a mutiny by some dissident soldiers. According to the statement:

> In the early hours of this morning, 15th January 1966, a dissident section of the Nigerian Army kidnapped the prime minister and the minister of finance and

took them to an unknown destination. The General Officer Commanding and the vast majority of the Nigerian Army remain completely loyal to the Federal Government and are already taking all appropriate measures to bring the situation under control.

Nzeogwu refused to accept that the game was up. He threatened to march on Lagos to complete his revolution. He claimed the army authorities in Lagos were planning to march on Kaduna to crush the mutiny. He told the officers and men to be ready to defend the Northern Provinces. It was clear to Babangida and other young officers that this lone actor on the stage of the nation's unfolding tragic drama had unleashed forces beyond his control on the country.

As the grim details of the coup began to filter on to the larger canvas of the national situation, the future military president realised that January 15, 1966, had become a watershed in the politics of the country. The coup had been bloody. Ademulegun and his wife had been killed. This shocked Babangida as much as it did the other officers. The killing of the premier and some members of his family pained him.

Nzeogwu led the assault on the premier's residence and shot Sir Ahmadu Bello, his wife and his security guard dead. Babangida, Katsina and Mayaki were very close to the late premier. Babangida says the premier "took a lot of interest in us. He was very generous to us. He used to give us money and anything we asked. The three of us happened to be his favourite young officers. Knowing that we had lost him made us feel bad."

The killing of Ademulegun was, Babangida says, "callous" but he was a soldier. Soldiers are not strangers to cruel and callous deaths. Babangida felt that the killing of the brigadier's wife was both cruel and senseless. She was "an innocent woman who had nothing to do with military matters. So, why kill her?" He still wonders.

Nzeogwu denied he had anything to do with the killing of Ademulegun and his wife. Babangida later found out that Nzeogwu lied about this. Ademulegun's killing was not an accident. It was part of the strategic plan. Nzeogwu bore grudges against the brigadier. Babangida said he "also knew that Nzeogwu committed an offence and Ademulegun was trying to discipline him." He does not remember what the offence was because the charge against the major "was not formalised" before the coup took place. He is sure it had to do with insubordination.

Nzeogwu was actually having problems with the military authorities at the time. Captain Udowoid wrote a letter to the brigade commander, accusing Nzeogwu *"of brain-washing officers against the government and planning a coup."* Ademulegun referred the letter to Col R. Shodeinde, Nzeogwu's commandant, who although did not recommend any actions against the major, advised that *"there is no smoke without fire even if it is smouldering fire."* Ademulegun duly made his report to Army headquarters in Lagos. He described Nzeogwu as *"a young man in a hurry"* and advised that he be *"closely watched."*[3]

It is quite possible that Nzeogwu got wind of this report. Udowoid quoted him as saying: "Wait until the day you will look at the senior officers through the sights of your rifle."

Some of those who knew Nzeogwu said he was contemptuous of some of his superior officers. He once referred to Aguiyi-Ironsi as a 'tally clerk.' He was also highly idealistic. And like all idealistic people, he tended to see the solution to every problem, no matter how complex, in rather simplistic terms. This was reflected in his confidential reports.

In his confidential report in July 1963, Lt Col H.M. Njoku, said Nzeogwu was a *"resourceful, calm and calculated"* man who, since he knew him in 1960, had *"made remarkable improvement in his social outlook and now shows good signs of maturity."*[4]

Nearly two years later in February, 1965, his boss at the NMTC, Col Shodeinde, commended Nzeogwu's hard work but noted that he was *"inclined to be easily upset when the views of others are contrary to his own, particularly officers of his own rank. Also in his enthusiasm he has the tendency to take too much for granted."*[5] His involvement in the coup and his subsequent handling of events showed those character traits at full play.

Nzeogwu was something of an oddity in the army. He did not drink. He kept away from female company. He withdrew to himself and devoted himself to work as a more creative compensation. He was a pretty complex character. Odumegwu-Ojukwu remembered him as an eccentric person. "Sometimes he (Nzeogwu) would shave his entire head and that would be his period of retreat. He wouldn't speak to people for weeks."[6]

Lt General T.Y. Danjuma, former Chief of Army Staff, said he and Nzeogwu were "very close friends. Nzeogwu was a charming (but) confused person. A bit flippant."[7] Nzeogwu took more than a passing professional interest in the politics of the country. He was very critical of the Tafawa Balewa administration and the behaviour of the politicians. According to Danjuma: "He had this method; he would start criticising government and then watch your reaction. If you joined him in criticising the government, then he would say well, we would fix them one day. He wanted Nigeria to look like China. An exuberant young man but he didn't know that China was China and is peopled by Chinese."[8]

Major-General Joshua Dogonyaro remembers the late major as "a very self-disciplined officer (who) was very conscious of his military profession." He recalled that Nzeogwu became increasingly interested in the political goings-on in the country. "The way he put it to you," said

Dogonyaro, "was that the civilians were trying to destroy this country and that it was not good to allow the civilians to destroy the country." Nzeogwu spoke contemptuously of some "ignorant and uneducated politicians" who were ruining the country. He also, according to Dogonyaro, often alleged that the politicians had corrupted some senior officers. Still, Dogonyaro said he was shocked to see Nzeogwu take up arms against the government and some military officers "because we never suspected anything like that happening in this country."

Some of Nzeogwu's close friends certainly saw nothing wrong or unusual with Nzeogwu's interest in the politics of Nigeria. Obasanjo, one of the closest friends the late major had, admits: "We were idealistic young men, inspired by the mood of nationalism that was sweeping through many parts of Africa at that time and as young army officers, we freely discussed the future of the Nigerian Army, Nigeria and Africa, and the condition of the black man in the world."[9]

Such discussions must have brought Nzeogwu into contact with some other idealistic young men, some of whom were young university graduates who had joined the army. Among them were Major Emmanuel Ifeajuna, a graduate of the University of Ibadan, who made a name as a high jumper in the Commonwealth Games in Canada in 1954, and Major Adewale Ademoyega, who claims to be the sole survivor of the five majors who planned and executed the coup. At the time of the coup, Ifeajuna was the brigade major in Lagos.

It still remains unclear who really led the coup. Obasanjo remains convinced Nzeogwu did. The general says that as the political "situation in the country grew worse, he (Nzeogwu) started to talk more unguardedly to identified officers, to work out a plan of action. He chose Major Emmanuel Ifeajuna ... as the officer to work with and to co-ordinate the south. The impression had been given by Ifeajuna that he was thinking of the same thing at the same time and they both hit off immediately."[10]

Muffet disputes that contention. He points out that although Nzeogwu was "the leader (indeed, the instigator) of the mutiny in Kaduna," he was not "the brains behind the plot."[11] John de St Jorre supports Muffet's view. He argues that "contrary to popular belief and Nzeogwu's own claim, it appears that the original caucus did not include him. Majors Ifeajuna and Okafor (commander of the Federal Guard) were the principal plotters and they brought Nzeogwu - dubbed by one writer, 'the Brutus of the coup' - in later since they needed an efficient and strongly motivated man to direct operations in the north." [12]

Ojukwu also believed Nzeogwu did not lead the coup. He contended that "Ifeajuna led a group of young officers, mostly of the rank of major and below and attempted to take over the government of Nigeria." Nzeogwu, he said, was credited with leading the coup because of the broadcast he made in Kaduna. "He did not (lead the coup). He actually joined that group."[13]

It is unlikely that the truth about Nzeogwu's actual place in the coup plot will ever be known. He ruled the Northern Provinces for all of four days. His revolution ended. But he succeeded in locking up democracy. Aguiyi-Ironsi assumed power as Head of the Federal Military Government and Supreme Commander of the Armed Forces of the Federal Republic of Nigeria. The man who did not dream of power became Nigeria's first military ruler.

On Monday, January 17, Aguiyi-Ironsi, accompanied by the head of the navy, Commodore Akinwale Wey, and the Inspector-General of Police, Alhaji Kam Salem, addressed a crowded press conference in the senate building, Lagos. He said that his "main concern is to restore law and order as soon as possible" and that how long he remained in power would depend on how long it took to return life in the country to normal. He set up the Supreme Military Council as the highest legislative organ in the country. Permanent secretaries functioned as both administrative and political heads of their ministries at the federal and regional levels. The former regional governors became advisers to the military governors of the regions. He appointed military governors for the four regions - Major Katsina (North), Lt-Col Francis Adekunle Fajuyi (West), Lt-Col David Ejoor (Mid-West) and Lt-Col Chukwuemeka Odumegwu-Ojukwu (East).

Nzeogwu and the other coup plotters were arrested. Ifeajuna escaped to Ghana but was later repatriated after President Kwame Nkrumah was also over thrown in a coup.

When the smoke cleared the scale of the killing of senior army officers by the coup plotters shocked Nigerians. In addition to the Sardauna, the Prime Minister, Alhaji Sir Abubakar Tafawa Balewa, his minister of finance, the flamboyant Chief Festus Okotie-Eboh, the premier of the Western Region, Chief Samuel Ladoke Akintola, had all been killed. The toll in the army was also heavy. Brigadier Zakari Maimalari, Brigadier Ademulegun, Col Kur Mohammed, Lt-Col Yakubu Pam, Col R. Shodeinde, Lt-Col Abogo Largema and Lt-Col Unegbe were dead. Of the officers killed, four (Maimalari, Pam, Largema and Mohammed) were from the north; two (Ademulegun and Shodeinde) were from the west and one (Unegbe) was from the Mid-West.

III

The Nigerian 'revolution' took off on the wrong foot. This dramatic development in the politics of this country ran into a cloud of mutual suspicions. To be sure, there was some relief at the going of the politicians. Their excesses generally denied them public sympathy. But questions turned to the real objectives of the coup. Like most things in Nigeria, both the north and the south perceived the mission of the military in politics differently. The south generally welcomed it with unguarded celebrations. According to St de Jorre, "In Lagos and other major towns there were popular demonstrations expressing support for Aguiyi-Ironsi's military government."[14]

The north was less jubilant. Its suspicion about the real motives of the coup was fuelled by several factors. The first was the region lost nearly all its senior military officers in the coup. They were Brigadier Zakari Maimalari, Commanding Officer, 2 Brigade, Lagos; Lt-Col Yakubu Pam, Adjutant-General of the Nigerian Army; Lt-Col Abogo Largema, Commanding Officer, 4 Battalion, and Colonel Kur Mohammed, deputy commandant, Nigerian Defence Academy, Kaduna.

The second source of suspicion by the north was that four of the five majors who struck were Igbo. Only one, Ademoyega, was Yoruba. It was easy for the north to put two and two together and arrive at the conclusion that the political dis-empowerment of the region was the real objective of the coup.

Aguiyi-Ironsi's policies did nothing to dissuade the north from this line of thinking. He had his own solution to the problems of the nation. One of these was to abolish federalism and replace it with a unitary system of government. On May 26, 1966, he issued decree 34 of 1966. The decree abolished the regions and unified the federal and regional public services. The former four regions were renamed groups of provinces. The Federal Military Government was accordingly renamed National Military Government.

Aguiyi-Ironsi believed he took the right decision because he was convinced "that the bulk of our people wanted a united Nigeria…(and) one government, …not a multitude of governments." He appointed a one-man commission headed by Francis Nwokedi on the unification of the public and judicial services of the centre and the regions. He acted even before Nwokedi submitted his final report to him.

The north was wary of the unification decree. What may loosely be described as the first northern reaction to it came in a letter published in the *New Nigerian,* a Northern Nigeria government-owned newspaper, on April 19, 1966. The writer, Alhaji Suleiman Takuma, was a senior producer with the NBC, Kaduna. He objected to the unitary system and argued that it was best for Nigeria to remain a federation. He pointed out that "the mad rush of application letters for jobs" in the north from the southern provinces raised the worst fears in the north about the real intentions of the coup plotters. He told Aguiyi-Ironsi that "a unitary government (would) not necessarily unite the people of Nigeria."

The head of state responded to Takuma the only way dictators do. He locked him up. Takuma must have correctly represented the feeling of the north. Three days after Aguiyi-Ironsi abolished federalism, protest riots broke out in Kano and quickly spread to some other towns in the north. The decree had grazed northern sensibilities.

The north had some genuine reasons to suspect that the unification of the public services was patently against its political and economic interests. The region lagged far behind the other three regions in Western education. It could not compete with them in a unified public service structure. As at independence in 1960, the north had only 41 secondary schools. The Eastern and Western regions had more than four or five times that number each. Here is a fair picture of the level of the disparity between the Northern and Western regions and what the north was up against: At independence, the Western Region had 1,250,000 children in primary schools; the north, the largest and the most populous region in the country, had primary school enrolment of only 250,000 children.

It was struggling to train indigenous administrative and other critical levels of manpower when the change of government interrupted it. The implementation of its northernisation policy was even affected by its lack of manpower. The south resented the domination of political power by the north before the coup. After the coup, the north feared the same thing from the south.

As Professor Jonah Isawa Elaigwu very well put it:

> The concentration of political and economic power in the hands of southern leaders had titled the delicate Nigerian balance. Political power had been the north's safeguard against the south's economic and educational advantages. With the military coup...the Northern Region's political advantage was destroyed. The South's advantage in the bureaucracy (which, if anything, was strengthened in authority by the coup) was greatly augmented. Thus, the efforts to strengthen and unify the civil services came to have political consequences.[15]

Aguiyi-Ironsi blamed the riots in the north on unnamed foreign elements. He remained unshaken in his resolve to have one Nigeria, one government. The emirs and chiefs in the north sent him a confidential memo advising him to abrogate the decree, return the country to a federation and try the coup plotters for treason. He had, indeed, promised to try them for mutiny and treason but he did not. He also ignored the memo.

Had the head of state been sufficiently sensitive to the mood in the military, he would have realised that officers of northern origin were becoming increasingly unhappy with his molly cuddling of the mutineers. The mutineers continued to draw their salaries even in detention. This special privilege granted them fuelled fears among the northern officers that the head of state was privy to, and fully backed, the coup and, therefore, had no intentions of punishing his 'co-conspirators.'

According to Danjuma:

> We (the northern officers in particular) had expected the so-called dissident elements, as General Aguiyi-Ironsi's announcement called them, to be tried. Then (the press) started saying the people who did it were national heroes and they should be forgiven. And the government was foolish enough to get carried away by it. It was an unpopular coup in the army because we said if you have to overthrow the government that is when you will need all hands on deck to run the country properly. Why do you have to wipe out half of the senior officers? These questions were not answered. Instead, we were subjected to all sorts of harassment.[16]

At the time of the coup, Danjuma was a major and staff officer, administration, in army headquarters. He recalls that his "immediate boss, Col Pam, was killed in that coup; my former battalion commander was killed in that coup."[17]

The simmering feeling of discontent and betrayal among the northern officers was soon brought to a boiling point, thanks to their political education by the young northern bureaucrats. They educated the young northern officers on the implications of Aguiyi-Ironsi's actions and how they affected the political and other interests of the north.

"They told us," Babangida recalls,

> that injustice was being done to the northerners. You could see a sudden awareness. Then they began to taunt us, telling us the Sardauna was killed, Balewa was killed, Maimalari and all those northern officers were killed. What were we going to do about it? There were publications in the *New Nigerian* along those lines. You could see a really orchestrated sort of thing. We were politically agitated.

According to Duba:

> We were young officers and we were left without any reasonable leadership. At that time, officers did not care where you came from; whether you were

Yoruba or Ibo. All they knew was that you were a fellow officer of the Nigerian Army. But then one night, we found out that one tribe, mostly Ibos, woke up and eliminated northern or Hausa officers of the rank of major and above. That was the time we started thinking that something had to be done; something for the interest of this country, for the nation, for the north and for our own safety. And when the northern students in the universities, particularly at Ahmadu Bello University, Zaria, started this campaign of Araba, we had interactions with them and they told us that they could not just sit down when such a thing was happening to them. It was at that time that things like politics began to interest us.

IV

For most of the early part of 1966, Babangida was only part of the audience watching the drama. Nine days after the military took over, he enrolled in Course 38 of the Young Officers' Course (ARMED C) in Britain where he received a four-month course in Saladin and gunnery. The course ended April 22. His confidential report from the course shows that he was still having some problems with the weapons of war but he had begun now to influence others. He came ninth in the Saladin course. His senior instructor noted that Babangida was willing to invest extra time and energy in the course. "His general attitude to the course," the senior instructor wrote, "and his time-keeping have been excellent and he has been an example to the others in his class."

He did not do that well in the gunnery. Both the chief instructor of the Gunnery School and the officer in-charge of the Gunnery Wing, agreed that Babangida was "a very cheerful and hard-working officer who achieved a satisfactory standard." With a touch of a wry military humour, the report went on to note that Babangida was "…a little uncoordinated and in practical work, seems to have more thumbs than he is really entitled to." He took 17th.

By the time Babangida returned to his unit from the course, the political situation in the country was virtually racing towards a dangerous precipice. In only three months' time, he would play his first role as one of the kingmakers in military politics in Nigeria.

Events moved rather rapidly in the army. After the May riots in the north, rumours were rife in military circles. The rumours had two parts to them. One part was that northern officers were planning a revenge coup; the other part was that Igbo officers were planning another coup to finish up the 'unfinished business' of January 15. It would appear that both sides believed these rumours and did more than look over their shoulders.

Aguiyi-Ironsi was aware that *esprit de corps*, the bond of comradeship that holds armies together, was breaking down, thus occasioning these rumours. But he put it down to lack of adequate information on the policies of his administration. He decided to try and rebuild trust and confidence of the officers and men in one another and in his administration. He assigned the task to his chief of staff, army, Lt-Col Yakubu Gowon. It is difficult to establish how much Gowon did and to what effect. Perhaps, the Supreme Commander acted a little too late.

About the middle of July 1966, Aguiyi-Ironsi, pressing on with his new doctrine of one Nigeria, one people and one government, announced he would rotate the military governors by posting them to groups of provinces other than their own. Hitherto, the military governors were indigenes of the group of provinces they ruled. This posting would, in his view, be in accord with the letter and the spirit of decree 34 that recognised Nigerians, not northerners, easterners, westerners or mid-westerners. Interestingly, although the north interpreted this rotational policy as part of the plot to subjugate it politically, Murtala Muhammed and subsequent military rulers from 1975 adopted it.

The Supreme Commander began a tour of the country that month to sell his policies and programmes to the people prior to the reposting of the military governors.

V

By early July, the northern officers had decided on a counter-coup. The inner caucus was made up of majors Murtala Muhammed, Yakubu Danjuma and Martin Adamu. They opted for a pre-emptive action to forestall the alleged plans by their counters from the eastern group of provinces. Members of the inner caucus sent emissaries to northern officers in military formations in some parts of the country. Lt Ahmadu Yakubu was one of those emissaries sent to Kaduna. "We knew something was in the offing," recalls Babangida.

Yakubu briefed the selected officers about the rumours they picked up concerning alleged plans by their colleagues from the east. He said that the rumours were so strong that they could not ignore them any longer. They had lost once; they were not prepared to lose again, he said. After the briefing majors Abba Kyari and Musa Usman and lieutenants Babangida, Sani Abacha, Yakubu Dambo and Garba Duba, were selected to co-ordinate what Danjuma admitted many years later as "revenge coup."[18]

Babangida nearly ruined the plan. Two days before July 29, the date set for the coup, he made "a slip." He told Lt Abdullahi Ahmed about it. Madiebo, commander of the recce squadron, reported the rumours he kept hearing about a coup plots by northern officers to Lt-Col W.U. Bassey, Ademulegun's successor as the brigade commander. Both of them agreed that Madiebo should nose around to find out if the rumours were more than rumours.

Somehow, Madiebo got lucky. Ahmed told him what Babangida told him the previous day. Bassey and Madiebo summoned Babangida. He knew he was in trouble because "they got to know that maybe, I knew something about it. They called me and I knew that I was going to be in trouble. So, I went and told them I didn't have any idea of what they were talking about. I told them I was chatting with Ahmed when I told him of the rumour I heard."

Babangida was subjected to a series of questions. He maintained his ground that he knew nothing about an impending coup. He heard a rumour and told his friend about it. And that was that. He was allowed to go but he knew he had become a marked man. He managed to get through to the co-ordinators and all of them went for a meeting at the Kaduna Gardens near the police firing range. There, he told the rest of the group of his encounter with Madiebo. The co-ordinators took whatever measures they believed were necessary to protect themselves. But they had no intentions of calling off the coup.

In continuation of his nation-wide tour to meet with traditional rulers, Aguiyi-Ironsi was scheduled to be in Ibadan from July 28 to 29. The coup plotters decided to begin the operation with his arrest along with his host, Lt-Col Francis Adekunle Fajuyi, military governor of the Western group of provinces. The first shots went off in Abeokuta. On the night of July 28, fighting broke out in the army garrison there. The garrison commander, an Igbo officer, was killed along with several Ibo soldiers. Lts Onoja and Ibrahim Sauda led the northerners.

Some published accounts blame subsequent developments on this incident by saying that it "beat the gun," thus suggesting, possibly, that a date other than July 29 was chosen for the revenge coup. Nasko said that the incident "prompted the counter-coup planners to hasten action." It is still not clear what exactly led to the fighting. Some unconfirmed accounts say that the garrison commander had called either a meeting or a party of mostly Igbo officers and that because of the growing distrust among the officers and men of the Nigerian Army, the northern officers interpreted the meeting or party as the final rehearsal for the second coup allegedly being planned by the Igbos. The northerners, according to this account, quickly decided on a pre-emptive action. They rounded up all those who attended the meeting or party and killed them. On the night of the incident, two northern officers, Captains Remawa and Bali, were said to have been locked up in Bali's office, suggesting that either they were not privy to the incident or the other group within the northern group did not trust them.

The fighting in Abeokuta had immediate ripple effect in other military formations. In Ikeja, Lagos, "the Abeokuta fighting touched off an expected barracks revolt. Northern soldiers pounced on their Igbo colleagues and killed many of them."[19]

In Ibadan, Danjuma and Lt William Walbe, took charge of the execution of the plan. They arrested Ironsi and Fajuyi. The rest of that is now history. Lt Sani Bello, aide de camp to the head of state, was caught in a delicate balancing act. He is a northerner but he was not aware of the coup plot. When the shooting started in Ibadan, Bello took steps to protect the head of state. But he was more or less lost because he was a stranger in Ibadan. His unit was in Enugu before he became ADC to Ironsi. The only officer he could think of immediately was Lt Ibrahim Umar Sauda, his classmate in Bida. He telephoned Sauda in Abeokuta and told him: "Look, things are getting tough here."

Sauda told Bello to hang on; he would drive his armoured vehicle all the way to Ibadan to help. That would have taken ages. Sauda remembered that Lt Mohammed Magoro and Captain Garba Dada were in 4 Battalion right there in Ibadan. Dada, who was the adjutant, was Bello's senior in Bida. Magoro was his classmate. Sauda told Bello to reach them to see what they could do. Magoro had no telephone, so Bello contacted Dada who promptly took steps that, Bello says, saved his life.

Bello and an Air Force officer, Captain Andrew Nwankwo, who was also with Ironsi, witnessed the death of Ironsi and Fajuyi at an isolated bush on the outskirts of Ibadan. Col Hilary Njoku, who was also with Ironsi, was said to have escaped with gunshot wounds.

It remains a painful experience for Bello. He liked Ironsi because he found him to be "very pleasant, a typical army man." He said Ironsi "looked hawkish from outside but inside, he was a very soft person, a loveable man." The head of state impressed the young officer, or as Bello referred to himself, "a miserable second lieutenant," when he went for interview as his ADC. He was late for the interview but he was the choice of the commander-in-chief.

In Kaduna, as soon as word about the shooting in Abeokuta was received, the co-ordinators swung into action. They rounded up the southern officers, mostly those from the east and the mid-west. Most of them were course mates of people like Musa Usman, Hassan Katsina and Abba Kyari. Babangida himself had been pretty close to some of them too, having worked closely with them. The northern officers did not want to burden their conscience with the blood of their military colleagues. They decided to save them.

All the officers were herded into protective custody at Kanta barracks. A day or two later, the officers, worried stiff about their fate, asked Nasko if any harm would come to them. He assured them that as long as he himself lived, no harm would come to them. But one of the northern officers, Lt Yakubu Dambo, was conducting his own private war against the eastern officers. He went to them at the Officers Mess, Kanta Road, and persuaded them that they would be safer and more comfortable in the state house.

Dambo then sought permission from Kyari to transfer the men. Kyari, innocently, gave his approval. When they were being taken out, they expressed their gratitude to Nasko for saving their lives. Nasko was unaware of Dambo's motives. To Babangida's shock, Dambo had all the five affected officers shot at a spot on the Kaduna-Jos road. The next day, in an attempt to cover up what Babangida still regards as "a dastardly act," Dambo floated a story to the effect that the officers had escaped and that someone had come with an aircraft to spirit them away. It was not a neat story. Dambo later confessed that the officers had been killed. Babangida's first boss in the recce squadron, the man who took him under his professional wings, Captain Isong, was among the dead. Dambo was one of the early casualties in the civil war on the federal side.

Two hundred days after Aguiyi-Ironsi took assumed office as Nigeria's first military dictator, he was dead. The coup that brought him to power had given birth to the country's second coup.

Chapter Five

The Rise of Yakubu Gowon

I had been brought to the position today of having to shoulder the responsibilities of this country
–Lt-Col Yakubu Gowon

For three days, July 29-31, Nigeria had no government. Aguiyi-Ironsi was dead but he had not been officially so declared. The official statement was that he had been kidnapped. The next most senior army officer after the head of state was Brigadier Babafemi Ogundipe. But he simply refused to step in. The situation was anything but clear. He decided to summon a meeting of senior military officers in order to reach a collective decision on the next line of action. But "when he found that even a sergeant would not take orders from Major Mobolaji Johnson or himself, he thought his seniority as next-in-command had been deflated beyond any reasonable doubt." [1] A soldier, presumably a northerner, reportedly told Commodore Akinwale Wey, head of the Nigerian Navy, that he was going to take orders only from his captain, presumably a northerner.

"The rebels," as the leaders of the coup were referred to in official circles, were holding out, notably in Ikeja cantonment. Again, as in the January coup, there was a problem with this one. Conceived and executed essentially as a revenge coup, 'the rebels' did not appear to have fully thought out the implications and their next line of action if they succeeded. For three agonising days, the nation waited for the resolution of this latest crisis in its series of crises since independence in 1960. The fate of the Nigerian nation was simply uncertain.

Ogundipe appealed to Gowon. Gowon found himself saddled with the enormous responsibility of resolving the volatile crisis. He was not part of the coup plot. But as the most senior northern officer in the army, the urgent task of resolving the impasse to save the nation became his unenviable lot. As soon as he knew on the night of July 29 that the commander-in-chief had been kidnapped in Ibadan and learnt of the identities of those involved, he tried to save the lives of Aguiyi-Ironsi and Fajuyi. Unfortunately, he knew too late and acted too late.

Gowon went to Ikeja cantonment where he met Major Murtala Muhammed and the others. As the most senior northern officer, they deferred to him. It is not clear if they had him in mind all along to succeed Aguiyi-Ironsi but in the circumstances, the majority of the officers who planned the coup accepted his leadership. They were willing to let him succeed Aguiyi-Ironsi. 'The rebels' ignored Gowon's argument that the military hierarchy be maintained. He accepted their demand. Or, rather, one of them. He flatly rejected the other demand, that northern troops be withdrawn from the south in a secessionist bid.

On August 1, 1966, Gowon, 31, became the new Head of State and Commander-in-Chief of the Armed Forces. The agony of waiting for a new leader was over. And a new chapter in the Nigerian political crisis opened.

Gowon's maiden broadcast that morning, showed the difficulties in which he found himself. He told the nation:

> I had been brought to the position today of having to shoulder the responsibilities of this country and the Armed Forces with the consent of the majority of the members of the Supreme Military Council, as a result of the unfortunate incident that occurred on the early morning of July 29, 1966.

The first casualty of the change of government was the unitary system of government. Indeed, the heading of Gowon's speech was: *No Trust or Confidence in a Unitary System of Government.* His decision to revert the country to a federal system of government must have come as a big relief to the north, the only region that was openly and violently opposed to the unitary system of government.

Gowon traced the July coup to the January coup in which "... a group of officers, in conjunction with certain civilians, decided to overthrow the legal government of the day.....by eliminating political leaders and high-ranking army officers, majority of whom came from a particular section of the country." The culmination of the crisis was that in "...in the early hours of July 29, 1966, ...the country was once again plunged into another very serious and grave situation - the second in seven months." Aguiyi-Ironsi and his host, Fajuyi, had been kidnapped and there was "no confirmation of their whereabouts."

Their death was not officially confirmed for another six months - that is, until after the Aburi meeting between Gowon and Ojukwu. After reviewing the political developments up to that point, Gowon came to what he admitted was "...the most difficult but most important part of this statement;" and that was "...the great disappointment and heartbreak it will cause all true and sincere lovers of Nigeria and of the Nigerian unity, both at home and broad, especially our brothers in the Commonwealth." But what he said next did not reflect the tone of the preceding statement. It was as if he changed his mind. He said:

> As a result of the recent event and the other previous similar ones, I have come to strongly believe that we cannot honestly and sincerely continue in this wise, as the basis for trust and confidence in our unitary system of government has not been able to stand the test of time.

His prelude to that sentence has haunted Gowon ever since. It is often cited as evidence that the north decided to secede from the federation and that Gowon who approved this demand by the officers who staged the July coup was persuaded by Britain at the last minute to drop it.

Gowon has repeatedly denied that he and 'the rebels' ever contemplated the break-up of the country. He clarified his position at an interview with *Drum* magazine. He told his interviewer:

> I certainly believe in the unity of Nigeria. If I didn't, I would not be here today. It was very easy at the time I took over to say "let everybody go his own way." The atmosphere then was conducive to such an action. I don't believe in unity by domination of any kind, whether by religion, population or size.[2]

Babangida also denies that their aim was secession:

> The clamour for the division of the country was more or less political. But militarily, I don't think we subscribed to the idea of dividing the country. I knew the whole intention. I don't agree the intention was to divide the country.

Before he formally assumed office as head of state, Gowon spoke with Major Hassan Usman Katsina, military governor of the northern group of provinces and his Mid-West counter-part, Lt-Col David Ejoor. Both of them accepted his leadership and urged him to put a stop to further bloodshed. He did not speak to the military governor of the Eastern group of provinces, Lt-Col Chukwuemeka Odumegwu-Ojukwu. Commodore Wey did on his behalf. As soon as Gowon made his broadcast, the crisis took a new turn.

On the evening of the same day, Ojukwu made his own broadcast from Enugu. He said that Ogundipe, by virtue of his seniority, should succeed the head of state if, indeed, Aguiyi-Ironsi was no longer alive. He did not recognise Gowon as head of state, only as chief of staff, army, and hoped that Gowon's early morning broadcast was only meant to restore peace in the country and not as a successor to Aguiyi-Ironsi.

Gowon was faced with two immediate and daunting tasks – restoring discipline and trust in the armed forces, especially in the army and heading the country down the path of peace. None of that was easy but within the first few weeks of his taking over, tempers cooled off in the armed forces. Babangida gives him a generous credit for that achievement: "I think credit should go to him for trying to restore normalcy within the military."

According to Babangida, Gowon was convinced that the source of instability in the country was within the military itself. One of the first steps the army authorities took in this regard was to effect some troop movements between the north and the south. This movement saw Babangida move with the A Squadron (recce) from Kaduna to Abeokuta. Its place in Kaduna was now taken over by the B Squadron from Abeokuta. The movement was effected in August that year.

However, the contest of will between Gowon and Ojukwu made the clouds hanging over the nation frightening. Each day took the country closer to the edge. Gowon then made a rather astute political move. He released Awolowo and the leading members of the Action Group from jail. They were tried, found guilty, and jailed on charges of treasonable felony in 1964. It was the right move at the right time. It won over the support of the West, meaning the Yoruba, for Gowon. That support was critical to the survival of the nation.

Gowon desperately tried to restore the confidence of Nigerians in their own nation. But in September, another round of riots broke out in parts of the north that led to the wanton killings of hundreds of innocent people, particularly the Igbo just when everyone thought that the fire had stopped burning. The riots were grist to Ojukwu's mill. The crisis entered a new and dangerous phase. Ojukwu portrayed the violence as pogrom, a calculated design to exterminate the Igbo. This, in his view, meant one thing and one thing only: the rest of the country no longer wanted the Igbo in Nigeria. The seed of his own alternative to the national problem dropped into the soil and would be watered through well-coordinated and effective propaganda machinery.

Gowon's pre-occupation was how to save the nation. The answer did not come easily. Ironically, the military authorities reached out for the politicians that had been driven out of power. Leading regional politicians were vested with the curious title of *leaders of thought*. Gowon instituted an ad hoc constitutional conference at which each region was represented by a delegation led by its leader of thought. After the September riots in the north, Ojukwu stopped the Eastern delegates from attending the conference in October and November, because he said he feared they were no longer safe and that he did not believe the federal government would protect them. Gowon did not want the conference to go on without the participation of the Eastern Region. Consequently, after all efforts made to persuade Ojukwu to allow the delegates back to the conference failed, he suspended it.

The Ghanaian army overthrew President Kwame Nkrumah in March 1966. Lt-General Joseph Ankrah headed the new government. Ankrah offered to mediate in the Nigerian crisis. He offered a neutral venue for a meeting between Ojukwu and Gowon at Peduase Lodge, Aburi, Ghana. Gowon and Ojukwu accepted Ankrah's mediation. The talks lasted two days - January 4 and 5, 1967.

Aburi raised some hope in the peaceful resolution of the Nigerian crisis. As it turned out, Aburi exacerbated the crisis. The Aburi accord, if implemented, would have been virtually the end of Nigeria as a country. Both sides accepted some form of a confederal arrangement - a moving apart of the regions - as a temporary measure while the people rebuild their trust in one another. It was the only option acceptable to Ojukwu and the Eastern Region.

The accord obliged the leaders to renounce the use of force in resolving the crisis. The most telling point was that under the agreement, virtually all the powers conferred on the Head of the Federal Military Government and Supreme Commander of the Armed Forces under Aguiyi-Ironsi's decree number one of 1966, were vested in the Supreme Military Council, SMC. All soldiers were to be withdrawn to their regions under new commands known as Area Commands to be headed by area commanders.

Aburi merely delayed what Ojukwu knew was inevitable – the secession of the Eastern Region. Ojukwu returned home from Aburi to a hero's welcome. There was no such rejoicing on the federal side. Savouring victory, Ojukwu began to badger Gowon into implementing the accord, on which, the East said, it stood. Ojukwu went ahead to release his own version of the accord. This was later waxed into a record. The federal government accused Ojukwu of distorting the accord to suit his own purpose. It was thus forced to release, most reluctantly, its own version of the accord. No one knew which was the authentic document. Aburi, far from heralding peace, became the new weapon for propaganda by the Eastern Regional government.

The SMC met without Ojukwu and approved the implementation of the Aburi accord on March 17. On the same day Gowon promulgated Decree No. 8 of 1967 to this effect. Nigeria became a confederal state in accordance with Ojukwu's wishes and demands. But he refused to be satisfied. He insisted the decree was far short of what was agreed. Few people now had any doubts about his ultimate intentions. Aburi was a waiting game.

Babangida and his colleagues felt concerned about the situation. Babangida soon came to know that the army authorities did not think that whatever was happening on the political front should affect the training of its officers. In early April, 1967, while Gowon and Ojukwu were grappling with the political problems of the nation, Babangida left for the D & M RAC Centre in Britain for a four-month course to learn to become an instructor in armoured vehicle maintenance and driving. In early July, his course was interrupted with only two weeks to go. He was recalled home. He did not have to wonder why.

While he was away, the crisis had escalated. But Gowon was learning the ropes fast. On May 27, 1967, he did what ethnic minorities in the country wanted the British colonial authorities to do before granting the country independence: he created twelve new states from the ashes of the four regions and appointed military governors for them. It was a deft political move, or in the words of Babangida, "a political master stroke," to checkmate Ojukwu in his secessionist bid. The move pulled the rug from under Ojukwu's feet in the ethnic minority parts of the Eastern Region. The minorities in the region had clamoured for their regions or states to free them from perceived Igbo domination. Their struggle was waged under the auspices of Cross River Ogoja State Movement. Gowon gave the minorities two states - Rivers and Cross River. The Igbo had their own state, East-Central State, headed by the only civilian to hold that position in the Gowon administration, a former university teacher, Ukpabi Asika. Asika, not being a soldier, he could not be a military governor. He was named administrator of the East-Central State.

Ojukwu was ready for Gowon. Three days after the creation of states, Ojukwu announced the secession of the former Eastern Region from the federation on May 30. He named it the Republic of Biafra. What everyone feared and what Gowon had tried so hard and so desperately to prevent could not be prevented.

A civil war to crush the rebellion loomed. Ojukwu knew Gowon would not let him get away with it. He was ready to take him on. His propaganda machinery was reved up at home and abroad. For one month, both sides psyched one another. Ojukwu declared that no black nation in the world could crush Biafra. On July 6, the nation took him up on his declaration. War broke out with the first shots in the Nsukka sector. The federal military government dubbed it "police action."

II

Babangida and other officers on courses abroad were recalled home. Lt-Col Yakubu Danjuma, who was on a staff college course in the United Kingdom, was also recalled. Babangida made a lasting impression on his instructors in the course this time around. He was rated highly. In his confidential report, his chief instructor described him as *"a very hard worker (who has) a splendid sense of humour. He has a sound knowledge of Saladin and will be an excellent instructor."* He had come a long way from Dehra Dun.

His close friend, Lt Shehu Musa Yar'Adua, met Babangida on arrival at the Ikeja airport, Lagos. On their drive back to Lagos island, Yar'Adua filled him in on developments in the country; the various efforts made by the federal government to appease Ojukwu, including decree number eight which legally killed the federal republic as it was when Babangida left for Britain and why Gowon insisted that the federal government was not going to war but merely taking a police action to force Ojukwu to give up his dream. The federal government issued military commanders with guidelines on the conduct of the police action.

Babangida is a fierce nationalist. As a young officer, he did not have much say in what the government and his superiors were doing. In military tradition, he was far too low in rank to play any meaningful role at the time. But whenever he had the opportunity, he never failed to make contributions on the political situation at the time. Many of his colleagues knew where he stood in the Nigerian crisis. Nigeria, he felt, must be saved. What happened in January and July were unfortunate. Perhaps, they were the necessary prices the nation had to pay to cement its unity.

Now, the nation had been driven to war. He felt sorry that the country had to shed more blood in its long journey into nationhood. Babangida abhors blood or the use of force to resolve issues. He has always believed that violence does not solve problems. It aggravates them. Dialogue was, and has always been, his preferred choice. As one of his close friends puts it: "He believes that as long as people keep talking, they won't resort to violence. Talking to each other makes suspicion impossible because it gives both sides the chance to understand one another's positions and points of view. If you understand the other man's position and point of view, there will be less friction and less trouble."

Both sides were still talking when Babangida left for the United Kingdom. That gave him hope that the crisis would be resolved and Nigerian leaders would go on with the task of building the necessary infrastructure for the nation's development. But the talks failed, hence the civil war. It made the young lieutenant sad that the Nigerian crisis had taken this turn but he appreciated the position of the federal military government. The government had no other choice than to crush the rebellion. Nearly three years after he left the Indian Military Academy where he received his professional training under the rigours and demands of a war situation, Babangida went to war to help save his own country from disintegration.

He was posted to 21 battalion in the 1 Division also known as One Sector, commanded by Col Mohammed Shuwa. The division operated from Nsukka, north of the former Eastern Region. Babangida entered the battlefield a couple of days or so after the capture of Nsukka in early July. Major Inuwa Wushishi was his sector commander.

As soon as he entered the theatre of war, it became clear to Babangida that it was "a miscalculation on the strategic or military thinking to regard the war as a police action." It was, indeed, according to him, "a miscalculation of the possible strength of the *enemy.*" Ojukwu himself was not that prepared for war either but his propaganda machinery simply overwhelemed this fact and created the impression he was prepared to crush the federal might. The federal government, according to Babangida, "lacked the basic intelligence of the level of Ojukwu's preparedness." In the heat of the crisis before the outbreak of the war, the East had been left with only one battalion. "Everybody," according to Babangida, "thought that was the only thing. We did not take into consideration that the time lag could have given Ojukwu a chance to retrain, reorganise, mobilize and equip the army because, definitely, he had at the back of his mind the intention to secede."

Ojukwu exaggerated the strength of his army when he declared that no black army in the world could beat it. A later account by Ben Gbulie in his book, *The Fall of Biafra,* shows that Biafra did not have the arsenal and men that Ojukwu boasted of. He had well-motivated officers and men who were prepared to fight for their "freedom" against those they called the "Nigerian vandals.' When what the federal government regarded as a limited military action began on July 6, 1967, the federal troops met stiff resistance from the rebel forces. The spirit and the morale of the rebel soldiers were high because the propaganda left no room for doubt about the justice of their cause.

Both sides grappled with shortage of men and materiel. Infantry officers and troops were in short supply on the federal side. Gowon did not want a general mobilisation. Instead, ex-service men, most of whom were demobilised between 1946 and 1948 after World War II, were pressed back into service.

This created some immediate problems for the Nigerian Army. The old soldiers had been out of service, and therefore, out of touch with the army for so long that most of them found themselves apparently lost in the theatre of war. Their reflex, as soldiers, had atrophied. They found the new weapons rather strange. New battle plans had been introduced since the end of World War II. These new weapons and the new battle plans needed to be taught and learnt. This required time, always a rather limited and valuable commodity in crisis situations. But the worst problem for young officers like Babangida was the reaction of the old soldiers to enemy fire. It was unhelpfully panicky. As soon as they heard firing from the Biafran soldiers, their immediate reaction was to return fire. It hardly mattered to them that the enemy was at a safe distance, out of the range of their firepower. In the circumstance, those they invariably killed were not the enemy soldiers but their own fellow troops operating in the forward line. In the early days of the war, therefore, the federal troops sustained most of their casualties from friendly rather than enemy fire.

The only solution was to retrain the ex-service men in the tactics of modern warfare, the use of modern weapons and inculcate in them the discipline of responding to enemy fire only when their commander so ordered. There were other problems such as the shortage of arms and ammunitions. They had to be imported. Again, that bought the secessionist forces valuable time.

The officer corps of the Nigerian Army before the war was predominantly from the south. Most of them were now in Biafra. In the words of one senior army officer, "the leadership had gone with Biafra. You needed the leadership to bring this hardcore army together."

Infantry officers and men are the hardcore fighting machines in wars. Armour officers and men play a supporting role, covering the infantry with their firepower. The acute shortage of infantry officers was a problem that needed to be addressed in a practical way. This was how Babangida, an armour officer, found himself on the driver's seat of an infantry officer. He was given command of an infantry battalion. He took over the command of 44 battalion, also known as The Rangers, from Lt David Ichoghol, who was relieved of command of the battalion by Danjuma.

Lt. John Inienger fought in the same sector with Babangida. He said Babangida's command of an infantry battalion was a "very rare feat" for an armour or recce officer. It was Babangida's lucky professional break. Both the war and his command of the infantry battalion brought him into contact with senior and junior officers who came to play important roles in his professional career and, ultimately, his becoming president.

Inienger was educated at the Nigerian Military School, Zaria and joined the army as a boy's warden. He was in the electrical and mechanical engineering, EME, corps training to be a vehicle mechanic just before the outbreak of the civil war. It was at about this time that he began to hear about Babangida. Inienger heard that Babangida was "a nice and competent officer."

When the war broke out, Inienger was in the first batch of officers to be given emergency training and commission. He was commissioned into the infantry corps in August 1967, and was "sent straight to the war front." He did not directly work under Babangida but his battalion operated side by side with Babangida's. Major Abdullahi Shelleng was the commander of the 22 battalion in which Inienger served but his immediate boss, Shelleng's second-in-command, the man who "really drilled me through the nitty-gritty of the war," was another old boy from Government College, Bida, Lt Mamman Vatsa. When Inienger finally met Babangida, the man he had heard so much about, he was mesmerised by the gentle lieutenant. "I found in him a very considerate officer, very accommodating, very understanding. He was always ready to help those who had problems without finding out where they came from or what regiment they came from."

Inienger proved his mettle in the war and was rewarded with higher responsibilities. In 1968, he was promoted a field lieutenant and was given command of a company. In normal circumstances, his rank entitled him to command a platoon. As a company commander Inienger worked more closely with Babangida, who had been promoted captain. In 1969, Babangida was promoted a major. Inienger moved up as a captain and a battalion commander. "We sat down in the mess to chat. We discussed our operational plans and so on. I really enjoyed working with him. Professionally, I want to say that apart from being a very competent officer, he is very understanding. Babangida does not believe in handing down orders. He believes in participatory leadership. No matter your rank, no matter your upbringing, he will want you to contribute in whatever he is doing," Inienger said.

A soldier-democrat was something rather unusual; in a war situation, even less so. Like Ifere before him, Inienger must have found this trait in Babangida a little confusing. One young man who met Captain Babangida about this time and in circumstances which he too must have found the equivalent of an oddity in a military man was 2Lt Yohanna Madaki. When Madaki met Babangida during the war, the latter was a staff officer in the brigade in Enugu. He was in charge of logistics - the provision of transportation and ammunition to the troops. The 4 Battalion was in a place called Uzala when it suffered casualties. The commanding officer and his second in command were both killed. The troops had no leader and were in disarray. The report that reached the brigade headquarters was that the troops had mutinied. There was an urgent need, therefore, to send a replacement. Madaki was chosen for this but his immediate boss decided that Babangida should break the news to the young lieutenant.

Madaki reported to Babangida that evening. He expected to be given the marching orders. Instead, the smiling captain he had never met, called him by his first name, clapped him on the shoulder and "explained the grave situation" to him in detail. He told Madaki he had been selected to save the situation because "they thought," recalled Madaki, "that I was the only one who could go and so he wanted me to prepare my mind before I went. The beauty with which he approached the matter made me not to see even the danger involved."

An impression was formed and a bond was forged between them that instant. Madaki was too happy to go. Early the next morning, Babangida went to him again and asked if he could move before eight o'clock. "He could have said: Move!" but he did not put it that way," said Madaki.

Madaki jumped into his vehicle and sped off towards the danger and the uncertainty out there but with a song in his heart. "The way he talked to me, I wanted to prove to him that he had not been wrong," Madaki said. He was one of the military governors under Babangida and was retired with the rank of colonel in 1987. He was wounded in the war but not in that particular attack. He found in Babangida the sort of officer he would like, in a manner of speaking, to do business with.

2Lt Haliru Akilu also met Babangida at the war front in 1968. He describes Babangida as "the conservative type of commander" in the mould of Field Marshall Montgomery or General Rommel, commanders who "do their job properly without much noise, without much show-off." Babangida conducted himself more or less like the legendary General Douglas McAthur. He seemed to dare death with some dash and bravado, taking risks that junior officers found both fascinating and troubling.

Inienger called him "a very adventurous man." Babangida quite often toured the various units either alone or with only his driver. According to Inienger, "most of the time you would find this man driving his Land Rover. Many a time, he visited us and we would ask him: 'Sir, do you have to come all this way alone?'" Babangida would simply laugh off their concern and assure them he was safe.

Considerate and courageous, Babangida was an example other officers felt obliged to follow. He showed compassion for the wounded and pity for the dead. Inienger saw a great deal of the future general and president during the war. He recalled:

> If there was anything that endeared him to the minds of his troops, it was his concern for the wounded. He would never leave behind wounded or dead soldiers. He would make sure they were evacuated to the rear by all means, no matter how difficult. I remember when an attempt was made to take Umuahia and it failed. He had to pull back and regroup. Some soldiers were shot dead. He insisted that their bodies be retrieved. This is the kind of action that endears a senior officer to junior officers and troops. In war, the ability of the troops to execute any act is dependent on the courage of the officer in command. If they discover the officer is the I-don't-care type, then they adopt the same attitude. But once they discover the officer is someone who never gives up, is someone who takes the welfare of the men at heart, then they fight behind him, they fight with him, they take his orders anytime, anywhere.

Babangida's boyhood friend, Captain Garba Duba, was in the armoured corps in the same sector too. After the capture of Enugu, the federal troops were directed to make it safe for the administrator of the East Central State, Mr Ukpabi Asika, to go there and set up his administration as a civilian equivalent of the military governors. Enugu was safely in federal hands. However, the secessionist soldiers were still shelling it from its outskirts. It was not safe enough for Asika and his team. It was necessary to clear a wide swathe of the capital to make it safe enough for the nucleus of the state administration.

Federal troops began the operation to push off the Biafran soldiers. At Agbani, 30 or 40 kilometres from Enugu, the federal troops came under heavy Biafran fire. Duba was shot. Babangida saw his dear friend go down and sprang into action. The fire was heavy but there was no way he was going to leave his best friend out there to bleed to death. He rushed in, unmindful of the bullets flying virtually all around him and lifted Duba off the ground. He carried him to the Land Rover and Duba was rushed to the safety of the rear and thence to the Orthopaedic Hospital, Kano, for treatment. One more evidence, in the words of Inienger, that "Babangida took risks, risks which some of us under normal circumstances would be scared to take."

Such acts of concern and bravery came to Babangida quite early in his life. His first rescue operation was in 1958 when he was in form two in Bida. His school was going for a sporting event known then as triangular sports at the Provincial Secondary School, Okene, when the lorry in which they were travelling was involved in an accident a few miles from Ilorin. The lorry hit a bump by a stream and the two front tyres came off. The games master, Alhaji Ladan Zuru, sat by the driver and watched in horror as the poor man lost control of the vehicle. Babangida and the other boys were singing, unaware of the wrestling contest between the driver and his vehicle. The lorry careened off the road and ended in a stream. Some of the students were thrown into the bush. Some of them were injured but none suffered serious injuries.

As the students picked themselves up, they became confused and were virtually running everywhere but to nowhere in particular. Alhaji Ladan was hanging from the front seat. He was confused and worried about the students. But only one boy, Ibrahim Babangida, remembered the teacher was missing. "Where is malam?" he shouted. The students popularly called Alhaji Ladan *malam*. Babangida rushed to the front of the lorry and found the teacher holding on to the door. He called the rest of the students and they freed him.

Care. Compassion. Sympathy. There is no one who has met Babangida and has not come away clutching at those nouns in praise of him. He so fascinated Akilu during the war that on one occasion, the latter, who was not in Babangida's unit, could not resist following him into battle during the push towards Umuahia from Okigwe and Igwube axis. Akilu nearly lost his life. A shell exploded not far from where he took cover. Everyone thought he was dead. He was lucky. When he reported back to his unit, his commander, Major A.A. Gora berated him.

Babangida has always combined his care and compassion with a sense of justice and fairness. He defended junior and other ranks from their seniors if he felt that the senior ones were taking advantage of their rank and position. One such incident that occurred in the officers' mess, in Enugu during the war both fascinated and frightened Akilu. As he recalled it, Major Gora lived the tough and rough life of the soldier. He drank quite a bit and this sometimes showed in his conduct towards others. On this particular day at the mess, he had ordered some drinks, which were duly served by the mess steward. It is not clear exactly what the steward did wrong after that but Gora blew up and started shouting at him.

Babangida watched the drama, which he knew would lead to the steward being punished by the major. He thought the steward was being unduly bullied and he intervened to save him from possible punishment. Gora was incensed. A shouting match ensued between him and Babangida. Akilu managed to calm both men down. It was the first time Akilu saw Babangida so angry that he "was prepared to exchange blows with a fellow officer". Babangida confesses it was the first and only time in his military career he was prepared to physically fight an officer. Gora, now late, was also a very brave officer.

Captain Gado Nasko was in the Second Division. But he heard a lot about his friend's courage in battle. "All the time, he featured prominently; his name echoed all over," he said.

Babangida's unlucky day came sometime in April 1969, during the push from Uzuakoli towards Umuahia. He was wounded. He took the bullet on the right side of his chest. Evidence, according to Inienger, that although Babangida was commanding an infantry battalion, he "operated as a recce officer. The role of the reconnaissance unit," he went on to explain, "is to go ahead of the fighting forces, to read the battle and assess the enemy capabilities. During our move to Umuahia, he was always striving to lead his people rather than stay behind. It was in this process that he was shot."

Inienger was an eyewitness on Babangida's unlucky day. He remembered

> vividly when he was shot. Unlike somebody one would expect who was shot to fall on the ground and start yelling or screaming, he merely held his hand in order not to discourage his subordinates. He held his chest and said to the of-

ficer next to him that he thought he had been shot and then he started walking to the rear. It was then he fell and somebody picked him up on a stretcher.

Babangida was taken to the Lagos University Teaching Hospital, LUTH, Idi-Araba, Lagos, for treatment. The bullet was lodged in his chest and he needed surgery to remove it. He confesses he "was quite frankly scared of surgery." He asked his surgeon, Professor Elebute, if he had a choice in the matter. Yes, the surgeon told him. He could either remove the shrapnel or leave it there. If he chose to leave it there, there would be no problem until may be, when he grew old. "So, I decided not to allow the removal of the shrapnel. I still carry it with me," he says.

Several of Babangida's military colleagues visited him in the hospital. Lt Joshua Dogonyaro was one of those who did. He found the major, as usual, in very high spirits. Babangida even joked about his condition, telling Dogonyaro he was not afraid of dying. "If I give up," he said, laughing, "that will not be the end of the world."

Despite his putting on a brave face, "a curious thing" happened to Babangida in the hospital. "The first thing that came into my mind was my God, I would have been dead and that would be all," he recalls. That would have been the end of his life and the end of the Babangida line. As the only surviving male child of his parents, if he died childless, the family tree would have stopping growing.

That fear, curiously, increased "the feeling in me that this time around, I just have to find myself a wife." He was 28 years old. His thoughts went back to all the girls he knew. He did a mental calculation on each of them, trying to assess the one with "whom I shall be able to live comfortably with." Like many a young officer with a promising career, Babangida, to quote his wife, Maryam, an officer generally, "did not miss the chance of a girl's company if (he) could help it."[3]

His mind settled on apparently the most beautiful of them all - a tall, elegant girl with the colour of ebony and big, dreamy eyes. Even as a young girl, she had this regal bearing. Her name was Maria Okogwu. Her mother, Asabe, was a younger sister to Garba Duba's father. Her father was from Asaba in what is now Delta State. He worked in the survey department, Northern Nigeria Ministry of Lands and Survey. His job took him to several parts of the north - Kaduna, Zonkwa, Kafanchan and Kontagora. It was in the latter town that he met and married Maria's mother. His other children were Sonny, Elizabeth, Edith, and Jummai.

Okogwu retired from the service and went back home where he later died. He left some of his children, Sonny and Maria, as well as the two youngest children with his wife in Kaduna, where they were schooling. Only Sonny had left school at the time. Maria was a student at the Federal Training Centre, Kaduna. The children's mother lived wirh her brother, Alhaji Muhammadu King, Duba's father, at Unguwan Sarki, Kaduna.

Babangida often went with Duba to visit the latter's parents there. He was more or less seen as a member of the family. Maria also frequently visited Duba and Babangida at their Kanta Road residence. She and Babangida were attracted to each other and became friends. As time went on, they knew they were in love but marriage was not on the cards. During the Nigerian crisis, Maria's uncle, Alhaji Muhammadu King, took her and her siblings under his protective wings and they took the surname, King.

Now in the hospital, Babangida could only think of Maria. As soon as he was well enough, Babangida left the hospital, met Maria and popped the question. She said yes. On September 6, 1969, Babangida and Maria were married at the marriage registry in Kaduna and topped it off with Islamic marital rites. His best man was Major Abubakar Waziri. Maria converted to Islam and changed her name of Maryam.

Mrs Maryam Babangida was to play a major role in defining the Babangida presidency as First Lady from August 27, 1985 to August 27, 1993. She brought glamour and panache to the office of First Lady. When she launched her Better Life for Rural Women Programme, Mrs Babangida took that little known office out of the closet and made the First Lady an active partner in governance. First Ladies after her no longer see themselves as trophy wives.

Now married, Babangida returned to the war front, a happier man. The task before the nation still had to be done. He was back where he left off - at Okigwe, commanding a battalion. This was now late in December 1969. About January 11 or 12, 1970, Danjuma toured the formations and told the officers and men at Okigwe the war was over. Ojukwu had run away. Biafra had surrendered. Babangida was thereafter posted to Afikpo where he became a brigade commander. He did not stay long in Afikpo. He was posted to Umuahia where he took over command of the 44 Battalion known as The Rangers which he commanded before he was wounded.

Inienger was glad to see him back in action. It turned out to be fortuitous for Inienger. Towards the end of the war, it became necessary to second one battalion from the First Division to the Second Division. Inienger's battalion was chosen. He did not like it and he was prepared to disobey the order. He had strong reasons:

> Here was I, having been used to my colleagues, having been used to my fellow officers, here were my men having fought side by side with battalions that we were used to. In this kind of setting, we were more than willing; we were so excited each time there was a mission because you were sure who was on your

right flank, you were sure who was on your left flank, you were sure that your rear was covered by people who were very committed, by people who were very seasoned.

He knew no one in the Onitsha sector. He became worried about his safety and that of his troops. The day he received the orders, he went to the brigade headquarters and he was told to move within 72 hours. If he had any hopes that someone would reason with him and choose another battalion for the assignment, those hopes were immediately dashed. As he left the brigade headquarters with worries etched on his young face, he ran into the one man it was his fortune to see at that particular moment: Major Babangida. The major always seemed to be at the right place at the right time. As soon as he saw Inienger, he knew something had gone wrong. Inienger poured out his problem to him in a torrent of words. Babangida heard him out. Inienger wondered if he would intervene to save him from his long trek into uncertainty. Babangida was going to do no such thing. A military order was a military order. It had to be obeyed.

He clapped Inienger on the back and told him: "John, you needn't worry. Given the kind of experience you have acquired here, you should have no fear."

Chin up, chest out, Inienger saluted the major and matched off briskly. "And so," he recalled, "I went because the words of encouragement I got from him really spurred me on. And that is one other quality Babangida has got. He has those soft words of assurance. He uses them to pacify officers when they are confronted with danger, when they are confronted with problems."

Akilu can testify to that. In 1978, Akilu had a problem. Some of his mates had been promoted temporary lieutenant colonels. He was not. He did not understand why. He had attended a junior staff college and had received consistently good reports from the commandant of the newly established Command and Staff College, Jaji, in Kaduna, Major-General G.I. Ejiga. "I felt really bad," said Akilu, so he wrote a letter of protest.

Somehow, he decided to send a draft of the letter to Babangida for his advice. Both of them had become very close by this time. Akilu's wife, whom he met in Babangida's house, is Mrs Babangida's cousin. When Akilu was going for a course in the UK, he stayed briefly with the Babangidas in Ikeja, Lagos. Babangida, Duba and another senior officer whose name Akilu couldn't now remember, took it upon themselves to see him, "a bloody captain," off to the airport.

Babangida wrote back to Akilu and advised him not to send the letter of protest. "Look, young man," Babangida wrote, "you must not write a protest letter. Leave it. When the time comes, you will be promoted." Akilu took the advice. It probably saved his career because he later found out that in the army, protest letters count against officers who write them. Akilu himself learnt from that "experience in advising my younger officers whenever they want to do something like writing or documenting things."

Fourteen days after Inienger moved into the unfamiliar terrain of the Second Division, the war ended. Babangida received a good confidential report during the war. In one report, which covered the period from July, 1968, to July, 1969, his immediate boss and friend, Lt- Col A.D.S. Wya, wrote:

> Captain I.B. Babangida is an intelligent, duty conscience (sic) pushful and hard working officer. As a commanding officer of a battalion, he has proved himself capable. In the operational field he can instil confidence into men under his command easily and has shown great initiative, sense of adaptability and co-operation. He is administratively intelligent. He is very social and regimental.

Wya noted something else that had crept into Babangida's character. For the first time since he was commissioned, his confidential report now showed he had begun to show that beneath the friendly, sunny disposition lurks a streak of self-assertiveness. Wya noted that Babangida *"easily falls out with his senior officers because of speaking out his mind openly and straight forward."*

Col Muhammed Shuwa, the general officer commanding the division, described Babangida as "one of the finest officers we have in this division." Babangida was doing more than inching his way up the ladder of his profession.

III

The Nigerian civil war ended on January 12, 1970. It took thirty months to crush the rebellion and save the country from disintegration. Ojukwu fled into exile in the Ivory Coast. Philip Effiong, a lieutenant-colonel in the Nigerian Army but a major-general in the Biafran Army, formally surrendered to Col Olusegun Obasanjo. The next day, Obasanjo escorted Effiong and other former Biafran officers and civilian leaders to Dodan Barracks, Lagos, where he submitted the instrument of surrender to Gowon. It was all over

Gowon, ever the man with a generous heart, did not gloat over his victory. He declared there was no victor and no vanquished. He did not set out to conquer a territory but to save the country. The Igbo had not been vanquished. As head of state, he had simply done his duty to his country. The war slogan was: *To keep Nigeria one is a task that must be done.* The task had been accomplished.

The greatest threat to the corporate existence of Nigeria had been averted. Yes, it left new physical and social problems in its wake: the reconstruction and the rehabilitation of the war-torn areas and the re-integration of the Igbo into the main stream of the Nigerian society. Gowon could not have had any illusions about the enormity of the task that faced him and the nation at that delicate period in its political history. He launched a programme famously known as the 3 R's – reconstruction, rehabilitation and re-integration.

IV

Umuahia was the last strong hold of the Biafrans. Babangida fought in that last theatre of the war. Umuahia was thickly populated. With the end of the war hundreds of people streamed back into the town from the bush. They were generally a sorry sight. Most of the children were suffering from kwashiorkor, a debilitating disease caused by malnutrition. The adults among them had no money. The Biafran currency was now worthless.

Babangida found himself playing a new role – trying to help rehabilitate the people. He shared the food meant for his unit with the people. But they needed more than food. They needed shelter and health care. Babangida allowed those who had houses to move back into them without hassle. Some form of shelter had to be found for those who had no homes of their own. Above all, hundreds of these people needed urgent medical attention. The situation was desperate.

Babangida's determination to assist the people in any way he could, brought him into contact with a medical doctor, Dr J.O.J. Okezie, who owned a hospital in Umuahia. Okezie later became federal commissioner for agriculture in the Gowon administration. His hospital, like almost everything else, had been badly affected by the war. It needed urgent rehabilitation and drugs to cope with the large number of patients – victims of the war – suffering from various ailments. Okezie had no money. But his hospital offered the best immediate prospects of helping the sick and the wounded. Babangida talked with Okezie and together, they planned the rehabilitation of the hospital.

The depth of Babangida's humaneness impressed Okezie. Despite the assurances from the federal government, the ex-Biafrans still trod with informed caution. But from what he saw of Babangida and from talking with him, Okezie believed he was genuine in his affection and his determination to lessen, as much as it was within his power, the sufferings of the people. He and Okezie became close friends. Their circle widened to include Dr Ernest Ezike, Dr Nwankwo, Professor O.K. Ogan and Sam Ihekwu.

Said Babangida:

> We tried as much as possible to assist them so they could stand on their own feet, feed their family and so on. We, as a unit, had enough fund which we could spare. We put this into the rehabilitation of the people, particularly the orphans.

His involvement in the rehabilitation of the victims was Babangida's bridge with a long span into the heart of the Igbo and Igboland. Most people in the former Eastern Region perhaps remember him more for his rehabilitation work in Umuahia than his role as a soldier.

Babangida was still in Umuahia when he received the news he had been waiting for on May 25, 1970: His first child, Aishatu, was born at St Gerrard's Hospital, Kakuri, Kaduna. The birth of the baby girl was announced in Part II order from Supreme Headquarters. His second child, a boy, Muhammadu, was born in the same hospital on February 2, 1972. They were followed by Aminu in 1977 and Halima in 1989 respectively. Halima had the distinction of being born in Dodan Barracks, Lagos, when her father was president.

Babangida returned to Kaduna in August 1970 to take on a new assignment as company commander and instructor at the Nigerian Defence Academy, NDA. Two months later, he was nominated with Major Paul Omu and five others for a company commander's course in the Officers Wing of the School of Infantry in the United Kingdom. The two-month course ended in November that year.

His confidential report from that course was, as usual, quite good. His instructors scored him high on hard work and popularity. They noted he *"showed that he was a capable and experienced commander."* But they found he had *"some difficulty with the (English) language. At first,"* wrote the officer commanding the division, Lt-Col T.G.H. Jackson, *"he was understandably unsure of expressing himself in a syndicate but he became more confident as the course progressed."* Nevertheless, Babangida left his mark on the school. Jackson gushed: *"He was (a) popular member of the course which gained from his presence."*

Babangida always tended to exhibit initial diffidence in unfamiliar environments. But once he mastered the environment, he never failed to turn on his greatest personal asset - his charm.

Back home from the UK, Babangida immersed himself in his job in the academy where he commanded the short service course company known as Ashanti. In his 1971 confidential report, his reporting officer, Lt-Col M.P.S. Adamu, commended him for having *"greatly inspired confidence in both his company officers and cadets with a tidy, logical mind."* He, however urged him *"to show a lot more interest in outdoor activities and games as a good example to his cadets on the one hand (and) against the tendency to put on weight on the other."*

Babangida gave up games and sporting activities. And it showed. Col H.S. Chandel, DY commandant of the academy, was, like Adamu, unhappy with Babangida's *"bulky physique."* As acting commandant of the academy, Chandel had cautioned Babangida in an earlier confidential report (December 14, 1970 to April 6, 1971) *"to take more active interest in games and guard against putting on extra weight."*

We are left to wonder why the all rounder in Bida and who, as a junior officer, impressed other ranks with his keen interest in sport, turned his back on the second love of his life and became a couch potato with a telling evidence on his physique.

Babangida, now a Lt-Col, left for the advanced armoured officers' course in the US sometime in 1972. On his return to the country in 1973, he was posted to the 4 Recce Regiment then based in Badagry as its commander. His close friend, Lt -Col Duba, principal staff officer in recce headquarters in Lagos, had raised that recce unit. Duba returned much earlier from the US where he too had attended the same course with Cols Ibrahim Taiwo and David Jemibewon and Lt-Col M.B. Mayaki. Duba said he formed the unit and kept it for Babangida mainly because he wanted him to stay in Lagos with him.

Duba even secured accommodation for Babangida at the Ikeja cantonment before his return. Duba credits Babangida with developing the unit into a regiment. It was in that command that Babangida's reporting officer made what turned out to be a prophetic statement about his prospects in the Nigerian Army. Brigadier G.S. Jallo said Babangida *"can be relied upon to act quite independently without much supervision. He is a smart officer with a high degree of cleanliness. Possesses lots of initiatives and discusses very well while maintaining a broad mind on all issues. Will go a long way in the army if he maintains his present standards."*

Babangida maintained those standards. Ten years after Jallo wrote that report Babangida achieved what all officers naturally regard as the ultimate in their professional military career. He became Chief of Army Staff. He had promised his friends he would one day ride NA 1. On January 1, 1984, the staff car bearing that number had Babangida in the owner's corner.

Chapter Six

The Baton Changes Again

There had to be a change
–Lt-Col Ibrahim Babangida

Sometime in January, 1975, Lt-Col Shehu Musa Yar'Adua took Lt-Col Ibrahim Babangida out on an evening drive in Lagos. Their initial subject of discussion was the gathering of army officers in Lagos for a military activity. The conversation later drifted to the state of the nation and the Gowon administration. Then quite suddenly, Yar'Adua stopped the car. He turned to Babangida and told him he was planning to topple the Gowon administration.

A few minutes of awkward silence ensued between them. A coup is a very touchy subject in the military. No one treats it lightly. It is not uncommon, in military politics, for some officers to trap fellow officers by broaching a coup plot. Babangida was on his guard. "I thought he was trying to size me up," he now says.

Was someone trying to set him up? He quickly dismissed that fear because he and Yar'Adua were too close and too trusting of each other for the latter to contemplate booby-trapping him. Although they were of the same rank, Yar'Adua was Babangida's senior by one term. Yar'Adua was course five and Babangida course six in the NMTC. Babangida asked Yar'Adua why he was thinking of a coup against Gowon. Yar'Adua reeled off a litany of complaints against the Gowon administration.

Most of what he said was not new to Babangida. After nearly nine years in power, some sort of disenchantment with the Gowon administration had set in. Allegations of corruption and ineptitude against him and the state governors were rife. The clamour for change was hardly muted. Babangida told Yar'Adua he shared his views on all the issues he raised. "I also shared the same conviction," Babangida admits. He says he was aware of "this strong belief that we needed a change, a new sense of direction. At that time, it was very clear to me that there was a general apathy, a general frustration within the society, so there had to be a change."

II

Gowon pulled the nation through a 30-month civil war. His humane attitude towards those who fought on the secessionist side, and his famous three Rs - rehabilitation, reconstruction and reconciliation - endeared him to the nation and the international community. But he knew better than most that the time had come for him to make a pronouncement on his plans for returning the country to civil rule. He chose the tenth anniversary of the country's independence, October 1, 1970, ten months after the civil war ended, to make this momentous announcement. He would return the country to civil rule on October 1, 1976.

It was a major step towards the future of Nigeria. The nation was upbeat at the prospects of civil rule. There were major tasks that Gowon had decided to accomplish to make Nigeria a wholesomely new nation by the time the civilians replaced the military at the helm of affairs. Perhaps, that was why he gave himself about six years. He reduced these tasks to his now famous nine-point programme. A new national census, the eradication of corruption, creation of more states and a new constitution were some of those tasks Gowon set for himself and his administration. Taken together, the nine-point programme, if successfully executed would indeed lay a strong socio-political foundation for the Second Republic.

Gowon created the twelve states on May 27, 1967, and whetted the appetite of Nigerians for many more states. Almost every community now demanded for a state of its own on grounds of a well-worn argument – self-determination. He thus took a wise step by making the creation of more states part of his nine-point agenda. It was a calculated response to public agitations; and for that alone, not a few Nigerians were prepared to let him get away with not returning the country to civil rule in 1976 as he had promised.

Nigeria had had problems with its head count. Census was, and remains, a nasty, political problem, tied up with sectional politics and the sharing of the national cake. The first national census conducted by the civilians in 1962 became so controversial it had to be cancelled and repeated the following year. The 1963 figures did not satisfy every regional interest but mercifully, the politicians chose to tolerate them. Many Nigerians felt that only a military administration could conduct a reliable census free from the sort of controversy that attended the 1962 and 1963 headcount.

Corruption was the main complaint the military laid at the door of the civilians that morning of January 15, 1966. Perhaps, pre-occupied with the crisis and the 30-month civil war the head of state could not give attention to the eradication of corruption. These and the rest of the tasks in the nine-point agenda were of more than a passing interest to all Nigerians.

Nigeria could afford to deal with the nine-point programme. The national economy was in good shape. Nigeria was no longer a struggling agrarian economy. It was virtually awash in petro-dollars that fuelled massive construction and development projects - roads, health institutions, schools, etc. A cement armada congested the ports - a cynical but fair indication of Nigeria's anxiety for rapid social development.

Gowon paid some attention to the welfare of public servants. In his budget broadcast of April 20, 1970, the head of state promised to review salaries and wages in the public sector. Fair enough. If the country had become richer, it should reflect in improved salaries and wages in the public sector. He kept his promise. Gowon set up the Salaries and Wages Commission headed by a well-known technocrat, the late Chief Jerome Udoji, "to review the existing wages and salaries at all levels in the public services, statutory corporations and state-owned companies and determine the areas in which salaries, wages and other remunerations in the private sector can be rationalised and harmonized with those in the public sector."

Salaries and wages in the public sector were so poor that there was a brain drain to the private sector where the pay was much better than in the public sector. Gowon had to arrest the drift for even a more pragmatic reason. The new, four-year national development plan he was working on would be hobbled by lack of administrative and professional manpower in the public services if the brain drain continued and robbed the public sector of trained and competent hands.

The Udoji commission completed its assignment and turned in its report sometime in 1973. In early 1974, the Federal Military Government released a white paper on its recommendations. The commission made some interesting recommendations on the structure of the public services to enhance productivity and stem the brain drain. Most people probably remember the commission today only for "the Udoji awards" – the windfall occasioned by the payment of nine months' arrears of wages and salaries in April 1974. The awards had the unintended effect of causing a spike in inflation but the windfall, the first of its type in living memory in the country at the time, made Gowon the man of the moment.

III

Gowon rode the crest waves of popularity. However, the payment of the Udoji salary arrears remains the harshest criticism of his management of the economy. Life is often so unfair that the best intentions do not always yield the intended results.

On July 8, 1974, trouble came to the administration from unexpected quarters. Godwin Daboh, a businessman, swore an affidavit before a Lagos high court, making allegations of corruption and abuse of office against one of Gowon's most flamboyant commissioners, Mr. Joseph S. Tarka. Daboh and Tarka, both Tiv from what is now Benue State, were close friends or business associates. The press and the nation hailed Daboh as an anti-corruption crusader. It was a stab at the Gowon administration.

The affidavit raised questions about one critical item in Gowon's nine-point programme - the eradication of corruption. Why was one of his commissioners found with alleged soiled hands four years after the general promised to eradicate it? Tarka protested his innocence but he was forced to resign as commissioner for communications.

Tarka was out but trouble dug in its heels. About six weeks after Daboh swore his affidavit against Tarka, the late Aper Aku, another Tiv man and former principal of the Federal Training Centre, Kaduna, went to a Jos high court on August 31 and swore to a 26-point affidavit alleging corruption and wrong-doing against the military governor of Benue-Plateau State, Police Commissioner Joseph Gomwalk. Aku too was hailed as an anti-corruption crusader by the press and the general public. He was not as lucky as Daboh. He was arrested for allegedly inciting the public against the government.

Gowon called Gomwalk to Lagos to explain himself. The public waited for what he would do about the allegations against the governor. Virtually all the military governors were rumoured to be steeped in corruption. Aku's affidavit was generally seen as evidence that this was indeed so. The public expected Gowon to begin the house cleaning with Gomwalk but the head of state took a dim view of Aku's action. He cleared Gomwalk of the allegations made against him by Aku. On his way to China for a state visit a day or so later, Gowon told airport reporters: "I am now satisfied, after listening to explanations and having had time to check all the relevant references as provided by Mr Gomwalk, that he has not been guilty of any wrong-doings as alleged by Mr Aku in his affidavit."[1]

In the general public view, Gowon's decision to clear Gomwalk smacked of double standards. The press and the public were roundly disappointed – and said so, often in a language famous for its lack of restraint. Why was Tarka forced to resign without the government raising a voice in his defence but Gomwalk was cleared by the same government? Gowon obviously felt he was the real target of those who were making allegations of corruption against his lieutenants. The federal military government took a tough stand. It banned affidavits against public officers.

The ship of the Gowon administration headed towards a rough sea. He had problems with another important item in his nine-point programme. The census was conducted in 1973. It too turned out, like others before it, not to be free of controversy. In the face of the controversy, the federal government could neither accept nor reject the figures. It simply let them hang in the air.

Gowon also dithered over the mounting demands for the creation of more states. Gowon took no concrete steps publicly towards his fulfilling this promise. Inertia appeared to have atrophied the government. Perhaps Gowon did not seem to feel the stiffening of the arteries of his administration. He carried on as if the country had unlimited patience with him.

IV

On October 1, 1974, Gowon stepped on a messy banana peel. Two years to the 1976 handover date he promised in 1970, the head of state stunned the nation. He had changed his mind on the return to civil rule in 1976. That date was no longer 'realistic.' He blamed the politicians for his decision to renege on his promise. The politicians, he said, had learnt nothing and forgotten nothing. To give power back to them at that point in time would be irresponsible. Gowon told the nation:

> Regrettably, from all the information at our disposal, from the general attitude, utterances and manoeuvres of some individuals and groups and from some publications during the past few months, it is clear that those who aspire to lead the nation on the return to civilian rule have not learnt any lessons from our past experiences. In spite of the existence of a state of emergency which has so far precluded political activity, there has already emerged a high degree of sectional politicking, intemperate utterances and writings which were deliberately designed to whip up ill-feelings within the country to the benefit of the political aspirations of a few. There is no doubt that it will not take them long to return to the old cutthroat politics that once led this nation into serious crisis.[2]

He said he was persuaded by a large number of "well-meaning and responsible Nigerians from all walks of life and from all parts of this country, as well as well-wishers of Nigeria at home and abroad (who) have called attention to the lack of wisdom and the dangers inherent in adhering to the target date previously announced."[3]

Therefore, he went on:

> Our assessment of the situation as of now is that it will be utterly irresponsible to leave the nation in the lurch by a precipitate withdrawal, which will certainly throw the nation back into confusion. Therefore, the Supreme Military Council, after careful deliberation and in full consultation with the hierarchy of the armed forces and the police, have decided that the target date of 1976 is, in the circumstances, unrealistic and that it would indeed amount to a betrayal of trust to adhere rigidly to that target date.[4]

Gowon promised to redeploy the military governors and appoint new federal commissioners with the bulk of them coming from the armed forces. He did keep his promise to appoint new federal commissioners in January 1975. But there were too few new faces to make much difference or even satisfy the Nigerian public that is usually intolerant of long political tenures. Gowon did not keep his promise to redeploy the military governors. There were strong rumours that he could not redeploy them because the governors had become so powerful they insisted that if he wanted them to go, then he too must go. Perhaps they were just rumours but it is important to remember that the military governors were also members of the Supreme Military Council, the country's highest legislative body. This, in itself, was not reason enough to believe the rumours; still, it could mean that the governors were in a strong position to have a say in their proposed redeployment. The public expected Gowon to effect the redeployment by March 1975. The month came and went but the governors remained very much at their duty post. Few then needed to be persuaded that the rumour had strong basis in fact.

Gowon genuinely believed his decision to prolong military rule beyond 1976 had the full support of his military colleagues. According to Babangida, sometime in 1974, Gowon called a meeting of senior military officers from the rank of colonel and its equivalent and above to brainstorm on the state of the nation. He told the officers of his fears about the 'unrepentant' behaviour of the politicians. He also told them about the various calls and representations he had received, asking him to stay on beyond the target date. What did his military colleagues think? he wanted to know.

Discussions centred on his either adhering to the target date or to continue in office but with a new target date. Some officers cautioned that the military was honour-bound to keep its promise of the 1976 target date. Those who favoured this option argued that it would be dangerous for the military to abort the dream of civil rule by 1976. These voices were in the minority.

The majority of the officers favoured continued military rule until the military authorities were fully satisfied that the civilians had learnt the needed lessons and were prepared to play the game of politics in accordance with its established rules. "A lot of them," according to Babangida,

> supported the idea (of not keeping to the target date of 1976). But my instinct tells me that they supported the idea because some of them felt that they would be beneficiaries of this new thinking. Quite a number of them who wanted redeployment of the governors and members of the SMC wanted to take up political appointments. You know, they just wanted Gowon to change them so they could get in. They wanted him to stay but because he did not effect those changes, some of them found it easy to go along with the idea of change of government.

V

Gowon was persuaded by the argument of the majority of those who attended the meeting. He decided to jettison the target date and continue in office. It was a costly mistake. By early 1975 anyone who wanted to topple Gowon had enough excuses to do so. The atmosphere, according to Babangida, "was (now) very ripe for change." Gowon's decision not to hand over power in 1976 alone was a good enough reason. What else did it show but that Gowon intended to cling to power?

Yar'Adua and Babangida having agreed that the atmosphere was ripe for change, their next line of action was to sell the idea to their close friends. Babangida credits Yar'Adua with being "the real, main actor in that coup. He made sure he selected those of us who were close to him."

The inner core of the coup plotters consisted of seven people. In addition to Yar'Adua and Babangida, there were Col Joe Garba, commander of the elite Brigade of Guards, Lt-Col Muhammadu Buhari, Col Anthony Ochefu, the provost-marshal, Col Ibrahim Taiwo and Col Abdullahi Mohammed. Taiwo and Babangida knew each other at the Provincial Secondary School, Bida. Taiwo, who was Babangida's prefect, was two years ahead of him in the school.

"We started building up a corps of friends, people of like minds," according to Babangida. It was more or less an easy task. Grumblings against the Gowon administration were so loud it was easy to find those who were prepared to help bring it down. The core group soon had a cast of committed supporters. They included Lt-Col Sani Bello, Col Paul Tarfa, Col Alfred Aduloju and Col Muktar Mohammed of the Nigerian

Air Force. Babangida brought Major General Muhammad Shuwa and Lt-Col Sani Sami into the plot at the last minute.

The coup plotters did not want power themselves. They decided they would get rid of Gowon but hand over to some other senior officers they believed had the courage to do what Gowon mulled over. From Babangida's own account of the plan, members of the inner core identified some senior officers in the army, the navy and the air force, to whom they would hand over once the coup succeeded. Brigadier Murtala Muhammed was the favourite choice as Gowon's successor as head of state. Brigadier T.Y. Danjuma was tipped to succeed Major-General David Ejoor as Chief of Army Staff. Danjuma was widely respected in the army for his courage and competence. For Muhammed's deputy as Chief of Staff, Supreme Headquarters, the group considered two men, Brigadier Olusegun Obasanjo and Brigadier Olufemi Olutoye. In the end, Babangida recalls, "we settled for Obasanjo (because) he works very, very hard and he also had a good experience in governance."

They did not want to involve the senior officers in the coup but according to Babangida, they needed their support to succeed. The senior officers had to be approached with caution. Taiwo and Yar'Adua were very close to Brigadier Murtala Muhammed. They were assigned to contact him. Other members took up similar assignments to contact Brigadier Theophilus Danjuma, Brigadier Olusegun Obasanjo, Brigadier Martin Adamu, Brigadier Olufemi Olutoye and a host of others to explain their mission to them individually. Obasanjo and Murtala Muhammed were in the Gowon administration as federal commissioners for works and communication respectively.

Murtala Muhammed was said, by one account to have told Yar'Adua and Taiwo: "Look, if you boys want to go on, you can go ahead. If it fails, I will try to protect you but I am not ready to be part of it." Babangida disputes the authenticity of this account. A similar statement was also credited to Danjuma. He reportedly told Taiwo and Garba who contacted him on the phone: "Make sure there is no bloodshed. Let me make this clear that I will do nothing to stop you, but I will not join you."[5]

Not all the senior officers who were briefed about the coup supported it. Brigadier Martin Adamu refused to have anything to do with it outright. He was their original choice to announce Gowon's ouster. When he was contacted, his answer was a blunt no. According to Babangida, Adamu asked the emissaries to tell him at what price he should do that sort of thing. "I think," said Babangida, "he wasn't willing to go against Gowon and so, he politely declined to have anything to do with our plan."

The group then settled on Garba as the coup announcer. As a core member of the group, Garba did not need to be persuaded. Garba, as commander of the Brigade of Guards, was Gowon's principal chief security officer. His role, therefore, had a nice ring to it.

By June that year, the plan was in top gear. Somehow, people sensed it. Sometime that month, Babangida ran into Murtala Muhammed in London. Muhammed told Babangida: "A lot of people know what you boys are doing because you can't keep your bloody mouths shut."

Babangida assured him everything was under control. They were going right ahead. Indeed, as far back as April 1975, Gowon was said to have been pretty certain there was a plot afoot to oust him. Just before he left for Kampala, in July to attend the OAU summit, according to one account, he called Garba and told him that if they wanted to topple him, he was not going to stop them but that they must make sure there was no blood shed.[6]

Babangida believes Gowon knew "that something was happening because there were always those checks and counter-checks between Abdullahi Mohammed and M.D. Yusuf at that time about a possible coup attempt. I think he knew it and as to when and so on, maybe he did not know. But he knew that definitely, something was going to happen. And I think, typical of Gowon, he would have told Garba something like, 'Well, I leave everything to your conscience.'"

If Gowon knew, why did he not stop it? Those who know him well say his Christian upbringing informed his attitude to the plot. He left the matter of saving or losing his throne severely in the hands of God.

A few days before the coup, Major Joshua Dogonyaro arrived back from an overseas course. He and Babangida had separated after the civil war. He was posted to the School of Armour in Ibadan. He went to Lagos to see Babangida and some of his friends. Babangida filled him in on the coup plan and why. "He told me," recalls Dogonyaro, "that we were losing grip of the administration and there was no longer a sense of direction. He said the military governors saw themselves as indispensable and were no longer working in line with the objectives of the administration."

Dogonyaro was surprised to see that Babangida had now become "more politically aware." Dogonyaro was persuaded by the "objectives for the change but without bloodshed." He did not play any significant role in it mainly because he was still on his disembarkation leave from his unit.

On the night of July 28, 1975, the country's third coup and the first bloodless one, was under way. Babangida assembled and briefed his troops on what they were about to do. The armoured tanks were rolled out, ready for action. The zero hour was set for 2 a.m. After he made sure everything was in order, Babangida went home and changed into his uniform. He went back to the troops and they pulled out of the Ikeja cantonment. Their primary assignment was to take over all the strategic points, known as KP zone. These included the studios of the Nigerian Broadcasting Corporation, NBC, (now Federal Radio Corporation of Nigeria, FRCN), Ikoyi, from where the announcement of the takeover would be made; Dodan Barracks and, according to Babangida, "most of the vulnerable areas between Ikeja and inside Lagos, down to the Brigade of Guards."

He reinforced these 'vulnerable areas' with his armoured vehicles. They had no problems with Dodan Barracks. The head of state was not there and in any case, Garba was in full control of his troops. Babangida went round "some few officers who were living in and around Dodan Barracks" and told them to report to the Lagos Garrison Organisation headquarters. One of those officers he so informed was Brigadier Godwin Ally, "a very decent man." There was another officer whose name Babangida cannot now recall. When he went to him, the officer simply refused to come out. No attempt was made to force him out. He was left alone.

The plan was executed faultlessly. Martial music on the early morning services of the NBC, Lagos, told Nigerians the military had once again moved against itself. Garba announced the overthrow of the Gowon administration, the dissolution of the SMC and the federal executive council as well as the retirement of the head of state, the military governors and service chiefs.

Gowon received the news of his ouster in far away Kampala, Uganda, where he was attending the summit of heads of state and government of the Organisation of African Unity, OAU. His immediate reaction was a cool, almost detached acceptance of his fate. After all, he needed no one to tell him, in the immortal words of William Shakespeare that the world is a stage. He had played his own leading role on the Nigerian political stage for nine years. If the end had come, so be it.

VI

The torch was seized from Gowon and given to Murtala Muhammed. In his first broadcast to the nation Muhammed said the change became necessary because:

> Nigeria has been left to drift. This situation, if not arrested, would inevitably have resulted in chaos and even bloodshed. ...The armed forces, having examined the situation, came to the conclusion that certain changes were inevitable.

Muhammed accused Gowon of virtually running a one-man show since the end of the civil war. "The affairs of state," the new head of state claimed,

> hitherto a collective responsibility became characterised by lack of consultation, indecision, indiscipline and, even, neglect. This trend was clearly incompatible with the philosophy and image of a corrective regime. ... The head of the administration became virtually inaccessible even to official advisers, and when advice was rendered, it was often ignored. The leadership, either by design or default, had become too insensitive to the true feelings and yearnings of the people. The nation was thus plunged inexorably into chaos.

The Federal Ministry of Information published Muhammed's first broadcast in a pamphlet titled: *Drift and Chaos Arrested.* The title summarised the rationale for the coup against Gowon. Muhammed and his new team wanted Nigerians to appreciate that they acted solely to save the country from drifting and ending in possible chaos.

When those who planned and executed the coup approached Brigadier Muhammed and told him of their decision to make him head of state, he gave them one condition. As Babangida recalls it:

> He told us we must come up with a plan, otherwise people would think we were taking over for the fun of it. Of course, we knew there was a clamour for political activities and a return to constitutional government. He said the only way we could give ourselves a stamp of legitimacy was to come out with a programme. The advantage of a programme was that it would enhance the stability of government because the people would see it and be patient enough to allow you to carry it out.

Babangida absorbed every word of the last two sentences when he took over the government in 1985.

Muhammed came into office and hit the ground running with a blueprint on those political, social and economic issues that the Gowon administration had allowed to linger. He and his team knew that Nigerians wanted action. They came fully prepared. With almost breath-taking speed, old structures gave way to the new. A new administrative structure was set up at the federal level. The Supreme Military Council was retained as the highest legislative organ of the military administration but state military governors were no longer members of the council. A new body, the National Council of State, incorporated in the country's constitution since 1979, was created. Military governors were members of this council. The federal executive council was also retained.

Two days after he assumed office, Muhammed announced the appointments of service chiefs, members of the new Supreme Military Council, military governors and corps commanders in the armed forces. Federal commissioners were appointed much later. Some of the coup planners either core or supporting cast, were appointed into the three bodies - the SMC, the National Council of State and the federal executive council. Babangida, Yar'Adua, Muktar Mohammed and Garba were appointed into the SMC. Yar'Adua and Garba were also appointed federal commissioners for transport and external affairs respectively. Abdullahi Mohammed, Buhari, Ochefu, Bello and Taiwo were appointed military governors.

Where Gowon was slow, Murtala Muhammed was fast. Where he was indecisive or vacillating, Muhammed was decisive. The census figures, riddled with controversy and over which Gowon had agonised for about two years, were thrown out as unacceptable. For planning purposes the country reverted to the obviously outdated census figures of 1963. He appointed a panel headed by Justice Akinola Aguda, an eminent jurist, to recommend an alternative to Lagos as Nigeria's new federal capital. A 50-member constitution drafting committee headed by one of Nigeria's most respected lawyers, Chief Rotimi Williams, was appointed to draft a new constitution for the second republic. Only 49 of the members carried out the assignment. Chief Obafemi Awolowo, protesting the manner of his being informed of his appointment through the radio, declined to serve on it.

Another panel headed by Mr Justice Ayo Irikefe of the Supreme Court of Nigeria looked into the creation of more states. Muhammed turned his attention to allegations of corruption against the Gowon administration. Probes were ordered into the tenure of the military governors, the administrator of the East-Central State and some federal commissioners.

The pace was breathless. Every action of government, no matter how weighty, and no matter who was affected, took *immediate effect*. The phrase became the hallmark of the administration's speed towards its set objectives. Muhammed ordered the purge of the public services at federal and state levels to rid them of dead woods, people with declining productivity and drunkards, etc. People once considered sacred and untouchable, tumbled from their high perches. There must have been an aim but there was hardly a method to it. Public service regulations on the sack or retirement of civil servants were ignored. People heard government decisions about their fate on the radio. Sometimes, this came to them in very embarrassing circumstances - either at work or in the course of their assignments in or outside the country. The babies were being thrown away with the bath water.

Still, Nigerians relished the daily sack and retirements. The newspapers employed the executioner's instrument, the axe, in casting their headlines. Daily, the axe fell on the high and the lowly. Inevitably, the axe was misused to chop off heads to settle personal scores. The nation was too inebriated by the new wine served in new wine glasses to worry about the implications of the ubiquitous axe as an instrument of administrative justice in the public services of the federation. It was Muhammed's show and it was a show playing to a large and appreciative audience.

Gen Muhammed announced his intention to pull the military back to the barracks by October 1, 1979. He thus gave himself four years in office. Within that time frame, he would tackle the creation of new states, give the country a new revenue allocation formula, choose a new federal capital, give the second republic a new constitution through the work of a constituent assembly to ratify the draft constitution, etc. The programme was neatly divided into credible phases.

With the administration in place, the core group, in Babangida's words, "more or less fizzled out." But that was only in the sense that they were not collectively, as a distinct group, involved in the routine administration of the country. Some of them held very visible positions. Col Joe Garba, for instance, was commissioner for external affairs. Babangida himself, in addition to being a member of the SMC, was the inspector of recce. As was noted earlier, Yar'Adua, Buhari, Bello and Taiwo, among others, also held political appointments in the government.

VII

Babangida and Yar'Adua were next-door neighbours in Ikoyi, Lagos. They were so close that they put a door in the wall separating their two houses. Both of them were strong members of the administration's kitchen cabinet. This group was referred to as the Lagos SMC. It dealt, in most cases, with emergency or urgent situations. Said Babangida: "If there were decisions that needed to be taken quickly, General Obasanjo would just call General Danjuma and the other service chiefs and those of us in Lagos. So, we would meet and he would brief us (and) we would take a decision. If someone raised an issue in the SMC and the time was too short to get everybody around, the Lagos SMC would consider it."

The group also frequently met and took positions on all sensitive or important matters due to be tabled before either the Federal Executive Council or the SMC. They did so with inputs from their military colleagues and young technocrats. Often, decisions of the kitchen cabinet were formalized at council meetings "with some adjustments."

Babangida became so good at soliciting for and obtaining these inputs that he took on another assignment. He became the "public relations officer of the administration." Three such young technocrats who made valuable intellectual inputs into government decisions were Dr. Yaya Abubakar, Dr Tunji Olagunju and Baba Gana Kingibe, all of whom rose in their career in the civil service. Abubakar retired as a permanent secretary. Olagunju remains very close to Babangida. He served the Babangida administration in various capacities, ending his formal services as minister of internal affairs. Kingibe, a former federal permanent secretary and a former ambassador, was secretary to the constituent assembly in 1988. He retired from the public service and entered politics and became national chairman of the Social Democratic Party, SDP. He was also Moshood Abiola's running mate in the 1993 presidential election annulled by Babangida.

It was as a contact man between the administration and the military that Babangida, perhaps, made his greatest contributions and learned enduring lessons in politics. He constantly briefed senior and junior officers on government decisions and actions. These briefings were particularly important for officers who were not living in Lagos. The primary reason for this level of contact was to give all the officers a sense of belonging to the administration. It afforded them the opportunity to make their contributions to government decisions. This boosted their morale. In turn, it enabled government to receive the necessary feedback from its primary constituency.

In his early days in the administration, Babangida was almost coy. Conscious of his status as the most junior officer in the council, he was guarded in his contributions to discussions in the council. General Muhammed soon put him at ease. He encouraged all the junior officers "to be forthcoming" with their own ideas. "Even when I thought we were talking nonsense," says Babangida, "he would still listen to us. That was when we started building a lot of confidence gradually."

Muhammed expected his younger colleagues to be uncompromising militants. He was surprised they were not. "So they thought we were fairly immature," says Babangida.

Muhammed was mercurial. His explosive temper was legendary in the army. Junior and even senior officers cowered before him. In the early days of his administration, if he felt strongly about something and anyone opposed it in council, he often flared up. But he was forced to learn that as head of state, he had to give and he had to take. Some of his colleagues were soon surprised to see that the head of state was even "cracking jokes at council meetings." He would even laugh. Babangida did not have problems with him. "I think I was reasonably in his good books."

One matter, however, nearly brought the two men on a collision course. In February 1976, the government received the report of the Justice Irikefe panel on the creation of more states. The panel had recommended the creation of additional states. Niger State was one of them. The panel recommended Bida as the capital of the new state. A council memo to this effect was prepared and circulated to all the members before the meeting. When Babangida, who is from the proposed state, saw it, he knew he could have a fight on his hands because "I was not going to sit in that council and get historical facts distorted."

He knew better than to confront the head of state. He resorted to doing what he had come to accept as the fact of government life. He lobbied his colleagues to support his position that Minna be made capital of the new state. Minna was the provincial headquarters of the then Niger Province. Babangida argued that it was the most appropriate choice as capital of Niger State because "Bida belongs to the ethnic majority (Nupe)" in the state.

He spoke with Col Sani Bello, governor of Kano State, and Yar'Adua, among others. He strongly argued that

> even if you take history, we have three emirates that got the staff of office from Usman Dan Fodio in Niger. I said Bida was one of them, Kontagora is one of them. Now, Kontagora can claim the same thing on historical basis, so you have no right to choose Bida while Kontagora is there. Historically, they are at par. They have first class emirs. So, the neutral place, of course, is Minna, which had been the provincial headquarters. We marshalled a lot of arguments.

His friends agreed to help lobby others to support Babangida's position. As they filed into council, Babangida was still apprehensive. He knew better than to take Muhammed for granted. He had not spoken to the head of state on the matter. He hoped Yar'Adua had done so. Babangida was pleasantly surprised when he saw the head of state smiling when it was the turn of Niger State. Minna had won over Bida. Yar'Adua had done the spadework.

Yar'Adua also needed the help of his colleagues. Murtala Muhammed wanted the then North-Central State (renamed Kaduna State by Muhammed) split into Kaduna and Katsina states. North-Central State was made up of two former provinces - Zaria and Katsina. Yar'Adua, from Katsina, was opposed to the creation of Katsina State. He too lobbied Babangida and others to support him. "We knew," said Babangida, "we were going to resist (the creation of Katsina State). Shehu didn't like it. A lot of other people didn't like it either." But Muhammed wanted it. When he found the arguments marshalled against his position, Muhammed blew up. Still, he lost and Katsina State was pencilled out. Curiously, in 1987, Babangida created Katsina State. Had Yar'Adua changed his mind or did he deliberately undermine his friend?

The Supreme Military Council was a watershed in Babangida's life. It was the most important institution for his political education. He recalls: "It exposed me to a lot of things. I got to know a lot of people in and out of government. Then, of course, political balancing, political intrigues. I was monitoring, studying and learning." He served in the council until the military hand-over on October 1, 1979. He was not there merely to serve. He was there to learn. And learn, he did.

Babangida's appointment into both the SMC and as inspector of recce pleased some and displeased others. He took over the inspectorate from a more senior officer, Brigadier Mamman Remawa. There were other recce officers senior to him. But Muhammed and Danjuma had no apologies for that. They wanted someone "who was effective." Babangida's colleagues did not quite see it that way. His seniors felt he was "being pampered." Officers of his own rank felt that he took advantage of the role he played in the coup to warm his way into higher political and professional positions. The late Col. A.B. Umar, who was in the NDA, pointedly told him that anyone in Lagos could have done what Babangida and the others did. No big deal. So, why the favoured treatment?

Babangida put all that down to "more or less envy. Of course, that sort of statement was very instructive to me because it showed that a lot of officers think that all you need for a coup to succeed is to take Lagos. But Dimka's coup showed that taking over Lagos alone cannot ensure the success of a coup."

Dogonyaro said the 'envy' marked "the beginning of the differences between him and his colleagues. They said he was full of himself." Dogonyaro was Babangida's colonel general staff. He said it worried Babangida that his colleagues saw him as overly "ambitious although he never portrayed that. Why they felt that way, he did not know." Dogonyaro advised his friend to ignore them and carry on with his work so long as he enjoyed the confidence of the head of state and the chief of army staff.

Dogonyaro told Babangida: "Your conscience should be clear. Once your conscience is clear and you know what you are doing, you don't have to bother about anybody. You don't sit down and then brood over the opinion of other people."

Babangida carried on with his military and political assignments. One of the grievances against Gowon was that he neglected to carry out the re-organisation of the army at the end of the civil war. The war had saddled the nation with a large army, most of whose personnel were poorly trained. The army needed to shed weight and become a small, well-trained, efficient and well-equipped army. Danjuma assigned Babangida the task of producing a blueprint for this re-organisation.

VIII

From February 5 and 6, the SMC discussed the report and recommendations of the Irikefe panel on the creation of more states, the Aguda panel on a new federal capital and a report of the commission of enquiry into the official conduct of the military governors and some federal commissioners in the Gowon administration.

On the evening of February 6, Muhammed announced the decisions of the government in a nation-wide radio and television broadcast. He created seven new states; four in the north, two in the West and one in the East. They were Benue (from Benue-Plateau), Niger (from North-Western State), Bauchi and Gongola (from North-Eastern State), Imo (from East Central State) and Ondo and Ogun (from Western State). Most of the old states or what remained of them were renamed. What remained of East-Central State was renamed Anambra, after the Anambra River. North-Central State became Kaduna State, after River Kaduna, and so on. Nigeria moved up with a 19-state structure.

The SMC also accepted the recommendation of the Aguda panel for a new federal capital. The panel recommended the present site, now named Abuja, which met its brief. It is centrally located and does not belong to any of the three major ethnic groups in the country.

A panel, headed by Mr Justice Owen Fiebai, a high court judge in Jos, Plateau State, was appointed to find a name for this virgin land. Perhaps, it could not find an original name. The name, Abuja, was appropriated from the neighbouring emirate of the same name. The federal government renamed the emirate Suleja after the incumbent Emir, Sulemanu Barau, who happened to be very light skinned. *Ja* is Hausa equivalent of light.

The report of the commission of enquiry into the affairs of Gowon's governors and the administrator of the East-Central State did not disappoint public expectations. The commission found all but two of them guilty of corruption and abuse of office. It was a devastating indictment of the Gowon administration. The two men who were found to be clean were Brigadiers Mobolaji Johnson (Lagos State) and Oluwole Rotimi (Western State). Muhammed described the former military governors as "a disgrace to their uniform." He dismissed them from the armed forces and the police *with ignominy*. All their landed properties and other possessions, allegedly acquired through corrupt practices were ordered to be confiscated by the state governments.

The punitive measures taken against the former governors met with popular public sentiment. They also bolstered the image and popularity of the Muhammed administration. It had vowed to fight corruption, abuse of office and indiscipline. Here was the evidence it would remain true to its word.

The Murtala administration might have been sincere in its fight against corruption and abuse of office but subsequent developments showed that the various commissions of enquiry did a hatchet job. They ignored common rules of evidence in their desire to play up to popular public sentiments. Public mood favoured crucifying these once powerful men who, in the classical movement of fortunes and misfortunes, had fallen from grace to grass. Hard evidence of guilt was not even sought for in many cases. In several other instances, some of those appointed to sit in judgment over the former governors were their political enemies. Given the public sentiment at the time, the former military governors could not have expected a better treatment.

Equity took a long time coming to some of these people. It came sixteen years later in 1991, through Babangida, a member of the SMC in the Murtala/Obasanjo administration. He put a patch on the frayed dignity of the former military governors. He restored their ranks to them - and thus wiped clean their slate of public shame. Their sins were forgiven. Two men lost out forever. One was the late Gomwalk who was implicated in the Dimka coup and executed. The other was police commissioner Audu Bako, military governor of Kano State and the architect of the state's famed irrigation and agricultural development projects. He died in virtual penury long before Babangida came to power.

Muhammed was a new age-Moses leading the nation to the Promised Land free from corruption, abuse of office, indolence, indiscipline, declining productivity, nepotism and all the other deadly sins. Only a week after the SMC took those momentous decisions, General Murtala Ramat Muhammed was shot dead on a Lagos street on his way to work on the morning of February 13, 1976.

Chapter Seven

The Dimka Coup

I did not save the day. God saved the day
—Col Ibrahim Babangida

Lt-Col Joshua Dogonyaro lived in Mayong Barracks, Yaba, Lagos. To get to his office in Bonny Camp, Victoria Island, on time, he usually left home before 6.15 in the morning. And because he left home before the NBC news at 7.00 am, he usually listened to the NBC news in his office.

On the morning of February 13, 1976, however, he did not tune his radio in his office. He was too busy to even remember. He had worked himself to the bones for two days "preparing postings for the new staff college in Kaduna." He had sat virtually through the night with his wife helping him to type some official documents to be submitted to his immediate boss, Babangida, that morning. Dogonyaro was reading over the report when one of his officers, Captain Jimmy Ojokojo, burst into his office, a transistor radio in hand.

Lt-Col B.S. Dimka of the army physical training corps was on the air, announcing the overthrow of the Murtala Muhammed administration. Dogonyaro muttered "nonsense" to himself. He thought it was a big joke. He believed Dimka could not stage a coup because "he was incompetent professionally and the type of people he would have around him must be drunks like him." Dogonyaro felt the Muhammed administration was so popular that there could be "no justification for (a coup) at that particular time. The time was not ripe for that action."

He was tempted to dismiss what he was hearing on the radio but something came back to him. He remembered that on at least three occasions, Dimka had spoken about his becoming head of state and "making Alhaji Maitama Sule a commissioner for something." Dogonyaro can't remember what post Dimka earmarked for Sule. Now, it appeared Dimka was serious about his ambition. "My immediate reaction," says Dogonyaro, "was that it (the coup) would not last because of the personality involved."

Someone called Dogonyaro from army headquarters and told him that the senior officers were on their way to Bonny Camp and he must provide for their security. He ordered Captain Kunle Togun, an acting battalion commander, to take appropriate action "for the security of the senior officers."

Dogonyaro telephoned Babangida's house. His wife told him the colonel was on his way to the office. Babangida did not know of the coup. Apparently, he too had not tuned his radio that morning possibly because he was pre-occupied with the major assignment before him. He was going for a meeting of the army top brass to present his report on the re-organisation of the Nigerian Army that morning. The meeting was scheduled for 9 o'clock. He arrived in his office quite early, as was usual with him. Little did he suspect that fate had a different assignment for him.

By the time Dogonyaro phoned Babangida's house, the latter was already in the process of carrying out the assignment, which brought him instant national recognition for bravery. Babangida had received his marching order to go and "flush out Dimka" from the NBC.

Babangida did not yet know it but he escaped an ambush on his way to the office that morning. He came to know this much later as the morning event began to unfold. Major I.B. Rabo was detailed to ambush Babangida on his way to the office. Rabo and his troops took up position along Ikoyi Crescent to the right of Babangida's residence. A jolt of instinct prevented Babangida from driving into the ambush. As his driver drove out of the house, Babangida noticed that the driver wanted to turn right. Instinctively, he directed him to make a left turn to Kingsway Road to avoid traffic congestion. Rabo and his men waited in vain for their quarry.

The drama was playing out in three places - Ikoyi, where Dimka and his men were holed up in the NBC; Bonny Camp, Victoria Island, where Danjuma and the other senior army officers were mobilising to crush the coup and Ikeja, where Babangida was mobilising men and materiel to return to Ikoyi to "flush out Dimka."

Cpl Ogiri Ochodugbo took Babangida to Ikeja on an army motorcycle. In the rather confused atmosphere, he had to rush carefully. He did not know who and who were involved in the came be known as the Dimka coup. On his way to Ikeja barracks, therefore, he decided to check what the situation was. Ochodugbo took him to the home of his friend, an Air Force Officer, Lt-Col Hamza Abdullahi. Babangida rang the barracks from there "to find out what was happening there." He was told that the boys "were there but there was nobody to come and give them any instructions." He felt safe. He took Abdullahi's car and drove to the cantonment and took over command of the barracks.

Again, he was lucky. The plotters had detailed Captain Adamu Alfa Aliyu, commander of the recce unit in Badagry, to take over Ikeja cantonment. Aliyu, "dead drunk," according to Babangida, arrived to find, to his shock, that Babangida had taken over. The armoured column, with Babangida in command, moved out of Ikeja barracks and headed for NBC, Ikoyi.

II

Major John Shagaya, commanding officer, 2, Guards Battalion, Bonny Camp, was returning to Port Harcourt that morning where he was participating in a weapons competition. He was sent to Lagos February 12 to collect some money. He knew nothing of what was going on but his driver had picked up some rumour of "some army disturbances." The driver, according to Shagaya, "showed reluctance and fear about taking the normal route to the airport because, according to him, he had heard rumours of army disturbances. I said I was the one to be afraid and that we should go. Not far ahead on our way, I came to the spot where Major-General R.M. Dumuje had just been shot and killed." (Dumuje was shot and wounded but he survived although Shagaya believed he was killed.)

Shagaya was in mufti and enjoying an early morning ride in a Mercedes Benz saloon car with ₦50,000.00 in cash. Near Creek Hospital in Ikoyi, Major Joe Kasai and Major Ola Ogunmekan who asked him where he was going intercepted him. He told them where he was going. Their next action told Shagaya something had gone badly wrong. He was ordered out of his car and ordered into their vehicle. Kasai and Ogunmekan began to argue over where Shagaya should be taken. Near the command mess on the Marina, they stopped the vehicle and almost began to fight. Shagaya took advantage of the situation, came down from the vehicle and sneaked away. Both men were too busy arguing to notice Shagaya's "escape."

Shagaya headed for his office. At the gate to Bonny Camp, a sergeant major refused to let him in. Then the sergeant major added the chiller: he had orders to shoot Shagaya. Shagaya knew better than to argue with an armed man with clear orders but something told him a little bravado would not make his rather desperate situation worse. He dared the sergeant major "to bloody go ahead and shoot me."

At that point, Kasai arrived at the gate. The sergeant major saluted him and let him pass. He ordered the sergeant major to let Shagaya in. Shagaya followed Kasai, who was also a battalion commander, to the latter's office. "There," said Shagaya, "I requested him to let me use his phone and he said I should go ahead."

Shagaya buzzed his office. Danjuma picked up the phone. Shagaya was confused. Could it be really Danjuma? What was the Chief of Army

Staff doing in his own office? Shagaya sent Captain Togun "to go and confirm." Togun did. Danjuma had moved his operational headquarters to Bonny Camp."

Dimka had not left the NBC where he made his dawn broadcast that stunned the nation, not least for its comic aside: he imposed a dawn to dusk curfew on the entire country. Babangida arrived at the station at the head of an armoured column. He was unarmed. He quickly took in the scene and noticed that "most of the boys who were involved in the coup were around the broadcasting house in open Land Rovers." They were all armed, of course. Dimka was also armed. He was surrounded by armed soldiers and junior officers, one of whom was 2Lt Samuel Garba, his aide de camp, who died in a shoot out there. Babangida said he found Dimka "drenched in alcohol."

Dimka spoke to him in Hausa: Ibrahim, *kai ne*?"[1]

Babangida: Bukar, you want to do something like this and you didn't tell me? We are friends. You should have told me.

Dimka: *Nka yi wasa;* if you play *wayo*, I will kill you.[2]

Babangida and Dimka were close friends. Now, fate had placed them on different sides. They found themselves confronting each other as enemies, the one to thwart the other's ambition in a possible shoot out in which either or both of them could be killed. Even for soldiers, it is a dilemma for friends to suddenly throw away years of their friendship because duty to the nation calls.

Col Conrad Nwawo and Major Nzeogwu faced a similar situation about ten years earlier when the former had the duty of persuading the latter to surrender to Aguiyi-Ironsi. Dimka remembered that incident. He warned that if Babangida had come to play a similar role, "I will gun you down." Babangida had his orders to flush out Dimka. But as he once told Ifere, what an officer is taught in a military institution must not be applied blindly. There are shades of grey in the stretch between white and black. If he could persuade his friend to surrender, he reasoned, he could achieve the same objective without bloodshed.

When Dimka saw Babangida, he knew something had gone wrong with his coup plan. As Babangida puts it:

> He knew that the whole bloody thing had collapsed because Danjuma ought to have been killed; I ought to have been killed and Obasanjo ought to have been killed. The fact that I was alive meant that his plan to kill all of us had failed. He knew something had gone wrong and that was why he started talking.

Dimka knew that Babangida's appointment as a member of the SMC and inspector of recce generated ripples in army circles. He decided to replay that before the man sent to make him a has-been. He told Babangida: "Sir, why don't you stay here and be part of us? You know, you are one of the most hated officers because people don't like you. You are not popular enough. Your relationship with senior officers is not good. Why not join us in overthrowing the government?"

Dimka then went on to catalogue General Murtala Muhammed's alleged 'sins' and why they decided to overthrow him. When he thought he was not making an impression on Babangida, he threatened to shoot him. Babangida told him that was okay. "I will be pleased to die when people like you are alive because I'll feel satisfied that I've a lot of friends who will take over my responsibilities. So, it is no big deal."[3]

Babangida still tried to reason with him, to persuade him to give himself up so that innocent people would not be hurt. Some civilian workers of the NBC had been trapped in the building. The director-general of the NBC, Christopher Kolade, was also there. If both sides resorted to a shoot-out, there was no telling the possible civilian casualties. He was trying to prevent that by reasoning with Dimka. He failed to persuade Dimka to give up and make it easier for everybody.

Babangida borrowed a civilian car and went back to Bonny Camp to brief Danjuma. The army chief was furious with him. He repeated his order and firmly told Babangida his order was for him to flush out Dimka, not to negotiate with him.

III

Lt Col. Mohammed Magoro lived in Ikeja cantonment. He was in the bathroom that morning and had just put on the shaving cream when he heard Dimka's announcement. He rushed out of the bathroom without shaving or washing off the shaving cream. He dressed up and rushed out to the residence of the commander of the armoured corps, Col Mayaki. Magoro banged several times before Mayaki opened the door. Mayaki was surprised, if a little amused, to see Magoro in his condition. Magoro was out of breath.

Magoro: Do you know what is happening?
Mayaki: No.
Magoro: You really don't know what is happening?
Mayaki: Frankly, no.

Magoro told him what he had just heard on the radio. Both men did not need to be told what to do next. They rushed out immediately so Mayaki could take over control of his troops.

Major Yohanna Madaki, staff officer, staff duties in Army Headquarters, lived in Ikeja barracks. He and Shagaya were members of the review panel headed by Babangida for the re-organisation of the Nigerian Army. He and Babangida had known each other from the civil war. He too did not hear of Dimka's coup before he left for work that morning. Like Babangida, Shagaya and Dogonyaro, it had been a tough week for him too, putting final touches to the report of their panel. When he got to his office and someone told him there had been a coup, he was tempted to laugh it off.

"I thought to myself," he said, "if there was a coup against Murtala (Muhammed) and all the generals and everybody who mattered were inside the conference, who then were making the coup?"

He couldn't understand that. But he resisted the temptation to treat the news as a joke. He went to Akinola, the director of military intelligence, to confirm what he had just heard. From his own account, Akinola did not know what was happening. He had been looking for Madaki to go to supervise the loading of ammunition to Angola. There were repeated announcements of the coup on the radio.

Madaki: "So, there we were, thinking about what was happening, what to do and so on."

Major David Mark came up to Madaki and suggested they should go and monitor what was happening in the other divisions. Madaki thought that could be dangerous. "I said if we went and were cut off, somebody could turn round and say we went to join them. So, let's go and get permission." They went to Brigadier Alabi, the principal general staff officer, for permission. Alabi promptly converted their permission to an order. He ordered Mark to go to the P & T and Madaki to go to the NBC. Madaki's "task was to go and find out who were the troops, how many they were, what were their weapons."

IV

The Dimka coup caught most people, including military officers, unawares. Its announcement did not follow the familiar script. It came late in the morning. Most workers were in their offices before Dimka came on the air. The director-general of the NBC, Dr Christopher Kolade, was already in the office before the coup got under way. He was in his office before Dimka arrived at the NBC to record his announcement. At 8.00 am Kolade was discussing some important matters with the commercial director when another senior official of the corporation rushed into his office to tell him he suspected there had been a coup because of the unusual movement of soldiers in the premises. Kolade felt that was rather strange. A coup at 8 in the morning was unusual. But he decided to go out and check. He headed for the continuity studio. As he was about to open the door, a voice behind him told him to stop because the soldiers were already in there. He turned to see who was talking to him. Abdulkarim Zakari, a continuity announcer. Kolade withdrew.

Dimka told Kolade that they had just killed Murtala Muhammed and taken over the government. He told Kolade he wanted to re-record his broadcast because someone had pointed it out to him that the curfew period, dawn to dusk, was wrong. It should have been dusk to dawn.[4]

At the NBC, Madaki established that those involved in the coup were from the physical training corps. He counted four, five or six soldiers, holding rifles there. He went to Bonny Camp to report his finding to Danjuma. When he heard that Danjuma had ordered that the radio station be blown up, Madaki said he protested, asking: "Why should we go and blow up the whole building because of four, five or six soldiers?" By the time he went back to the NBC, however, firing was going on, with "small grenades being thrown at the building." He thought it was wrong "to use maximum force for one man."

In returning to the NBC to carry out Danjuma's orders, Babangida faced one problem. No one knew the position of the elite Brigade of Guards, the closest army unit to the NBC. Were they involved in the coup? If they were, it would complicate matters. It meant there was going to be fighting between them and the loyal forces led by Babangida.

Col. Sani Sami, Babangida's former classmate and friend, was commander of the Brigade of Guards. "We were not sure of Sani Sami's loyalty, which side he was on," recalls Babangida. There was only way to find out. See Sami. Babangida thought that was his best option. He would go there himself. "I volunteered to get to that bastard because I said he was my classmate. I should be able to reach him." Again, it was a calculated risk. If Sami were involved, Babangida would be in trouble.

Lt Col Christopher Ugokwe and majors Shagaya and Jimmy Ojokojo moved out with the troops and headed for the NBC. Babangida headed for Sami's office "to make sure he had the Brigade of Guards in control because we later found out that the Brigade of Guards unit in Bonny Camp had even taken up positions" on the side of the coup plotters. He was still concerned about the safety of civilians in the NBC. He told his officers "to make sure all civilians are evacuated. I don't want any civilians killed." His order to Ojokojo who had a bullhorn was: "Urge the civilians to get out and the soldiers to lay down their arms. Don't just bump into them."

If Babangida thought that getting into the Brigade of Guards would be easy, he soon found he was mistaken. "It was hell." The soldiers were out on the road protecting their turf. They would not let anyone in. Luckily for Babangida, one of the junior officers recognised him and allowed him in. He found Sami in his office, "looking confused." He was surprised to see his friend. "Ibrahim," he admonished Babangida, "you keep on taking unnecessary risks."

Babangida could not tell if his friend was involved with Dimka but before the smoke of the abortive coup cleared, suspicion swirled around Sami in army headquarters of his alleged involvement. Babangida does not believe Sami was involved in the coup. He insists that "people wanted to suspect him because his troops were involved but quite frankly, I would want to exonerate him. Agreed, he was very close, just like me, to Dimka but I still don't want to believe he knew anything about it."

Dogonyaro and Shagaya still think there was enough reason to suspect Sami's involvement. Dogonyaro, who ascribes to himself a prominent role in it (curiously, his role appears to have been forgotten by others), maintained that Sami sat on the fence. Shagaya was one of the young officers who played a prominent role in turning Dimka's dream into a nightmare. He said he took Babangida in his own car to the Brigade of Guards where they found Sami eating *suya*⁵ in his office while all around him hell was breaking loose. The colonel was "looking confused and very hostile." Shagaya said there were "speculations that Dimka crossed the Dodan Barracks fence to Sami's office and had tea there."

This might have been improbable, given the circumstances, but Shagaya is prepared to believe "this could be true" because he claims that on the day of the coup, Sami "selected all the Warrant Officers who were to counter the coup and locked them up. And as early as November 1975, he had selected all senior non-commissioned officers, NCOs, who were Christians and sent them out of the Guards Brigade. Brigadier Bali and I told him this was wrong and we protested to Danjuma." It appears there is no love lost between the two men.

There are necessarily different perspectives to the Dimka story. Although all accounts give Babangida credit for aborting it, there are some rather fanciful recollections by some other people who played bit parts in it. Some of these recollections tend to indicate that Babangida took an undue credit for the role that others played to flush out Dimka from the NBC. The passage of time has certainly affected the recollections of some of those who took part in it. This is hardly unusual.

Sami, for instance, offers a different account of the coup and his role in stopping Dimka dead in his tracks. According to his own account, he was eating breakfast that morning when he heard shooting. He abandoned his food immediately and rushed to the door. His wife tried to stop him. "Where are you going? Don't you hear people shooting?" she asked, crying.

Sami told her he was the chief security officer to the head of state. "I will sacrifice my life," he told her as he jumped into his staff car. This is how he recollects the day and his role in aborting the coup:

> I went straight to Dodan Barracks and met so many people. People were running helter skelter. Nobody knew exactly what was happening. There wasn't a single staff officer in the office. The former governor of Kaduna State, Col Sarki Mukhtar was then my brigade major and Col Mohammed Wase was then my adjutant at headquarters. Mukhtar was nowhere to be found, unfortunately. Wase and I took it upon ourselves. We mobilised anything we could get around Dodan Barracks, around my headquarters, to defend the headquarters. Wase and I arrested the first six people who came to take over command of my headquarters, to take over possession of all the vehicles and all the ammunitions we had in the headquarters. We arrested them all. And that was how we saved the whole of Dodan Barracks and my headquarters at the time. I rang Danjuma and told him of the action we took and he commended me. But thereafter, the president (Babangida) came. And I am proud of it and I say it openly to everybody, if not because of that singular action that we took, Dimka could have succeeded in his coup.

Sami was clearly anxious to set the record straight by telling it as he saw it. He said he had suspected Dimka of a coup plot long before he struck. But when he raised the alarm, no one seemed to take him seriously. "Dimka's coup," Sami insists, "did not take anybody by surprise because I have today in my records, five letters that I wrote to Gen. Danjuma alerting him about the possibility of a coup by Dimka because he used to organise tribal meetings in Dodan Barracks itself."

He admits that Dimka "took all the soldiers" in his command to execute the coup. He blames his predecessor in office Major-General Joe Garba, for indirectly making that possible. The "worst thing Garba did for the Nigerian Army," according to Sami, was that he picked all the soldiers guarding Dodan Barracks "from one particular part of the country: Langtang, Shendam, all to defend Gowon." Garba, now late, was from Langtang in Plateau State.

Sami said that when he took over the brigade, he "wanted to command, not to be a figure head," so, he decided to "re-shuffle the command. I came up with a proposal dispersing all the senior NCOs from one particular tribe but later they said I should stay action. And Dimka was able to penetrate the system because most of the chaps were from his area."

Sami is reluctant to let someone else take credit for aborting the Dimka coup. Some of his recollections, which were not corroborated by other actors, tend to cast Babangida in a subordinate role. Sami said his office was attacked by some of Dimka's boys when Babangida was there. One of the two people who were never arrested for their part in the coup, Sgt Clement Yilda, according to Sami, "fired into my office. He wanted to kill us. Unfortunately, he couldn't."

Although Babangida said he instructed Ojokojo to use a bullhorn at the NBC, Sami claims it was he who used a megaphone "to tell Dimka to surrender or we were going to deal with him." According to him, he and Babangida talked to Dimka over the fence. Dimka, according to Sami's account, told Babangida and Sami that if they were not careful with him, he was going to demolish Dodan Barracks. "So," according to Sami, "it was because of that that we went quickly to mobilise armoured cars through Danjuma."

He admits that Babangida tried "to persuade" Dimka to surrender. He credits him for "an act of courage because to go calmly and boldly to confront an enemy when you didn't know the strength at his disposal" was a brave act. His recollection as to what point in the crisis Babangida went "calmly and boldly" to confront Dimka at the broadcasting house is unclear.

From what has been established, Babangida remained in Sami's office while his men were clearing the NBC of Dimka and his men. Evidence that his men had the upper hand soon came with the arrest of majors K.K. Gagara, Rabo and others. They were brought to Sami's office and ordered to be locked up in the guardsroom. Shagaya and Ojokojo reported back to Babangida that Dimka had escaped.

There were some conflicting reports about this initially. His ADC, Lt. Garba, was shot and left to bleed to death at the NBC. But nothing was heard of Dimka. Initial reports said he had committed suicide by jumping into a pond behind the corporation. This later proved to be incorrect because attempts to fish him out were negative.

From what has been pieced together about his last hours in the broadcasting house, Dimka did not wait for Babangida's return. After talking with him, he knew his game was up. If Babangida returned, it would be a bloody fight. He calmly walked out of the station. His own account at his trial showed he went back to his house before melting into thin air for several weeks. The police at a checkpoint somewhere in the East eventually arrested him. He was said to be escaping to the Republic of Cameroun.

V

The coup was quashed. The government was saved. But Murtala Muhammed was dead. He was waylaid, shot and killed with his ADC on his way to the office. Muhammed distanced himself from the rather imperial grandeur of the Gowon administration. He did not move into the official residence of the head of state in Dodan Barracks. He was casual about his own security. He preferred the anonymity of being lost in the Lagos traffic among the people to the noisy exhibition of power with the full panoply of out-riders. It was important to his administration to cultivate a new image of power - fewer exhibitions, more execution; a good public relations gimmick that went tragically awry on February 13, 1976.

Col Ibrahim Taiwo, military governor of Kwara State, was also killed in the failed coup. The federal military government at about 6.30pm that day made the formal announcement of the abortive coup. The government said an attempt by some dissident elements in the army to topple the Muhammed administration had been checkmated. Obasanjo, who succeeded Muhammed, formally announced Muhammed's death in his first broadcast to the nation on February 14.

Babangida became the star in that brief, bloody drama. As far as the Nigerian public was concerned, everyone else played a supporting role to Babangida in it. He was the hero. He heard of Muhammed's death much, much later. It made him "sad, very sad indeed." An emergency meeting of the SMC was convened that afternoon at which the Chief of Staff, Supreme Headquarters, Lt-General Olusegun Obasanjo, was confirmed head of state in succession to Muhammed. Lt-Col Musa Yar'Adua, the commissioner for transport, was promoted brigadier and appointed Chief of Staff, Supreme Headquarters. At the venue of the meeting, Major-General Emmanuel Abisoye, GOC, 3 Division, Jos, commended Babangida for his role in quashing the coup.

Abisoye: Look, I was told you saved the day. How did you do it?
Babangida: No sir, I didn't save the day. God saved the day.

Babangida remains modest about his role, insisting he did no more than his professional duty as a soldier to the nation. February 13, 1976, was the end for Gen. Murtala Ramat Muhammed. It was the stepping-stone to greater things for Col Ibrahim Babangida. His confrontation with Dimka, unarmed, remains the stuff of hero worship in the armed forces and the public. It cast the colonel in a Hollywood role - the brave, good guy against the bad guys who killed Murtala Muhammed.

A myth was bound to grow around him. It did. There was an outpouring of encomiums from his fellow officers. Magoro saw Babangida the day after the coup. The latter had gone to Ikeja Military Cantonment to "find out exactly what was happening there." There was no doubt that the news of Babangida's role had preceded him in nearly all the military formations. Officers and men discussed him and the role he played. It is remarkable that after all these years the opinion of some of these officers about Babangida's bravery has not changed. A sampler of such opinions:

Major-General Mohammed Magoro:

> It was a display of courage. You can relate what he did at the NBC to what he did at the war front when he single-handedly evacuated Duba who was shot, under heavy enemy fire. But this was even a bigger risk because it was not a battlefield. This was a military coup. In a military coup, you don't know who is where; you don't know whether the chap you would be talking to is against you. What that meant was that anybody within the NBC could have opened fire on him. But for him to have summoned the courage not to remain inside the armoured car but to have gone out physically to speak to Dimka, yes, it was a display of courage and self-confidence.

Major-General Sunday Ifere:

> He had done it before. Remember the capture of Umuahia? He was using his coolness and bravery to convince Dimka. Dimka too had confidence in him and he was willing to listen to him. Babangida did not have any other magic. If they had sent any other man to go and talk to Dimka under that tense situation, Dimka could have blown up the person. It was because he was calm and brave and popular that he was able to accomplish the feat.

Major-General Gado Nasko:

> It was a brave action. He is brave and fearless. It takes a lot of courage for one to go and face people who are armed, more so for someone who was listed among those to be killed. Babangida was one of those listed to be killed in that coup. As a military secretary, I recommended that he and the late Major-General Mamman Vatsa be awarded a medal for their role in aborting the coup. Vatsa also played a major role because he was the first to make the announcement that he was not supporting the coup.

Although the military authorities did not act on Nasko's recommendation, Babangida and Vatsa got their reward. They were promoted brigadiers ahead of their mates.

Major-General Abdulsalami Abubakar, who, as Chief of Defence Staff, succeeded Abacha as head of state and moved up as a four star general in 1998:

It needs courage to go and face somebody with a gun when you are unarmed. Agreed, as a soldier you are taught to fight but it needs some extra courage to do what he did. Normally, an officer would try and go with his troops to disarm somebody who turned rebellious but to go unarmed needs more than ordinary training.

Brigadier John Mark Inienger:

Confronting Dimka! Yes, of course, it was just like facing a mad man. Here is a lunatic you have heard has been chopping people's heads off and you say, okay, I am going to disarm him and you walk straight to him. The act of walking straight to the man needs courage and conviction, call it spiritual conviction, call it whatever. So, there was this belief in Babangida, born out of his conviction, born out of his courage, that Dimka would never kill him. It was a risk. Very few people can take that risk but he did. It was an act of courage that needs to be commended.

The myth became the man. A star was born. Mohammed Haruna, editor-in-chief of the defunct *Citizen* newsmagazine and one of Babangida's younger friends, captures the public perception of Babangida in these words:

There was this aura of an invincible person, somebody who went out there and confronted Dimka unarmed. I mean you saw him there at the airport and you could see that he was the star of the crowd sitting there and everybody surrounding him; you could see that everybody else was revolving around him.

For several days after the incident, Babangida felt uncomfortable with himself. How did the whole thing escape him? He was the government's listening ear. More embarrassing for him was the fact that most of those who took part in the coup were his boys.
Babangida admits:

I had a relationship with virtually everyone that was involved in the Dimka coup. All of them were my boys at one stage or the other. I saved them from either financial or marital problems. These were boys who could walk into my house any time and eat whatever they found. I used to enjoy discussing military affairs with them. We would discuss some of the famous generals like Rommel and Montgomery. They were very interesting to be with but they were very vocal and very, very militant.

Major Clement Dabang was one of those fiery young Turks in the army. He suffered from stomach ulcer and could therefore not eat 'normal' food. His doctor placed him on a special diet. Mrs Maryam Babangida often prepared this for him. Gagara also visited the Babangidas regularly. He had free use of their family vehicles. So did Major Joe Kassai.

One of those implicated in the coup, to Babangida's great shock, was his friend, Col Wya. He and Babangida were together less than 24 hours before the coup. So, how come the latter never had an inkling of what was afoot?

One possible explanation is that there are still doubts about Wya's involvement. He was most probably implicated on purely circumstantial evidence. Here is one account of how Wya found himself among the coup plotters. He visited Dimka in his house the night before the coup and found him drunk at what looked like a party going on in his house. He then left Dimka. On the basis of this visit, he was arrested along with Dabang and the others. He too was tried and convicted by the military tribunal. When his sentence came before the Supreme Military Council for confirmation, however, the council was split 50 per cent for and 50 per cent against his conviction. The head of state, General Obasanjo, allegedly cast the deciding vote that sealed Wya's fate.

Babangida still does not believe that the coup plot was hatched by the man the world knew as its leader - Dimka - because "he did not have the intellectual capacity to sit down and plan a coup." He thinks it was most probably the brainchild of the young Turks - Dabang, Gagara, Kassai and others. These officers, mainly majors, captains and lieutenants, apart from being very vocal and militant, were very politically aware. They had their own ideas about how the country should be run. They freely discussed politics and, like Nzeogwu and his group, their opinion of some of the senior officers was not high. They were in love with socialism and thought aloud of a socialist revolution in the country.

It is not clear if this was their mission on February 13, 1976. Nor is there evidence that Dimka shared such fanciful ideals with them. In his famous broadcast of the attempted take-over, Dimka referred to those behind it as "the young revolutionaries." The group did borrow a leaf from Major Nzeogwu.

Dimka, certainly, cut a poor image with his colleagues in the army. Those who knew him well refuse to give him any credits for coherence in thoughts, words or deeds. Babangida believes his friend was a willing tool in the hands of "frustrated senior officers" like Tense, Wya and Major-General Iliya Bisalla, all of whom, among many others, were tried, convicted and executed for their alleged role in the coup.

Dogonyaro dismisses Dimka as a drunk who could only get "drunks like him" to support his coup against Muhammed. Dogonyaro was a member of the panel that investigated the abortive coup and those implicated in it. He saw Dimka during his trial and "I looked at him with very bitter eyes and (a) stern face and he said, 'My brother, what have I done to you? Have I killed your son? Why are you looking at me like that?' I said to him, you are a disgrace." Dogonyaro, like Dimka, is from Plateau State. Most of those implicated in that coup were from that state.

The execution of the coup did little to burnish Dimka's poor image among his colleagues. It even reinforced it. The coup started very late in the morning. There was no co-ordination among the plotters. The senior officers among them appeared to have left the execution in the hands of the junior officers.

Babangida said the Dimka coup was "an ego thing, a sort of 'we too can do it.'" Dimka's speech was more memorable for its gaffe and brevity than for an articulation of their motive for change of government. Its brevity reflected lack of defined objectives; the gaffe, such as the imposition of a dawn to dusk curfew, reflected haste in its writing. Dimka said: "I bring you good tidings. Murtala Muhammed's hypocrisy has been defeated. His government is now overthrown by the young revolutionaries."

According to the Federal Military Government the coup plotters had two main grievances and two major objectives. Their first grievance was that the Murtala Muhammed administration was going communist. They wanted to stop this. The second was the promotion of brigadiers to generals. Shortly after taking over, Muhammed, a brigadier, was promoted a four star general; Brigadiers Obasanjo and Danjuma moved up as lieutenant generals.

The government claimed the plotters were particularly piqued by Danjuma's promotion and his appointment as Chief of Army Staff. This, according to a later government statement, was Bisalla's personal grouse. Although he too was promoted a major general, the "leap" by his mates had left him behind. Their objectives, according to the government, were to restore Gowon and all the former military governors to power and reinstate all retired or dismissed public officers.[6]

The biggest drama centred on Gowon. Government alleged that he was aware and approved of the plot to return him to power. In the view of the government, the involvement of a good number of officers and men of Plateau State origin was proof that Gowon knew. Even Dimka's link with Gowon through the marriage of the latter's elder sister to the former's relation, Mr. S.K. Dimka, then Commissioner of Police in charge of Kwara State, was used by the government to reinforce its belief in Gowon's alleged complicity. Police Commissioner Dimka was, of course, arrested, tried, convicted and jailed for his alleged involvement in his relation's misadventure.

Gowon strongly protested his innocence. He wrote to Obasanjo to this effect. He pointed out that as soon as he heard of his own overthrow, he pledged his loyalty to the new administration. As a man who values honour and integrity, he was not about to soil that pledge freely given with perfidy. He was particularly worried that "I have been virtually condemned by my government without giving me, first, a chance to defend myself, my good name and honour and that of my family...." He admitted that he received Dimka and "a mixed group" of Nigerians who had called to see him in his house in London "on the night of December 21st, 1975 but pointed out that he was "experienced enough militarily and in the art of government not to engage in serious discussion of planning a coup with (such) a mixed group" as visited him that day.[7]

The general fought and lost the battle to clear himself and his name. Public sentiment was against him. Murtala Muhammed had been assassinated at the height of his popularity. The Federal Military Government was not unaware of this. It stripped Gowon of his four star rank and dismissed him from the Nigerian Army. He was declared a wanted man.

It was Gowon's luck to live with the mud in his face for six long, agonising years. President Shehu Shagari washed off some of that mud in 1982. He granted Gowon state pardon. It was short of Gowon's demand. He insisted he had committed no crime and, therefore, there could be no question of a pardon. Shagari's action was more an attempt to put "the tragic event of the civil war behind" than a reflection of his personal conviction of Gowon's innocence because he also pardoned the former Biafran leader, Chukwuemeka Odumegwu-Ojukwu, who had been in self-exile in Cote d'Ivoire since the end of the war in January 1970.

Shagari did not restore Gowon's army rank. In effect, he remained a dismissed general. He held on to the half bread. In 1986, Babangida scrubbed the mud from the general's face. The first indication of this came at the convocation of the University of Jos that year at which Gowon was conferred with an honorary doctorate. In his speech at the occasion, Babangida referred to Gowon by his military title of general. It had taken ten years. But at last, someone had taken his protestation of innocence seriously. In God's mysterious way, the man who vindicated the stand of the former head of state was one of those who sat in judgement over him at the SMC in the heat of passion of the abortive coup.

Actually, Babangida had never believed that Gowon was involved in the Dimka coup:

> I knew and I believe very strongly that Gowon didn't know about the plot. The mere mention of Gowon was an afterthought by Dimka. I would say anybody who knows General Gowon, and I think a lot of us who know him, know he will not be a party to things like this. I still maintain it. Dimka was looking for

someone with a high degree of credibility. He must have been advised to do that because he knew he couldn't just go and call himself head of state. No one would take him seriously.[8]

Did Babangida defend Gowon in the council? Apparently no. It was a wrong time for a levelheaded assessment of the possibility of Gowon's involvement with Dimka. Babangida confirms that the circumstances simply made it difficult for anyone to express a rational view on the allegation against Gowon. He says Gowon "should understand the situation in which we found ourselves. There was a coup, people were killed, people were mentioned. You felt bad you lost a good head of state. Naturally, there was people's reaction. I think it was a natural consequence of what came out but I think once the dust settled down, people would reflect and start thinking and see that most of these things did not happen."[9]

VI

General Murtala Muhammed remains a folk hero. The spontaneous outpouring of public grief at his death remains poignant. On the first anniversary of his assassination, the Obasanjo administration, still hyphenated as the Murtala-Obasanjo regime, issued a ₦20.00 note with his bust on it as the nation's final rite of honour to him. The government went ahead with the execution of the political programme begun by him and returned the country to civil rule on October 1, 1979.

With the countdown to civil rule, Babangida faded more or less into the relative anonymity of the professional soldier. He became the first commander of the Armoured Corps in 1977 and moved to Bonny Camp headquarters of the corps. Dogonyaro remembers Babangida's time in the corps as the height of its "development and progress. Armoured fighting vehicles were introduced by way of tanks. (The) T55 rolled in during that period." Lt-General Alani Akinrinade, who succeeded Danjuma as Chief of Army Staff in October 1979, commissioned the tanks.

Babangida regards his chairmanship of the panel on the re-organisation of the Nigerian Army as one of his major professional assignments. It was here, perhaps, inadvertently and perhaps because of his visibility after the Dimka coup, that he came under close watch by his superiors. There were rumours that he was ambitious and that he was planning the overthrow of the Obasanjo administration. A series of intelligence reports described him as "a dangerous person" who should be watched. Babangida got wind of these rumours and reports. They bothered him. He insists he had never nursed a political ambition, at least, not then.

He was never confronted with these rumours or reports. He did not volunteer to stanch them either. But he confided in some of his close friends the rumours bothered him. He told Madaki he suspected they were planning to arrest to him. He vowed to resist any arrest. Luckily, it never came. Maybe his superiors could vouch for him. However, two incidents showed that not a few people were possibly jittery about his 'ambition.'

When he presented his panel report on the re-organisations of the army, he recommended no changes in the armoured corps. He wanted it left intact. One senior officer noticed this and asked why he didn't "plan how the corps was going to be." According to Madaki who was a member of the panel, "they said they were not going to accept the re-organisation until the armour was planned." He genuinely felt that there was no need to touch the corps. His action was misconstrued. "So," Madaki recalls, "people then said he didn't want to touch the armour because he wanted to use it."

Interestingly, other officers who wrote a similar report did not elicit the same reaction as Babangida's. Nasko, for instance, who was commander of artillery, argued that the artillery be left intact. The engineering corps was not touched either. In the end the armoured corps was created as a division.

The second incident was this. Madaki received a message from the director of the Nigerian Security Organisation, NSO, (now SSS) telling him he had just received reports of armoured vehicles moving towards Ikeja. He was instructed to go and check what was happening. He went there and found that the vehicles were brought in from Kachia in Kaduna State. They were off-loaded from a train and were being driven to Ikeja Military Cantonment.

Madaki did not report back his finding to his superior. Instead, he did a rather curious thing. He ordered his duty officer "to make sure the cantonment was secured." The officer was a little over zealous in carrying out the order. He locked up all the gates into the cantonment and prevented some officers who were returning to their quarters from entering the cantonment. There was some panic. Was Babangida about to strike?

The apparent confusion was soon cleared up but someone had to pay for it. Dogonyaro met Madaki the next day and asked him to produce the officer who locked the gates of the cantonment. He had to be disciplined. Madaki refused. He argued that even if the officer exceeded his brief, he was still carrying out a legitimate order. He offered to be punished instead.

The matter was then taken up with Babangida who told Madaki: "You bastard, you are standing my officer up." He laughed it off and commended Madaki for his principled stand. Case closed.

Babangida continued to enjoy the confidence of his superiors. Danjuma remained fond of him. Babangida accompanied the army chief in all but two of his official visits to overseas military establishments. Some of his colleagues and superiors interpreted this tour privilege as evidence that Danjuma was grooming Babangida as his successor.

Babangida proceeded to the newly established Army Command and Staff College, Jaji, near Kaduna, for his staff course on January 10, 1977. He completed the course on July 1 with an overall rating of C+. His grade was not great but his instructors raved about his performance in the course. He was described as "a charming, intelligent and mature officer (whose) attitude throughout the course was both constructive and helpful. He remains calm under pressure." The commandant believed Babangida "has the potential to rise very high in the army."

Back at his post in Lagos, Babangida immersed himself in his assigned political and regimental duties but more of the latter. He had set his sight high. He was aware of the favourable reports about him. In one unguarded moment, he told a close friend that he would one day ride NA 1, the official car of the chief of army staff. Meaning, his ambition was to become chief of army staff. He still had some bridges to cross to get there.

Late in 1978, the government formally lifted the lid on political activities and approved the formation of political parties. Only one week after the politicians received the nod from the military administration, Awolowo announced his new political party, Unity Party of Nigeria, UPN. He left no one in any doubts that he would run for president in 1979. He had resigned as commissioner for finance and deputy chairman of the Federal Executive Council soon after Gowon set the 1976 hand over date to prepare for his resumed political career and his well-known ambition to rule the country. He was a tried and tested hand in the game.

Babangida took the possibility of Awolowo becoming the next president seriously. He was a quiet admirer of Awolowo, particularly his discipline. Babangida thought it was time to begin to prepare for a new president and commander-in-chief. He could be Chief Obafemi Awolowo.

Late that year, Babangida discussed this possibility with Dogonyaro.

Babangida: Dogo, I think we have to start thinking seriously about the future of the army.

Dogonyaro: What about its future?

Babangida: Well, 1979 is around the corner now. We will be handing over to civilians. There is need for us to go back and study our books thoroughly and keep ourselves abreast because the handwriting is on the wall.

Dogonyaro: Why do you say so?

Babangida: Because I believe that Awolowo has confidence in, and respect for people who are mentally sound, who are intellectually up to date. It looks as if Awolowo could be the next president and if so, we have to buckle up, unless you want us to get out of the army. But we won't do that. So, let us stop drinking and begin to study.

Dogonyaro: I will not stop my drinking. Let's go ahead and do our reading.

After this discussion, according to Dogonyaro,

> We read so many books, trying to make sure that we were mentally alert, sound professionally and academically too in the event that we had to come across people that would like to do some screening because we didn't know what form the civilian administration would take. And if you have a person like Chief Awolowo on the seat, you better be sure of what you are doing.

Babangida, like a good scout, likes to be prepared. He is always one step ahead of others; always in a state of mental alert, antenna out. It is entirely in keeping with his character that when some of his colleagues gave little thought to the Second Republic, he decided it was time to prepare, to look beyond the military regime into the future of the service under a civilian commander-in-chief. Whatever that future would be, Babangida was not going to be found professionally wanting by his new civilian boss. Most certainly, by the time he told Dogonyaro it was time to get back in shape professionally, he had covered several miles himself.

Early in his military career, Babangida took a course in speed-reading, which enables him to absorb a mass of reading materials quickly while others are plodding through it. And because he reads fast, he also thinks ahead and therefore, stays ahead. In the army, his superiors admired this trait in him. One of them once said that Babangida is the only man he knows who knows exactly where he will be in ten years' time. Dogonyaro thinks it is a fair comment on his friend and commander-in-chief. "I would agree to the extent that he is a man who knows what he wants, how to get it, how to go about it."

Once he decides where he is going to be or what he is going to do at any given time, Babangida begins to meticulously prepare for it - studying and consulting others. He likes to bide his time, always sure the right moment will come. When he is ready, when that time comes, he makes his move and no one can dissuade him. He calls it his 'stubbornness.' Interestingly, he likes to move along paths less travelled.

His staying ahead of others has not always won him many friends. Those who are poorly prepared and find themselves out-distanced by him, regard him as both ambitious and arrogant. Ambitious? Certainly. Arrogant? Not likely. But there is always a detached air of superiority about him. His neatness from his primary school days, his choice of the armoured corps, his generosity to the point of denying himself something so that others can have it, his ability to listen to others as if he is conducting a therapy session and his willingness to stick out his neck for his friends - all these combine to give him that detached air of superiority that some people find wonderful and others find disagreeable.

He has always been careful with that image. To make it blatant is to risk being arrogant. As a devout Muslim, he would hate to feel he is superior to others. That is not the kind of humility his religion teaches him. He learnt to protect that image in three ways: hard work, friendliness and a fierce protection of his own secrets. No matter how close anyone is to him, the essential Babangida mind stays closed to everyone but the man himself. He opens the window into the recesses of his mind only a little. No two people who look in come up with the same view of what they saw. This opens him to various interpretations best summed up in the words of Dogonyaro: *shrewd, crafty, cunning.*

VII

In 1978/79, the road to Dodan Barracks and later Aso Rock was shrouded in the mist of the future. Did Babangida give any thoughts to that road? Perhaps not, but the feeling in military and civilian circles was that the country had not heard the last of the man who flushed out Dimka from NBC. He was a rising star in the military. On August 5, 1978, Babangida was promoted temporary brigadier. He was confirmed in March of the following year. Each climb up the ladder of success opened new roads to him. He insists he thought nothing more than to make a two star general. His close friends think so too. They dismiss any suggestions he nursed any ambition to rule this country.

Sani Bello waxes rather philosophical about this and argues that "there is no man without ambition. He could probably have put as his ambition that the highest he would make was probably an army chief." As to political ambition, Bello remains unshaken in his view that his friend did not entertain that sort of ambition. "I don't think he had a planned, articulated ambition to be a head of state through the bullets. Whether he was involved in all coups or not, I do not think it was a single-minded desire from 1966 to hope for a head of state through the bullets because it is dangerous."

On July 30, 1979, only two months before the military handover, Babangida returned to school. He was one of the 40 pioneer students of the newly established National Institute for Policy and Strategic Studies, NIPSS, at Kuru, Plateau State. The institute, a brainchild of Obasanjo, was set up under decree 20 of 1979, to provide a forum for initiators and executors of policy from all sectors of the economy. It offers a one academic year senior executive course to students drawn from mainly the public sector with a sprinkling of students from the private sector. The courses are in six broad areas, namely, policy and strategy, the domestic environment, regional studies, defence and security, international relations and international organisations as well as science and technology.

Babangida says the institute "was conceived as the premier centre for the conduct of study programmes, research and policy analysis. It was also set up to evolve ideas, new techniques and skills, as well as policies and new directions to guide decision-makers at the very highest level. The National Institute was, in short, designed to function as the chief source of ideas for strategies pertinent to national consolidation, betterment and survival."[10]

The students do research work and write a thesis on a subject of their choice. Babangida wrote his thesis on civil-military relations. His choice of subject showed what pre-occupied him. His feeling was that the survival of democracy would depend to a large extent on how the military and the civilians related in the Second Republic. After fourteen years in power as absolute masters would it be feasible to confine the military to the barracks? That question was the core of his thesis. Babangida thought the situation was delicate. He thought that people were not giving a serious thought to just how delicate this issue was.

To the first question, Babangida added another: Would the military return? Those who tried to answer that question argued that only good governance would keep the military out of politics permanently. How good is good governance and who is to judge?

Babangida used Gowon's ouster as a case study for his thesis. He analysed the reasons that made Gowon change his mind about 1976 and came to the conclusion that the general broke his promise because some senior officers who wanted political appointments misled him. That, Babangida says, "just shows how military officers are sometimes a bit selfish." Their being a bit selfish (in pursuit of power) might affect military-civilian relationship in the Second Republic, unless the military and the civilian leaders fully understood the dynamics of their relationship. Babangida articulated his worries and solutions brilliantly in his dissertation. He left the institute with one of the best academic records - alpha.

A little over eight years after his graduation from the institute, Babangida acknowledged the contributions of the institute to his personal development: "The National Institute invokes in me memories of an atmosphere for serious reflection, of rewarding intellectual exchanges as well as inspiration vital for the challenges of our time."[11]

NIPSS, certainly, opened Babangida's eyes to the enormous challenges facing Nigeria as a nation and the role its military must play in meeting those challenges. It provided him a unique opportunity to bounce some of his ideas off his fellow students as well as lecturers. By the time he graduated early in 1980, these ideas had taken root in his mind. The motto of the institute, **Towards a Better Society**, became an eternal spring, watering the roots of his new ideas.

T.B. Ogundeko, a retired major general and the first director-general of the institute, believes the policy objectives of the Babangida administration were largely shaped in NIPSS:

> When you look at some of the things happening in the Babangida administration, like the formation of transport, aviation and health policies, I often wonder whether this is not a rub-off on his participation at the NIPSS course because these are some of the issues they discussed thoroughly at syndicates and seminars.[12]

The military sparkled as an exemplary institution in the country. But beneath that sparkling surface, there was quite a bit of murk. It was riddled with petty jealousies and petty personality clashes. It pays for officers to keep their ears to the ground. Babangida always kept his ears to the ground. He enjoyed a wide circle of contacts in the army, the navy and the air force. His antenna was always out. It often picked up all sorts of signals. He used those signals to save a good number of his close friends from trouble.

One of those he could not save was Col Sani Bello, military governor of Kano State in the Murtala/Obasanjo administration. A former deputy adjutant-general of the Nigerian Army, Bello was the principal staff officer, Command and Staff College, Jaji, when his career in the army was cut short. He was a brilliant and well-spoken officer with a streak of cultivated disdain common to intelligent people. He received alpha grading from the staff college.

Early in June 1979, Babangida stumbled on a discussion among some very senior officers in which Bello was the subject. He did not like the comments one general made about the colonel. He quickly sought out Bello to find out what the trouble was between him and the general.

Babangida: Hey, Sani, what have you done to this bloody general? I heard him complaining against you.

Bello: How can a general start complaining against a blooming colonel?

Bello told Babangida that if the general had anything against him, "he should have had the guts to call me and dress me down." The general never called him, according to Bello, because "he had no guts. He was a bloody chicken."

Bello knew there was no love lost between him and the army boss, Gen. Danjuma. Although Babangida did not mention the "bloody general" by name, Bello knew who he was. Babangida advised Bello to keep his "ears to the ground." He too would do the same. Both men thought no more of the incident. On August 21, Bello heard from the "bloody general." He received a letter of retirement, telling him his services were no longer required in the Nigerian Army. He was stunned. He was being retired "for no offence, no criminal records, no charges." The "bloody general" had got him. He knew why.

According to him, "Danjuma and his Obasanjo man said I was too much for the army. They said I had my sights beyond the confines of the army." He did not know what that was supposed to mean. Bello could not contest his sudden retirement, unfair though he still believes it was, because army regulations give no room for redress in such matters.

The news of Bello's retirement crashed on Babangida like the waves. He was very unhappy to see his friend go. As young officers, all of them had dreamed of making it to the rank of a two star general. Now, only one step away from a one star general (brigadier), the sun had set on Bello's ultimate professional ambition. Babangida could not save him.

Babangida was in the habit of sticking out his neck to save those close to him from trouble, sometimes at a risk to himself. He has an impeccable sense of justice and fair play. He believes that punishment must be used as a deterrent to future infractions and not to destroy. This did not often square with the strict, regimental attitude towards crime and punishment in the army. And he was often criticised for being soft on people who committed offences.

In January 1976, Babangida presided over a court marshal. Madaki, Shagaya and two others were members of the panel. The court tried a colonel in the Nigerian Defence Academy accused of embezzling soldiers' pay, deceiving soldiers and nearly causing a mutiny. He was Babangida's course mate. The colonel was found guilty as charged.

Madaki voted for the maximum punishment - immediate retirement from the army. Babangida felt it was too severe. He always favours tempering justice with mercy. Shortly after he became president in August 1985, he demonstrated that when he opened the prison gates and let out the former public officers who had been locked up by his predecessor, Major-General Muhammadu Buhari, most of them without any formal charges. The purpose of punishment, he said then, should be reformative, not destructive.

"Why," he asked Madaki, "do you want to punish this man as severely as that when other people are doing the same thing?" Madaki said it was the colonel's fault he allowed himself to be caught and so, he must be punished in strict accordance with the law. Shagaya supported Babangida in recommending a lighter punishment. But without a unanimous decision of the court, Babangida refused to send his recommendation to army headquarters. Under the regulation, as chairman of the court, he could have ignored Madaki's dissenting vote but he insisted on a unanimous verdict. He has always been a consensus man.

Madaki did not like Babangida's stand. He went and confronted him in his office in Lagos and told him: "You are a member of the Supreme Military Council and you know there is stealing in this army and you want to leave this man? If you do that, I am going to take it that you are not the same tough disciplinarian."

When Babangida told him that the man was his course mate, Madaki replied that "the army does not know a course mate when it comes to this kind of thing."

They went back to Kaduna to review the verdict. Again, Madaki found he was still alone with his minority view. One other member of the court came from the same state with the accused colonel. He pleaded with Madaki to support a lighter sentence. He pointed out that if the colonel was "severely punished," back home he would be asked to explain why he did not save him. Reluctantly, Madaki understood that "this is Nigeria." He relented.

In August 1985, Major-General Babangida, Chief of Army Staff, brought his compassion down on the side of the same Madaki. Madaki had presented a paper critical of the army at the Law Week of the University of Ibadan. He was shocked to learn that "people were calling for my head." Babangida defended him. He rather liked what the colonel said in his paper.

Bello thinks loyalty is Babangida's "greatest attribute. Once he is with you, he sticks by you through thick and thin. He doesn't give you up easily. I have known quite a number of his friends that I may consider liabilities but he kept them because of his personal loyalty to them. He kept them against all advice, against all odds, even when they were working against him. Loyalty is probably his source of strength."

His loyalty is sometimes not reciprocated by those to whom he gives it. In the army, this tended to create minor problems for him. As president, it was a source of frustration for some of his aides. The general likes to go the extra mile in personal relations. To him, a friend is someone you don't disown, no matter what. He, certainly, may have derived his strength and his magic from this attitude but there is a reverse side to this personal coin: Loyalty and his desire to protect his close friends blind him to their faults. On at least two occasions as president, as we shall see later in this book, it brought him to the brink of disaster.

VIII

In June 1980, Babangida went to the US for a short course. In May 1981, he was posted to Army Headquarters as Director of Army Staff Duties, DASD. This was a very strategic appointment too. His star and his profile were rising. Few people failed to notice that. On March 1, 1983, Babangida, Buhari, Vatsa and several others were promoted major generals. The *Triumph* newspaper, owned by Kano State Government, saw their elevation as a bribe to stop them from toppling the Shagari administration. Obviously, suspicion about Babangida's ambition was still strong. By this time, rumours of an impending return of the military were widespread in the country. Almost everyone could hear the clock ticking, taking the Second Republic towards its date with history.

2nd Lt Ibrahim Babangida

Babangida and other army officers with General J. T. U. Aguiyi-Ironsi, GOC, Nigerian Army and later head of state

Babangida doffs his hat

Babangida at the war front

General Muhammed congratulates Lt. Col Babangida

First taste of political power; Babangida takes his oath of office as a member of the Supreme Military Council before the late head of state, General Murtala Muhammed

Chapter Eight

The Second Republic

The task ahead is enormous
–President Shehu Shagari

After nearly fourteen years of military dictatorship, Nigeria returned to civil rule. The Murtala/Obasanjo military administration had kept its promise. Alhaji Shehu Shagari assumed office on October 1, 1979, as Nigeria's first executive president under a new, military-minted constitution that replaced the British parliamentary system with the American type executive presidential system.

Shagari took office in controversial circumstances. Chief Obafemi Awolowo, presidential candidate of the Unity Party of Nigeria, UPN, challenged his victory at both the presidential election tribunal and the Supreme Court of Nigeria. Under the rules of the game, a presidential candidate had to win in at least two-thirds of the nineteen states. The electoral act stipulated 13 states to be two-thirds of 19 states. Shagari won in twelve states and had problems with the thirteenth – Kano. He won two-thirds of the votes cast there. He did not win on the first ballot, and, therefore, in accordance with the electoral act, he would have to face his nearest political rival in a run-off election.

Chief Richard Akinjide quickly solved the problem. In his forensic mathematics, he established that two-third of 19 is not 13 states but twelve states and two-thirds of the votes cast in the thirteenth state. A presidential candidate needed to win twelve states plus two-thirds of the votes cast in the thirteenth state to win outright on the first ballot. It meant that Shagari had won on the first ballot. The Federal Electoral Commission, FEDECO, accepted Akinjide's argument and declared Shagari the president-elect. The Federal Military inexplicably allowed this obvious forensic travesty to stand. It was to dog the Second Republic from the vocal UPN publicity machine that declared Shagari's victory a stolen mandate.

Chief Obafemi Awolowo, presidential candidate of the Unity Party of Nigeria, UPN, disagreed with Akinjide and FEDECO. He challenged Shagari's victory at both the election tribunal and the Supreme Court. Both confirmed Shagari although the Supreme Court cautioned that its judgement in the case not be cited as a precedent. It deliver a patently political judgment because in the wisdom of their lordships, it was safer to let Shagari keep the electoral prize, not least because world leaders had begun to congratulate him.

Shagari took office with a disputed electoral victory. He faced a crisis of legitimacy right from his first minute in the exalted political office. Awolowo and his supporters remained firm in their belief that Shagari "stole" the presidency from Awolowo. It did not make for a fortuitous beginning for the Second Republic.

Shagari was an astute politician. He appreciated what he faced should the other four political parties, UPN, PRP, NPP and GNPP, chafing over his victory, decide to make things difficult for him in and outside the national assembly. He decided to bring all the parties in to form an inclusive government of national unity. He told his political opponents that since the elections were over, "we must act as good sportsmen, set aside differences and harness our energies to the task of nation-building."[1]

His decision was eminently sensible. He did not win them all but it was good enough that he won over only the Nigerian Peoples Party, NPP. The UPN trundled up an impossible condition its leaders very well knew Shagari would not accept. The party said it would participate in the government of national unity if the president would implement its four cardinal programmes. The president rejected the condition.

The Peoples Redemption Party, PRP, was divided over the invitation. Its leader and presidential candidate, Malam Aminu Kano, did not think it was a bad idea but the younger and militant elements in the party were opposed to it. A compromise position adopted by the party was that there must be a national government based on a compromise manifesto of all the political parties. The NPN rejected the condition.

The Great Nigeria Peoples Party, GNPP, did not even bother to give Shagari's offer much thought. Its leader, the rather jocular Alhaji Waziri Ibrahim, a minister and Shagari's colleague in the Tafawa Balewa government in the First Republic, rebuffed Shagari.

The NPN and the NPP formally entered into what Kingsley Ozurumba Mbadiwe christened accord concordiale. In a simpler term, it was a pragmatic strategy intended to make things easy for the NPN in the national assembly. An agreement of convenience, if you like. Interestingly, both parties appeared to have understood its terms differently. The agreement did not attempt to shift the ideological positions of the two parties, if indeed they had any. Under the sufficiently vague terms of the accord, the two parties agreed to set up a special agency for the development of backward states and those affected by national disasters, geographical location and war. They also agreed to set up a review committee to amend certain sections of the constitution deemed likely to promote political instability. They would examine the agitations for the creation of more states, the problems of local governments and the controversial Land Use Act as well as the payment of adequate compensation to those whose property was compulsorily acquired by the federal government.

With the accord, the two parties controlled 52 of the 95 members of the Senate and 244 of the 449 members of the House of Representatives. It was the kind of control Shagari wanted to protect his bills from legislative harassment and filibuster.

Under the terms of the agreement, the two parties shared the top offices in the national assembly as well as ministerial appointments. Senator Joseph Wayas of the NPN was the senate president with Senator John Wash Pam of the NPP as his deputy. The post of Speaker of the House of Representatives went to an NPP man, Edwin Umezeoke. Idris Kuta of the NPN was his deputy. The NPP was also given six ministerial appointments. Still, the agreement turned out to be a bargaining chip.

It was not cast in the stone. The marriage of convenience between the two parties became inconvenient for them rather too soon. The first test of the accord came in the national assembly during the confirmation of Shagari's ministerial nominees. The senate took three weeks to confirm 13 nominees and another four weeks to confirm eleven more. This was in clear violation of Section 135 (6) of the constitution which stipulated that ministerial nominations be cleared by the senate within 21 working days or be deemed to have been so cleared unless the list was returned to the president before the expiration of the deadline.

Akinjide's nomination as attorney general and minister of justice was the most controversial. The UPN hated him and worked hard to block his appointment. Akinjide authored the forensic mathematics that gave Shagari victory on the first ballot. This was a mortal sin, as far as the UPN was concerned. The UPN believed that in a run-off election, which it presumed would be between Shagari and Awolowo, the latter would have won. The party held Akinjide responsible for Awolowo's 'loss' of the one political prize that eventually eluded him.

The real surprise when the Accord Concordiale came into effect was that not all the members of the NPP in the national assembly supported it. Such members ignored the accord and teamed up with their UPN colleagues to block Akinjide's confirmation by the senate. Akinjide managed to squeeze through the screening and was confirmed by the senate. The incident introduced bad blood into the agreement early in its life.

NPN leadership waited for payback time. It came in February 1981 when Shagari sent a list of ambassadorial nominees to the senate for confirmation. NPN senators refused to support the confirmation of four nominees from the NPP. The NPP felt betrayed. Both parties began to trade accusations of bad faith.

Later that year, Shagari announced his decision to appoint presidential liaison officers, known as PLOs, in all the states. The non-NPN-controlled states objected to the appointment. They said it was unconstitutional. Dr Nnamdi Azikiwe, presidential candidate of the NPP, urged Shagari to drop it. Shagari refused. He argued that the constitution permitted him to appoint as many advisers as he needed to get his job done. The president maintained that the PLOs would supervise federal projects in the states; they would not interfere with the state governors.

The accord wobbled until July 6, 1981, when it came to grief. For reasons not made known to the public, the NPP decided to pull out of the agreement. It gave the NPN a six-month notice - this was a requirement under the agreement - to terminate the accord. The NPN chose not to have NPP around anymore. It terminated the agreement effective immediately. All the NPP ministers were ordered to resign but Shagari retained some of them – evidence that he had broken the ranks of the NPP with obvious implications for that party.

The fate of the Second Republic was tied up with the accord. Its termination and the bad blood it generated had serious political consequences for the country. The NPP felt deeply wounded. In July 1979, the party had teamed up with the UPN and the GNPP to form the Progressive Alliance with the expressed purpose of preventing the NPN from winning the presidential election. PRP joined the alliance in 1980. With the accord, NPP left the fold but when the agreement broke down, it re-joined the other three political parties in the Progressive Parties Alliance, PPA. The governors of states controlled by the four parties called themselves progressive governors and began regular meetings under that aegis. It was a forum for wresting power from the NPN in the 1983 general elections. The country was inevitably put in an inter-party war mode.

II

Nigeria has a poor history of politics of conviction. For most Nigerian politicians, politics is simply a win-win game by individuals for the benefits of individuals. When the NPN leaders moved into the backwaters of the other political parties before the 1983 general elections they found hungry and greedy fishes waiting eagerly for the bait. The party hauled them into its net one after the other. And one after the other, each of the other four political parties was convulsed in divisive intra-party disputes and all of them were eventually factionalised.

The factionalisation weakened them so thoroughly that only the NPN went into the 1983 general elections intact. Just how hard the NPN worked to crush its rivals was reflected in the results of all the elections. In the presidential election, Shagari won in sixteen of the 19 states. This time, there was no controversy over what constituted two-thirds of 19 states. In the governorship elections, the NPN won 12 states, five more than it did in the 1979 elections. Its closest rival, the UPN, managed three; the NPP, three and the PRP one. Both the GNPP and the sixth party, National Advanced Party, NAP, did not win a single state.

GNPP lost its two states, Borno and Gongola, to NPN; PRP lost one state, Kaduna, to NPN but retained Kano State; NPP lost one state, Anambra; UPN lost two states, Oyo and Bendel, but captured Kwara.

The NPN made big gains over its 1979 fortunes in the senatorial election. It won all the senatorial seats in ten states and Abuja, which gave it a total haul of 61 of the 96 seats. UPN again emerged as the party's closest rival with only 16 seats; NPP came in third with 13 seats; PRP, five and GNPP, one, NAP, nothing. Interestingly, GNPP's lone seat was won in Kwara State.

Leaders of the NPN believed they chalked up these victories as evidence of the growing national popularity of their party. They were, however, the only people impressed by the magnitude of their victories, judging by the number of suits challenging most of them. This was not particularly unusual. Such reactions traditionally attend all elections in the country.

Still, the 1983 landslide victories of the NPN were too good to be true. Awolowo was so overwhelmed by it in the presidential election that he did not even bother to contest Shagari's victory this time around because "...the rigging was so massive it would have taken a month just to prepare the case; to collect the facts and figures."[2] The Nigerian Labour Congress, NLC, said "only a fool will say we had an election."[3]

The NPN made its political gains against one disquieting background: deterioration in the national economy. When Shagari assumed office in 1979, the national economy was relatively healthy. In the American ritual of a president's first one hundred days in office Shagari observed his first hundred days in office and spoke of how well he had managed the economy. He said:

> We have, during the last 100 days, witnessed tremendous improvement in our economic situation. When I assumed office on 1st October 1979, the daily cash balance of the Federal Government with the Central Bank was in the red to the tune of ₦521, 748.00. On that day, the country's reserve stood at ₦2, 376,824,653.00. Within three months of our coming into office, we have been able to reverse this unhealthy financial trend, which plagued the Federal Government since July, 1976. Today, I am happy to say that our financial position both internally and externally, is improving steadily which is a good sign of

hope for a prosperous future."[4]

Shagari was upbeat about this because an improved economy meant there would be enough money for him to tackle three national problems that formed the manifesto of his party, namely, the decline in agricultural productivity, inadequate housing in urban and rural areas and the mishmash in policies that had badly affected the quality of education in the country. And he did try to tackle them with mixed results.

He threw out Obasanjo's Operation Feed the Nation and replaced it with his own Green Revolution Programme. He also launched low-cost housing estates in all the states. His time saw a burgeoning number in tertiary institutions – universities, polytechnics and colleges of education.

One more important thing in celebrating the rosy picture of the national economy: Shagari dismantled the cost-saving measures, known as austerity measures, introduced by the Murtala/Obasanjo administration when a dramatic fall in the price of crude oil resulted in less money in the national kitty. Car loans were suspended under the austerity measures. Now, civil servants could obtain vehicle loans and allowances once more.

The flipside to it was that with the dismantling of the austerity measures labour moved to press for higher wages. Labour had been chaffing at the salaries and conditions in the public service long before Shagari came into office. The gains of Udoji bonanza had been wiped clean with inflation running at two digits. Labour wanted another general review of salaries and allowances.

Shagari's honeymoon with the NLC actually lasted all of three months. In early 1980, the congress dusted off its shopping list and confronted the Shagari administration with it. It added fresh demands it made to Obasanjo. The congress demanded a new national minimum wage of ₦300.00 per month. Negotiations over this and other demands between the government and the congress continued until early 1981 when they apparently broke down. In April 1981, the NLC called out its members on a nation-wide strike that lasted for two weeks.

Shagari had been disturbed about the wildcat strikes in the country. In his May Day speech that year, he chided the workers for going on frequent strikes "without ... using the machineries that have been established for resolving trade disputes."

In the first nine months of the new civilian administration, there were 247 officially registered trade disputes involving 144,886 workers. The nation lost over one million man-days.[5]

The federal and state public services are the largest employers of labour in the country. Political appointees such as ministers and commissioners as well as top civil servants, tend to see themselves as representatives of their states and ethnic groups in government. One area in which they try to satisfy the interests of their states and ethnic groups is employment in the public service – ministries, ministerial departments as well as government-owned companies and parastatals.

For the civilians coming in from the cold, as it were, after nearly fourteen years of military rule, the anxiety to meet the demands of state and ethnic groups was feverish. The federal and the state public services soon ballooned. Soon, they began to burst at the seams with more and more workers now being offered jobs that existed more or less on paper. Ministries and government-owned companies and parastatals were saddled with employment load they could not carry. Where vacancies did not exist, they were created to meet the exigencies of political rewards or investments. In some cases, three or four persons were employed to do a job meant for only one person. All of them ended up doing nothing - and getting paid for it.

By 1982, recurrent expenditures of the federal and state government outstripped capital votes. What this meant was that governments were spending more money on salaries and allowances and office maintenance than on the provision of social amenities and other capital projects. Still, they could not even pay the wages and salaries as and when due. Salary arrears piled up. Primary school teachers bore the brunt of this unfortunate development. Only a few states, notably Lagos, Sokoto and Kano, were able to pay primary school teachers. Almost all the other states had to close down primary schools for as many as nine months because teachers refused to continue to work on an empty stomach.

When the military returned to power four years and three months after the handover, the inability of federal and state government to pay workers' salaries regularly as well as the bloated bureaucracy, were cited as evidence of the poor management of the nation's economy by the civilians. As Brigadier Sani Abacha put it: "In some states, workers are being owed salary arrears of eight to twelve months and in others, there are cries of salary cuts, yet our leaders... continue to proliferate (*sic*) public appointments in complete disregard of our stark economic realities."[6]

Being able to pay civil servants was considered such a big achievement that state governors routinely informed the world each time they made that Olympic grade.

Despite all pretensions to the contrary, the nation's economy had exchanged its ruddy complexion for an anaemic one by 1981. Developments in the world oil market had resulted in oil glut. Nigeria was forced to reduce its oil production quota. Production thus declined from 2.09 million barrels a day in January that year to 1.86 million barrels a day in March. This went down to 1.116 million barrels a day in May and an all-time low of 0.64 million barrels per day in August. By early 1982, it hit the bottom with half a million barrels a day.⁷ Declining oil production meant a drastic fall in the nation's earnings from its single most important source of revenue.

Shagari was not unduly worried by this critical development. In January 1981, he launched an ambitious Fourth National Development Plan (1981-1985) in which he envisaged a total expenditure of ₦82 billion. The entire plan was to be financed mainly from internal sources. He predicated the plan on crude oil price of $55.00 per barrel and a daily production quota of 2.19 million barrels. Yet the Organisation of Petroleum Exporting Countries, OPEC, had pegged Nigeria's quota at 1.3 million barrels per day.

The contradiction here is difficult to understand. In his 1981 budget speech only a few days earlier Shagari had admitted that "the revenue expectations for 1981 are bedevilled by the somewhat unstable and unpredictable nature of the crude oil market." The developed countries, he rightly pointed out, "have been stockpiling oil. For this and other reasons," he cautioned Nigerians, "the oil producing countries may be compelled to cut back production in response to market trends."⁸

OPEC member nations were, indeed, compelled to do just that. A year after he launched the nation's most ambitious national development plan, Shagari responded to the changing fortunes in the nation's economy by introducing cost-saving measures similar to Obasanjo's - a belated admission that the economy was in trouble.

To be fair, oil had been good to Shagari. Between October 1979, when he took over and 1982, when the oil glut redefined the nation's wealth, Nigeria earned ₦44.77 billion from crude oil exports. It was more than the nation earned in nine years of the Gowon administration. Much of it had been frittered away. Shagari was faced with accumulated trade arrears of over ₦4 billion; medium and long-term loans of ₦10.6 billion and yearly budget deficit of between ₦427.4 million and ₦0.2 billion. External loans by the 19 state governments totalled $8 billion by March 1983.⁹

The country could not meet most of its international financial obligations any more. Because of liquidity problems, the Central Bank of Nigeria could not honour letters of credit. Manufacturers could not import their raw materials and spare parts. They too were forced to introduce cost-saving measures, notably retrenchment of their staff because of low capacity utilisation. This and other developments bewildered the nation. The austerity measures, were, obviously, too little, too late to repair the damage that had been done to the economy. Basic commodities such as milk and sugar acquired some importance and were christened 'essential commodities.' The federal and state government embarked on a massive and indiscriminate importation of rice from Spain, the US and Thailand.

Despite the apparent rice armada, its artificial scarcity persisted. Merchants and politicians induced the scarcity of the essential commodities. The most vulnerable socio-economic group - the low-income earners – queued up in long lines to buy the essential commodities. The queues were the most visible evidence that the national economy was in trouble and its management by Shagari left much to be desired.

To make matters worse, corruption thrived in various forms. One area that bothered Shagari was contract costs. He set up the Adamu Ciroma panel to make a comparative analysis of project costs between Nigeria and selected African countries – Kenya, Libya, Egypt, etc. Nigeria outranked them all, in some cases by as much as two and half times the cost of similar projects in those countries. Nigerians began to feel the ominous shadow of the military. And Shagari faced open press hostility from the opposition camp that stoked the fire of public disenchantment with the administration.

The 1983 elections provided the press with much of its ammunition for the war against the government. In its editorial of October 1, 1983, the *Nigerian Tribune* owned by Awolowo, said Shagari was "assuming office on borrowed time." The paper published a John F. Kennedy quotation: *Those who make peaceful change impossible make violent change inevitable,* on its front page daily.

Triumph newspaper owned by PRP-controlled Kano State government, published an editorial in its issue of August 21, that year with the ominous title: *Violent Change Inevitable.*

The National Concord, freed from its compulsory support of the NPN and the Shagari administration with its publisher, M.K.O. Abiola's ditching of the party, began to raise its voice against the Shagari administration. Yakubu Mohammed, deputy chief executive officer of Newswatch Communications Ltd., was editor of the **National Concord**. When he joined the paper as deputy editor in 1980, he "met an editorial policy which was totally, purely, unashamedly pro-NPN." The paper would not even report Awolowo. But as soon as Abiola left the NPN, the Concord publications turned 360 degrees and became hostile to the NPN and the Shagari administration. Its editors and reporters might be innocently doing no more than reporting what they considered to be good news but its jump in circulation from less than 100,000 copies a day when the chief supped with the NPN to over 400,000 copies a day in early 1983 when the grape had turned sour, was evidence its readers welcomed both its anti-NPN stance and its daily fare of *good news*.

Abiola was bombarded with all sorts of documents from mostly anonymous sources, most of which were forgeries, on the alleged corruption or perfidy in the government. He also brought some authentic documents, some of which were handwritten, relating to corruption that he gave to his editors for publication. Some of these documents were strongly believed to be from military sources. So, "The *National Concord*... part from its editorials, was coming out almost every day with fresh evidences of rot in the government."[10]

One of such major stories was published in its issue of December 30, 1983. In it, the paper gave details of government expenditure between 1979 and 1983 on the National Assembly. It contained juicy cases of financial profligacy, inflated contracts and bribes. The publication, however, was part of the orchestrated media reports on the heavy cost of democracy to a nation whose economy had been ravaged through mismanagement.

The press was, perhaps, innocently but certainly naively, psycheing the people into believing that the cost of democracy was so heavy for the nation that democracy itself was anything but good for Nigeria. The verdict of the press more or less was: this is a bad government, a government we don't deserve. It was the kind of story the military wanted to hear, the kind of evidence it needed to act. The press actually preached to the converted.

Within the first few weeks of his second term, Shagari created a ministry of national guidance headed by Nigeria's former ambassador to the United Nations, Alhaji Yusufu Maitama Sule. Its brief was to promote ethical revolution in the country. It was Shagari's take on tackling corruption as well as moral degeneracy in the country. The philosophy appeared to be: Put the nation back on the path of moral rectitude and you kiss corruption good-bye.

Shagari went before the National Assembly on Friday, December 30, 1983, to present his ₦10.944 billion 1984 appropriation bill. He promised to "revamp the economy and continue to pilot our nation on the path of political stability as well as provide increased development in order to improve the quality of life and security of the individual." In what appeared to be a veiled reference to the rumours of a coup against him, the president said: "I will need the guidance of God in order to achieve these objectives."

III

God's guidance had taken Shagari that far, allowing him to complete his first four-year term and renew his mandate for a second term in August 1983. What he perhaps did not know was that he was lucky to have stayed in office that long. The military were on his tail less than two years after he assumed office. Some young elements in the military began to snort about the conduct of the civilian administration since 1981.

"We thought, quite frankly," recalls Babangida, "that the country was heading towards a disastrous situation, both economically and politically, and therefore, there was the urge to intervene in the whole process."

That urge was restrained for nearly three years to prepare the ground for the tiny seed of doubt about the ability of the civilians to run the country to grow. The politicians themselves watered the seed of doubt. They cultivated larger than life images of themselves. They lived life to the hilt in famous world capitals and cities. They made wild allegations of corruption against one another. The more frustrated and marginalised amongst them openly canvassed military intervention.

Discussions about what to do to save the country, according to Babangida, "became a topical issue within the officer corps. Anywhere you went, you found officers discussing what was happening."

Three separate groups planned Shagari's ouster. These were the Buhari group, the Idiagbon group and the Babangida group. The three men held strategic military appointments. Buhari, a major general, was the General Officer Commanding, 3 Infantry Division, with its headquarters in Jos, Plateau State. Babangida, also a major general, was director of army staff duties and planning in army headquarters and Brigadier Tunde Idiagbon was the military secretary.

Sometime in early 1983 during an army sports week in Jos, Buhari reportedly told Brigadier Muhammadu Gado Nasko he was going to take over from Shagari and that he would "prosecute all the rogues" in the Shagari administration. Nasko said Buhari sought opinion on his intention to make Major-General Domkat Bali his chief of army staff. Nasko told him Bali was a fine officer but that he was not firm enough for such a rather demanding position. He advised that he should be made minister of defence instead.

Accounts of how the three groups and another said to be made up mainly of lieutenant colonels fused are sketchy but by about the first quarter of 1983, they had become one formidable group. Members of the inner corps drawn from the three services, were Babangida, Buhari, Brigadier Ibrahim Bako, Idiagbon, Air Vice-Marshall Usman Mu'azu, Brigadier Mamman Magoro, commandant, Army School of Infantry, Air Vice-Marshall Hamza Abdullahi, Mohammed Abdullahi and Commodore Murtala Nyako.

It is not true that Bako, who died in an ambush on his way to Aguda House to arrest President Shagari on the night of the coup, was the prime mover in the coup against the president; nor was he ever tipped to be the head of state. In fact, Buhari did not even want Bako to participate in it because he was said to be flippant. However, because he was close to

Shagari, he was able to convince the other members to assign him the role of arresting the president.

The group toyed with three different dates to effect the change of government. The first was in the first quarter of that year. This was changed because it was felt that although the Shagari administration had become unpopular, for the coup to enjoy a popular support, it needed something more dramatic than Shagari's unpopularity. The second plan was to move in just before the general elections and abort them. Again, this was changed. This is how Babangida explained it:

> We thought it wasn't proper because we would be accused of sabotaging the electoral process. So, we said the best thing was to allow the election to go on. In our analysis, we felt that those who were presidential aspirants would accuse us of aborting their presidential ambition. So, we decided we were going to allow the elections, everything to go through.

It was both a gamble and a calculated plan. If the elections did not produce a change of government, particularly at the centre, the coup planners reckoned that the losers would accuse the winner of electoral fraud and, therefore, support a military intervention. The gamble worked. The election produced howls of protests. If calls for the military to return were muted before the elections, they became loud after the elections. These encouraged the coup planners to set a new date: October 1, the day Shagari and the state governors would be sworn in for a new term.

Nasko was not a member of the inner group but they often sought his opinion. When they sought his opinion on the October 1 date, he marshalled a strong argument against it. He argued that the country's international image would suffer an irreparable damage if they toppled a civilian regime on the day it would be sworn into office and that foreign diplomats invited to the swearing in ceremony would be embarrassed. He said he was not against the takeover "but the timing was inappropriate because of the international implications." He won. The coup was called off at the last minute.

IV

Shagari was not unaware of the rumours of a coup. He had received enough hints to know that a military intervention was again in the offing. Some of his senior aides picked up oblique remarks from military personnel that they were not happy with his administration. The coup plot had even leaked to the president. Shagari confirms in his autobiography that sometime in November 1983, the governor Plateau State, Chief Solomon Lar, told him that there was a plot to remove him from office. Lar's wife had picked the information from her sister married to a senior army officer in Jos, who, pressed by his wife for keeping late nights, confided in her he was attending meeting on the removal of the president.[11]

Babangida did not seem to like Shagari's rather passive nature. He often joked about the president's style of administration to his civilian friends but he dropped enough hints to show he thought Shagari could do a better job of ruling the country by acting differently. He once told one of Shagari's close friends: "Ah, ah, this man doesn't seem to know what he is doing. I mean, as a leader, he could just think of creating some kind of a diversionary something and while the public is concentrating on that, he will have time to tackle issues and get himself organised."

Babangida took his own advice here. He used this tactic to keep Nigerians talking throughout his time in office as president for eight years.

Shagari reportedly confessed to a visiting special envoy of the Cameroonian president sometime in 1983 that there had been eight unsuccessful attempts to overthrow him.[12] If so, only one of such attempts ever became public knowledge. That year, a Maiduguri-based businessman, Alhaji Zanna Bukar Mandara, was arrested, charged, tried and convicted on charges of financing a coup against the president. Shagari resigned himself to fate. He would often tell his aides who advised him to take steps to forestall his overthrow that the military were free to come and take over if they felt he was not doing his best. As far as he was concerned, he said, no one could take power from him unless Allah who gave it to him decided to take it back and give it to someone else. And if that was Allah's decision, then so be it.

Shagari's resigned attitude irritated some of his senior aides who urged him to be firm with the military. They advised him to retire the officers whom they believed nursed a political ambition. Two men were always mentioned: Buhari and Babangida. But the president resisted all attempts to act against them. He knew they were good and popular officers and part of the cream in the army. He had no reason to doubt their loyalty, despite what people said about them.

Events moved much faster than Shagari was prepared to admit. On Thursday, December 29, the president was busy on two important things. He was putting final touches to his 1984 appropriation bill, which he would present to the national assembly the next day. He was also working on his traditional New Year message that he wanted to record before leaving for Abuja, the nascent federal capital, where he would spend his New Year holiday. In the midst of these preparations he was said to have received a telephone call from London. The caller reportedly told him there was a plan to topple him that weekend. He allegedly mentioned Babangida as the prime mover of the putsch.

If this information worried Shagari, he did not let on. He went ahead with his preparations. The next day, he presented the budget to the national assembly and recorded his New Year broadcast. He went for the Friday prayers.

At 5 pm that day, Shagari flew to Abuja in the company of some of his ministers and political associates. Abuja was a city after the president's heart. He was building it in a hurry. The new city became his equivalent of Camp David to which he often retreated for some rest. Most of the ministers and members of the national assembly had also left Lagos for the New Year holiday.

After his dinner and evening prayers in Akinola Aguda house, Abuja, the presidential lodge named after Mr Justice Akinola Aguda who headed the panel appointed by Murtala Muhammed to recommend a new federal capital, Shagari went into his study to do some work. He was aware of the high degree of agitation among his personal staff. Some of them had heard the rumours of a coup plot against the president. Indeed, according to Shagari, his ADC, Captain A. Anyogo, had told him after dinner of Lt Col Ogbeha's visit during which he told the captain that a coup against the president was afoot and that he should arrest him at mid-night and keep him until the arrival of senior officers from Kaduna.[13]

The captain pledged his loyalty to the president and took steps to protect him and his family. But as the hands of the clock moved inexorably towards the zero hour, the president and his staff naturally became increasingly apprehensive for their own safety and the safety of the president. Shagari remained stoical. His personal physician, Dr Dalhatu Sarki Tafida, noticed that despite his attempts to remain calm, the president's inner turbulence was clearly wearing him out. He advised that the president should flee. Shagari refused.

In Lagos, the coup plot was moving towards its climax. Babangida and Idiagbon were co-ordinating most of the activities in the north and certain parts of the west and the east. The members of the inner core had worked on the coup broadcast and chosen the announcer, Brigadier Sani Abacha. By the evening of December 30, they were reasonably sure they would pull it off. Contacts with Abuja confirmed that the security around the president would be no match for the group led by Col Ibrahim Bako and Lt-Col Jonathan Tunde Ogbeha.

Babangida and Air Vice-Marshall Muktar Mohammed went to the Flag Staff House, the official residence of the Chief of Army Staff, Lt-Gen. Inuwa Wushishi, that evening to tell him they were taking over. They knew they were taking a risk. If he did not support them, he could move against them. The army boss was both angry and shocked. But they told him there was nothing he could do about it. He could no longer count on enough loyal officers and men to crush the coup.

In Abuja, Shagari, now tired, was beginning to think the coup scare had blown out with the wind. He was mistaken. Not long after he went to bed, shots rang out not far from Aguda House. The coup men and the loyal soldiers had had a brief encounter in which Bako lost his life. It was at this point that the security men spirited the president out of the lodge to safety in the home of his minister of state for External Affairs, Alhaji Hassan Mohammmed and later to a farm owned by a retired air force officer, Group Captain Usman Jibrin, on the outskirts of Nasarawa in what is now Nasarawa State. The Shagari presidency had become history.

Chapter Nine

The Augean Stable

"...corruption has become so pervasive..."
–Major-General Muhammadu Buhari

In the early hours of Saturday, December 31, 1983, Brigadier Sani Abacha, accompanied by armed soldiers, stormed the studios of the FRCN, Ikoyi, Lagos. A few minutes later, martial music blared from the radio station. The soldiers had struck again. And the Second Republic was history. And again, as on January 15, 1966, the military men accused the civilian administration of corruption and the mismanagement of the economy. Said Abacha:

> You are all living witnesses to the grave economic predicament and uncertainty, which an inept and corrupt leadership has imposed on our beloved nation for the past four years. I am referring to the harsh, intolerable condition under which we are now living. Our economy has been hopelessly mismanaged. We have become a debtor and a beggar nation. There is inadequacy of food at reasonable prices for our people who are now fed up with endless announcements of importation of foodstuff. Health services are in shambles as our hospitals are reduced to mere consulting clinics without drugs, water and equipment. Our educational system is deteriorating at an alarming rate; unemployment figures including the [sic] graduates have reached embarrassing and unacceptable proportion. In some states, workers are being owed salary arrears of eight to twelve months and in others there are cries of salary cut, yet our leaders revel in squandermania, corruption and indiscipline...

These, he said, forced him and his colleagues in the armed forces "to effect a change in the leadership of the government of the Federal Republic of Nigeria and form a Federal Military Government."

The Second Republic had lasted all of four years and three months. The return of the soldiers was not without some anxious moments. Repeated announcements of the takeover were broadcast on the network service of the FRCN from Lagos but little else was known in the other parts of the country. Those who did not tune to the services of the FRCN early enough that morning, did not even know there was a coup. The presence of a few soldiers in some areas of Lagos not considered particularly strategic was not seen as anything unusual that morning. S.G. Ikoku, special adviser to Shagari on assembly matters, did not hear of the change of government until nearly 9. 00 am that day at the residence of Shagari's powerful minister of transport, Alhaji Umaru Dikko.[1]

The situation in the states remained unclear. Some of the brigade commanders only learnt of the coup through the radio announcements. They had no prior knowledge of it. They received no orders save Abacha's instruction that commanders who allowed those he said were wanted but whom he did not specify, escape would have themselves to blame. Even as late as 6 pm, some state radio stations gave reports, which suggested that the operation was confined to Lagos. However, there was no counter announcement indicating that it was either a coup scare or that it had failed. Nigerians were repeatedly told by an unidentified announcer to wait for further announcements. And wait, they did.

Since no one raised a voice against the coup announcements, it became evident that the soldiers were in control. Speculations then turned to who was behind it. Dikko had no problems with that. He instantly identified Babangida as the "moving spirit behind the coup" with the support of retired Major-General Shehu Musa Yar'Adua.[2]

Dikko's conclusion was based on the widely held view that Babangida was the man to watch because he was the man most likely to topple the government. What was now certain, given that the coup announcer was a one star general, was that senior military officers were behind it.

The most important announcement the nation waited for finally came nearly twenty hours after Abacha's dawn broadcast of the takeover. At 1.00 a.m., January 1, 1984, Major-General Muhammadu Buhari, GOC, 3 Infantry Division of the Nigerian Army, assumed office as Head of State and Commander-in-Chief of the Nigerian Armed Forces. The general was born in Daura in what is now Katsina State, on December 17, 1942. He too received his initial military training at the NMTC, Kaduna, before proceeding to the Mons Officers Cadet School in Aldershot, UK. He was commissioned a second lieutenant in January 1963.

In addition to several military appointments, he had a stint on the political turf as military governor of Borno State and later federal commissioner for petroleum and energy in the Murtala/Obasanjo administration. His superiors described him as a fine and disciplined officer.

His broadcast that night ended the second longest wait in the nation's political history. The first was after the coup, which ousted the country's first military ruler, Major-General J.T.U. Aguiyi-Ironsi on July 29, 1966. It took three days for Gowon to emerge as the new head of state.

Buhari said the change of government "became necessary in order to put an end to the serious economic predicament and the crisis of confidence now afflicting our nation." He said the military "dutifully intervened to save this nation from imminent collapse." ³

He laid four main 'sins' at the door of the civilian administration. One was the mismanagement of the economy. Buhari acknowledged there was "a world-wide economic recession (but) in the case of Nigeria, its impact was aggravated by mismanagement."⁴

The second was the conduct of the 1983 general elections. The head of state said the elections "were anything but free and fair." All the six political parties were to blame because "the only political parties that could complain of election rigging are those parties that lacked the resources to rig. There is ample evidence that rigging and thuggery were relative to the resources available to the parties."⁵

The third and fourth sins were corruption and indiscipline, the "two evils in our body politic (which) attained unprecedented height in the past four years." Indeed, said the new military strong man, "corruption has become so pervasive and intractable that a whole ministry has been created to stem it."⁶ He was referring to the newly created Ministry for National Guidance that Shagari had hoped would launch an ethical revolution in the country.

He ended his broadcast with this famous exhortation to his compatriots:

> This generation of Nigerians, and indeed, future generations, have no other country than Nigeria. We shall remain here and salvage it together.⁷

A twenty-one member Supreme Military Council, SMC, was sworn in the next day. Two leading members of the coup planners were assigned the next two important positions after Buhari. Babangida became Chief of Army Staff. If it was true, as was pointed out earlier, that this was his ultimate professional ambition, he had attained it. Idiagbon became Chief of Staff, Supreme Headquarters. Air Vice-Marshall Ibrahim Alfa and Rear-Admiral Augustus Aikhomu were appointed Chief of Air Staff and Chief of Naval Staff respectively. Abacha was appointed a member of the Supreme Military Council and the General Officer Commanding the strategic Second Mechanised Division of the Nigerian Army with its headquarters in Ibadan.

The country reverted to the legal and administrative structure of the Murtala/Obasanjo administration with the Supreme Military Council as the highest legislative body in the country. The two other organs at the centre were the Federal Executive Council, which replaced the council of ministers, and the National Council of State.

II

The return of the military was widely hailed by the populace, particularly by the members of the other five political parties swamped by the NPN in all the elections. There was some relief for the politicians but for a different reason. A takeover by the senior officers rather than the young radical elements in the armed forces that had been feared all along meant that they would be spared the fate that befell Ghana at Flight Lieutenant J.J. Rawlings' first coming in 1979. With some relief, Ikoku told his wife: "There is no coup."[8]

His wife must have been puzzled at this but his assessment reflected Edwin Madunagu's assertion that "Buhari's military intervention in political governance was a rescue operation for the Nigerian ruling class which between August and December 1983 faced a real threat of direct radical challenge."[9]

Suspicion persists that the coup was a pre-emptive strike to prevent the younger elements from taking over. The belief was, and is strong, that a group made up mainly of lieutenant colonels, was also planning to topple the Shagari administration. Lt-Cols. David Mark and John Shagaya were mentioned as possible leaders of this group. The group was said to have fused into the senior officers' group at the Port Harcourt army games in 1983 when each group discovered that the other existed.

If this was so, then the theory that the 1983 coup was a pre-emptive strike by the major generals must be dismissed as merely speculative. It has been difficult to get at the truth of this junior-officer-group theory, strong though it was and, perhaps, is. Dogonyaro, then a colonel, said no such group of junior officers existed "because I don't see how David Mark and Shagaya would move separately from me and the others." He was aware of only one group - and that was the group that took over.

Babangida does not dismiss the possibility of the existence of another group of mostly junior officers "because at that time everyone (in the military) was talking" about the state of the nation. He was aware that "there were stories about another group of young officers but (this group) wasn't as pronounced as people portrayed it." He believes that such talks "could also have been a disinformation, a ploy so as to hasten the execution" of their own plan. Later developments and the strong presence of junior officers in the Babangida coup and his administration, as we shall see, advise against an outright dismissal of the second group theory.

III

The next few days after the coup saw Nigerians and the press behave true to type. The ousted administration had a generous quantity of tar thrown in its face. No one, from Shagari down, was spared. Nothing good was said about them; nothing good was written about them. They no longer had any friends. Villains don't enjoy such luxury. It was a big, warm welcome once again to the military, the ultimate saviours of the nation The federal government-owned *Daily Times* heartily welcomed the return of the military because

> the nation... had for long been emotionally bruised. Indeed, an atmosphere of inexorable futility and despair hung over the nation for years. The country had for long been in travail while the Robin Hoods amongst us lurked around free and undismayed. ....political power and authority were abused consistently. (The politicians) were egocentrics bereft of both intellectual and moral fibre. They wallowed in self-deceit and in their pursuit of material wealth, power and authority, lost every twinge of moral compunction.[10]

Former Chief of Army Staff in the Murtala/Obasanjo administration, Lieutenant-General Yakubu Danjuma, blamed the civilians for the military intervention. He argued that "democracy has been in jeopardy for the past four years (1979-83). It died with the 1983 elections. The army only buried it."[11]

Buhari made the same point even more strongly. He told members of the diplomatic corps four days after he took over that "the economic mess, the corruption and the unacceptable level of unemployment could not be excused on the grounds that Nigeria was practising democracy. Democracy at that price was certainly not in the interest of the people of this country, nor indeed would it be acceptable anywhere."[12]

The military administration wasted little time in getting down to the business of cleaning up the Augean Stable. The constitution was suspended. All political appointees lost their job. They were all hounded into detention, collectively accused of corruption. Buhari had promised to bring them "to book." Buhari, accompanied by Idiagbon, addressed a world press conference in Lagos on January 5. They made quite an impression on the reporters and the nation. They wore black berets said to be the symbol of revolutionaries. The black beret was popularised by the late Chinese leader, Mao Tse-Tung and Fidel Castro of Cuba. Buhari and Idiagbon surprised the journalists by taking copious notes of the questions they were asked. There was something radical and yet friendly about them. And when Buhari said their regime was an offshoot of the

Murtala/Obasanjo administration, a country still enamoured of Murtala's charisma, was won over.

The general read a sixteen-minute statement to the press in which he reiterated his earlier charges of economic mismanagement and corruption against the civilians. They had run down "the buoyant economy" bequeathed to them by the Murtala/Obasanjo administration. They showed neither competence nor seriousness in responding to the global recession and its effect on the country. He said the legislators failed "to check the drift of the executive since where they were not active collaborators, they were pre-occupied with other things of no benefit to the people whom they represented."[13]

Three points, reflecting the mindset of the new government emerged from that press conference. These were:

- The new military administration had no time-table for return to civil rule yet.
- The government would pursue the recovery of public fund allegedly stolen by former public officer holders.
- All those detained by the government would be held until investigations proved each of them innocent of allegations of corrupt enrichment against them.

He underlined these points again 19 months later in a widely reported interview with the Federal Radio Corporation of Nigeria, FRCN, Kaduna, on July 24, 1985. He said that when they took over, there was "no agreed policy that one will serve for such and such years." They would, therefore, continue in power "until the economy of the country has returned to its stable footing and law and order restored in the society." Only then would they begin to think "of how many years one would serve."

Detainees would remain behind bars because there was "no guarantee that if you release someone with a case to answer, he will not run away."[14]

It is important to note at this point that Buhari was honest enough to confess that the military could not perform magic. Nigerians must, therefore, learn to moderate their expectations of how fast the military would turn the economy around. He cautioned: "Let no one, however, be deceived that workers who have not received their salaries in the past eight or so months will receive such salaries between today and tomorrow, or that hospitals which have been without drugs for months will be provided with enough drugs immediately."[15]

A few months later, Buhari admitted that "we have not been able to act as fast as possible as people think the Murtala/Obasanjo regime did because we took over from a system entirely different, which was on for four years and which had run two elections and the political orientation of Nigerians had been adversely affected."[16]

The administration moved on other fronts. The pursuit of former public officers and their "collaborators" in the private sector went on. There is a sadistic streak in most Nigerians. The rough treatment the former movers and shakers of the society were subjected to by the military administration became a soap opera playing to a bemused national audience. The corrupt, as far as the country was concerned, were being given their comeuppance.

The security agents took advantage of the public mood and soon exceeded their brief. National Security Organisation, NSO, operatives virtually roamed the length and breadth of the country, arresting and intimidating people. Under the provisions of decree number two which permitted the Chief of Staff, Supreme Headquarters, to detain persons suspected to be a security risk, hundreds of Nigerians and foreigners were arrested and detained. Most of them never found out what their offences were. The law, in the hands of the unscrupulous, had become an unfortunate instrument of fear, intimidation and extortion. The actions of these security agents did not win the government many friends. It won it many enemies and created an unfortunate climate of fear in the land.

The government, certainly, did not set out to create a climate of fear but it did little to reassure Nigerians that the security agents were acting beyond their legal brief. Instead, it piled it on. In six months, the regime issued 22 decrees, each of them specifically targeted at what it considered to be its immediate problems or those of the nation. The most controversial of these were decrees 2, 3, 4, 13, 16 and 20.

Decree number 3, known by its official title of *Recovery of Public Property (Special Military Tribunals) Decree 1984*, came into effect on December 31, 1983, the day the Shagari administration was overthrown. Through this decree, the government set up panels to investigate the assets of former public officers and the tribunals to try them.

Each tribunal, according to section 2 (a), (b) and (c) of the decree, "shall consist of a chairman who shall be an officer of the Armed Forces not below the rank of colonel or its equivalent; three other officers of the Armed Forces not below the rank of Lieutenant-Colonel or its equivalent; and a serving or retired judge of the High Court of like jurisdiction who shall, amongst other things, assist the tribunal in determining questions of law."[17]

This decree brought the administration face to face with its first public opposition. The Nigerian Bar Association, NBA, objected to the tribunals being headed by military men. The association insisted judges should head them to ensure that the laws were correctly interpreted and applied. When the government remained adamant, the NBA ordered all lawyers to boycott the tribunals in protest.

Chairmanship of the tribunals was hardly the worst aspect of the decree. The penalties it prescribed for conviction were stiff. Section 11(1)(a) of Part III of the decree provided "imprisonment for a term not less than 21 calendar months"[18] to life jail, depending on the magnitude of corrupt enrichment of the accused. The minimum sentence tied the hands of the tribunals. They could not use their discretion to make the punishment fit the crime, which is the standard practice in common, law. The decree tailored the alleged crime to fit the punishment. Each accused person was presumed guilty until he could prove his innocence. An age-old legal norm that an accused be presumed innocent until proven guilty was thus stood on its head.

The second challenge to decree number three came from one of the detainees, Chief Bola Ige, former governor of Oyo State. He was brought before the tribunal on charges of corruptly enriching his party, the Unity Party of Nigeria, UPN. Ige, a lawyer, took his case to a Lagos High Court where he argued that he could not be tried for his alleged offences because when the decree came into effect, he was no longer a governor and could not, therefore, have committed any offences in an office he no longer held.

The administration was stung by this legal twist. Its implication was clear. It meant that all the former public officers being detained, some of whom would face the tribunals under decree number three, must be set free. By the effective commencement of the decree, none of them could have committed the offences laid at their door.

The Federal Military Government promptly enacted *The Federal Military Government (Supremacy and Enforcement of Powers) Decree 1984* also known as Decree 13, in case anyone had any lingering doubts about the superiority of its laws to all other laws in the land. This was an amusing repetition of history. The Federal Military Government of General Yakubu Gowon was faced with a near identical situation in 1970. The Western Nigeria Government issued an edict empowering it to seize personal property alleged to have been corruptly acquired by former public officers in the region.

The family of one Lakanmi affected by the edict challenged the government in court. The case went up to the Supreme Court. In its judgement in *E.O. Lakanmi and another versus the Attorney-General for Western State and others,* the court invalidated the edict and added non-sweeteners to the effect that what happened on January 15, 1966, was not a revolution.

The Federal Military Government said thank you to the court with the promulgation of decree number 28 (*Supremacy and Enforcement of*

Powers) on May 9, 1970. The decree provided that "any decision whether made before or after the commencement of this Decree, by any court of law in the exercise or purported exercise of any powers under the constitution or any enactment or law of the Federation or any state which has purported to declare the invalidity of any decree or any edict (in so far as the provisions of the edict are not inconsistent with the provisions of a decree) or the incompetence of any of the governments in the federation to make the same is or shall be null and void and of no effect whatsoever as from the date of the making thereof."[19]

Decree 13 told the courts not to interfere with whatever the Federal Military Government considered necessary to do "with a view to assuring the effective maintenance of the territorial integrity of Nigeria and the peace, order and good government of the Federal Republic of Nigeria."[20]

Section 1 (b) (i) provided that:

No civil proceedings shall lie or be instituted in any court for or on account of or in respect of any act, matter or thing done or purported to be done under or pursuant to any Decree or Edict and if any such proceedings are instituted before, on or after the commencement of this Decree the proceedings shall abate, be discharged and made void.

The hands of the courts were tied. The effective date of decree number 3 was rolled back to October 1, 1979. In its blind fury, the administration had decreed the Second Republic illegal. This had a horrendous implication. Everything done under valid and prevailing laws between October 1, 1979, when the military handed over to civilians and December 31, 1983, when the military returned to power, were, by implication, declared illegal and, therefore constituted criminal offences where the government so desired. Ige and the others were roped in.

IV

Controversy was to dog Buhari's almost every step. His next controversial step put a dampener on the euphoria in the press. In his first major press interview granted to Yakubu Mohammed, editor of *National Concord,* Ray Ekpu, chairman of the editorial board of the Concord group and the late Dele Giwa, editor of *Sunday Concord* in January, 1984, Buhari purportedly promised to "tamper with press freedom." If so, he kept his promise. On March 29 that year, Buhari signed into law a new decree, *Public Officers (Protection Against False Accusation) Decree*

1984, better known as Decree Number 4. Section one of the decree is worth quoting in full:

> *The Federal Military Government hereby decrees as follows: -*
>
> *1 (1) Any person who publishes in any form, whether written or otherwise, any message, rumour, report or statement, being a message, rumour, statement or report which is false in any material particular or which brings or is calculated to bring the Federal Military Government or the Government of a State or a public officer to ridicule or disrepute, shall be guilty of an offence under this Decree.*
>
> *(2) Any station for wireless telegraphy which conveys or transmits any sound or visual message, rumour, report or statement, being a message, rumour, report or statement which is false in any material particular or which brings or is calculated to bring the Federal Military Government or the Government of a State or a public officer to ridicule or disrepute, shall be guilty of an offence under this Decree.*
>
> *(3) It shall be an offence under this Decree for a newspaper or wireless telegraphy station in Nigeria to publish or transmit any message, rumour, report or statement which is false in any material particular stating that any public officer has in any manner been engaged in corrupt practices or has in any manner corruptly enriched himself or any other person.*[21]

The decree stunned the press for at least two reasons. The first was based on two fundamental errors, namely, that for the first time in the history of the country, a law was specifically made to protect public officers from the press, thus limiting the professional, moral and constitutional rights of the press to make public officers accountable for their decisions and actions; secondly, that the decree did not even excuse the accuracy or truth of the published information.

The press felt betrayed. The press believed it made it possible for the military to return to power. It saw itself as having played as patriotic a role as the military itself in the ouster of the civilian regime. To curb its powers in any way smacked of ingratitude on the part of the military administration.

The public also felt betrayed and outraged by the decree. Why would a military regime out to clear the Augean stable now seek to specifically shield public officers from the prying eyes of the press? The press almost uniformly described the decree as "draconian" and "obnoxious."

Any hopes that the head of state would listen to press and public protests over the decree were dashed when the first two journalists Nduka Irabor and Tunde Thompson both of the *Guardian* newspaper were charged before a tribunal set up under the decree. The two men had reported a story on the impending appointment of new ambassadors. At worst, the story was speculative, nothing more. Perhaps, what offended Buhari was that the story gave rise to a flurry of pilgrimages to Dodan Barracks by those said to have been pencilled down for the appointment as well as other hopefuls who intensified their lobby for ambassadorial appointments.

It is difficult to see how the publication contravened the decree. The speculation might not have been entirely accurate but to conclude that it was false or calculated to ridicule or bring any public officer into disrepute was laying it on rather more strongly than even the law envisaged. The tribunal found the two men guilty as charged and jailed them one year each on July 4, 1984. Their newspaper was also fined.

The press and the public ignored the more pernicious provision of Decree 4. In its editorial comment on the conviction of Irabor and Thompson, *Sunday Tribune* acknowledged that Decree 4 "is good to the extent that it obliges newsmen to check their facts before publishing. (But) it is bad and unacceptable because it seeks specially to protect public officers as distinct from other Nigerians. We submit," the paper went on with a touch of legalese, "that this is a bogus legal erection around public officers to protect corruption, incompetence and racketeering."[22]

Section 2 of the decree was actually where the biggest problem was. It empowered the head of state to ban newspapers or magazines and withdraw the licence of any electronic media if he was satisfied that their behaviour was inimical to public interest. This provision is worth quoting in full:

> 2 -(1) Where the Head of the Federal Military Government is satisfied that the unrestricted circulation in Nigeria of a newspaper is or may be detrimental to the interest of the Federation or any part thereof, he may by order published in the Gazette, prohibit the circulation in the Federation or in any part thereof, as the case may require, of that newspaper; and, unless any other period is prescribed in the order, the prohibition shall continue for a period of twelve months unless sooner revoked or extended as the case may require.
> (2) Where the Head of the Federal Military Government is satisfied that the unrestricted existence in Nigeria of any wireless telegraphy station is detrimental to the interest of the Federation or any part thereof, he may by an order published in the Gazette -
> (a) revoke the licence granted to such wireless telegraphy station under the provisions of the Wireless Telegraphy Act 1961; or
> (b) order the closure or forfeiture to the Federal Military Government, as the case may be, of the wireless telegraphy station concerned.

This provision was a new and dangerous element in the saga of press and government relations in Nigeria. The press had had some experience of being banned. In the First Republic, some regional governments banned newspapers they considered inimical to their political interests from circulation in their regions. The Obasanjo administration banned *Newbreed*, a monthly magazine, in 1978. But the right to ban those publications was not exercised under any existing laws. It was exercised on whim. Decree 4 provided the legal prop for such whims or arbitrariness.

It is difficult to see which is the lesser evil - a ban exercised as a whim or one exercised with a legal backing. Further debate on that is outside the scope of this book. Suffice it to say that read together with the other provisions, Decree 4 was a tough law whose every brick appeared to have been ironically provided by a press that had lost its way in the nation's partisan and intolerant political wilderness.

Decree 4 was not the first law in Nigeria designed to regulate the conduct of the press. The first of such laws was "*The Newspaper Ordinance No.10* of 1903 (that) contained provisions for regulating the publication of newspapers in what was then Southern Nigeria, there being practically no newspapers in circulation in Northern Nigeria at the time."[*] The exclusion of the north in the 1903 ordinance was remedied in 1917 with a new law that applied throughout the country, the *Newspapers Ordinance* of August 9.

That ordinance was more or less succeeded by *The Newspapers Amendment) Act, 1964* enacted by parliament. It was the first federal press law made to take care of new developments in a nation now ruled by the natives themselves. The Act caused uproar in parliament as well as in the press. The controversy centred on Section 4, which provides:

> *(1) Any person who authorises for publication, publishes, reproduces or circulates for sale in a newspaper any statement, rumour or report knowing or having reason to believe that such statement, rumour or report is false shall be guilty of an offence and liable on conviction to a fine of £200.00 or to imprisonment for a term of one year.*
> *(2) It shall be no defence to a charge under this section that he did not know or did not have reason to believe that the statement, rumour or report was false unless he proves that, prior to publication, he took reasonable measures to verify the accuracy of such statement, rumour or report.*[23]

"The emphasis," Elias noted, "is on the falsity of the statement, rumour or report."[24] Decree 4 stressed the same points.

---

[*] Elias, T.O. *Nigerian Press Law*, Evans Brothers Limited, 1969, page 1

Buhari's Decree 4 was a re-enactment of Obasanjo's Decree 11 right down to the title, Public Officers (Protection against False Accusation) Decree 1976. Section 1 (1) of that decree provides:

> *Any person who publishes or reproduces in any form, whether written or otherwise, any statement, rumour or report alleging or intended to be understood as alleging that a public officer has in any manner been engaged in corrupt practices or has in any manner corruptly enriched himself or any other person, being a statement, rumour or report which is false in any material particular, shall be guilty of an offence under this decree and liable on conviction to be sentenced to imprisonment for a term not exceeding two years, without the option of a fine.*[25]

Decree 4 was, therefore, Decree 11 made more comprehensive. The noose got tighter around the neck of the press. That decree did not generate as much heat as Decree 4. It is difficult to see why. It was as a strong a gag law as they come. The only lame excuse one can offer is that the times were different. The press must have become more alert or more daring to do battle with a military administration than it was in the late seventies when the Obasanjo administration was in power.

Perhaps, a more valid reason is that because journalists did not even bother to read Decree 4, they saw it as a monster in its entirety. The view persists that the decree made it an offence to publish facts about public officers who abused their office if those facts embarrassed them. Not true. The word embarrass does not feature anywhere in that decree either. Ridicule and disrepute do. They are not synonyms for embarrass. Perhaps, the law would have had a more friendly reception if its intentions were to protect all Nigerians from false publications.

Public officers in Nigeria are fond of chiding the press. On September 18, 1979, for instance, Obasanjo, as head of state, said that

> certain sections of the press have shown a tendency towards the negative approach capable of wrecking this country. In the so-called civilised countries of East and West people cherish their institutions and build them up. Criticisms are constructive and aimed solely at exploring areas of their strength, which they fortify, and guard jealously. The media is used to educate and not to incite. Rather than seek to besmear, divide and destroy, their concern is to instil internal cohesion. This contrasts sharply with the negative approach adopted by some Nigerian journalists who indulge in vicious, sensational journalism, unmindful of the fact that, by their actions, the prestige and stability of the country is to that extent affected, possibly with unpredictably grave consequences for the well-being of the citizen.[26]

Buhari had been a victim of a rumour stoutly paraded as a fact in the press. The rumour centred on an alleged $2.8 billion said to be missing from the account of the NNPC at the time Buhari was the commissioner for petroleum and energy and chairman of the board of NNPC in the Murtala/Obasanjo administration. Shagari was more or less badgered by the press into setting up a commission of enquiry into it to ascertain the truth. It turned out that Tai Solarin, the old school master who earned quite a reputation as a social critic and who started it all, had picked up the rumour from one of the most unreliable places for a reliable information: a local bus. Buhari never forgave the press. The press did not forgive him either. He told the Voice of America at an interview in which he was asked about the purpose of Decree 4:

> We have a difficult society in which once an accusing finger is (pointed) at you, people virtually, hardly listen to what happens after that. For that reason, any newspaper or journalist who intends to write anything against any person in government or the government is encouraged by this legislation to make some research so that he can defend himself.[27]

Buhari went ahead with his house cleaning. But he was saddened by the fact that the judiciary had become elitist. "The richer you are, the more likely you are to get justice."[28] And when you are dealing with rich and influential people such as former public office holders, you must resort to extraordinary means that cannot be subverted by the powerful. Buhari meant business. The tribunals handed down stiff sentences on former public office holders. Some of the governors collected enough jail sentences to last them three or four life times over. The SMC confirmed all the sentences brought before it.

With Buhari, it was an all out war against societal vices. One of these was the trafficking in hard drugs. Not many Nigerians knew much about cocaine and other hard drugs at the time; other than that the country had become a transit route for drug barons and their mules. A new breed of young millionaires was, however, springing up from drug trafficking. Nigeria was a transit route but a big one, for the drugs on their way from the Far East to Europe and the United States. Buhari moved to stop the trafficking and the use of young Nigerians, male and female, as mules, as carriers are known in the trade. He issued Decree 20 to deal with the menace.

The decree prescribed death for drug traffickers. Three young Nigerians ran foul of the law. They were tried by a special military tribunal, convicted and shot by a firing squad. There was a public outcry but Buhari offered no apologies for backdating the decree to about when the four drug traffickers were arrested at the Murtala Muhammed International Airport, Lagos. They were arrested before the government issued decree 20.

As far as the head of state was concerned, the death penalty was the right way to attack the drug menace because "Nigeria is being used by highly-influential people, rich people in the society who are prepared to destroy both their society and other people's society to make money. We definitely felt... we must not allow Nigeria to be used for destroying others and for that we decided to permanently keep those involved out of the society and we have no regret for it."[29]

In his twenty months in power, Buhari waged the battle for a better society on all fronts. As Felix Adenaike, a veteran journalist, put it: "They confronted students. They confronted labour. They confronted market women. They confronted public servants. They confronted the press. They confronted doctors."[30]

IV

Babangida kept very much in the background, pretty conspicuous in his lack of public involvement in matters political. He granted only one major news media interview and that was to *The Guardian,* in March 1984. For the rest of the time, it would seem he was merely watching events unfold. But he certainly was not because he knew trouble was brewing around him.

A crack appeared in the leadership of the military administration within one year of its coming to power. Babangida found himself on one side and Buhari on the other as the crack widened. Both men, naturally, attracted sympathisers and willing recruits to his cause. The crack began, as it often does in such cases, as the handiwork of sycophants. Some officers ingratiated themselves with both the head of state and the chief of army staff by peddling tales of evil planning, one against the other. They told Buhari to watch out: Babangida was out to get his job. Babangida's alleged political ambition was painted in rather frightening colours.

Another group of sycophants told Babangida to watch out: Buhari was going to get him by retiring him. These tales soon poisoned the atmosphere between the two men and in the administration. Power play soon became the pre-occupation of the principal officers in the administration. The crack widened with each passing day, drawing major and bit players to both sides. Once the seed of distrust had been sown, all it needed to take root was to constantly water it with more tall tales, each taller than the other.

Babangida gave the impression he did not take these tales seriously but he did. However, he tried not to rush into anything because he said he had enough experience in government to appreciate what he called 'environmental problems' that rulers face in Nigeria:

> One of the problems of power is that once you get there, you become a prisoner of the environment. Environmental insecurity sets in. People will come to you with tales of what people are planning against you. Tell you ABCD are planning a coup. Or they tell you they saw ABCD talking XYZ and they must be up to no good. Unless you have this broader outlook to understand people and learn to trust them, you will be tempted to put almost everyone in prison or get everybody out of their job.

Both Babangida and Buhari had wanted the top job after Shagari's ouster. At Bonny Camp, Lagos, where the coup planners set up their headquarters, Babangida summoned a young and brilliant officer, Major Abubakar Dangiwa Umar, the colonel GS in the Directorate of Armour that morning, threw some poems at him and told him to go and write a speech for the new commander-in-chief who had still not been named.

Umar, one of Babangida's students in the Nigerian Defence Academy, Kaduna, was not involved in the coup. But he had to do as his boss commanded. It is not clear if Babangida's action was an indication that he was sure to become the new commander-in-chief or he was merely carrying out part of his assignment in the change of administration. What is clear is that Buhari emerged as the new head of state. Babangida settled for the post of Chief of Army Staff.

Two reasons have been given for this. One was that Babangida did not enjoy the support of the Nigeria Air Force. Both the army and the navy were said to have supported him. The plausibility of that explanation is affected somewhat by the fact that if the army and the navy supported him, he could have won two to one. The second reason was that Babangida conceded the leadership of the new administration to Buhari in due regard to seniority. Again, those who find this explanation credible must remember that a coup is an aberrant action, which respects neither procedure nor seniority. If Babangida had the upper hand, he would not have surrendered to Buhari. A more valid explanation will be found in Babangida's action twenty months after Buhari became head of state.

His move was preceded by rumours of a coup plot. In October 1984, the London *Observer* reported that 47 abortive coup plotters were executed in an underground firing range at the Ikeja cantonment. The government strongly denied this. In May 1985, Lt-Col Tanko Ayuba, commander, corps of signals, denied rumours that he led an abortive coup. Two months later, Babangida himself warned soldiers against peddling rumours of a coup.

Perhaps, the most telling public evidence that things were steadily falling apart in the administration came from Buhari himself. In an address to officers and men of the Nigerian Army at the Ikeja Cantonment February 6, 1985, he warned that "any officer who feels too big for his office or duties should quit or (he) would be shown out."[31]

Was it a veiled reference to Babangida?

Babangida denies that he nursed any political ambition even at that time. He says he was happy with his job as the army boss. It was the ultimate professional crown he had worked for. He went on to implement some of the re-organisational structures he had been involved in formulating since the Murtala/Obasanjo administration, which resulted in "a massive redeployment of officers" in which the right men were placed in the right job. He was also satisfied with the performances of the Buhari administration "because it addressed the immediate situation. There was a concerted effort to address the economy to arrest the drift; the general lack of discipline in the society was also addressed."

Try as he would, Babangida could not shake off the feeling that the eyes of the head of state were on him, watching him *a la* Big Brother. The seed of distrust sown between him and Buhari was watered daily by events - planned and unplanned - which stretched their relationship to a breaking point. That point nearly came early in 1985. By this time, Babangida had become thoroughly frustrated. As Chief of Army Staff, he was a key member of the Buhari administration but he found himself increasingly checkmated and sidelined by the head of state. His advice was often ignored.

The rumour mill was in full, feverish production, churning out stories of conflict in the administration. Rumours of Babangida's impending retirement from the army were pretty rife. These rumours could not but have deeply affected Babangida. As often happens in matters of this nature, unrelated developments have a way of presenting themselves as evidence, if anyone needed one.

Sometime in 1985, Brigadier Aliyu Mohammed Gusau, an intelligence officer and a very close friend of Babangida, was accused of involvement in an import licence deal during the civilian administration. There was import licence racket in the Shagari administration. Buhari set up a panel headed by Nasko to probe the allegation against Mohammed. Mohammed told the panel Babangida was aware of what he did. Babangida recalls that he knew Mohammed helped someone to obtain an import licence "and to me that was a normal thing for people to help their friends."

Mohammed refused to speak to the author on his case. Col Haliru Akilu, director of the Directorate of Military Intelligence, said the allegation against Gusau was "a cooked up investigation by Lawal Rafindadi (director-general of the National Security Organisation, now State Security Services) just to rope him in." According to Akilu, the allegation had to do with the importation of rice by the son of Alhaji Yakubu Wanka. One million naira was said to have been "paid to someone through Wanka from the proceeds of the rice."

The Nasko panel did not invite Babangida to testify before it. Military tradition does not permit junior officers to probe their senior. "Moreover," Nasko explained, "we felt that Babangida as a member of the Army Council (to which the report of the panel would be submitted for further action) could be asked of his role in the charges at that forum." The council, chaired by the head of state, had Idiagbon and Babangida as members.

The council met over the matter. Buhari felt strongly that Aliyu Mohammed Gusau should be retired. Babangida objected to this action on two grounds. First, he felt that the setting up of the Nasko panel was procedurally wrong. As the Chief of Army Staff, he argued that if a disciplinary action must be taken against an army officer, he and not the commander-in-chief should initiate it. Secondly, he felt that "there was no thorough investigation to find out what happened" because no such report was presented to the council.

The council deferred its decision at its first meeting. But it was clear to Babangida that his friend's days in the army were numbered. He knew "the feeling was very strong that the retirement should actually be accepted and implemented." The vote was clearly two in favour of retirement and one against.

Babangida found this painful. He and Mohammed had been friends for some twenty-six years as at that time. They first met in Makurdi during the Nigerian civil war when Mohammed, a genial, young officer, was fresh from the Nigerian Defence Academy. Now his army career was coming to an early and sudden end.

Babangida felt obliged to save him. He was even prepared to "take the rap" for whatever Mohammed did wrong. "I felt he was my subordinate, he was my friend and above all, he was in my service. So, I had every reason to be interested in what happened to him," Babangida says.

It was much more than that. Babangida's reaction, whatever the obligations of friendship might have demanded of him and whatever might have been the merits of the case against his friend, was dictated more by what the incident represented or portended for him than anything else. He interpreted it as conclusive evidence that Buhari was, indeed, out to get him by first getting his friends.

Babangida was convinced that he and some of the officers described as "ambitious characters" were being monitored by the security agencies. He said: "Our telephones were tapped to know what we were talking about; what we had said and what we hadn't said. Sometimes our movements were checked to know where we went and what we had done or not done."

Babangida was frustrated. He wrote to Nasko, intimating him of his intention to resign his commission. He would not wait around to be humiliated out of the service by the head of state. Nasko, always a cool-headed officer, felt that Babangida was making "a selfish and self-defeating move." He advised him against resigning. "I asked him if he would be happy to leave and watch the system suffer from the sidelines." But Babangida "insisted he could no longer bear things but I persuaded him not to resign; rather, he should allow them to ask him to go first."

Babangida took the advice of his childhood friend. He chose to take his annual leave. Nasko, commander of the corps of artillery, was appointed acting Chief of Army Staff. Then Babangida changed his mind without explanation. He cancelled his leave and decided to go for a military exercise at Gumel in Kano State.

Buhari was aware of this exercise. It was routine. Nothing to it. Or so he thought. It was Babangida's last military exercise as Chief of Army Staff.

Chapter Ten

In the Saddle

We do not intend to rule by force
–President Ibrahim Badamasi Babangida

August 26 and 27, 1985, were public holidays to mark the Muslim festival of *Eid El-Kabir.* Major-General Ibrahim Babangida returned from watching a military exercise in Gumel August 24. A week earlier, he received birthday cards from his wife and close friends. He was 44 August 17. He does not usually celebrate his birthday. But that year, it was a special occasion for him. He held family prayers to thank Allah for all He had done for him and ask His blessings for what he was about to do in ten days' time.

Since his pilgrimage to Mecca, Babangida has always taken his religious obligations much more seriously. He regards all Muslim festivals as solemn occasions. He usually spends his *Eid El-Kabir* with his family in his hometown, Minna. He flew into Minna in a light aircraft August 26. Lt-Col David Mark, military governor of Niger State, met him on arrival. They drove to Babangida's country home set on a small hill where his relations and friends waited to receive him. His only surviving sister, Hajia Hannatu Gambo, was also there. She usually prepares his *sallah* meal as part of the family tradition. It is the only occasion her famous brother eats her food. She always looks forward to it. She collected her *sallah* gifts and left, promising to bring in the food early the next day.

Babangida was relaxed, joking with his friends and relations. None of them knew how truly worried the army boss was that night. He maintained his calm, as he does whenever a storm of agitation rages in his mind. Tea was served late in the evening after which his visitors left. Now alone, the storm threatened to burst. Sleep had deserted him. He tried to read but the words on the pages were a blur. He could not make them out. The question kept popping up in his mind: *What if something goes wrong?* For want of a better thing to do to calm himself, Babangida drove out alone in his private car. He had nowhere to go in particular. He drove aimlessly around the town. He later visited two of his close civilian friends. He returned home. The loudest sound in the house was of his heart pounding in his mouth. He jumped out of his seat when the phone rang. It was Mark. He called to tell him he was in touch with Lagos and that there was nothing to worry about. Everything was working according to plan.

The plan was what worried Babangida. And the plan was a coup to topple the Buhari administration. Mark, a signals officer, was part of that plan. As soon as Babangida flew into Minna, Mark set up a communication facility to monitor what was going on in Lagos so he could keep Babangida informed of developments. A coup is a dangerous adventure in the military. Few people appreciated that better than Babangida who had taken part in three successful coups including the revenge coup of July 29, 1966, which brought Gowon to power.

Anything can go wrong, even at the last minute. Before he left Lagos that afternoon, he went through the details of the plan once more with the inner core he likes to refer to as 'my co-conspirators. Everything seemed all right. The plot had not leaked. He went over the speech with the man chosen to make the announcement on the network service of FRCN, Brigadier Joshua Nimyel Dogonyaro. Satisfied, Babangida left the rest severely in the hands of Allah.

Babangida is an early riser. But on August 27, 1985, the telephone woke him up. Mark was on the line. He spoke only two sentences.

Mark: Congratulations, Sir. It is all over.

II

"I, Brigadier Joshua Nimyel Dogonyaro..."

Major-General Gado Nasko was in his country home, Nasko, near Kotangora. He had just finished his morning prayers when Dogonyaro came through on the radio. Oh God, he sighed. A coup? He wondered who was behind it. He reached for his phone. It was dead. He used a military radio to get in touch with the commander of the artillery unit in Kotangora. The officer, who did not quite know what was going on, assured him that they stood by him and would take instructions from him on what to do. Nasko prayed to Allah, asking Him "not to allow me to make a bad choice (in the event of a power tussle). Miraculously," the general recalls, "Babangida came into my mind."

Some assurance from the Almighty Himself! Nasko had always hoped and prayed that the problems between Buhari and Babangida would not come to this. Just before he left for home on the *sallah* holiday, Akilu told Nasko, according to the latter, that it "had become inevitable to remove Buhari before more havoc was done." He tried to dissuade the colonel from that course. He advised that if Buhari was no longer acceptable to the military, then the Supreme Military Council should remove him. Akilu argued that "if they dared to do that, Buhari would kill all of them in the council chambers." In any case, he had come merely to inform Nasko, he said. They were going ahead with their plan whether Nasko supported them or not, Akilu said. Dogonyaro's dawn broadcast confirmed their determination to go ahead went ahead.

Nasko reached Lt-Col Adetunji Olurin, commander, 1 Brigade of the Nigerian Army, Minna, on phone and asked the colonel if Babangida was safe. Affirmative. He asked if he could talk to Babangida. Olurin said he would get in touch with him and let Nasko know. Olurin kept his promise. He called Nasko and assured him Babangida was all right and was preparing to leave for Lagos. Babangida promised to send an aircraft later to pick up Nasko because, according to the latter, "he did not want the two of us to be in Lagos at the same time."

III

Hajiya Hannatu Gambo rose up early to prepare the *sallah* meal for her brother. At about 11 am, the food was ready. Her husband's driver took her to the general's house. She noticed from the gate that the house was unusually quiet. She expected to see the usual crowd but only a few beggars were outside the gate. She went into the house. It was empty. She found the steward and asked where the general was. He told her he had been taken to Lagos about an hour earlier. The steward could not tell her who took him to Lagos and why. She had prepared to return to Lagos with him. And now this. She wondered what was going on. She had no one to turn to immediately for an answer to the big question: *what has happened to my only brother?*

Had her worst fears about her brother come true? "I was very apprehensive," she recalls. Twenty-two years ago when she learnt that her brother had joined the army, she wept because she said she knew "the army is a risky job." She wept silently as she returned to her house.

IV

Lt-Col Haliru Akilu, director of Military Intelligence, co-ordinated the coup plot in Lagos. Like everyone else involved in it, he too had a sleepless night. He was up all night, co-ordinating the activities of the various groups. By early morning of August 27, he knew it was all over for the Buhari administration. He received field reports confirming that everything went according to plan and that the coup was a success. It was a bloodless coup; just as they had planned.

Akilu chartered a six-seater aircraft and despatched lieutenant colonels Tony Ukpo and Tanko Ayuba to Minna to accompany Babangida to Lagos. It was generally but wrongly believed that the aircraft belonged to Babangida's good friend, Chief Moshood Abiola

In the aircraft taking him to Lagos, Babangida took out his prayer beads. He still could not steady his nerves. He felt grateful to God that there were no reports of casualties during the operation. What was more, it had succeeded, ending all his fears and anxieties. It had been weeks of preparations and uncertainties; weeks during which he developed cold feet because of the risks involved in toppling a military administration. The last night was the worst for him. He was worried about the "boys" who were carrying out the operation. If anything went wrong, they would go the way of all abortive coup plotters. They would be tried, convicted and executed by firing squad. He too would go down. He would not forgive himself. Now, thank God, it was all over.

An unmarked car awaited Babangida in the presidential wing of the local airport. The entire airport complex was desolate because all flights had been suspended. Lt Col John Shagaya, commanding officer, 9 Brigade, Ikeja, received Babangida on arrival at the airport and drove with him through the deserted streets of Lagos to Bonny Camp. There, Babangida met Major General Sani Abacha, Brigadier Dogonyaro, Akilu and his other "co-conspirators." There were 23 of them from the rank of captain to major general and equivalent in the Nigerian Navy and the Nigerian Air Force. Most of them, according to Babangida, were "young generation officers." Some of them were his former students in the NDA; some worked with him and others were close friends he had cultivated during and after the civil war. They were the "boys" who executed the plan.

Even as he continued to receive congratulatory messages from those around him, Babangida knew there were tasks ahead of him, not least that of explaining his mission in government to a nation that had grown cynical about 'saviours' in uniform. He began a series of consultations with officers around him. His new administration began to take some shape.

V

While Babangida and his men huddled in their operational headquarters in Bonny Camp, Nigerians were kept wondering what was happening. They stayed indoors, glued to their radio sets. The absence of a counter announcement meant the coup had succeeded and the 20-month administration of Major-General Muhammadu Buhari had ended. Dogonyaro's was the only voice of the new man. Save for his dawn broadcast relayed every 15 minutes or so, nothing else was heard from anyone else. Dogonyaro, director of the Armoured Corps, told the nation that he and his colleagues in the armed forces decided to shove aside Buhari in order to "restore hope in the minds of Nigerians and renew (their) aspirations for a better future."

He painted an unflattering picture of the ousted administration. He accused it of a multitude of sins to convince Nigerians that the armed forces had, as usual, done the right thing in the interest of the nation. He claimed that "a select few members" of the Buhari administration had ignored the "concept of collective leadership" and "arrogated to themselves the right to make the decisions for the larger half of the ruling body." This attitude, the brigadier said, made the government squander the goodwill of Nigerians who welcomed it "with unprecedented enthusiasm." He and his colleagues, he told "fellow Nigerians," could no longer remain "passive and watch a small group of individuals misuse power to the detriment of our national aspirations and interest," and so they decided to act to arrest the "present state of uncertainty and stagnation."

An apprehensive nation was told to wait for further announcements. At 2 p.m., more than eight hours after Dogonyaro's broadcast began, the NTA showed Babangida, surrounded by Shagaya and others, getting into his official car in Bonny Camp. He merely waved to and smiled at reporters keeping vigil in the new seat of power. He said nothing. No one told the reporters anything. Was he the new man of the moment?

It took another one hour and fifteen minutes before anything else of significance happened. The day being a public holiday, the NTA was transmitting earlier than its daily schedule. At 3.15 p.m., Abacha appeared on television. He was the announcer of the Buhari coup. Had the kingmaker become the new king? Nigerians held their breath for an answer. Apparently not.

Abacha said he "once more found it necessary to address the nation on very crucial national issues." He too, like Dogonyaro, accused the Buhari administration of betraying the hope of Nigerians because "most of the economic and social ills that plagued this nation during the civil administration" had not disappeared nearly two years after the military take over. He berated the regime for its incompetence in dealing with the economic and other problems facing the country. He said the Buhari administration "lacked the capacity and (the) capability of leading this nation out of its economic and social predicament," thus making the change of leadership necessary.

The armed forces, Abacha said, decided to do its national duty by choosing a new man who would do a better job of pulling the nation out of the rut in which it was stuck. The man chosen was Major-General Ibrahim Badamasi Babangida, the Chief of Army Staff. He would take on the title of president, the first military ruler in Nigeria to do so. No applause. The nation looked on rather quizzically.

The military men were clearly enjoying the drama of the moment, no matter that they were playing to a largely cynical, if apprehensive, audience. The script was written and directed by Babangida himself. He had worked out a sure, deliberate step every inch of the way. For nearly 15 hours after Dogonyaro's broadcast, Babangida was seen publicly twice but not heard. He allowed the nation and reporters to have a glimpse of him more than one hour before and after Abacha formally named him leader of the new military team in government.

At 4.17 p.m., Babangida was seen on television again. He was all smiles but otherwise silent. The television showed a man in control and yet a team player. He was seen conferring in Bonny Camp with a group of senior officers. They included Dogonyaro, Shagaya, Ayuba and Madaki. He wore the equivalent of an officer's business suit - a long sleeve khaki shirt with the lower end of the trousers tucked into his boots. Businesslike, yet casual. He cut the picture of the friendly neighbour, a smiling, friendly man ready to wrap his arms around you. He wanted to be seen as an officer and a gentleman. It was the picture Nigerians responded to as soon as the smoke of the take-over cleared up. It was too early to realise then but the evidence was unmistakable that Babangida wanted to be seen as a different man who wanted to be a different military leader. The sorcerer's apprentice had come of age.

VI

In Minna, Hajiya Hannatu was virtually reduced to your everyday picture of a confused, helpless woman. No one could tell her why her brother was taken to Lagos. But she suspected he might be in trouble with the government. Someone burst into her house at about 6 p.m. to give her husband the news: Babangida had been named president of Nigeria. Her husband rushed in to tell her. She took in the news slowly, wondering if someone was playing a cruel joke on her. Then a few others came with the same news. She smiled, wiped her tears. "I thank the almighty God," she said.

VII

At 9 p.m., Babangida made his grand entry on the nation's political stage. He was 44 years old. Few men could have had a better birthday gift. Four months of intense planning had borne the desired fruit. The nation had waited for his maiden broadcast on radio and television for some 15 hours. Babangida won a reading competition in the primary school. His voice is a cross between the shrill and the loud, this side of feminine. He employed that gift on television that night. His performance was memorable less for what he said than how he said it. He was always a rapid reader. He went through his speech as if he was in a hurry to get it over and done with so he could devote his attention to more urgent tasks at hand.

There was something different about the man. He departed from the format of maiden speeches by military leaders, which are usually laced with threats designed to show their toughness and psychologically cow the populace. Babangida's was friendly; no fire, no brimstone. He was appealing and persuasive. He was not going "to rule by force (but) with the consent of the people." He merely offered himself in the service of his nation.

He came, he told the nation, because the Buhari regime which initially "received a tumultuous welcome (became) alienated from the people." He repeated charges made by Dogonyaro and Abacha. Babangida was a leading member of the Buhari team but he refused to share responsibility for its failure. He held two men responsible - Buhari and Idiagbon - the head of state and his deputy. He accused Buhari of being "too rigid and uncompromising in his attitude to issues of national significance." Idiagbon "arrogated to himself absolute knowledge of problems and solutions (and) used the machinery of government as his tool."

Against this background, his administration, he said, would chart a new course for the nation hinged on two planks. First, he said, "We do not intend to have all the answers to the questions." Secondly, his government would "create an atmosphere in which positive efforts shall be given the necessary support for lasting solutions." His government, in other words, would only lead all Nigerians as a team in finding solutions to the nation's various problems - social, economic and political. Babangida then went on to make, perhaps, the important statement in his broadcast when he said:

> Fellow Nigerians, this country has had since independence, a history mixed with turbulence and fortune. We have witnessed our rise to greatness followed with a decline to the state of a bewildered nation. Our human potentials have

been neglected, our natural resources put to waste. A phenomenon of constant insecurity and overbearing uncertainty has become characteristic of our national existence.

And so? So, he would make all the difference, said the new president. "My colleagues and I," he went on, his voice on an even keel, "are determined to change this course of history."

Bravado? Perhaps. But lest anyone thought he was immodest, the same sin of commission he had accused his predecessor of, the new president told Nigerians he and his colleagues believed that to succeed, they needed the "consent of the people (because) we do not intend to rule by force."

This declaration of intent was novel in a military administration. Was it merely a public relations gimmick on which to anchor his legitimacy and win the support of the people? It remained to be tested. One thing, however, was clear even so early in the day in the life of the Babangida administration. Babangida was determined to leave more than mere footprints in the tortuous footpath of the nation's political history. He would leave the Babangida mark. He left that mark in the primary school when he won the reading competition. He left it in the secondary school as one of the best all-round students in academics and sport; he left that mark in the various military courses he attended; he left that mark during the Nigerian civil war where he showed his bravery and compassion in the conduct of the fighting and the treatment of refugees and he left that mark in the armoured corps that he nursed into a full-fledged corps.

As Chief of Army Staff, he gave the army a new lease of life, having been closely involved in the plan to transform it into a small, mobile, well motivated and a well-equipped fighting force. To stand out has always been his burning ambition. It underlined his choice of the elite armoured corps; it underlined the most glamorous discharge of his professional duty - the quelling of the Dimka coup in 1976. His sole purpose in government was "to make this country better, different."

In spite of the promise his maiden speech held, the lukewarm attitude that greeted Dogonyaro's dawn broadcast did not automatically translate into a warm welcome for the administration. The national mood was subdued, not least because his emergence portended, the public feared, another long winter of military rule. If the new president expected the nation to throw its arms around him that did not quite happen. Cynicism in the country was more than ankle deep. Nigerians remained guarded. Good and pious words by past administrations had not buttered parsnips. The reception accorded the Babangida administration, according to *The Nigerian Chronicle,* a Cross River State government-owned newspaper, was "the most subdued that Nigerians have shown in similar circumstances" although the paper admitted that the new regime "came at the appropriate psychological moment to release Nigerians from the tension of silence, the groan of dismay and the sigh of helplessness."

You could not blame Nigerians for their cautious welcome to the new military administration, argued the *National Concord,* because "they are wary of seemingly new heroes."

Newswatch magazine wrote in a rare editorial comment:

> If Nigerians have not been noticeably exuberant in welcoming the Babangida government, it cannot be for lack of love; it can only be an expression of their disappointment with successive governments that Nigerians had presented with a bouquet of flowers only to be given a scorpion in return.

Babangida was very well aware of the enormous problems he faced. Much as Nigerians tend to welcome the overthrow of civilian administrations by the military, they still hunger for democracy. A new military regime in 20 months could only mean that the return to democracy would be a long way away. Babangida's immediate task was to dispel this gloom of cynicism. He knew that Nigerians were daring him to prove he was going to be different. He knew that cynicism had become a national ethos. Nigerians tend to see in any government action a hidden motive inconsistent with the common good. Babangida wondered why: "Is there perhaps hidden in our attitude a belief that we do not have a stake in the present as well as the future of this country?"

Babangida says he is a good student of people and environments in which he finds himself. The cynical environment presented him with a challenge he saw as a piece of cake to him. Buhari even made it easier for him. All he needed to do was to be what Buhari was not. Babangida took on the trademark of the constant, toothy smile. Nigerians found his sunny disposition wonderful and refreshing. He was evidently generous with his friendship. The doors to his office and home were open to all comers. He had promised to rule with the consent of the people because he did not pretend to have all the answers to all the national questions. Now, he was demonstrating it by welcoming individuals and groups and listening to whatever they had to say. Nigerians began to warm up to him as the ticking clock counted the inexorable march of time.

The new president wasted little time keeping the promises he made in his maiden broadcast. He had deplored the prolonged detention of former public office holders by the Buhari administration because "there is no moral reason to detain somebody for one year and eight months without preparing a formal charge against him." In line with his "intention to uphold fundamental human rights," Babangida threw the gates of the country's prisons open and the former movers and shakers of the Second

Republic walked out into freedom. He pitched his action on a high moral ground. He reminded Nigerians that no matter how sorely disappointed they must have been with the civilian administration of the second republic, "we must never allow ourselves to lose our sense of natural justice," adding that "the innocent cannot suffer for the crimes of the guilty."

He did not quite receive the applause he expected from Nigerians for this action. Some Nigerians wanted more than a pound of flesh from the politicians whom they blamed for all the problems, real or imagined, in the country. They loved to see them suffer either long jail terms or prolonged detention. Luckily for the president, such people, no matter how vocal, appeared to be in the minority. Nigerians generally welcomed the rough treatment the Buhari administration gave to the former public office holders but their prolonged detention without formal charges became counter-productive and earned the regime some deficit in public support.

The protection of human rights was dear to Nigerians. They were not about to lose sight of that. Still, Babangida found it necessary to explain the rationale for his action. "Our action," he told the nation in his independence anniversary broadcast on October 1, that year, "was inspired only by the ideals of justice and fair play (and) must not be construed as an attempt on our part to excuse, cover up or condone corruption in public life."

Babangida went on to set up three judicial panels to review the cases of all the former public officers. The one headed by Mr. Justice Mohammed Bello, a justice of the Supreme Court of Nigeria (and later Chief Justice of Nigeria) reviewed the cases of all former public officers convicted by the various military tribunals. Another panel, headed by Mr Justice Samson Uwaifo, a judge of Benin High Court (later justice of the Supreme Court) tried all those whose trials had not been concluded by the military tribunals. Mr Justice Akinola Aguda, a former chief judge of the then Western State and later of the Republic of Botswana, headed the third panel. It reviewed the cases of those convicted under the *Exchange Control (Anti-Sabotage) Decree 7* of 1984.

That panel also looked into the cases dealt with by the *Special Military Tribunal (Miscellaneous Offences) Decree 20* of 1984 which provided the death penalty for illegal dealing in petroleum products, unauthorised tampering with NEPA wires and meters and NITEL cables. This panel also reviewed the cases of drug traffickers convicted under this decree. Babangida had amended this particular decree and substituted life imprisonment for the death penalty for offences under it. He was acting like a man who was ready for power and was willing to exercise it to a maximum, dramatic effect.

The Uwaifo panel was of special interest to Nigerians because it reviewed the case of former President Shehu Shagari and former Vice-President Alex Ekwueme. The panel found, on the strength of the evidence before it, that they had no case to answer and ordered their release from detention. Its decision did not have too many takers. The public believed that Shagari bore responsibility for the alleged corruption that ravaged the economy under his watch. The public bayed for a pound of flesh. Some critics of the panel's decision argued that if those who served Shagari went to jail for corruption, then the former president must at least bear the moral blame for what they did and must be punished too. To set him and his former vice-president free, they argued, was to make a mockery of the entire process of cleansing the Augean Stable.

But the tribunal was legally right in its decision. Those who criticised it did not care to know that no specific charges of corruption were brought against the two men. Natural justice did not permit the law to punish innocent people because of public sentiment, no matter how strong it might be.

Babangida acted quickly to end the public debate over Shagari and Ekwueme's fate. Government said that the tribunal had discharged its legal responsibility in accordance with the country's common law tradition. The final decision, the government said in a public statement, rested with the AFRC. The council, the government assured the public, would consider the political implications of the panel's judgment before arriving at a decision that might satisfy everyone. Shagari and Ekwueme remained in detention. The public awaited the council's decision with keen interest.

The decision came on June 27, six clear months after the panel gave its judgment. The AFRC took a middle course to assuage feelings on both sides. Babangida said that government was "aware that legal justice is not necessarily social justice (but) government is anxious to emphasise that while the rule of law must be respected, the issue of the ex-politicians must also be handled politically and administratively."

Taking these into consideration, he said the government had decided that Shagari and Ekwueme be released from detention but restricted to their local government areas until 1990. They were banned for life from holding elective or public offices.

VIII

It is not really known when or for how long Babangida began his meticulous plan for the country's ultimate political prize. But he was not afraid of dropping hints that if he had the chance he would do things differently from what he saw other leaders of the country do. He masked his criticisms as the expression of genuine concerns of a concerned patriot.

Rear-Admiral Murtala Nyako, Flag Officer, Western Naval Command, was a member of the Armed Forces Ruling Council. He was also a member of the president's inner circle. Nyako was the first military governor of Niger State, Babangida's home state. It was during his tenure there that Nyako met Babangida and they became close. He does not think that Babangida plotted his rise to political power. But he admits that he and Babangida sometimes discussed the problems of the country in general terms. According to him, "we didn't just sit down and say what is wrong with Nigeria? Never did. Never. With me, we never did but we could raise an issue and discuss it."

Babangida was in the corridors of power for a long time. He saw, he listened and he learned. And he discussed with his military colleagues and civilian friends, particularly the bureaucrats of his generation, some of whom he became friends with early in his military career in Kaduna. It would be unfair, of course, as Nyako warns, to attribute this to his "scheming for power."

The decision to topple Buhari was taken in May 1985. As was pointed out in an earlier chapter, 23 officers drawn from the three services were involved in the planning and execution. Although Babangida admits he was their leader, the accounts of some of those close to him and who were among the group of 23, seem to indicate he was reluctant to get involved at the beginning.

Akilu's version gives the impression that the coup planners reserved the right to choose who was to succeed Buhari as head of state. He said they had a 'war' "convincing (Babangida) to accept this after everything was almost finished" but he told them "he didn't want anything." The coup planners, according to Akilu, then "sat down and scouted round and looked at who should be the leader of this country; all the generals were lined up from himself to the GOCs. Then we came round to the army headquarters, looked around at those in the army. Outside that, it was General Nasko, commander of artillery. So after going round all the generals and brigadiers, one had no other choice but to press on Babangida. We told him: 'Look, you are the only hope now.' He was very, very reluctant."

Was he, really?

Yes, says Major Abubakar Dangiwa Umar, also a member of the group. Umar was the administrator of the Federal Housing Authority under Buhari and a military governor under Babangida. He said Babangida wasn't himself for the coup. I think he was urged on. I must be frank with you, he was urged on. I know several times we sat and he said he didn't want to go on. He told me several times and I know in November 1984, we sat with him and I told him that I thought a coup was not wise. And so, unlike what many thought that he was willing, that he was enthusiastic to take over or he was manoeuvring, several times he changed the dates of the coup because he was hesitant. At one of our discussions, I told him: 'Look, you can't continue discussing a coup and postponing dates and hoping that nobody would get to know or you will not be arrested. So, do make up your mind on what to do."

Babangida took the advice. In May, he told his group it was time to get moving. Was Babangida really reluctant or opposed to a coup against Buhari? The answer, from what has been pieced together so far, is no. It is true that he felt frustrated with the administration. It is also true he refused to show he was jumping at the suggestion to topple it. His cool reluctance was a ploy, not his refusal to take his turn in the musical chair. Perhaps, as he admitted, he was worried about the bloody consequences of failure. It was important for him to weigh the pros and cons and be reasonably certain that the coup would succeed. Everything he did was a calculated step every inch of the way. He dramatised his problems with the administration sufficiently to make those close to him really worried.

Sometime in late July or early August 1985, Babangida's childhood friend, the late Kere Ahmed of the Nigerian Television Authority, NTA, was leaving for Japan on a course. He went to bid the Babangidas good bye and found the general in an unusually pensive mood. He wondered what might be the trouble. He asked the wife, Maryam, what was wrong with him. "Ask your brother," she snapped and left the room.

Ahmed, who knew the general's problems with the administration, felt really concerned. When his wife left the room, Babangida tried to tell Ahmed what the trouble was.

"In trying to explain to me," recalled Ahmed, "I found him picking his words carefully which was an indication that he was trying to hide something from me." Ahmed was not making much sense of what the general was saying.

Then Akilu walked in. Babangida felt relieved. He asked the colonel to explain things to Ahmed. "Akilu then surprisingly took me away from the house to the compound and tried to reassure me that I shouldn't worry; that things would be all right by the time I came back from Japan."

Ahmed did not ask any more questions and Akilu did not say much more but Ahmed said he "suspected that something was going to give." They had taken to speaking in tongues, as it were, in Babangida's official residence, according to Ahmed, "because the whole house was bugged."

Babangida played the reluctant leader to a dramatic effect. He gave the impression he was allowing his subordinates to pressurise him into staging the coup. But as usual, he had his acts together. He did not want the coup to be seen as a solution to his personal problems with the administration. That would debase the philosophy of his leadership and paint him in bad colours as an ambitious man. He wanted the coup to be seen as a patriotic act - and he as a man who risked all, not to save his neck but to save his country from "drift and the stifling climate" created by an administration increasingly behaving as if its mission was to save Nigeria from Nigerians.

Well, the coup succeeded and Babangida came into office with a script that benefited from his years in the corridors of power. He began to follow it by doing those things he knew would earn him instant public applause. He took the boot to the backside of the Nigerian Security Organisation, NSO, headed by Lawal Rafindadi, a former ambassador. NSO was dreaded in the Buhari administration because its operatives terrorised the populace. Armed with photocopies of detention papers signed by Idiagbon, they indiscriminately arrested and detained hundreds of people. Politicians, former public office holders as well as local and foreign businessmen, were harassed, arrested and detained. Many paid for their freedom. Extortion became both routine and rampant. NSO operatives who roamed the land as if they were a law unto themselves cowed Nigerians.

Babangida wisely promised to overhaul the Organisation as a matter of priority. Not quite one month after he took over, he kept his promise with a ringing sense of the consummate dramatist. He ordered that the detention cells of the NSO be thrown open to the public and the press. What Nigerians saw truly shocked them. Hundreds of people, Nigerians and foreigners, walked out of those cells looking like the skeletal versions of their former selves. Babangida wanted "the public (to) see that we did not create any imaginary (stories)" about the Buhari administration.

The president later re-structured the intelligence agencies in the country into three intelligence units - the State Security Services, SSS, for domestic security, National Intelligence Agency, NIA, for external security and the Defence Intelligence Agency, DIA, as the umbrella security outfit for the armed forces.

There were muted criticisms of the regime's decision to open the detention cells to the public, public applause notwithstanding. There were obvious implications for the agency. For one, it undermined its moral authority as an intelligence agency. For another, it exposed the nation's intelligence agency as both fraudulent in design and Gestapo in action. But Babangida sought to demonstrate one strong point: we won't subject people to such inhuman treatment because it is both wrong and immoral. He was telling the nation: *See, this is part of the reason my colleagues and I came to the conclusion that the country deserved something better than the Buhari administration.*

This was part of the general's winning formula, which derived from his commitment to uphold and protect human rights. Every action in those early days was a brick with which he was constructing the bridge of trust between himself and the nation over the ravine of cynicism. It was an important bridge. Babangida stood on it and stretched out his hands to the nation, inviting everyone to cross over. No one who saw those outstretched hands and the trademark smile doubted his sincerity. Babangida was moving on to convince a cynical nation that he meant to be different in every sense of the word.

"As we do not intend to lead the country where individuals are under the fear of expressing themselves," Babangida had told the nation on that unforgettable evening of August 27, "the *Public Officers (Protection Against False Accusation) Decree* No. 4 is hereby repealed." He went on to assure the media they would be free "to disseminate information.... without undue hindrance."

Note that word again: *undue.* As Chief of Army Staff, he let it be known that the Buhari administration would not permit *undue radicalism.* Now, the press would be allowed to do its duty *without undue hindrance.* This value-loaded word was a significant pointer to the working of his mind. It boiled down to this: *I respect the freedom of all Nigerians to do or say as they please but I reserve the right to set the limits of how far they would go.* No one bothered about such pointers or fine distinctions in those early days. When it dawned on Nigerians that despite all gestures of human rights protection, Babangida was still a dictator, they had one rude shock after another.

Babangida was as good as his word. The only two victims of decree 4, Tunde Thompson and Nduka Irabor, both of the *Guardian*, were released from jail and granted state pardon. The abrogation of decree 4 was a deft public relations move, a political master stroke even. The rambunctious Nigerian press had found itself gagged by the decree. The feeling in the press flowed down to the people. Few things could be worse than to prevent Nigerians from talking or writing to the press as they please.

Encomiums poured forth. Naturally. The late Dele Giwa, the first editor-in-chief of *Newswatch* magazine, described the new president as a "surprise gift to journalism and the country." *The Guardian*, not easily given to adulation, felt sufficiently elated by the development and cheered the general on in an editorial:

The government's open declaration of emphasis on human rights, followed by the immediate release of some 87 detainees, has given a tremendous push to optimism, to the belief that the new government will be just and humane and that the necessary redress to the evils perpetrated by the Buhari regime will be swiftly accomplished.

Ordinary Nigerians hailed the administration. A Lagos resident, Sunday Jobson, welcomed the abrogation of Decree 4 "because it [i.e. the abrogation of the decree] has given journalists and Nigerians as a whole the opportunity to partake and contribute towards a better Nigeria."

Babangida had unleashed the winning streak. Soon, the ice of cynicism began to thaw and human traffic poured across the bridge. Right from the first day, Babangida cut a new picture for himself and his administration. His taking on the civilian title of president was instructive. He was later to explain that this was in conformity with the 1979 constitution. His predecessor had used the title, head of state, used by all the previous military rulers in the country. Since Ironsi, the highest ruling organ of all military regimes in Nigeria was the Supreme Military Council, SMC. Babangida chose a new name for his own organ: Armed Forces Ruling Council, AFRC.

He did not choose a new name for the sake of it. It was part of his policy of inclusiveness. To demonstrate it, the AFRC had 28 members - nine more than the SMC under Buhari. This was to enhance broader representation of the armed forces in the government. The Chief of Staff, Supreme Headquarters, again a title used since Gowon, was renamed Chief of General Staff and the incumbent, Commodore Ebitu Ukiwe, took charge of political matters. Buhari and his number two man, Idiagbon, are both s from the north. Babangida chose as his number two, a Christian, an Ibo from the east. In a country sensitive to religious and ethnic balancing act in the power equation at the state and national levels, it was a wise and sensitive move. The appointment of his service chiefs, military governors as well as members of the AFRC reflected, as much as possible, his policy of inclusiveness.

There was every indication he had planned for this pretty carefully; evidence that he had studied other leaders before him, learned from their mistakes and inadequacies; evidence he knew how to approach Nigerians and win them over to his side. The Babangida mystique which was but a tiny seed in Minna and Bida, had now begun to blossom in a thousand petals with the colours of the rainbow.

One sure step after another showed a man who was prepared for power and the exercise of it. He did not throw out Buhari's ministers with disgrace, as had been the case in the past. Instead, he organised a send-off dinner party for them at which he thanked them for serving their country when it needed them. He even retained some of them in his new cabinet. He reached out to Nigerians in his choice of ministers.

He appointed Prince Bola Ajibola attorney general and minister of justice. Ajibola was president of the Nigerian Bar Association, NBA, which was very critical of the harsh decrees of the Buhari administration. He was instrumental in the decision of the association to boycott the special military tribunals unless they were headed by retired or serving judges rather than by military officers. The Buhari administration ignored the lawyers. Ajibola's appointment was like telling the lawyers the new administration believed they had a genuine case in their protest. The NBA was more than mollified.

Thirty-four days after he took over, Babangida seized one more opportunity to demonstrate a style of governance calculated to make a loud statement in winning friends and influencing people. On the silver jubilee independence anniversary of the country, the heavens opened in Lagos. Soldiers and school children participating in the national parade were soaked. When Babangida arrived to take the salute, an aide tried to protect him from the rain with an umbrella. He promptly brushed him aside. There were loud cheers from the capacity crowd at the Tafawa Balewa Square. Nigerians were mesmerized as they watched their president standing there in the rain, taking the salute.

Later that night, at the state party, stewards asked him to pose for photographs with them. He obliged. Their lucky day. The day after the parade, Babangida personally wrote letters to the headmasters and principals of schools in Lagos whose pupils participated in the independence anniversary parade, expressing his "heart-felt greetings and deepest appreciation" for the children's patriotism when they "marched and cheered with enthusiasm and fervour" in spite of the "heavy rainfall."

By the time he clocked his first 100 days in office, the ice had thawed. Its clear water reflected the unique style of one man. Few people could now hold back their admiration of him. Ray Ekpu of *Newswatch* magazine wrote in his column in the magazine: "Babangida has within the few weeks we have seen him operate, brought charm and class into the business of government. Whoever wrote his public relations script must be a pro. But I have a feeling that the president is the writer of his own script, his own public relations man."

Ekpu went on to describe his smile and his gait - some of the other things that made him different from those before him on that high horse: "He has a warm, natural smile that plays around his lips; he walks in a springy manner as if an electronic lever has been put under the soles of his shoes, and as he walks, he exudes confidence that infects his own environment."

Babangida's admirers began to fall over themselves. His charm and simplicity demystified governance. About two weeks after he took over, Babangida was conferring with the visiting British Foreign Secretary, Sir Geoffrey Howe, when a crowd of reporters and press photographers burst in, breaching protocol in the process. But the president hardly showed any signs of irritation. His officials and the journalists were more than pleasantly surprised by his attitude.

He had obviously struck the right cord with the press. In his first 100 days, he granted more interviews to local and foreign news media than his predecessor did in 20 months. He became the first Nigerian leader to grant an interview to the *Nigerian Tribune*. The *Tribune* group of newspapers, owned by the late Chief Obafemi Awolowo, had a reputation as a vocal and decidedly hostile critic of all federal governments, civil or military. Every leader, therefore, kept the *Tribune* group of newspapers at a respectable distance. Not Babangida.

When the *Tribune* asked for an interview, he granted it. Some of his close friends thought it was foolish. No gesture, they felt, could change the *Tribune* from what they saw as its avowed mission - to oppose, with every means at its disposal all leaders of the country but Awolowo. The president defended his decision to bring the newspaper group in from the cold. He reminded his colleagues that "you cannot sit down and listen to one side of the story. It is always better to listen to the people with dissenting voices."

The president's gesture paid off. The *Tribune* group crossed the bridge to Babangida, lauding his human rights policy and easy-going style. Its hostility ceased. In any case, Folu Olamiti, editor of the *Nigerian Tribune,* was one of the journalists detained by Buhari. Babangida released him and the others, including Haroun Adamu from detention.

Three other people also crossed that bridge. Babangida granted an audience to Tai Solarin, the old school headmaster who earned his reputation as a strident critic of all governments in the country. He reciprocated by hailing the new regime. The new leader also charmed Professor Wole Soyinka, who became the first African to win the Nobel Prize in Literature in 1986. He gave the new administration the pass mark as a government that listens. But by far the biggest fish that found itself in the Babangida pond was Chief Awolowo. He and his wife went to Dodan Barracks on a courtesy call on the president and the First Lady. Awolowo told reporters he was reciprocating the president's love for him and his family.

Babangida had reached out and touched everyone.

In his first few days in office, he had mended all the fences cracked by his predecessor. All the interest groups as well as labour and students unions could count on him as a friend – the Nigerian Labour Congress,

NLC, the National Association of Nigerian Students, NANS, and the Nigerian Medical Council, NMA, among others. The last two had had a brush with the Buhari administration.

The traditional institution received a cruel jolt in the hands of that government as well. Two first class traditional rulers, the Emir of Kano, Alhaji Ado Bayero, and the Oni of Ife, Oba Okunade Sijuade, were punished for their unauthorised visit to Israel. They were suspended from office for six months each. Traditional rulers throughout the country felt humiliated by what the government did to their two colleagues. They were apprehensive, not least because some of the elite in the country had begun to question the relevance of the institution in a modern society. Babangida needed to put the traditional rulers at ease.

On his 38th day in office, he invited first class traditional rulers throughout the federation for a meeting in Lagos. As "fathers of the nation," he told the glittering gathering of emirs, obas and chiefs,

> you play a very major role as the main stabilising agents in any society. The peaceful co-existence of citizens therefore rests on your shoulders squarely and I expect that as part of your contribution to the success of the government, you will ensure the stability of the country.

He said he would set up a forum for a periodic exchange of views with the traditional rulers. He promised that he would take measures to safeguard their role as "impartial advisers." The temperature in the traditional institution came down. Babangida had won their hearts. His own view had always been that the military administration could use the traditional institution "to reach everybody."

He reached out to women too as a special interest group in the country. He did not appoint a woman to his cabinet. He took two steps to make up for that. He directed each of the military governors to appoint at least one woman into his cabinet. He also appointed the first woman to head a Nigerian university. A mathematician, Professor Grace Alele-Williams, was named vice-chancellor, University of Benin. This was his first foray into the academia.

Babangida held his first meeting with vice-chancellors of the country's universities on November 16, 1985. He promised he would uphold academic freedom because his government "regards academic freedom as an indispensable ingredient of all the freedoms."

It was an important pledge. There had been a steady erosion of academic freedom over the years. But the pledge came with a condition that, in the euphoria of the time, might have been ignored by the university community. Babangida told them that:

> When the emphasis shifts away from the conception of the academic calling, and moves to the idea of self-defined and self-determined mission to change society as a primary objective and to make this central focus of activity without proper and due regard to the will, wishes and beliefs of society, then the academic has changed into something completely new and problematic for himself and for the society which supports his activity.

In other words, there was a limit to academic freedom. Obviously, Babangida did not intend to let anyone step beyond the threshold. The university dons would do well to remember that. It was also a veiled reference to the radical, leftist lecturers. The lecturers in this group were usually accused of stirring up students' agitation.

Was he the true friends the lecturers? The answer came in its own good time, as we shall see – and wiped the smirk from the faces of the university teachers.

Chapter Eleven

The Parting of Ways

One of the most painful things I have ever done
–Ibrahim Badamasi Babangida

Only four months after Babangida took over and was still grappling with winning the confidence of Nigerians and the international community, the devil stepped out of the shadows. In early December 1985, a coup plot to overthrow him was discovered. If Babangida found this shocking, then he certainly found it even more shocking because it allegedly involved one of his childhood friends, Major-General Mamman Jiya Vatsa, minister of the Federal Capital Territory. They had been friends since their secondary school days in the Provincial Secondary School, Bida. Babangida felt shattered.

In a way Babangida perhaps saw it coming. Rumours of his alleged disagreements with Vatsa preceded him to the presidency. Babangida found himself increasingly forced to explain to some of his close military and civilian friends that there was no truth to the rumours of disagreements between him and Vatsa.

In August that year, Vatsa was in the entourage of the Chief of Staff, Supreme Headquarters, Major General Tunde Idiagbon, to Mecca for the holy pilgrimage. They were still in the holy land when Babangida toppled Buhari. Before Vatsa went to Mecca, Babangida went to him and told him that he came to ask for his forgiveness if he felt he had wronged him in any way. Both men joked about the stories people were spinning about them. As far as Babangida was concerned, that was the end of the matter. He appeared to be mistaken.

The rumour did not die. Babangida recalls that by October that year, the rumours more or less intensified. Some of their mutual friends were worried. Some of them went to Babangida to find out what the problem was. But I kept "telling them that to the best of my knowledge, there was no such thing."

The rumours of disagreements between them, however, soon took a new turn for the worse. The rumours now had it that Vatsa was allegedly plotting to overthrow Babangida. Some other officers were also mentioned in the alleged plot. Babangida phoned Nasko and asked him if he believed Brigadier Abdusalami Abubakar would plot his overthrow.

Nasko said no. The president asked him if he would believe if he heard that Vatsa would do the same thing. An alarm went off in Nasko's brain. He didn't like what he was hearing. His instinct told him some people were obviously trying to set the president against some of his close friends. He told Babangida of his fears in this respect and advised him not to let people push him down that dangerous path.

Vatsa too picked up the rumour of his alleged coup plot. He was worried that Babangida had not mentioned it to him. He was sure Babangida knew what was going on. He decided to confront him, partly to find out how much he knew and partly to deny his alleged involvement. Sometime in late November 1985, during tea break at an AFRC meeting, Vatsa went to Nasko and told him he would like him to be present when he confronted Babangida over the rumours of his alleged coup plot. Nasko told him it would not be right for him to be there unless Babangida approved. Vatsa secured that approval.

There were some awkward moments at the meeting. It was as if each man was sizing up the other, trying to find telltale signs of honesty or dishonesty on one another's face. Vatsa said he picked up the rumour of his alleged coup plot against the president from his own wife. He denied knowledge of any such thing. He said that he had brought Nasko with him as a witness to his assurance that he was not part of any such plot against his childhood friend. Babangida let a few anxious moments roll by. He put on his best smile and told Vatsa:

> Look, old boy, there is a rumour going on about a coup and everybody's name had been mentioned. The only person whose name has not been mentioned in that coup is myself because I cannot stage a coup against myself. Look at Nasko who is sitting next to you; some people even mentioned his name but because of my relationship with you, I never found it necessary to call you and tell you because I trust you. I can vouch for you. This is rubbish. Let us forget it. By my training or my belief, if I tell you that you are being suspected of planning a coup against me, it means my sincerity towards you is incomplete. So, forget it and let's go on doing our business.

Nasko was shocked, to put it mildly, to learn that he too had been mentioned in connection with the alleged coup plot. He asked Babangida why he did not tell him. Babangida told Nasko not to worry. "I trust you, so why should I bother?" The meeting ended. It turned out to be the last meeting between Babangida and Vatsa.

When Nasko saw Babangida again later that evening, the president told him his gut feeling was that Vatsa was involved in the alleged coup plot. He said he noticed some nervousness in the normally self-confident minister for the Federal Capital Territory. Vatsa was evidently so unsettled that he had asked Babangida if he was going to be executed "now that everybody suspected him." It was an unusual question for a very senior army officer who knew the rules.

Less than two weeks after this meeting, the arrest of those suspected to be involved in the alleged plot began. Vatsa was picked up a week after the arrests began. His wife, Safiya, was devastated. She continued to protest her husband's innocence to Nasko. She phoned him constantly to complain about the arrest of her husband "without any concrete evidence."

At first, Nasko felt obliged to offer his shoulders to the distressed wife of a friend in trouble. Vatsa had told his wife that Nasko was the only reliable friend he had in the government. Nasko soon found it necessary to lengthen the distance between them. Vatsa and the others were still being interrogated and more arrests were being made. Security agents were tailing Mrs SafiyaVatsa. Nasko did not want to be implicated in any way. He said it "came to a point I had to warn her of the grave security implications of her visits" to his house. Mrs Vatsa, according to Nasko, insisted "there was no concrete evidence to prove her husband's guilt."

Some in the military hierarchy thought otherwise. A few days before Vatsa was picked up, Abacha had gone to Nasko "with conclusive documents to prove Vatsa's complicity." That appeared to erase any further doubts in Nasko's mind. He asked Mrs Vatsa if she was aware that Lt-Col Musa Bitiyong, deputy quarter master-general and a close confidant of her husband, had been arrested. Nasko said Mrs Vatsa was shocked by the news but quickly recovered from her shock and argued that Bitiyong's arrest alone proved nothing against her husband and that in any case, she was sure Bitiyong would not say anything damaging against him.

But unknown to her, Bitiyong had implicated her husband. Bitiyong told the investigation panel he received ₦50,000.00 from Vatsa for the coup plot. Vatsa admitted he gave Bitiyong some money but that it was to help him get started in farming.

Babangida was actually informed of the coup plot late in October that year by military intelligence. He appeared to have been calm about it. At the opening ceremony of the 1985 Chief of Army Staff training conference in Lagos on November 4, Babangida made a veiled reference to saboteurs and promised the government would deal with them with "incisive professional skill."

It is not clear if he was dropping a hint that he knew of the plot afoot. By the first week of December, the plotters reportedly appeared ready to move. But a firm date had not been set. They toyed with either December 19 or 25. Neither was to be. Their arrests aborted the plan. On December

20, the public was officially informed of the alleged plot. In a broadcast on radio and television, Major-General Domkat Bali, Chairman, Joint Chiefs of Staff, said that "officers from all the services were recruiting followers and concluding plans for the violent overthrow of the government."[1]

According to Bali, the coup plotters had four grievances against the government. These were the retention of some former public officers in government, human rights, involvement of middle-level ranks in public office and the rejection of the IMF loan. Vatsa was arrested on the eve of Christmas, four days after Bali's broadcast. On March 5, 1986, he and nine other officers from the army, the Air Force and the navy, having been tried and found guilty of the alleged coup plot by a military tribunal, were executed. The tribunal condemned twelve of them to death. On appeal, the AFRC reduced the death sentence of two majors to life jail. It was a tragic and unedifying end to Vatsa who was also popularly known as the Emperor of Abuja.

The coup plot caused Babangida considerable personal pains because apart from Vatsa, some of the men involved were also close to him, particularly, Lt-Col Mike Ioryorshe and Lt-Col Musa Bitiyong. Babangida and Vatsa played roles that frustrated the Dimka coup and earned them promotion ahead of their course mates. Vatsa was commanding a brigade in Calabar and was one of the first commanders who promptly denounced the Dimka coup and announced his loyalty to the Murtala Muhammed administration.

Vatsa loved literature. He wrote poetry. He was very active in both the development and the promotion of literature within and outside the army. There is something poignant about his fate captured in one of his poems in Pidgin English in which he wrote:

> *Judgment Day*
> *That Day*
> *Na waa.*

If Vatsa actually participated in the coup as alleged, a question arises as to why he would want to plot to overthrow his childhood friend? That question may never be satisfactorily answered, partly because Vatsa is no longer alive and partly because some of the stories about their alleged friction are exaggerated and rather too fanciful. The wives of the two men were even drawn into the tales of alleged rivalries between Babangida and Vatsa. Vatsa and his wife were said to have always loathed Mrs. Babangida and that Mrs Vatsa must have goaded her husband to topple Babangida because she too wanted to be First Lady. Such stories are not strange in matters of this nature in which suspicion is often readily dressed up as a fact in hyperbolic proportions.

Still, something may be made from this fact. Babangida did not involve Vatsa in all the coups in which he participated. In the 1983 coup against Shagari, Babangida admits that "to a certain extent, we did involve him but not fully (because) we were a bit careful because he was once a brigade commander of the Guards Brigade. He also worked briefly I think with Shagari. But I owed it a duty as a friend to let him know what was happening."

In Babangida's 1985 coup against Buhari, Vatsa was not informed either. Some of their mutual friends were not happy that Babangida retained Vatsa as minister of the Federal Capital Territory. Shagaya was one of such people. He argues that Babangida's decision to retain Vatsa reflects the president's inherent personal weakness of "too trusting, pretending not to be able to harm. In the case of Vatsa, I am sure he didn't want to be castigated in Niger State as destroying everybody, even his own people, on his way to the throne. But a lot of us didn't share in that his sentiment towards Vatsa. We didn't like his retention."

Shagaya's main grouse was that he believed Vatsa nursed a political ambition. He argues:

> Don't forget that the fact that both of them were from Niger State, the fact that they were classmates, the fact that they were course mates did not mean each did not have his own ambition. It didn't mean they didn't have their independent ways they would want to see things happen. And it didn't remove individual greed to attempt power seizure.

Shagaya says that in 1975 he "had had cause to accuse Vatsa of vaunting ambition. He called Mark and told him what I had told him. I repeated myself and left him and afterwards, he sent Mark to me to call for a truce as it were. But I told Mark to inform him that the cultivation of friendship comes naturally and not by any form of inducement."

Shagaya says he was not surprised when he heard Vatsa was linked to the coup plot "because I had suspected him much earlier." He said both the president and his wife, Maryam, would bear him witness. "I had had to prevail on IBB to ban the taking of pictures at council meetings by anybody because Vatsa was fond of taking our pictures each time we went for council meetings. I had to cause a law or an order to be passed to ban such an act."

But some other officers did not suspect Vatsa of anything. Duba said he "initially couldn't believe it because I said it wasn't possible. We grew up together, worked together, fought the civil war together, sleeping in the same trench, sharing the same room, the same food, drinking from the same cup and we were just like brothers. I couldn't believe such a thing was possible. I was so shocked and found it hard to believe until later when the facts came."

Duba dismisses the stories of rivalry between Babangida and Vatsa as unfounded. Babangida and Vatsa taught in the NDA. Duba says Babangida was responsible for bringing Vatsa from Jaji to become quartermaster general of the Nigerian Army. As far as Duba was concerned, the two men had cordial relations. "I don't know of any signs of Vatsa's animosity towards Babangida," he insists.

As fate would have it both men came to an eternal parting of ways. Babangida had the painful duty of approving the execution of one of his close friends. It was his painful duty to submit a memo to the AFRC on the judgement of the tribunal headed by Major-General Charles Ndiomu. Babangida instructed Major Mahmud Santuraki, his intelligence officer when he was the Chief of Army Staff, to write a draft of the memorandum to council for him. He told the major "to place himself in my position" in drafting the memo. Santuraki, according to Babangida, "did a very good job. Very tough stance he took."

While the major was working on the draft, Babangida was consulting with a wide spectrum of officers in the armed forces "to pick their brains and see how they felt." Opinions were hardened against the coup plotters. Everyone voted for the death penalty as stipulated by law. Babangida says he had hoped to sway the council from voting for the execution of the men. He knew he was swimming against the tide. There was a precedent in 1976. Incidentally, Vatsa was secretary to the Major-General Emmanuel Abisoye tribunal that condemned Dimka and the others involved in the abortive coup against Murtala Muhammed to death.

Babangida said that those he consulted pointedly told him that anything other than the death penalty would have serious implications for the military. There would be strife and disaffection and a feeling that there were different strokes for different people in the armed forces, he was told. And remember, they reminded him, according to the president, the case of Flt Lt Jerry Rawlings of Ghana who was imprisoned for plotting a coup and who engineered another coup from prison and emerged to become head of state.

Despite the weight of argument in favour of execution, Babangida says he found it "so painful" that he left the conclusion in his memorandum open. "Deep inside me," Babangida says, "I knew that if I should be given the chance, I would not have put him (Vatsa) on the stake to get him fired. Deep in here, it was there. It was one of the most painful things I have ever done, God knows. So painful."

The sentence was carried out on March 5. Babangida was informed. Bali informed the nation on television early that evening. The president was later shown a video recording of the execution. "It really made me uncomfortable that day. It was a nightmare," he says.

One of the early callers in Dodan Barracks that night confirmed this. He said he met Babangida in an uncharacteristically subdued mood. "You could see how the unfortunate incident weighed on him. I think if he were not the president, he would have openly wept" this early caller said.

Babangida, certainly, was devastated by the involvement of his friend in the coup plot but he did not find the plot itself particularly unusual. He knew only too well that there were others in the armed forces angling for political power and given the right excuse or atmosphere, they too could push him out. In September 1985, he called a meeting of the caucus of the administration, "the conspirators, the people who did the coup, the same Group of 23" and advised that each of them should make "at least two to five friends, confidants within the military" to enable them enlarge their support base. If they did not do that, he reasoned, their colleagues would see them as privileged people. This would breed envy and once envy has taken root, there is no knowing where its branches will reach.

"I told them," Babangida recalls, "that this was necessary because just like we took up arms and ousted one of our colleagues, we could never rule out the possibility of somebody ever taking up arms against us. So, I don't think we were surprised that other military officers wanted to take over. We expected that it would happen."

The nation was not prepared for another change of government so soon after Babangida took over. Nigeria was not yet a banana republic, all things considered. Initial public reaction to the coup plot was outright condemnation of the plotters. There was an outpouring of support for the administration. Solidarity marches were almost spontaneous in various states. States, such as Benue and Cross River, whose indigenes were implicated in the plot, found it expedient to publicly denounce them and distance the rest of the people from their intended action. Failure, as they say, has no brothers. The men had failed. Now, they were alone, all alone, carrying their own cross.

The public reaction was genuine, even if there was some attempt by those who are usually smarter than others in such things to reap personal benefits from it. Babangida had invested in public goodwill right from his maiden broadcast. The public did not wait to be asked to make returns on it. It felt obliged to do so. Nigerians saw the regime essentially as a military government with a human face. Or, as Professor Wole Soyinka put it, it was a government that listened.

The IMF debate was still on when the plot was uncovered. It is difficult even now to see why this was something the coup plotters would object to. Public condemnation of the coup plot might also have been informed by the fact that Nigerians were getting increasingly tired of the musical chairs; this also informed their cynicism when Babangida took over barely four months earlier.

Despite the robust condemnation of the men, however, by the time the tribunal returned its guilty verdict on thirteen of the coup plotters, public sympathy for the government had run its course. It now turned the other way. Appeals were made to the government to spare their lives. However genuine the appeals were, they demonstrated a vital lesson to the regime early in its life. There is inherent fickle-mindedness in the public. To take its support for granted in all things and in all circumstances is to ignore the law of mutability. Certainly, the public must have been disappointed when the guns rang out and silenced those men forever.

Why did a listening government ignore public pleas to temper justice with mercy? Expression of such a surprise reflects a poor reading of the military mind, which knows two colours - white and black. All the various shades of grey in between are ignored. By plotting the fall of the government, the men had become enemies. The only way to deal with an enemy, as in war, is to kill him. And that was it.

Chapter Twelve

Rocking the Boat

Nigeria's economic woes claim another government
–Newsweek

Babangida needed no one to tell him that the Nigerian economy had become, rightly or wrongly one failure of almost every Nigerian leader before him. *Time* magazine reminded him any way. The magazine urged him to "act quickly and decisively on the economic front, whatever might be his plans in other areas, because "in Nigeria, unpopular or ineffective leaders do not last long."[1]

Few things are more contentious in Nigeria than the management of its economy. It was a sore point between the military and the civilians, among civilians and among the military. The young majors, who toppled Abubakar Tafawa Balewa, cited mismanagement of the economy as one of the reasons for their action. The brigadiers and colonels who ousted Gowon similarly accused him of inept management of the economy. Buhari found Shagari guilty of the same failure on the economic front. Abacha who announced the coup, said that the "…economy has been hopelessly mismanaged. We have become a debtor and beggar nation."[2]

There was some exaggeration there but it was true that the economy was not faring well. Buhari confessed it was even worse than he had thought. The problem with the economy did not start with Shagari, although the military roundly blamed him entirely but unfairly for it. It only worsened on his watch. Crude oil was, and is, responsible for about seventy-three per cent of the country's foreign earnings. An oil glut during the Murtala/Obasanjo administration in 1978 caused a sharp drop in earnings from which Nigeria did not fully recover before Shagari took office as president despite the cost-cutting measures known as austerity measures, imposed by Obasanjo to rein in public sector spending.

Another oil glut hit the world market in 1982. Awolowo saw it coming a year earlier and said so. Shagari and his party faithfuls dismissed Awolowo as an idle prophet of doom. It turned out that Awolowo was right. When the glut hit and took a large chunk of the foreign exchange earnings down with it, Shagari was forced to re-impose austerity measures. He reaped the whirlwind. The austerity measures fuelled widespread social discontent that possibly smoothened the way for his ouster.

In April 1983, Shagari sought external financial help. He applied to the International Monetary Fund, IMF, for a balance of payments support facility of $2.7 billion. Negotiations for the loan were still going on when the military sacked him.

Buhari initiated measures to restore the confidence of the international business community in Nigeria as a credible trading partner they could do business with. His major worry appeared to be Nigeria's ₦18.3 billion external debt burdens. Creditors denied Nigerian exporters credit facilities. Buhari decided to pay off the debts as soon as possible. He committed 44 per cent of the gross national earnings to servicing them.

Although the administration continued the negotiations with the IMF for the bridging loan facility, it rejected the conditions stipulated by the IMF. Foreign creditors tied the re-opening of credit lines to Nigeria's acceptance of the fund's approved package or conditionalities for re-vamping the economy. There was a stalemate.

As an interim measure, government introduced counter-trade – a modern trade by barter by which crude oil was bartered for imports of essential goods and commodities. It was a sensible interim measure to prevent an import-dependent nation from grinding to a halt. In any case, it was a preferred alternative to the loan, according to Idiagbon, because "the IMF has never cured any economically sick country."

Buhari had to go because under him, according to Babangida, the economy was still burdened with "huge foreign and domestic debts, a rapidly declining per capita income, a high rate of unemployment, severe shortages of raw materials and spare parts....and a high rate of inflation (that resulted) in "deterioration in the general standard of living."[3]

That charge does not take away from Buhari the fact that he was committed to reviving the economy. Indeed, as far as he was concerned, that and cleaning "the society of the cankerworm of pervasive corruption" were his two primary objectives in government. His strategy for reviving the economy was by "efficiently exploiting and harnessing all available human and material resources in order to improve the quality of life of all Nigerians."[4]

Babangida went ahead to dismantle Buhari's interim economic measures. He did not think the country should commit more than 30 per cent of its earnings to service its external debts. He also felt that counter-trade forced "Nigerians.... to buy goods and commodities at higher prices than obtained in the international market"[5] (and) "mainly benefited government officials who used (it) to line their own pockets."[6]

It is not clear if Babangida openly opposed counter-trade during the Buhari administration, of which he was a very senior member. He must have kept his views to himself. He admitted that as he prepared to topple Buhari, he consulted widely but discreetly on the problems of the economy and the most appropriate solutions to them. He wanted to know the merits and the demerits of counter-trade and its place in the management of the economy. Most of the people he consulted did not approve of counter-trade as a sound economic management strategy. What the economy needed, he was told again and again, were not palliatives but structural reforms to diversify and strengthen its base. Babangida was fully persuaded that the country's path to economic redemption lay through the road less travelled: structural reforms. His 'consultants' were unknowingly preaching to the converted.

However, Babangida surprised those who expected him to throw out counter-trade. Instead, he retained it but decided it would no longer be used for "the exchange of consumer items and foodstuff" but for "project financing ... in those areas of critical importance to the nation's industrial and technological development as identified in the Fifth National Development Plan."[7] Counter-trade was not such a bad idea after all.

Business Week, an American business magazine, found it necessary to advise Babangida "to meet the economic goals he accuses deposed leader Muhammadu Buhari of failing to achieve."[8]

Babangida believed that there were four main problems besetting the economy. These were:

- Decrease in our domestic production while our population continues to rise.
- Dependence on import for both consumer goods and industrial raw materials.
- A grossly widening gap between the rich and the poor.
- The big role played by the public sector in economic activities with hardly any concrete results to justify such a role.

Babangida had an interesting take on how to get the economy out of the woods permanently. His thesis was that good economic husbandry is a product of good governance. Good governance in the country could best be brought about with the institution of a new political order.

He unfolded this thesis in his first independence anniversary broadcast on October 1, 1985. Babangida blamed the problems of the national economy on the "intermittent bad government (that had) left us a legacy of economic mismanagement and a chain of political instability." If Nigerians wanted a change, then they had no option but "...to begin a most vigorous search for a New Political Order capable of ensuring sustained economic growth and social development. It is only within such a framework that we can properly address these and other urgent tasks that lie ahead."[9]

He came to this conclusion, he says, from "reading history of how nations developed." This led him to believe that "self-reliance" was the key to the problems of the Nigerian economy. His decision to ban the importation of maize, rice and vegetable oil "just two to three months after we took over," was consistent with his new thesis on the economy. He wanted "to shift the attention of the nation from the buying and selling syndrome and parasitic services to the more enduring domain of increased total real production, rising labour productivity and greater efficiency of investment." [10]

He took calculated steps. But first, he had to deal with the IMF's bridging loan. In his maiden speech as president, he had promised to "break the deadlock that frustrated the negotiations with a view to evaluating more objectively both the negative and positive implications of reaching a mutual agreement with the Fund."

He then did something unusual for a military regime. He threw the decision on the matter open to the Nigerian public as if to prove to Nigerians that he meant it when he said that he and his colleagues did not "intend to have answers to all the questions." He warned that whatever the people decided, there would be no easy choices for the nation.

Abubakar Abdulkadir, managing director, Nigerian Industrial Development Bank, NIDB, headed the special committee that organised the IMF nationwide public debate. Babangida inaugurated the committee on September 25, 1985, and charged it "with the specific task of conducting a national debate on the desirability or otherwise of Nigeria obtaining the loan."

Nigerians responded to this novel idea with great enthusiasm. For nearly three months, they engaged in a lively debate over the loan. The voices of those who supported it were effectively drowned by those opposed to it. Dr. Ibrahim Ayagi, who was the managing director of Continental Merchant Bank at the time, was the leading light in the opposition camp. He and the others opposed to the loan succeeded quite beautifully in demonizing the IMF/World Bank as the destroyer rather than the builder of Third World economies. Their prescriptions, the opponents of the loan argued, did not work for Brazil, Turkey and other countries and so, they would not work for Nigeria either. To take the loan was to mortgage the future of the country to the IMF.

The committee submitted a preliminary report on the debate to Babangida in early December 1985. Its reports, preliminary or final, were never made public but it was easy to guess which way the wind blew. Abdulkadir noted in his preliminary report that "never in the history of Nigeria had people been so sharply divided on a sophisticated matter as the IMF loan." From what he saw of the debate, he could only conclude that Nigerians were "united in their determination to solve the economic (problems) facing the country" despite the sharp division among them "on the modalities."

After reading the preliminary report, Babangida, anxious to unfold his economic development blueprint, concluded that even if the debate continued for much longer, the feeling of the country towards the loan would not change. Quite suddenly, he ended the debate and addressed the nation on it in a radio and television broadcast on December 12. He praised the wisdom of the AFRC in throwing "the question of the IMF loan open to debate in obedience to our absolute faith in the capability of Nigerians to rally round Nigeria in order to ensure the success of our great efforts to achieve national salvation through deep and lasting reforms of the state and the planned restructuring of the economy."

Of the debate itself, he said:

> The IMF debate has proved to be a unique occasion for the people of this country. Opinions have been expressed by a wide spectrum of the society, each person acting to the best of his or her knowledge with the purest of motives and all in the interest of Nigeria.
>
> It has, in particular, helped to awaken the conscience of the nation and to raise our democratic ideals in a way that no other public issue has done in recent times. Without any doubt, the nation is the better for it; and this augurs well for the future.

Thank goodness, the people had made their own decision on a matter that sorely touched them and the future of the country. Babangida stopped short of applauding that decision but noted that it was "not at all clear from the evidence that the additional sacrifice involved by obtaining the loan is less than the additional sacrifice entailed in not taking the loan. But what is clear," he went on in his broadcast, "is that whichever option we take will involve a lot of sacrifices by our people."

Babangida weighed both options and the report of the presidential committee, and came

> "to the conclusion that for now the path of honour and the essence of democratic patriotism lies in discontinuing the negotiations with the IMF for a support loan. This is clearly the will of majority of our people on the issue. We have, therefore, decided to face the challenge of restructuring our economy not through an IMF loan, but a determination of our own people to make all the sacrifices necessary to put the economy on the path of sustained growth; doing so at our pace and on our own volition.

Babangida felt confident that the nation was now ready to begin a new journey along "the path of economic reconstruction, self-reliance and democratic patriotism."

It is debatable if this rather grandiloquent encomium poured on the people by the president on the IMF debate was truly deserved. What was clear is that the debate served a very useful purpose for the Babangida administration. First, it won it public admiration because it created two very important and valuable illusions – the illusion of participatory democracy in a military government and the illusion that the people's will had prevailed and would prevail all the time in the administration that did not have the answers to all the questions. Secondly, the debate showed that it was possible, even in a cynical Nigeria, to mobilise public opinion in whatever direction the government so desired. These illusions became valuable lessons that Babangida applied in at least two other instances – a new political order and a new foreign policy for the country. He let Nigerians debate what they wanted in each case.

It has been argued that Babangida knew exactly where he was going on the IMF loan and that even if the debate had been in favour of the loan, he would still have rejected it in favour of his homegrown strategy for tackling the economic problems. This was not off the mark. Babangida, obviously, had his own ideas on how the economy should be best managed. He believed that the problem with the economy lay in its faulty structural base. Unless that faulty structure was changed to respond to the nation's needs, an effective management of the economy would be difficult, no matter how hard and honestly anyone tried. The austerity and other measures taken by Obasanjo and Shagari, in Babangida's view, basically mistook the scarecrow for the enemy. They tackled the symptoms, not the illness. He would tackle the illness.

The IMF debate presented a simplistic scenario of the choices before Nigerians for taking or not taking the loan. The basic goal was revamping the economy. Two roads led to that. The IMF road was a bridging loan with conditionalities firmly attached to it. Those conditionalities gave the fund the right to dictate how the economy should be managed. The sore point in that was the value of the nation's currency, the Naira. All such prescriptions or conditionalities of the Fund involved what was called a 'realistic value' of the currency of the country in need of the IMF shock treatment. It always results in the devaluation or downward adjustment of the local currency.

The other road was the one that Nigerians had to construct by themselves. This was Babangida's choice. He wanted Nigerians to be the collective managers of the national economy by the choice they made in the light of what confronted the nation. This, of course, would exact some prices. Were Nigerians prepared to endure the discipline necessary to restructure and revamp the economy? The IMF debate said yes to that. Babangida welcomed it because it squared with his own thinking. It is thus easy to see was why the president took one look at the preliminary report of the presidential committee and was instantly convinced those who were opposed to the loan had won the debate in favour of home-grown prescriptions.

While the IMF debate was still going on, Babangida declared a 15-month economic emergency. The only time the country had an economic emergency was during the civil war, 1967-70. A national economic emergency decree gave Babangida discretionary powers. All workers in the country were to contribute five per cent of their monthly pay into the National Economic Emergency Fund. He defended this on the grounds that "all of us must make hard choices involving great difficulties and requiring sacrifices from everyone and every sector, including the Armed Forces."[11]

Perhaps, the real reason for the economic emergency was to buy him time to see his way clearly through the problems. He admitted this at an interview in which he gave three real reasons for it:

> First, it will afford us time to be able to give a good stock taking of the problems as far as the economy is concerned. Secondly, it will also give us time to plan on the economy and third, to reflect on the last four Development Plans of this country. So, we have a stock taking that gives us time to plan and then look back to reflect on what went wrong in the previous economic Development Plans. That will give us a very good take-off point.[12]

II

The story of the Nigerian economy has been a tale of strange paradoxes. In the seventies and eighties, all the traditional economic indices pointed to a buoyant economy. An oil boom fuelled gigantic development projects in the building and construction industries and other areas of economic activity. Hundreds of foreign investors and entrepreneurs flocked into the country to share in the burgeoning national wealth. Industrial and commercial expansion attracted workers from other countries in the West African sub-region.

Gross Domestic Product, GDP, was healthy. In nearly ten years (1970/71- 1979/80) it ballooned from ₦9.443 billion to ₦18.740 billion. Even when the economy received its first jolt in 1978 forcing the Obasanjo administration to institute austerity measures, the picture was only bleak, not harrowing, by Third World standards. The Naira was strong. It was almost at par with the British sterling and exchanged at one Naira to US $2.50

These indices told only half the story. The structural foundation of the economy was weak and therefore, the gross national product did not reflect the *real* level of Nigeria's economic development. The country had slipped into the dangerous economic zone of a mono-economy. Its dependence on one major source of revenue – crude oil – was almost total. By the time the military left the stage on October 1, 1979, after nearly fourteen years in power, the economy remained "backward, underdeveloped, disarticulated and dependent."[13]

Awolowo once referred to the Nigerian economy as a "street beggar economy." At independence in 1960, octopal foreign interests through their multi-nationals such as UAC and UTC controlled the economy. They dominated the distributive and retail trade in the country. Foreign interests also controlled the fledgling manufacturing industries. Buhari believed that Nigeria's first National Development Plan (1962-68), "correctly identified"[14] the problems of the economy yet it was to be financed to the tune of fifty per cent through foreign financial assistance tied to foreign aid. It was, of course, true that "the colonial state, through deliberate administrative manipulation and discrimination, under-developed indigenous entrepreneurship and relegated it to a compradoral role in the economy."[15]

The Second National Development Plan (1970-1974), arguably the best articulated national development blueprint ever produced by Nigerians for Nigeria since independence, was ambitious in its scope and profound in its philosophy of social and economic development. Its authors hoped that the plan, if properly executed, would turn Nigeria into:

1. a united, strong and self-reliant nation;
2. a great and dynamic economy;
3. a just and egalitarian society;
4. a land of bright and full opportunities for all citizens; and
5. a free and democratic society.

Still, in 1985, when Babangida came to power the country could not boast of "a great and dynamic economy." The economy was still beset with a very weak industrial and technological base; helpless dependence on massive importation of machinery, spare parts and raw materials and poor infrastructural facilities such as power, water and roads.[16] In other words, not much had structurally changed in the development and the management of the economy. The oil boom succeeded beautifully in making the country a rentier state, not an industrial one.

Babangida moved one step at a time, dropping hints of his economic policy. When he swore-in his first set of ministers, he said he would reduce budget deficit to no more than four per cent of the Gross Domestic Product and tackle the size of public expenditure, the sure breeder of inflation in the country. He promised to "…create the basic industry in order to reduce Nigeria's dependence on imported raw materials and to stimulate agriculture so that Nigeria could be self-sufficient in food production."[17] Heard that before? Certainly, but here was, as they say, a new sheriff in town.

Babangida seized every available opportunity to preach his new economic gospel. One of the key passages in that gospel was the attraction of foreign investments into the country. At a seminar organised by the African-American Institute and the Nigerian-American Chamber of Commerce in Lagos on September 25, 1985, he expressed regret at the frustrations prospective investors faced from "bureaucratic insensitivity and endless procedural hurdles. He promised to eliminate them and provide "workable incentives" to foreign investors. He noted at his first patron's dinner of the Nigerian Institute of International Affairs about two months later that "the reality remains today that we need foreign investors in order to accelerate and realise some of our national economic objectives."

There were, in fact, several interesting verses in Babangida's new gospel of a new economic order. Here is one that derives its relevance from what he called his government's "slogan for survival and orderly development." He was referring to his Mass Movement for Economic Reconstruction, Social Justice and Self-Reliance, better known by its acronym of MAMSER. It was recommended by the political bureau in line with its preference for taking the country "a little to the left."

This verse deals with reliance as a consequence of "economic reconstruction," that, according to him,

> involves a radical review of our external dependency, building our production process more on our own natural and human resources, switching our growth engine from trading to production, avoiding waste and vanity, shedding all pretences about our affluence, reversing our past life-styles, and accepting the pains of structural adjustment. We must create social justice aimed at promoting equality of opportunity in all spheres of our national life….We are convinced that self-reliance is the strategy for building a new society, where our people can develop the consciousness of being the masters of their own destiny.

He dropped another hint at the graduation ceremony of the seventh executive course, NIPSS. Babangida served notice of tough economic measures in the offing to address the immediate problems of the economy. A past master at drama, Babangida was systematically working on the people, softening them up and preparing them for his economic programme, complete with the bitter pills they must swallow if things must change for the better.

The press encouraged Babangida to take the road not yet travelled in his economic development programme. He must show the will to tackle the fundamental problems of the economy. He must arrest inflation and unemployment and create an enabling socio-political environment to attract foreign investments. His number one priority must be food production. Small-scale farmers must be provided with the necessary agricultural inputs to increase their acreage. The IMF deadlock must be broken quickly because "the entire economy cannot continue to be held hostage to this single issue."[18]

The Triumph, a Kano State government-owned daily, favoured a total restructuring of the economy. It advised the president to ban the importation of completely knocked down parts for the vehicle assembly plants as well the importation of malt, barley and wheat. It also wanted defence spending to be reduced. [19]

One man who was unimpressed by Babangida's move on the economic front was Dr. Junaid Mohammed. He was a member of the House of Representatives from Kano State in the Second Republic. He dismissed the economic emergency and other decisions that Babangida took in the early months of his administration as "...mere a public relations exercise or a sinister diversionary tactic for buying time rather than an honest-to-God approach to come to terms with a real problem. A credible national emergency must be predicated and justified on the basis of concrete, easily discernible threat to the national survival, security, socio-economic, institutional and political wellbeing. Importation of rice does not constitute such a threat." [20]

Mohammed argued that the president's entire economic package was an ill-thought-out policy to win popularity. He had a point. The Babangida regime was new in office and was still feeling its way through public cynicism. It was not out of place for it to take populist measures to win the support and the confidence of the people.

Still, the ban on the importation of rice should be put in its proper context. Through manipulation by businessmen with the active collaboration of politicians in the corridors of power in the Second Republic, rice was elevated to a national staple diet. Federal and state governments imported rice on a massive scale. The rice armada choked the ports and became a national embarrassment. The Shagari administration, perhaps, meant well but the massive and indiscriminate importation of rice from Thailand, Spain and the United States, did not do the reputation of his administration much good. Babangida's decision to ban the importation made a good political and economic sense.

There was a voice of caution too from the academia. The University of Lagos branch of the Academic Staff Union of Universities, ASUU, warned that Babangida's bias towards free enterprise could not pull the country out of its economic predicament and could, indeed, prevent the actualisation of his admittedly "laudable (economic) goals."[21]

Babangida knew he was more or less under sentence of death in the management of the economy. He admitted to a foreign newspaper that he risked losing public support if there were no positive results in the economy within the 15-month economic emergency period.[22] He knew tough decisions had to be made. As he put it:

> We have been a very, very lucky country; got independence on a platter of gold, blessed by God with abundant natural and mineral resources, blessed by God with very good and capable manpower, blessed with people who are well-travelled and, therefore, are able to have a lot of ideas and vision of what they would like to see in their own country. But despite what you have, you still have to take some tough decisions, you have to make life uncomfortable for others; things have to go bad before they get better. Perhaps, we underestimate the capacity of the Nigerian to withstand shock.

Babangida felt that Nigerians were over-governed and this contributed to the general impression held for so long by them that government was Father Christmas, able and willing to provide all things for all the people all of the time:

> When I came in, I believed there was too much government in the life of the Nigerian. Everything is government. Even to clean his house, the Nigerian would love to see government come and do it.

Eight years later, he was disappointed to find that the "mentality still persists." By the time he announced the 1986 budget, his first and Nigeria's 26th, Babangida had arrived at the broad outlines of his economic policy and programme. The main objectives of the policy, enunciated in the 1986 budget, were:

1. to restructure and diversify the productive base of the economy in order to reduce dependence on the oil sector and imports;
2. to achieve a fiscal balance of payments viability over the medium term and
3. to lay the basis for a suitable non-inflationary growth over the medium and long-term.

He built the budget "around policies rather than around projects." With a total expenditure of ₦10.935 billion, the 1986 budget was ₦334 million less than the 1985 budget estimate of ₦11.269 billion. For this and other reasons, the president was confident that "the 1986 budget marks a watershed in the difficult journey towards economic recovery."[23]

It did, indeed. The 1986 budget was the window to the structural adjustment programme, the very controversial economic reform programme on which Babangida staked his reputation and patriotism. In his view, if Nigerians had rejected the IMF prescription, it followed that they had voted for homegrown solutions to the economic problems to be applied "at our own pace and on our own volition, consistent with our own long-term national interest."[24]

What also emerged in that budget was one of the pillars of his economic and social development policies, the Directorate of Foods, Roads and Rural Infrastructure, DFRRI. The directorate was to be funded from about ₦900 million savings from the partial withdrawal of petroleum subsidy that year alone. This was the first major rural development programme for the country since independence. DFRRI would open feeder roads to facilitate rural-urban contact "and to uplift the living conditions of the peasantry who constitutes the overwhelming majority of our citizenry."[25]

Defence had had the highest sectoral vote in federal budgets for nearly two decades. This had always been a subject of intense public debate, particularly since the end of the civil war. Past Nigerian leaders wisely avoided tinkering with it for fear of provoking the military. As Chief of Army Staff in the Buhari administration, Babangida defended this lopsided allocation of fund to the military. His position on this changed somewhat as president. In the 1986 budget, he reduced the recurrent expenditure for defence from ₦806.570 million in 1985 to ₦742.392 million. Its capital vote came down from ₦319.1 million the previous year to ₦164.666 million. The 1986 defence budget was ₦218.591 million leaner than that of 1985.

In 1992, in the twilight of his presidency, Babangida restored defence budget to its primacy. That year, its vote of ₦3.004 billion was eleven per cent of the total federal budget, the highest sectoral allocation.

His defence budget reduction and some other cost-saving measures, including the partial withdrawal of petroleum subsidy in 1986 convinced the IMF and the World Bank that Babangida was taking the right steps in the management of the economy. They had prodded past administrations to withdraw petroleum subsidy and allow the oil companies to charge economic rates without success. The withdrawal of subsidy on petroleum products is always a touchy subject in the country. Nigerians generally feel they are entitled to it as citizens of a major oil-producing country. It has not always been easy to dismiss that sentiment.

Babangida's counter argument was that the country could no longer tolerate a situation in which it was "cheaper to buy petrol than to get drunk (because) a litre of petrol was much, much cheaper than a litre of Coca-Cola or Star lager beer."[26] That argument, a familiar and favourite line of defence by the government and its acolytes, ignored the fundamental difference between petrol and beer and soft drinks. Petrol is a necessity the society can ill afford to do without; beer and soft drinks are luxuries the society can afford to do without.

Government was spending ₦1.4 billion annually on petroleum subsidy. Babangida felt this was too much. He withdrew 80 per cent of the subsidy on petrol and diesel from January 1, 1986. This took the price of petrol from 20 kobo per litre to a princely 39.5 kobo per litre. It touched a raw nerve in the nation. It met with nation-wide protests.

He also decided to commercialise or privatise government parastatals and companies. This too, was not a particularly popular decision. And like the removal of petroleum subsidy, this too did not go down too well with the public. But that decision too has to be put in context.

Federal and state governments owned a variety of industrial and commercial ventures. Some of them were obviously of doubtful social benefits. It is difficult to justify public investments in breweries and distilleries, transport, distributive trade, electrical and electronic appliances and fisheries. Between 1980 and 1985 government investments in its wholly or partially-owned companies and parastatals totalled ₦23 billion. Annual subventions came to ₦11 billion. Annual returns on these huge investments and subventions came to a princely ₦933,701,134. Repayments on the subventions netted the government ₦67, 959,735. Of this, ₦26,124,463 was earned from interest payments on the subventions. Certainly, in the words of the president, these public ventures "have come to constitute an unnecessarily high burden on government resources."[27]

In 1981, Shagari was worried about the poor returns on federal government investments in its companies and parastals. He set up a commission headed by Gamaliel Onosode, a well-known technocrat, to study their operational problems and make recommendations on how to make them viable. The commission confirmed that nearly all the enterprises had become a burden on the federal and state governments. It observed that "many of the problems which seem internal to the parastatals derive from the realities of the social and political environment in which they operate. To propose only reforms internal to the parastatals or in their relations with government as the answer to the problem of getting the parastatals to satisfy public expectations" would, perhaps, miss the point.

It recommended, however that "commercially-oriented parastatals able to subject themselves to the discipline of the capital market should be encouraged to borrow money, on their own, or issue bonds."[28]

It established that the socio-political environment in which these enterprises operated made it difficult for them to perform. In other words, even if they were not viable, the politics of retaining them at public expense must not be ignored. Shagari bought that argument and chose to play safe in an area he knew had political booby traps. But his decision to set up the commission brought the problems of public enterprises into public focus. He had opened the Pandora's Box.

Buhari too appointed a study group, headed by Ali Al-Hakim, the then managing director of the Bank of the North, with the brief to review the financing, profitability and performance records of public ventures. Its findings confirmed those of the Onosode commission. It found that these ventures were hamstrung by a multitude of operational problems ranging from vague and conflicting objectives, inadequate autonomy, inflexibility in decision-making process, inappropriate capital structure, ineffective and inefficient management to over-staffing. It, therefore, recommended selective privatisation of public enterprises.

Privatisation and commercialisation of public enterprises made eminent economic sense but their fate could not be decided solely on the basis of economic imperatives. The point made by the Onosode commission could not be entirely ignored. Public ventures come in handy for political patronage as sources of employment for political supporters and cronies. Board appointments rank next in social and political importance to those of ministers and commissioners.

The political cost of tampering with the status quo must be carefully weighed. It was important to take into consideration public feelings about the government enterprises. Nigerians cherish the feeling of collective ownership of public ventures. Babangida soon found the people in whose interests he took the steps he did, were not prepared, no matter what the statistics said, to change their views or shift their positions as joint owners of these enterprises. They wanted the status quo to remain.

Those who favoured continued public funding of the enterprises argued that commercialising them would deny the people the right to subsidised and cheap services. The public would be forced to pay economic rates. Privatising them amounted to outright deprivation of the people of their property. A new avenue, they said, was being created to make the rich richer and the poor poorer and more deprived.

Buhari appreciated these points and even supported them. He agreed with the findings of the Al-Hakim study group and its recommendation for selective privatisation of public enterprises. But he did not intend to do it in a way that might make the rich richer and the poor poorer. He said it "would be unfair for (his) administration to sell to a few people so that people who buy those shares will just realise so much profits."[29]

Some state military governors under Babangida opposed the privatisation option. Lt-Col. Abubakar Umar, military governor of Kaduna State, said the plan did not enjoy everyone's support and warned against carrying out the programme at the expense of the people. Primordial fears of tribal or sectional domination of the economy were dragged into the debate. Fears were widely expressed over the possibility of the rich from the more economically advantaged sections of the country cornering all the enterprises to the disadvantage of the other sections lagging behind in private enterprise. In plain language, the north would be the worse off.

There was no dissuading Babangida. He strongly believed that the policy would reduce bureaucratic impediments in the operation of the enterprises, enhance efficiency in the management of resources, reduce disguised and open subsidy, boost the development of the nation's capital market, attract foreign capital and even free resources which government could invest in other vital areas of the economy. "The privatisation exercise (was) not an exercise to transfer publicly acquired properties to a few hands as some populist propagandists would make their audience believe," [30] he argued.

He promised that

> ...the divestment process will, however, give special encouragement and preference to groups and institutions like the trade unions, universities, pension funds, voluntary associations, patriotic unions, youth organisations, women societies, local governments and state investment companies. Care will also be taken to avoid the divested holdings from being concentrated in the hands of few individuals or few areas of the country.[31]

Everyone would have a piece of the cake. This point was underlined at the inauguration of the Technical Committee on Privatisation and Commercialisation, TCPC, headed by Vice-Admiral Augustus Aikhomu, Chief of General Staff. Babangida told the committee "to ensure equity and broad-based spread in the allocation and allotment of shares."[32]

The programme took off two years after its announcement in the 1986 budget. Decree 25 promulgated early in July 1988, gave legal backing to the privatisation and commercialisation, partly or wholly, of 86 public enterprises. TCPC was charged with carrying out the programme. The affected enterprises were divided into three broad categories. The first comprised partially privatised companies such as commercial and merchant banks, in which the government retained its equity shares of between five and 60 per cent. Government reduced its equity holdings in the second category such as agricultural co-operative and development banks from 100 to 70 per cent. Oil marketing companies fell into the third category. Government equity shares in companies in this category were brought down to only 40 per cent. It let go its majority share holding in paper and steel mills, sugar companies, fertiliser and cement companies, among others. Government held onto its shares in motor vehicle and truck assembly plants but freed hotels, abattoirs and 59 other enterprises from its hold.

The Manufacturers Association of Nigeria, MAN, welcomed the programme but it doubted that since government control "will still be dominant... the crippling inefficiency that has paralysed government enterprises over the years would be eliminated under a regime of commercialisation and partial privatisation."[33]

III

Babangida's ultimate goal, of course, was the restructuring of the country's economic base. The Structural Adjustment Programme, SAP, was his answer to the problems and the vagaries of the national economy. But the acronym, SAP, soon became the object of both veneration and derision in the public. The programme was to last from July 1, 1986 to June 30, 1988. The rest of 1988 was to be used to consolidate its gains. The policy objectives of the programme were:

- to restructure and diversify the productive base of the economy to lessen its dependence on oil and imports
- to achieve viable fiscal and balance of payment positions
- to lay the basis for sustainable low inflationary growth
- to lessen the dominance of unproductive investments in the public sector and increase the growth potential of the private sector.

Babangida's enthusiasm over the programme was palpable. He said:

Our structural adjustment involves new uses of wealth, new property relations, new products and production processes, new attitudes to work, new consumption habits and new interaction with the rest of the world. It seeks to harmonise what we consume with what we produce, using our own domestic endowment of human and material resources.[34]

The programme was a robust articulation of his philosophy of government as an agent of development. The business of government is to initiate and implement the right policies, create the right atmosphere and let "all citizens (be) producers, workers and consumers."[35]

SAP was innovative in the economic management of the country but it was not saying anything particularly new. After all, "adjustment is part of the process of existence of any human beings or human institutions."[36] But the question was: Whose SAP was it? Was it the much-resented and derided IMF formula for ailing Third World economies? Its critics believed so. Government insisted it was its own homegrown version. Nigeria's homegrown alternative would be equally tough on the people but it was merely pain before gain.

Suspicion remained strong that the IMF and the World Bank had hands in the programme. The experts felt Esau's hairy hands but heard Jacob's voice. Periodic inspection visits by officials of the Bretton Woods Institution to monitor the implementation of the programme appeared to confirm the suspicion and fuelled opposition to it. A World Bank publication confirmed that Babangida presented a budget reform package to the IMF and the World Bank in 1986. It said that the budget reform package

> …contained a package of export incentives incorporating trade liberalisation but without a change in the import licensing system. The petroleum subsidy was reduced by 80 per cent, and a commitment was made to privatisation. Although an exchange rate adjustment was mentioned, the Naira was not devalued.
> Nigeria's creditors, and the World Bank and the IMF, did not accept the package of reforms in the absence of devaluation measures. Thus, in August 1986, the government announced its structural adjustment programme, whose central feature was a two-tier system to devalue the Naira.[37]

Professor Bolaji Akinyemi, Minister of External Affairs, referred to SAP as *The Babangida Formula*. The World Bank was one of the first international institutions to praise the programme. Its representative in Nigeria, Ishrat Husain, described it as the "most comprehensive economic adjustment programme in Africa so far (and) a role model in Africa for free-market changes and responsible government."[38] President Ronald Reagan of the United States praised SAP as "a reflection of President Babangida's leadership, courage and vision."[39] The US ambassador in Nigeria, Princeton Lyman, described it as "one of the most exciting economic reforms in Africa."[40]

These lavish praises for the programme from quarters suspected to have a hand in it provided its opponents with enough ammunition for a sustained barrage of criticisms. However, despite the initial misgivings, the programme promised exciting and challenging times for Nigerians.

Self-reliance took on a new meaning. However, the programme, as Nigerians soon found out, was not an instant magical cure for the economy; nor was it intended to eliminate poverty in one fell swoop. While thousands of Nigerians took up the challenges of SAP by going into small and medium-scale private ventures, others waited for the magic manna they believed the proponents of the programme promised. It never came because no such manna existed.

In the early eighties, the World Bank and the IMF pushed Shagari to devalue the naira. They believed the national currency was over-valued. This was one of the conditions the Fund attached to the country's application for a bridging loan of $2.7 billion requested by the Shagari administration. Shagari rejected that condition.

Buhari too refused to consider an outright devaluation of the Naira. Instead, he "adopted a gradual depreciation of the Naira exchange rate in 1985."[41] The value fell from $1.22372 to the Naira in December 1984 to $1.2046 at the end of January 1985. About four months after Babangida took over from Buhari, the Naira exchanged for $1.0004.[42]

This was still unsatisfactory to both the IMF and the World. They insisted that the key to any meaningful economic reforms in the country lay in the devaluation of the Naira, import liberalisation, privatisation of public enterprises and the removal of all subsidies, particularly on petroleum products.

Despite his courage to dare, Babangida shied away from outright devaluation of the Naira. Instead, he decided to allow market forces to determine its value relative to the dollar and other world currencies. His economic advisers believed this was a better option for the country.

The Bretton Woods institutions demanded that the Naira be devalued by between 50 and 65 per cent. The president's economic advisers believed that if the market forces were allowed to determine the *realistic* exchange rate, it would be much less than what the World Bank/IMF wanted. Their prediction was that the Naira would find its level between ₦3.00 and ₦3.50 to the dollar. Whether that was the *realistic* value was debatable. In any case, the novelty of the idea was irresistible to Babangida with his well-known fondness for innovation.

The new exchange mechanism took off on January 27, 1986, with a Second-tier Foreign Exchange Market, SFEM. Government introduced "a floating exchange rate mechanism tied to market-determined forces"[43] through SFEM.

The new foreign exchange mechanism consisted of two tiers. The first was the official exchange rate for public service transactions. Private foreign exchange transactions were funded through the second tier, SFEM. The SFEM rate was determined by market forces at bidding sessions attended by the banks at the Central Bank of Nigeria. Babangida promised that SFEM would be operated like other open markets - free from undue bureaucratic bottlenecks. Sellers and buyers would be free to interact. His hope was that through this mechanism, the rates at the two tiers would converge before the end of the programme. Their convergence would be the *realistic* value of the naira. His economic advisers predicted this would be about four naira to the dollar. Their worst case scenario was five naira to the dollar. The president himself, "talking as a layman, an ordinary man who has no idea about what the economy is all about,..was looking to see a situation where the exchange rate will be ₦3.50 to ₦4.00 to the dollar."[44]

Babangida was praised for choosing this option. SFEM was described as a timely "semi-official market from where importers will purchase foreign currency at a more realistic exchange rate."[45] There was some degree of relief in the foreign exchange market with the introduction of this option. Industrialists and importers who always faced the difficulties of obtaining letters of credit appreciated the relative freedom under SFEM that enabled them to buy their foreign exchange needs.

Import licences were abolished. For the first time in its history, Nigeria operated two parallel rates of foreign exchange. Professor Samuel Aluko, a professor of economics and one of the biggest critics of SAP, predicated that the "hawking of the Naira" would ultimately have a deleterious effect on the economy.

He did not speak too soon. Within two weeks of SFEM, the Naira was effectively devalued by 66 per cent. Within two months, five Naira bought one US dollar at the official rate. The parallel rate was between ₦6.50 and ₦7.00 to the dollar. The consumer index, a function of inflation, rose from 5.4 per cent before SFEM to 10.2 per cent in less than one year of the new foreign exchange regime.

The SFEM option turned out to have served a limited political objective. It ultimately undermined the policy objectives of the structural adjustment programme. Once the market forces were let loose on the Naira, no one could hold them back. The storm burst in the face of the government. The press accused the government of taking "the back door route to the devaluation of the Naira, thus throwing the whole economy into an unknown wilderness."[46] *The Nigerian Tribune* predicted that the Naira "will collapse in the free-for-all that will ensue"[47] Prices of goods and services rose immediately in response to the new development in the foreign exchange market. This was the beginning of the difficulties that gave the programme a bad name.

Government tardiness in handling the new exchange policy was partly to blame. For almost three months after the president announced the new policy, nothing was known about it. There was no enabling law. Its operational method was not spelt out. The business community was in a quandary. The enabling decree was finally released on September 23 and took effect from September 29. By the time the decree came into effect, suspicion was rife that government had taken a loan from the World Bank to fund SFEM. Said *Lagos News:* "We are having a World Bank loan in place of the IMF loan to start the second-tier exchange market. Is there any practical difference between the two?"[48]

Babangida was forced to deny in his independence anniversary broadcast that year that government took a World Bank loan to fund the foreign exchange.

The foreign exchange market, it soon became clear, had become the Achilles heels of the structural adjustment programme. Rules were changed in response to predictions gone awry. The bidding session was changed from weekly to fortnightly in October 1986. The Dutch auction was introduced in April 1987. Under the old system, bids for foreign exchange were arranged in descending order. A line was then drawn at the point where the amount offered for sale was exhausted. The average of bidding above the line was taken. This became the official rate until the next bidding session. This method was criticised on the grounds that it encouraged high bids by the banks. The banks tended to outbid one another in order to meet the foreign exchange needs of their customers.

Under the Dutch auction, a bank bought forex at its bid rate and re-sold at one per cent above that rate. Again, this created a new problem - the emergence of multiple rates. To avoid this new problem, this method was scrapped. Government, clearly, was beginning to catch at the straw.

In July 1987, SFEM was scrapped and replaced with Foreign Exchange Market, FEM. This was supposed to mean that the official and unofficial rates had merged. But they did not. Both rates remained in effect, with Naira rapidly losing at the parallel market. In 1989, government tried another system. It "replaced the auction with the inter-bank foreign exchange market, (IFEM), allowing the Central Bank to determine the exchange rate on a daily basis."[49]

In less than one year *Babangidanomics* had resulted in "the increasing dilemma of the ordinary man."[50] The deregulated economy was frustrated by the weak foundation on which the new foreign exchange regime was built. The Central Bank did not have enough foreign exchange to meet the burgeoning demands of the banks and their customers. At the best of times, the CBN could meet only 25 per cent of these demands. The alternative market, even with a higher rate, became the more viable option for importers. This, invariably, meant higher prices.

The scramble among companies and individuals for foreign exchange at the official rate led, inevitably, to corrupt practices in the banks. Corrupt bank officials charged commissions under the table on the foreign exchange they sold at the official rate. At the beginning, the commission was ₦1.50 per dollar. Within six months, it was ₦3.00 per dollar. In effect, the lower rate at the official market was meaningless.

The ordinary man could not escape the consequences of the travail of the national currency in the foreign exchange market. Chukwuemeka Odumegwu-Ojukwu summarised the dilemma of the ordinary man in these words: "In the past, you needed a pocketful of Naira to bring home a basketful of goods; now you seem to need a basketful of Naira in order to bring back a pocketful of goods."[51]

Professor Aluko believed the government was more concerned with "manipulating the exchange rate value of the Naira than in structurally transforming the Nigerian economy from an essentially primary producing to an industrial one."[52]

The barrage of criticisms against the programme was unrelenting. Babangida fought back, maintaining that there was no viable alternative to the programme, whatever anyone might say. The country had taken an irrevocable step in the management of its economy. As he put it: "We cannot return to the pre-SAP days of over-valued Naira and unbridled spending of more than we earned."[53]

Even Babangida had begun to appreciate the fact that the odds were piling up against him. The economy had turned sluggish and made the pains of SAP sharper for the most vulnerable socio-economic class, the poor. The critics of the adjustment programme gratuitously played up these pains. Eghosa Osagie, a professor of economics at the University of Jos, argued:

> The most frightening aspect of the Nigerian structural adjustment (programme) is the adverse effects on the living conditions of vulnerable groups such as children, women, students, the unemployed, the sick, the elderly and surprisingly enough, the rudimentary middle class which is being wiped out by the effects of structural adjustment.[54]

Perhaps, the most telling criticism came from Obasanjo. At a public function in November 1987, the former head of state said:

> It appears to me that we now have a structural adjustment programme, which seems to drastically reduce the living standard of all classes of productive workers except speculators and commission agents. If we are substantially dictated to, let us tell those who preach trade liberalisation and other harmful measures to us, and which they do not practise on the ruins of their own economy and at great hardship to their own people, that they are leading us along the path of great economic decline, social dislocation and turbulence and political consequences that we can ill-afford. Adjustment is part of the process of existence of any human being or human institution. It is part of our daily expe-

rience. But adjustment must have human face, human heart and milk of human kindness and must not ignore what I call human survival and dignity issues of employment, food, shelter, education and health.[55]

Obasanjo's criticism shook Babangida although he told *Newswatch* magazine that the former head of state's criticism "did not bother me as a person."[56] He maintained that his belief in the efficacy of the programme remained strong. But from this point on, according to one of his close aides, his personal frustration with the relentless barrage of criticisms of the programme began the slow but steady process of corroding his own confidence in it. He still put up a brave face, somehow convinced that he would prove his critics wrong because "we are on course in our determined search for a stable developmental path, anchored on a sound economic foundation that can enable us to assert ourselves proudly and confidently in the comity of nations."[57]

Nine months later, however, he admitted that the programme was in some difficulties because "not everything has gone the way we wanted them to. We have problems in implementation."[58]

The Manufacturers Association of Nigeria released its study on the effects of SAP on industries in August 1988. It showed that capacity utilisation was still low - 35 per cent. The study blamed it on "inadequate and inefficient infrastructural facilities, high interest rates, especially for the small and medium-scale manufacturing enterprises, sharp increases in the cost of imported inputs arising from the devaluation of the Naira."[59]

Enormous pressure built up on the economy. Most of the small and medium-scale industries were unable to obtain foreign exchange to import their raw materials and spare parts. They were forced to either close down or drastically scale down their production. It resulted in the loss of jobs for hundreds of workers. Although Babangida still argued, with some justification, that "Nigerians are now a more rational, cost-conscious and efficient people,"[60] public frustration with the programme was on the boil. Something was bound to give.

In May 1989, it did. So-called anti-SAP riots broke out in Lagos and quickly spread to other major towns across the country. Babangida refused to accept the riots were a spontaneous reaction to economic pains caused by SAP. He believed instead that his detractors, who merely used SAP as "an excuse to wage war against the government in order to destroy the credibility of the military institution."[61]

At the inauguration of the Armed Forces Consultative Assembly on June 5 that year, Babangida spoke at length about the sinister objectives of the critics of the programme. He was, he said, "aware of agitations for the termination of SAP" but he was not prepared to yield because

> This administration is committed to the programme because there is no viable alternative. We cannot and we should not abandon this programme mid-way because the pains of trying to re-introduce it at a later stage will be worse than the current pains.[62]

He did not deny that there were problems with the programme. But in spite of them, he believed SAP was making a satisfactory progress. He underlined that point:

> The reports we have received and which we would like the opponents of SAP to know is that the prevailing situation in Nigeria is by far better than in any other African country. It is even better than the condition in most Third World states.[63]

The riots broke out when the ADB men were in Nigeria for a conference. A delegate to the conference was quoted as saying that "the pains of the structural adjustment are such that they are not widely spread. In particular, the poorer population does not benefit in the same pact as the other people in the privileged positions."[64]

Babangida had to do something to show that the programme was not a punishment designed by the rich to punish the poor. In the wake of the riots, therefore, he unveiled some populist goodies to give SAP a human face, if not the milk of human kindness. The highlights of what came to be known as SAP relief package were:

- All vacancies in primary and secondary schools to be filled immediately
- National Directorate of Employment to give jobs to 62,000 unemployed graduates and semi-skilled labour
- ₦100 million extra budgetary grant to be released immediately to fund job and food boosting programmes
- Federal and state ministries of works to use direct labour massively and also offer jobs to engineers and surveyors
- All schools to establish farms to boost nation's food production
- Importation of spare parts duty free
- Mass transit in Lagos to be given special attention
- Mass importation of drugs
- Easy access to foreign exchange by pharmaceutical companies to be facilitated to ease the importation of drugs and medicaments
- Importation of mass transit buses and spare parts at a cost of $30 million to the government.

These measures constituted a panic reaction to the criticisms of the programme. More importantly, they showed that SAP had begun to exact its political price. The relief package was calculated to shore up public confidence in SAP but it was an embarrassing evidence that a) government had lost its bearing and was clutching at the straw to salvage its image and b) government was stubbornly sticking to a programme which, even if it did not admit it in so many words, had proved obviously disastrous for the economy, the country and the people.

SAP was admittedly good in conception. Its philosophic base was unimpeachable. So, what went wrong with a programme that promised so much, not the least its radical approach to the management of the nation's economy? There is a one-word answer: implementation. Babangida himself admitted this. The Guardian newspaper observed, quite correctly that "because of poor execution, distortions have befogged and bogged down a programme that was expected to move the country forward."[65]

The first year of the programme was, perhaps, its best year. Government showed a determination to faithfully prosecute it. Trade liberalisation which saw the abolition of import licences, the scrapping of the commodity boards and the removal of virtually all import restrictions as well as the devaluation of the Naira through the instrumentality of market forces, all took place in the first few months of SAP. Ironically, the seeds of public disenchantment with the programme were also sowed during this period. The promise of a quick fix was a fundamental error because when there was no evidence of this, the apostles of the programme were stymied. In the 1988-89 period "the programme stalled and, in some areas, such as controls on the budget deficit and the growth of money supply, it even regressed."[66]

SAP faced domestic politics. Labour and student leaders agitated for a kinder, gentler SAP. Government, anxious to respond to domestic politics, hacked at the pillars of the programme in attempts to accommodate some flexibility. It backed away from total withdrawal of petroleum subsidy. The anti-SAP riots taught the government the elementary lesson that no matter how well-intentioned its actions might be, it could not take the people's support for granted. By 1989, the main planks of SAP had become rusty. The economy was more or less ignored as Babangida pursued another agenda - the political programme.

IV

A piece of luck. In late 1990, Iraq invaded Kuwait to annex the country it said was once an Iraqi province. The United States and its Western allies ordered Iraq to withdraw. It refused. Early in 1991, the United States led its allies into a war to liberate Kuwait from Iraqi occupation.

The war disrupted oil supplies from the Gulf region. The price of oil suddenly rose. The price increase brought a $12.1 billion windfall into the national coffers. However, with this windfall, "fiscal discipline broke down once more (because) established budgetary procedures were by-passed and the strategic planning processes that had been established under the structural adjustment programme were largely ignored. Of major concern was the expenditure of oil revenue without any apparent budgetary authorisation."[67]

Fiscal indiscipline leads to deficit spending. In 1991, the federal government deficit was ₦35.5 billion. Babangida failed in his promise to end deficit spending.

To see SAP primarily as an economic management tool with a time frame, as Babangida did, was to vest it with a limited vision. This was Babangida's number one mistake. SAP was bigger, much bigger than that. It was essentially a process for national economic transformation at the micro and macro levels. The programme butted its head against the walls of entrenched economic and political interests. Those interests fought back.

Again, Babangida prosecuted the economic war with some pity on the "enemies." Thus, by 1989,

> rent-seeking interest groups who lost out during the initial period of the structural adjustment programme, had resurfaced and undermined the reform process. For example, the closure of several inefficient industries prompted the Manufacturers Association of Nigeria to seek and obtain greater protection. The government also lost much ground on trade liberalisation to large agricultural interests by increasing the number of items under import bans.[68]

The cynical manipulation of the exchange rate regime, the orchestrated noise about the pains of the programme, local and international pressure on the government to lift the ban on the importation of wheat, rice, barley and malt as well as the World Bank/IMF insistence on trade liberalisation all exerted tremendous pressure on the programme. Trade liberalisation was clearly inconsistent with the programme. Self-reliance cannot be reasonably pursued simultaneously with trade liberalisation. The World Bank/IMF saw no contradiction in this policy.

SAP was a national challenge. Its philosophy of self- and national-reliance was in tune with modern economic thoughts and development. The programme offered options for Nigeria's development strategy. It remains an irony that the opportunities the programme offered were frittered away in a needless pre-occupation with limited and immediate gains. For instance, manufacturers failed to take advantage of the policy objectives of the programme to search for alternative local raw materials for their industries. Some half-hearted efforts made by the breweries to use sorghum in place of malt and barley, were abandoned for the easier option of imported raw materials.

Necessity failed to become the mother of invention in the country under the programme. SAP sought to pull government off the back of Nigerians. The National Economic Reconstruction Fund, NERFUND, the National Directorate of Employment, NDE, Peoples Bank of Nigeria, PBN, the Directorate of Foods, Roads and Rural Infrastructure, DFRRI, were all part of the core policy of the programme.

SAP led to a phenomenal growth in the financial sector, thanks to deregulation. The number of commercial banks, for instance, rose from 28 in 1985 to 66 in 1990. There were twelve merchant banks in the country before SAP. In 1990, four years after the programme was introduced, there were 54 of them. The number of finance and mortgage institutions rose from almost nothing in 1985 to 600 in 1990. The abuses to which they were later subjected could not be blamed on SAP.

The economy was Babangida's greatest source of worry when he took over power in 1985. He set out to cure the structural defects of the economy and make it modern, healthy and progressive. SAP was his tool of choice. Babangida displayed courage of his personal vision and conviction. But he did not realise his promise because in his own words, "the economy proved to be a more difficult nut to crack."

He blames the failure of his economic reform programme partly on what he calls "the human factor" and partly on the fact that Nigerians have no stomach for difficulties, discipline and the patience required to prosecute long-term plans. Despite his personal frustrations with the results of the programme, Babangida left office in 1993 holding strongly to his belief that he chose the right development tool for the country because:

> We have unleashed a lot in terms of political awareness, in terms of economic liberalisation to such an extent that you just have to work to make it. There will come a time when the next generation will have no alternative but to work. It is a matter of time. The culture has to change.

It can be said, with some justification that the failure of Babangida's economic reform programme was, to borrow the title of David Stockman's controversial book, a *triumph of politics.*

The General steps out

*The signature smile. Babangida steps in as president,
August 27, 1985*

Babangida and members of his Armed Forces Ruling Council

Babangida and First Lady Maryam Babangida with British Prime Minister Margaret Thatcher and her husband, Dennis

Babangida, First Lady Maryam with Queen Elizabeth II and Prince Philip at Buckingham Palace

Babangida and the legendary Nelson Mandela

Babangida with fellow African leaders

Babangida with F. de Klerk, president of South Africa

Babangida with Flight Lt Jerry Rawlings of Ghana

Babangida talks to reporters

*Babangida with his first Chief of General Staff,
Commodore Ebitu Ukiwe*

Babangida with the late PLO leader Yassir Arafat

*Caring mother. First Lady Maryam Babangida
and her baby daughter, Halima*

*The family man. Despite the pressures of office as president,
Babangida still found time to cuddle his last child, Halima*

Chummy, chummy. Babangida and the late Chief M.K.O. Abiola

Major Gideon Orkar (1st left) and his fellow coup plotters at their trial. Their failed coup against Babangida redefined his presidency

Hand in hand. Babangida and General Sani Abacha

His winning ways. Babangida with the late Chief Obafemi Awolowo

At the launch of the Peoples Bank at Ajegunle, a suburb of Lagos, Babangida pays out the first loan granted by the bank to Mrs. Hannah Ilodibe (first right). In the middle is the managing director of the bank, Mrs. Maria Sokenu

First Lady Maryam Babangida. She brought glamour and panache to the office of First Lady in Nigeria

Babangida with Vice-President Admiral August Aikhomu (2nd right) and service chiefs at an independence anniversary parade

Chapter Thirteen

A New Political Order

Our political programme must be gradual, purposeful and effective
—President Ibrahim Babangida

Babangida, certainly, came away with some vital political lessons during the Murtala/Obasanjo military administration. He put them to good use as soon as he assumed office. It is, therefore, easy to see some similarities between his script and the Murtala Muhammed script.

General Murtala Muhammed began his brief reign by showing that he *was* not Gowon. He came up with a definite political programme that touched all the areas where Gowon prevaricated – return to civil rule, creation of more states, posting of military governors outside their states of origin and selecting a new virgin land for Nigeria's new federal capital. His prompt dealing with these lingering issues made him very popular.

Babangida similarly showed he *was* not Buhari. Buhari had no programme for returning the country to civil rule. He made no secret of that. At a world press conference in January 1984, he said that the Supreme Military Council had not discussed a transition to civil rule programme because

> I think the problem we have now is how to revive the economy of the country, ensure discipline at home and respect abroad. After that we will think of what to do next.[1]

Nigerians generally welcomed the return of the military in 1983 but interminable military rule was out of the question. No one knew this better than Babangida. Five and half months after he took over, he took a pragmatic step to show the people he shared their anxiety for the return to civil rule. He inaugurated a 17-man Political Bureau on January 13, 1986. The primary brief of the bureau was to provide the framework for a new constitution and "time sequences for the transition (to civil rule) to be achieved by October 1, 1990."[2]

Babangida did not want to fix the economy before returning the country to civil rule. It was a wise political move. In his independence anniversary broadcast in October 1985, he had said that

> ...what really lies at the bottom of our past dilemma is the absence of a viable political arrangement. The political history of this nation is partly one of disillusionment with politics and politicians. We must, therefore, begin a vigorous search for a New Political Order.

He returned to the same theme one year later in his 1986 independence anniversary speech in which he said that "the establishment of a viable political system is...an essential prerequisite for the achievement of our national goals and objectives" and one, which his government would "be proud to bequeath to posterity."

With the inauguration of the political bureau, Babangida set out on a political odyssey with the ultimate objective of fundamentally restructuring Nigerian politics. The bureau, headed by an educationist, Samuel Cookey, was given the following five terms of reference:

- Review Nigeria's political history and identify the basic problems which have led to our failure in the past and suggest ways of resolving and coping with these problems;
- Identify a basic philosophy of government, which will determine goals and serve as a guide to the activities of government;
- Collect relevant information and data for the government as well as identify other political problems that may arise from the debate;
- Gather, collate and evaluate the contributions of Nigerians to the search for a viable political future and provide guidelines for the attainment of the consensus objectives;
- Deliberate on other political problems as may be referred to it from time to time.

Babangida believed that Nigeria needed a political system "capable of ensuring sustained economic growth and social development."[3] The country's main political problem was "the absence of a viable political arrangement."[4] This problem could not be resolved unless and until a unique political system was found for the country. The bureau's task was to find this magic political formula. The president told the bureau at its inauguration:

> I would like to warn that this administration does not want a regurgitation of the political models of the so-called advanced countries of the world. If this were our desire, we would not have wasted your time, and ours, by inviting

you here. Rather, we would simply have turned to the many volumes and various encyclopaedias on these alien constitutions. We cannot, indeed, we must not, lift foreign models (because) we share neither the political history nor the political cultures of these lands.[5]

The president was travelling on a well-beaten track. In 1975, the late General Murtala Ramat Muhammed set up a 50-man Constitution Drafting Committee, CDC, and tasked it with finding such a unique political system for the country. The 49 wise men (Awolowo refused to serve on it) found no such system. Instead, they fell back on an existing political system - the American style executive presidential system. The military administration adopted it in the 1979 constitution for the Second Republic.

The British parliamentary system carried the watering can for the country's political problems in the First Republic. There was no empirical evidence for this. But no one needed any. If the 49 wise men and the military believed the answer lay in the wholesale importation of the American model, then they must be right in the sentiments of the times. If military intervention is a measure of the failure of a political system, then the system imposed on the country in the 1979 constitution too failed and must be regarded as unsuitable for the country.

Was Babangida merely in motion? It is doubtful that Babangida seriously believed that there was a new political formula waiting to be discovered by the bureau. It would be more sensible to say that what he wanted was a radical shake-up in the country's political system. He intended to do more than run a transition programme. His ambition was to lay "such foundations for political stability as will render unnecessary military intervention as a vehicle for alternating or changing governments."[6]

He had his own ideas on how to go about it. He was in love with ideas. He needed the collective inputs of the nation for two good reasons. The first was to enable him measure his ideas against those of the rest of the country. The second and more important reason was to convince Nigerians that they and their president were taking a collective decision to reshape the polity.

The bureau went to work. Its members met 149 times in nine months and visited all the then 301 local government areas in the country. It received 14,961 memoranda. Oral submissions brought in 1,723 recorded audio and videotapes. Its members pored through 3,933 press clips in the great search for the new, unique political system waiting to be discovered.

II

Babangida was in a hurry for change. Only five months into the work of the bureau, he announced one of his most controversial decisions - a ten-year blanket ban on all former public office holders since independence in 1960. "The time has come for a new generation of men and women to take up the leadership mantle of this country," Babangida said with presidential finality

Again, he did what the Obasanjo administration refused to do in 1978. The Constituent Assembly tried to persuade that administration to ban the same people. The administration refused. Obasanjo was being sensible. If he had caved into that demand, Chief Obafemi Awolowo would have been the most prominent victim of the ban because of his indictment by the Coker Commission.

The fuss kicked up by the ban was predictable. Those affected by it denounced it in purple prose. Nigerians being such excitable people, it is often difficult to correctly gauge the depth of public reactions to matters of this nature. On the face of it, the ban enjoyed wide, if not popular, support. It was a courageous decision anchored almost entirely on the shifting sands of public sentiment. Babangida was aware that many Nigerians blamed civilian leaders for all the political, economic and social problems of the country. Public sentiment favoured marginalising those of them who had been in government over the years. Even if Babangida did not share in that sentiment, he appreciated the import of identifying himself with it. Time to give younger people a chance to have a crack at the leadership of the country.

Clearly, the president had drawn a line in the sand. The ban served its immediate political purposes. It unleashed a carefully calibrated military propaganda to whip up public sentiment against those affected by it. The objective was to create a watershed in the politics of the country - the past for the former leaders whose failure invited the military into government and the present and the future for the young Nigerians as yet untainted by the lures of lucre and power.

Government expressly forbade the so-called new breed politicians from fraternising with the so-called old breed, also known in military parlance as *discredited politicians*. Events, as they sometimes do, proved the fallacy of this great divide in the life of the Babangida administration. Seven years after the ban was imposed, it was lifted. It had failed to achieve its purpose. Hardly surprising. The blanket ban was a cop out on the part of the Babangida administration. The military chose to punish everyone rather than separate the innocent from the guilty. Most of those affected by the ban committed no more grievous offence than that they served their country. They had to be punished, according to Babangida's sense of justice typified by his confessed belief in "collective punishment." Civilians who served military regimes were not affected by the ban. Babangida's argument was that they were called to serve their country under the military. Hardly a great defence of a decision long on sentiment.

The bureau ploughed on with its task. In his broadcast on February 3, 1986, Cookey listed 28 items for public debate. Almost nothing of importance was left out in its work - politics, the economy, interest groups, the tiers of government, bureaucracy and development. Although Nigerians responded with memoranda to the bureau, the quality of their contributions to the form of government best suited to the country betrayed a frayed national nerve over frequent constitution-making as a solution to the country's political problems. It is only in a nation which has run out of new ideas that the following could have been suggested for consideration as forms of government: *communocracy, trumbatism, womenocracy, culture-based one-party* and *triarchy*. If that was a joke, then as William Churchill would say, the titter ill-accorded with the tocsin.

Awolowo had warned that the search by the bureau would be fruitless. The fault, he argued, was not in the system but in Nigerians because "we have not got the temperament that is suited to the successful functioning of any of the two systems."

Fourteen and half months after the bureau began its search, it ended. At the formal submission of the report to government through Aikhomu, Cookey exulted:

> If our recommendations are accepted and implemented, Nigerians can, with firm and conscientious leadership, move into an era of political stability, balanced development and true national greatness based on the principles of social justice, economic self-reliance and unity.[7]

His positive exaggeration was silent on the failure of the bureau to find that unique magic political formula for the country. Like the 49 wise men before them, members of the bureau opted for the same American-type executive presidential system for the country. It argued, and this was hardly original, that "the presidential system is the best for Nigeria (because) the need at this point in our political history (is) for a single, popularly-elected executive with its merits of unity and energy."[8]

The Constitution Drafting Committee, CDC, made the same point almost ten years earlier in rejecting the parliamentary system. In recommending the executive presidential system in preference to the parliamentary system, the committee said that the "energy in the executive is a leading character in the definition of good government (because) the unity of a single executive clearly conduces more to energy and despatch."⁹

Much of the script by the bureau agreed substantially with Babangida's idea of the new Nigerian nation he was trying to build. The route to the new nation lay in a transition programme designed as "a training process that would eradicate the ills of Nigeria's political system."¹⁰ It faulted the Murtala/Obasanjo transition programme as "defective and inadequate."¹¹

Babangida found this argument utterly persuasive. His more durable alternative was

> ... a broadly-spaced transition in which democratic governance can proceed with political learning, institutional adjustments and at sequential levels of politics and governance, beginning with local government and ending at federal level. From our past experience, our political programme must be gradual, purposeful and effective (to enable the regime lay) such foundations for political stability as will render unnecessary military intervention as a vehicle for alternating or changing governments.¹²

Most of the recommendations of the bureau hardly made any waves. Some of them were patently curious. For how long should the Babangida administration stay in power? Nigerians have always had a remarkably ambivalent attitude towards this question. They recognised military rule as an aberration but an aberration they were willing to tolerate as a rationalised inevitability – and only for a period brief.

When Buhari took over in 1983, some well-informed politicians and traditional rulers recommended a minimum of 50 years for the military. This, certainly, did not reflect the majority of public opinion but it showed the ambivalence of Nigerians to military rule.

The Babangida administration chose its own terminal date of October 1 1990. The bureau approved the 1990 terminal date as the wish of most Nigerians. It then proceeded to work out the "the time sequences" for a three-year transition programme. But four of its members disagreed with the 1990 terminal date. Their minority report recommended October 1, 1992. They argued that 1990 did not provide enough time for the political education of the people, which was necessary for the success of the third republic.

It was up to the AFRC to decide. The council set up a select committee to study the recommendations of the bureau and produce a government white paper on them. The committee, headed by Major-General Paul Omu, submitted its report on May 18, 1987. Curiously, it accepted neither 1990 nor 1992 recommended by the majority and the minority members of the bureau respectively. The committee chose a new date - October 1, 1995.

It was easy to see the purpose this third option served. It gave the AFRC two extreme options - 1990 and 1995 - and a middle ground - 1992. The council opted for the middle ground "in the circumstances (and given) the major issues which must be tackled before military disengagement."[13]

The socialist alternative proffered by the bureau stood on thin ice. Socialism was crumbling in Eastern Europe at that time. Less than a year after the bureau ended its assignment, the USSR, the bastion of socialism, disintegrated and the constituent states of the socialist republic went their separate ways.

The AFRC rejected the socialist alternative for the rather funny reason that it would amount to the "imposition of a political ideology on the nation"[14] but accepted the agency for social mobilisation recommended by the bureau as an essential component of the socialist alternative. The truth is that Babangida found them mutually exclusive. He needed the agency, named Mass Mobilisation for Social Justice, Self-reliance and Economic Recovery, MAMSER, to propagate his new political order. He launched MAMSER on September 2, 1987. He said that the nation needed MAMSER "to inculcate new values, politically educate the adult, socialise the young and mobilise the masses for participation in the new order."[15]

Babangida's burning ambition was to bury the past. The bureau helped along. Its recommendation for a two-party system to be substantially funded by the government agreed entirely with Babangida's own idea of a new political system. The revolutionary impact of this recommendation must be appreciated against the background of Nigeria's political history. Since independence from British colonial rule in 1960, Nigeria had operated a multi-party system. The one-party system, which took root in many newly independent African countries never found strong advocates in Nigeria. Political parties in the country tended to exploit certain weaknesses in the socio-political system to the detriment of the corporate interests of Nigeria.

In the First Republic, the three leading political parties, NPC, AG and NCNC, were regionally based. The smaller political parties were more of political pressure groups fighting for certain vested interests such as the creation of new regions, revenue allocation and promoting and protecting the peculiar political interests of the minorities. Each of the big parties drew the bulk of its followership from its own region. So jealously did each party guard its regional turf that it did not tolerate other parties fishing for support in its backyard. The intolerance that characterised the politics of the First Republic left ugly marks on the national psyche. Most

Nigerians would rather not have that kind of politics again. Babangida knew that popular opinion favoured the de-regionalisation of politics.

The Murtala/Obasanjo regime too appreciated this and addressed it in the enabling law of its transition to civil rule programme. The electoral act of that administration made it mandatory for all political parties to have a national spread. They were required to have offices in at least two-thirds of the states of the federation. However, this legal requirement was observed mainly on paper. No physical proof of the offices was required and none was given.

The parties easily settled back into the old mould of regionalism as more or less reincarnations of the parties of the First Republic. Thus in the Second Republic, the biggest parties were firmly rooted in the old regions. NPN was "northern;" UPN "western;" and NPP, "eastern." PRP was NEPU. The GNPP was essentially the Bornu State Movement.

There is much to be said for the bureau's belief that the two-party system was "the best for Nigeria at this time."[16] It argued that it would scale down the degree of competition, always fierce in Nigerian politics. The bureau also recommended substantial funding of the parties by the government to "control the role that money should play in the fortunes of political parties and candidates at the polls."[17]

Babangida found these recommendations irresistible. He was convinced that the two-party system would "..avoid the noise, the clamour, the confusion and the violence which had been the bane of our partisan political experience (and) put an end to the inter-ethnic and inter-personal feuds which dominated the pattern of partisan politics in the past."[18]

The two-party system received an enthusiastic welcome throughout the country. Its generally wide acceptance even encouraged General Obasanjo to canvass for a one-party system in his new book, *Constitution for National Development*. Still, there were possible fears over the two-party system. The strongest was the fear of its polarising the country along religious lines with Christians predominating in one and Muslims in the other. Babangida says he was "very, very scared" about this ugly possibility. He was not alone. Some of his colleagues in the AFRC also feared that the two-party system "might lead to polarisation." Babangida read press reports and opinion pieces about the possibility of the two-party system dividing the country along north-south or Christian-Muslim fault lines.

Somehow, Babangida overcame his fear and "kept on insisting (to his AFRC colleagues) that "the two-party system would not polarise the country along religious or geo-political lines" because, as he put it:

> I want to believe that as long as everybody in this country accepts that (we) will remain a united country, then the question of going along religious lines is

out of it. I hope the people who are coming to take over the leadership of this country are not going to see themselves as representatives of religion A or B. I have not the slightest doubt whatsoever that there will be no polarisation along religious lines as far as the two-party system is concerned.[19]

But the fears about the possible religious divide were not unfounded. Religion had become a strong factor in Nigerian politics. The "smuggling" of Nigeria into the Organisation of Islamic Countries, OIC, by the Babangida administration blew the ashes from the smouldering face of religious fire. A fierce verbal war pitted Muslims against Christians. Everyone was apprehensive that the strong feelings among Christians and Muslims could polarise politics along those lines and weaken the two-party structure.

Babangida's confidence in the two-party system was put to the test three years later in the local government election of December 1990 on party basis. The two-party system was a success. Neither religion nor regionalism was a factor in how the electorate voted. It was a pleasant surprise to everyone. Babangida could then beat his chest and say that the two-party system was a "very dangerous (and) risky" gamble which he thought "was worth taking." He dared and he won.

In recommending government funding of political parties, the bureau was reacting to a lingering problem of party control in the country. Rightly or wrongly, rich members of the parties have always been accused of controlling them. There were no rules guiding the founding and the funding of political parties. Naturally, but perhaps unfairly, a member's influence in the parties was in direct proportion to his financial muscle. Educated but financially-challenged Nigerians felt alienated from politics. More correctly, they were marginalised. Money politics was a common slogan but a troubling spectre in the politics of Nigeria. The recommendation for a partial public funding of the parties was based on the need to free parties from the clutches of the rich. Babangida was not quite satisfied with this halfway house. Something more radical and more sweeping was needed. He knew what to do.

III

The transition time-table released under the legal backing of Decree 19 of 1987 (*Transition to Civil Rule Programme*) set events in motion. The timetable spelt out quarterly schedule of activities between 1987 and 1992.

The work of the bureau and the decisions of the AFRC on its recommendations were to form the framework of a new constitution for the Third Republic. A Constitution Review Committee headed by Mr. Justice Buba Ardo, who was deputy chairman of the Constituent Assembly in 1977/78, was inaugurated on September 7, 1987. Its assignment was fairly straightforward, namely, to review the government white paper on the report and recommendations of the political bureau and the 1979 constitution and incorporate other fresh, relevant ideas for consideration by a constituent assembly that would, in turn, meld the committee's views into a new constitution for the Third Republic.

To those who believed the country did not need a new constitution because the 1979 constitution was fundamentally unimpeachable, Babangida's reply was that the constitution is the fundamental law of the country and, therefore, "the crucible within which the right attitudes and the proper way to behave may be given a chance to evolve."[20] His ambition was to give the country "a document which will prove acceptable, workable, adoptable, enduring and suited to our particular circumstances, needs and temperament as a people now and in the foreseeable future."[21]

Babangida's great gift was in his ability to convince the country, at each stage of his political engineering, to trust him. His sentiments always seemed to be the product of an intellectual approach to the problems of the country. He was a great political salesman.

The review committee went to work. While this was going on, two developments critical to the transition programme took place. Sixteen days after he inaugurated the CRC, Babangida was on the move again. And again, the honey and the vinegar. He created two new states, Akwa Ibom, from Cross River State, and Katsina from Kaduna State. That was the honey.

He extended the ban on former public officers to include civil servants, police and military personnel and businessmen who, from October 1, 1960, were found guilty of corruption or abuse of office. These fell into the first category. They were banned from public office for life. The second category comprised all politicians who held elective, appointive and party offices in the first and second republics, even if they had no stains. The third group were Babangida himself and all those who served in his administration. The ban on the last two groups was to last only for the life of the transition programme. And that was the vinegar.

The president offered three reasons for his action. The life ban was imperative because "such people have forfeited every moral right to vie for, or occupy any position of responsibility or leadership in this country." Secondly, "..the civilian leadership had (not) learnt any lessons." The third reason was to facilitate "the emergence of a new political leadership which Nigeria desperately needs."[22]

It was now easy to see that Babangida's ambition to re-make the country in his own image had become an obsession. While a good number of people believed that the cultivation of a new leadership was both necessary and imperative, his politics of massive exclusion was showing vital signs of naiveté. He was beginning to win without conquering. The chickens waited to come home to roost.

The second major development at this stage was the conduct of local government election on non-party basis on December 12 that year. The grand political experimentation programme of the administration shifted into gear two. Doubts linger as to what the elections were meant to achieve. Perhaps, it helped to ventilate the political system. Perhaps, it helped the new breed politicians to test the waters. Perhaps, it was to test the efficacy of the blanket ban. Whatever was its objective, Nigerians welcomed the opportunity to return to the hustings once again.

The elections were conducted only three months after the National Election Commission, NEC, which replaced the Federal Electoral Commission, FEDECO, was inaugurated. Eme Awa, a retired professor of political science, was appointed its chairman. The elections showed, disappointingly, that violence and election malpractices were indestructible. Glaring cases of malpractices forced NEC to cancel 312 councillor and chairmanship elections in ten states and Abuja. Lagos State managed to stand out. So bad were the malpractices in the state that the entire elections were cancelled.

The diseases had been scorched, not killed. The late Kingsley Mbadiwe could hardly hide his glee at the turn of events. He delivered this withering judgement: "The disease which it (the ban) was meant to cure - election malpractice - is much more with us in the (new) political system."[23]

The repeat election of March 1988 was more successful. Babangida's faith in the rightness, if not the justice of his actions, was rekindled. A few months later, he told the tenth graduating students of the tripartite military institution, the Command and Staff College, Jaji, that he was confident the military would leave the control of government "in the hands of a new breed of leaders who shall detest the culture of deceit, election fraud as well as a culture of violence." He spoke too soon.

IV

The CRC submitted its report on March 1, 1988. It received 438 memoranda from the public. It would appear that the quality of public contributions to its work showed the lingering doubts on the need for a new constitution. The committee concluded its report with these telling statements:

> From the memoranda received from the public, the political bureau's findings and input from government, it seems reasonable to conclude that there was nothing fundamentally wrong with the 1979 constitution. However, ambiguities and lacunae in certain of its provisions and difficulties in the operation of some of its institutions have been encountered, thus justifying such changes and attempts at clarifications as contained in this report.[24]

It was now time to call in the representatives of the people to decide on the final shape and content of the new constitution. The 567 members of the Constituent Assembly, who were partly elected and partly nominated by government, received their charter from the president on May 11, 1988. Anthony Aniagolu, a retired justice of the Supreme Court of Nigeria, headed it. The assembly did not receive a carte blanche from Babangida. At its inauguration, he drew the boundary beyond which they were not to step:

> The Constituent Assembly does not possess the power to create states or alter state or local government boundaries. I should also state categorically that the Assembly should not indulge itself in the fruitless exercise of trying to alter the agreed ingredients of Nigeria's political order, such as federalism, presidentialism, the non-adoption of any religion as state religion and the respect and observance of fundamental human rights. I should also add the two-party system, the ban or disqualification placed on certain persons from participating in politics and belief in basic freedoms, including the much-cherished freedom of the press. Your job is to improve on these agreed political issues and not to change them.[25]

The work of the political bureau showed that Nigerians had more or less exhausted new constitutional ideas. Babangida refused to be despaired by public cynicism. He hoped the Constituent Assembly might "..come to achieve the distinction of being our last and final experience in constitution-making." He, apparently, could not see into the future of Nigeria even from that vantage position as president. Events were to prove him wrong. His was not the last constitution. Two more constitutions followed but as at the time he spoke, the future was shrouded in a fog of mystery that only God could see through.

Constitution making is a serious business demanding time and intellectual vigour. But the members of the Constituent Assembly failed to realise this. They did not have all the time in the world to ratify the draft constitution but they acted as if they did. Instead of tackling the important recommendations of the constitution drafting committee, they bogged themselves down with a long debate on the president's no-go areas. What remained of their energy was dissipated on the unfinished business of a shari'a court of appeal at the federal level and the status of Abuja, the new federal capital. The debate on the shari'a court of appeal and the status of Abuja generated such heat and acrimony that the federal government had to withdraw them into the no-go areas. Such was the lethargic attitude of the members to the work of the assembly that absenteeism forced the chairman to lower the quorum from 300 to 200.

While the assembly plodded on with its work, Babangida struck again. On September 1, 1988, Sam Orji, chairman of Enugu local government, was removed for what government said were his "actions, utterances and activities." Orji was elected chairman in the 1987 local government election on non-party basis. His removal served notice that the first experiment in some form of diarchy in the country was heading for grief. To justify its action and re-assure the nation, government resorted to a nebulous explanation: security advised its action. No one was convinced. It was the first in a series of sabotage against the transition programme by the government itself for reasons that were never clear.

Eleven months after Orji was removed, government dissolved all the local government councils in the country, five months before the end of their tenure. Government explanation, as bland as they come, was that the action became necessary to prevent the chairmen and councillors from using government facilities to push their political ambitions. It made little, if any impression, on the decidedly cynical public. The transition programme was being increasingly subjected to cynical manipulation by the military. As *The Nigerian Tribune* put it:

> The dissolution of elected local government councils three weeks ago is the most recent and serious indication of a wide gulf between the theory and practice of the transition programme. It exposes the dilemma of authoritarian supervision of a democratic order.[26]

Where the government acted outside the purview of existing laws, as it often did, it simply redressed it with a retroactive decree with the appropriate ouster clauses. Decree 15 of December 1989, was promulgated five months after the federal government dissolved the local government councils. Section 34 of the decree empowered the president to remove an elected chairman and a vice-chairman as well as dissolve any local government councils. No offence for this punishment was prescribed in the decree.

Shock treatment became a regular feature of the transition programme. On March 29, 1989, Babangida administered one more shock treatment. He added to the long list of those disqualified or banned from contesting elective offices during the transition programme. This time, the ban had nothing to do with offences or alleged offences but to safeguard some institutions critical to the implementation of the programme. Chairmen and members of MAMSER, NEC, National Population Commission, Code of Conduct Bureau, National Revenue Mobilisation Commission and DFRRI at both federal and state levels were banned, according to the president, "to create an environment for free and fair elections during the transition period and in order to ensure total impartiality on the part of the key institutions charged with central elements in the political transition programme."[27]

Decree 9 of 1989, which legitimised this ban, also amended decree 25 of 1987 to give more teeth to it. It now became an offence under the new decree for a banned or disqualified person to sponsor or campaign for any candidates or fund a political party. The penalty for infringement was stiff - ₦250,000.00 fine or five years imprisonment or both.

Balabare Musa, first civilian governor of old Kaduna State and a leftist with a penchant for defiance, soon ran foul of this decree. He was arrested for founding and funding a political association, the People's Liberation Party, contrary to the provisions of the decree. He spent five months in detention.

The submission of the draft constitution on April 5, 1989, marked a new phase in the transition programme. Babangida had begun to worry about who should succeed him. He hinted, rather darkly, that he would

> not hand over political power to any person or persons, no matter how distinguished or wealthy but to a virile civilian political organisation which is openly committed to the proper use of power in the national interest. Those who think otherwise and who are now parading themselves as aspirants in 1992 would be disappointed in the end.[28]

Perhaps, not many people took the hint of what was to come.

The AFRC was the final authority on the draft constitution. A four-day marathon meeting of the council ended on May 3. That evening, Babangida practically kicked off the journey into the Third Republic. The timing was vintage Babangida. He was due to travel to Great Britain on a state visit, the first by a Nigerian leader since Shagari. He wanted to demonstrate to the nation and the world that he meant business with the transition programme. His 44-page broadcast to the nation was more or less all things to all people. He lifted the ban on politics and gave the green light to "Nigerians other than those disqualified.... to form and promote political associations."[29] He also announced the new constitution for the federal republic.

The new constitution bore little resemblance to the Constituent Assembly draft. The AFRC went through the document with a sharp pencil. Few of the recommendations of the assembly survived. The council would not permit Nigeria to become a welfare state because, "defining Nigeria as a welfare state will circumscribe future political operators who might consider the notion unnecessarily restrictive..."[30]

Free education, free medicare for certain categories of Nigerians, financial autonomy for the judiciary, (a sore point between the executive and the judiciary since independence), restoration of the post of head of civil service scrapped in the 1988 civil service reforms and a host of other provisions approved by the assembly, were pencilled out by the council.

Rather than accept the recommendations of the assembly on the ages of those eligible for elective offices, the ruling council chose to reverse itself because "we do not see the rationale for ignoring the early maturity of today's Nigerians - talented and well-educated young persons in their twenties and early thirties who can man key sectors of our economy and, by extension, our polity."[31]

The assembly, like the CRC, had recommended higher age brackets. The AFRC prescribed the following age limits: president, 35 years; governors and senators, 30 years; members of the House of Representatives and state assemblies and local council chairmen, 25 years and 21 years for councillors. The council voted down the single six-year term for president and governors. The two terms of four years each for the president and governors as in the 1979 constitution was retained.

The assembly, perhaps, with a dark sense of humour, decided to tweak the whiskers of the military. Section 1 (4) of the draft constitution provided that "Any take-over or control of the government of Nigeria by any person or persons other than in accordance with the provisions of the present constitution, shall remain a punishable crime at all times under Nigerian law."

This was practically a rewording of section 1 (2) of the 1979 constitution. That provision did not stop the military from taking over in 1983. What the draft provision sought to do was to make it possible for anyone who takes over to be tried for treason even after leaving office. The AFRC would not countenance it. As Babangida explained it:

> We took the view that there are sufficient constitutional and other legal provisions to deal with this form of breaches of the constitution. In any case, we felt that all crimes should be and indeed are, punishable offences. Hence it appears tautological to imply that a specific offence is a punishable crime. We also view it as superfluous to say that breach of Nigeria's constitution could be punishable under any law other than Nigerian law.[32]

In a flash of sarcastic humour, Babangida handily dismissed such a far-reaching constitutional provision with obvious implications for the growth and sustenance of democracy in the country. The action of the council betrayed a collective sense of *us versus them* on the part of the military. It was a case of self-interest being promoted above national interest. The provision could not have prevented military adventurism in politics *post* Babangida. What it merely sought to demonstrate was that laws are needed to protect democracy from undemocratic forces.

In a calculated charade, the military allowed the civilians to have their say but not their way. The way belonged to the military. The Obasanjo administration did not treat the draft of the 1979 constitution submitted to it by the Constituent Assembly as a sacred document either. Despite protests by the civilians who felt, quite wrongly, that the assembly, being elected representatives of the people was superior to the Supreme Military Council, that council went ahead to "tamper" with 17 provisions in the draft constitution.

Was the whole process of constitution making from the political bureau through to the Constituent Assembly an expensive circus? Many Nigerians were asking this and similar questions. If the military had the monopoly of movement, why did it allow the civilians the motion? Aniagolu, chairman of the assembly, did not believe money spent on the making of the constitution was a waste. "I think all the money spent on the Constituent Assembly was money well-spent, especially considering that we were carrying out a democratic process of teaching and learning which is expensive. If we try to equate the learning process with money spent, we are not preparing the country for a lasting democracy,"[33] he argued.

He may be right. Democracy thrives on the illusion that it is participatory. The civilians wrote the constitution, the military merely took out the provisions with which they disagreed or found unacceptable. After all, responsibility for the new republic was entirely that of the military.

The promulgation of the constitution into law threw up another problem the assembly wisely avoided. This was, in effect, the introduction of a diarchical arrangement. It has always been a sensitive issue since the former president, Dr Nnamdi Azikiwe, propounded it in 1974. Babangida, aware of this, had sought to re-assure the country that

> the idea of diarchy never featured in our political programme because we are aware that diarchy is either a permanent state of affairs involving power-sharing between the civilian and military personnel in government or a permanent veto power for the military personnel in government.[34]

That is a constructionist definition of diarchy. With the constitution becoming the supreme law through decree 12 of 1989, Nigeria was operating a hybrid political arrangement that was part constitutional and part dictatorial. This was clearly diarchical. Babangida might not have intended this but from this point on, the transition programme made diarchy inevitable. It came into full bloom with the election of governors and state legislatures in 1991.

V

The race into the Third Republic claimed its first casualty even before it started. Professor Awa was removed as chairman of NEC in controversial circumstances on February 28, 1989. His sudden sack gave rise to a new round of speculations about the fate of the transition programme. Was Awa removed because he refused to dance to the tune of the military? Duro Onabule, chief press secretary to the president, dismissed such questions. He said that "there is nothing sacrosanct about changes or appointments of any person into public offices."[35] You cannot argue with that.

Awa tried to take his sack in stride, saying, "the chairmanship of NEC is a very hot seat..... I have tried to do this job very honestly to ensure a free and fair election, but perhaps, somewhere along the line, there has been a clash with the normal trend in Nigerian politics..."[36]

In plain English, he lost his job because, to use a well-worn expression, he probably refused to play ball. More than one year after his removal, Awa claimed government interfered with his work. He said he had maintained an uncompromising posture on the interpretation of decree 23 of 1987, the enabling law of the commission. His view was that the decree clearly vested the power to approve and register the two political parties on the commission, not the AFRC. Apparently, the council did not wish to accept a subordinate role to the commission. It simply amended the decree and transferred the power from NEC to itself.

The case was closed with Aikhomu's clarification that "The reconstitution of the NEC was based on the urgent need for a much better organisational structure with a firm grip of responsibility."[37]

Humphrey Nwosu, a professor of political science, and Awa's former student, stepped into the shoes of his old teacher. He brought élan and dash to the office. Barely 12 hours after Babangida flagged off the politicians, Nwosu announced a series of stringent guidelines for the formation of political associations wishing to be registered as political parties. The initial public response to the formation of political associations was rather cold because of the apparent confusion over the bans and disqualifications. This initial response was in contrast to what happened as soon as Obasanjo lifted the ban on politics in 1978. Response was immediate. Within 24 hours, several political leaders announced their political associations. In Obasanjo's transition, no one was banned or disqualified. The government openly encouraged political associations even before the ban on political activities was formally lifted that year.

In 1989, however, the politicians and security agents were engaged in a game of hide and seek with the politicians. The old breed and the new breed could not meet openly because the government forbade it. New breed politicians who met with the old breed risked being banned or disqualified. The situation advised a retreat into the cellar. The comprehensive nature of the bans and disqualifications enmeshed NEC, the transition to civil rule tribunal headed by Fred Anyaegbunam, a retired high court judge and the various high courts in the untidy drama of clearing and disqualifying politicians who contested their ban or disqualification. In most cases, no clear-cut criteria were used.

Nigerians tried not to allow the confusion dampen their enthusiasm for civil rule. In the first two weeks of Babangida's clarion call for the game to begin, some 40 political associations were formed. In another two weeks, there were 88 associations. Many of them existed only in hand outs and newspaper announcements. Their founders simply wanted to be noticed by the more serious-minded politicians. NEC stipulated a registration fee of ₦50,000.00 for each political association wishing to apply for registration as a political party. It also required each association to submit membership forms and passport photographs of all its members. Suspicion runs deep in Nigerian politics. These conditions constituted a financial burden most of the associations could not bear. When the deadline for submission of applications came on July 19, 1989, only 13 of the associations submitted their papers.

The electoral law required NEC to verify the claims of all the political associations. This was clearly an impossible task. The commission did not possess the executive capacity to carry out this function. Five weeks after it received the submissions, the commission submitted its own report to government. The report was a classic study in organised ambiguity. NEC could not make up its mind on which two of the 13 associations to recommend to the AFRC. It passed the buck to the council. It recommended six of the associations to the ruling council to choose any two it pleased. The associations recommended to the council were Peoples Solidarity Party, PSP; Nigerian National Congress, NNC; Peoples Front Party, PFN; Liberal Convention, LC; Nigerian Labour Party, NLP and Republican Party of Nigeria, RPN.

In the commission's assessment, none of the associations met the requirements for registration because all of them "... made exaggerated claims about their membership size and organisational strength."[38] Nwosu virtually foreclosed a favourable consideration of his recommendation of any of the associations by the AFRC. In his report, he observed:

> Virtually all the associations derive their roots from the politics of the first and second republics in varying degrees.... There is a little substantial difference between the associations as reflected in their manifestos and policy papers. More critically, they failed to offer concrete and viable solutions to the social, political and economic problems of the country. All the associations have (a) poor financial base and therefore, stand to be hijacked by the wealthy individuals within them. Virtually all the associations are rent by factionalisation as a result of power struggle which portends ill for the Third Republic.[39]

The politicians, not without some trepidation, settled down to await the final word from the AFRC. It came on October 7. Another shocker. The AFRC simply accepted NEC view that none of the six associations was fit to be registered as a political party. What was more interesting was the decision by the council that left on their own, the politicians could not get their acts together. Something had to give. The right of the politicians to form parties gave.

In a nation-wide broadcast that evening, Babangida explained the rejection of the associations by the council with a culinary metaphor: "All we are saying is that we will not serve our people yesterday's food in glittering, new dishes."[40] All the associations, the president said, were, horror upon horrors, "surrogates of banned or disqualified politicians."

The politicians having failed, the responsibility fell on the council to form the two political parties for them. Babangida was prepared for this 'assignment.' He wasted little time in giving the country two new political parties - the National Republican Convention, NRC, and the Social Democratic Party, SDP.

Reactions to the two parties formed by the AFRC were mixed. However, there were no fundamental disagreements with it. Criticism of the parties as government parastatals came much later, not least because of government decision to fund and house them at every level. The politicians were prepared to accept whatever prescriptions the military thought necessary to cure the lingering political ills of the country and get it moving.

The grass-roots concept of the parties was entirely Babangida's own idea, which he sold to the AFRC with "a lot of effort." As he put it:

> This grass-roots concept came about because I had seen some campaigns being

conducted in remote places like the Philippines where senatorial candidates were virtually going to the people in their houses, telling them, 'I am this, I am vying for this job; vote for me.' This was something that had never happened in Nigeria and I felt that maybe it would be a good idea to start inculcating this idea in our politicians so that those who want to serve can go and sell themselves to the electorate. I told my colleagues I wanted to see a situation where a man running for an elective office comes to my house and says to me: 'Look, old boy, I am running for this thing. Will you support me? This is my plan.' Or he can even stay on the street and as people pass by, give them hand bills, soliciting for their vote. This is the sort of thing I wanted.

He felt so strongly about the two-party system that at one stage in 1989, he considered an unusual step to bring it about:

We toyed with the idea that if we are going to get more than four or five viable political associations, then the best thing would be to call the political party leaders together, put them in a room and say, 'Look, this country belongs to you. What we want is for you to talk among yourselves and then come and tell us what you want. It is your country and you should be able to bury your differences here and now and decide this is what you want. Come out with one or two parties only.'

He abandoned this idea when he found there was an easier way out. "From all the noises that went on," Babangida knew that the politicians were largely divided into two ideological camps - right and left. They were all speaking the same language, offering the electorate the same thing. He also realised that the politicians did not quite appreciate the fact that they were basically offering the people the same manifestos with only minor differences in emphasis and language.

He watched the unfolding drama of the political associations. By the time NEC submitted its report, recommending six instead of two of the 13 political associations for registration, Babangida was ready for his move.

Convinced that the politicians would fail to get their act together, he began to work on creating two parties himself. He first bounced this idea, like most of his ideas, among members of his kitchen cabinet. Most of them found his argument utterly persuasive and supported it. His next step was to work on the concept. Jonah Isawa Elaigwu, at the time a professor of political science at the University of Jos, and a member of the Presidential Advisory Council, is Babangida's close friend. He was involved in some of the president's steps towards the new political order. The president sold his idea of the two-party system to him. Elaigwu too bought it.

The two men met for several nights discussing the modalities after which they prepared a position paper on the grass-roots political concept for the AFRC. The idea was to simply create two political parties, one with leftist and the other with rightist leanings. Or, as he later put it, "a little to the left and a little to the right." The names of the parties chosen by Babangida reflected this unclear ideological divide in today's world. Before he formally tabled the position papers at the AFRC, Babangida enlisted the support of his close associates in the council. He encouraged them to discuss his ideas with some leading politicians and political scientists and report their reactions to him. He received reports of no substantial disagreement.

As part of his new deal, he wanted to discourage or abolish money politics in the country. He wanted his two new parties to have no founders and joiners. He wanted every member to be a co-founder and a co-joiner. More importantly, he did not want to leave room for wealthy members of the parties to hijack them. This, then broadly, was the concept of his grass-roots political parties; ideal parties in which all members were equal and none more equal than others. Fantastically idealistic but he believed it was a workable proposition given the history of party politics in Nigeria.

The political bureau did a lot to help Babangida along with his innovative political ideas. The bureau, also anxious to discourage money politics in the Third Republic, recommended substantial public funding of the political parties. Babangida decided there was no room for a half house. Instead of the substantial funding recommended by the political bureau, he decided that government would fully fund the parties and build party headquarters for them at the national, state and local government levels.

Babangida offered the nation a new political arrangement - parties founded and funded by the federal government. Chances of marginalisation of party members because they were poor, were theoretically minimised. The president offered rational explanations for the decisions of the council. National exigencies for one. Babangida admitted that the decisions of the AFRC "may be traumatic to the present system. But we have come to the conclusion that it may be necessary for us to jolt the system a bit if we are to successfully establish a two-party system."[41] No one needed telling. After all, "our political problems require(d) radical solutions."[42]

Ray Ekpu of *Newswatch* magazine did not think the action of the council was as radical as the president would want the country to believe. "Each of (the two parties) is an amalgam of the rejected parties. The NRC has the intestines of the defunct Nigerian National Congress, Liberal Convention and the Republican Party while the SDP has the ribs of the defunct People's Front and Peoples Solidarity Party. Each of them is old wine in a new skin,"[43] he argued.

NEC was directed to draft the constitutions and the manifestos of the two parties for ratification by the AFRC. Babangida left nothing to chance. It was his show. NEC duly submitted these documents on November 3, 1989. A month later, government released the constitutions and manifestos. These documents, which are normally vital to political parties, were severely deficient. They were too similar to reflect the different ideological spectrums the parties were supposed to represent. No matter. Babangida had got his wish.

Still fearing that the parties might divide the country along religious or regional lines, Babangida took a keen interest in the election of the party executives. To defeat that bogey required that each party must be seen to accommodate the religious and the regional mix. He and his colleagues began a quiet campaign among the new breed politicians because "we want(ed) to defeat this argument about north and south, religious beliefs and so on."

There is no direct evidence that government dictated who was who in the party executives but there is some evidence that the leadership that emerged had the tacit support of some leading members of the AFRC. Tom Ikimi, a Christian from Edo State, became national chairman of the NRC. He is a close friend of Vice-President Aikhomu. The SDP had Baba Gana Kingibe, a Muslim from Borno State, as national chairman. He is a former diplomat and a close friend of the president. Kingibe was one of the young bureaucrats Babangida cultivated as a member of the Supreme Military Council in the Murtala/Obasanjo administration. It, certainly, was not a fluke that the two men led the parties. Nor was it by accident that Kingibe and Ikimi are minorities from the north and the south respectively.

With the party executives in place, government then asked to make their own inputs into their respective constitutions and manifestos. This, certainly, was an attempt by the government to satisfy those who insisted that it was wrong to impose the constitutions and the manifestos on the parties. The parties submitted their contributions to the AFRC for approval. There were very few changes in the constitutions and manifestos. Indeed, the most important contribution the parties made was the choice of their flags and emblems. NRC's emblem was the eagle. Its flag was white. A horse was the emblem of the SDP; and green the colour of its flag.

The new political order was shaping up.

Chapter Fourteen

The Shuffle

Shall we continue to try a system that has failed us?
–President Ibrahim Babangida

Shortly before Babangida gave the politicians the go-ahead in 1989 to form political associations and prepare for the return to civil rule, he was confronted with a tempting option. Some of his officers were still not convinced that the politicians could be trusted to rule the country in accordance with the rules of the game of politics. These officers were members of his kitchen cabinet, his trusted men, nicknamed the 'IBB boys.' They did not support the return to a full-blown civilian regime. They preferred some form of arrangement in which the country was ruled by a sucession of "civilianised" military men. They canvassed what they called the 'Nasser model.'

Gamal Abdel Nasser was a colonel in the Egyptian army. He and 89 other officers in the Egyptian army, known as Free Officers, staged Africa's first coup d'état on July 23, 1952. They overthrew King Faruq. Nasser was the leader of the Free Officers movement. He, however, allowed General Muhammed Naguib to assume power as prime minister after the overthrow of the king. Nasser was the power behind the Naguib thrown. He shoved Naguib aside in 1954 and took over as prime minister from 1954-56. In 1956, he drew up a new constitution for the country that formally abolished the monarchy and replaced it with a one-party presidential system. Nasser dropped his uniform and became the sole candidate in the first presidential election in 1956. He won the election and remained president until his death in September 1970.

Egypt has been ruled by a succession of military men since then. Nasser's successor was Anwar Sadat, a colonel in the Egyptian army and a member of the Free Officers movement. He took part in Nasser's coup in 1952 and served the Nasser administration in various capacities. Islamic fundamentalists assassinated him on October 6, 1981. Hosni Mubarak, a general and former Chief of Staff of the Egyptian Air Force, who was also in the Sadat regime, succeeded him as president. Thus military men in mufti have ruled Egypt since 1952.

Babangida's kitchen cabinet argued that this model would end coups in the country and ensure national stability and a succession of disciplined leadership drawn from the armed forces. Military regimes in the country had not been stable either. One set of officers had overthrown another set three times since the first coup on January 15, 1966. Threats of recurring coups were real. In their calculated view, their suggestion would end the game of musical chairs between the military and civilians and within the military itself. This, to them, seemed reasonably grounded on empirical facts. They also believed it would satisfy the local and international communities yearning for democracy and meet the peculiar political exigencies of Nigeria.

Actually, this same group of people canvassed this idea at the preparatory stage of the coup that brought Babangida to power but he demurred. Their return to the same argument four years later showed that its attraction for them remained strong. This time, they argued that Babangida and some senior officers should retire from the armed forces and contest elections as 'civilians.'

Had Babangida had accepted this option then or even from the beginning, his transition to civil rule programme would have been much shorter than the even original terminal date of 1990. It was a tempting option and one that Babangida wrestled with. He refused to give in to the temptation. He feared that the complexities of Nigeria and its politics would be hostile to the Nasser model.

He preferred what he regarded as the more pragmatic option of an elaborate transition programme that would achieve his three fundamental objectives: a) a restructuring of the polity on the basis of a two-party system fully or partially funded by the federal government and, therefore, protected from being hijacked by the moneyed class; b) the entrenchment of a new political culture borne out of the learning process envisaged in his transition programme and c) the emergence of new breed politicians with a more nationalistic outlook and temperament than the older generation of politicians.

Babangida was convinced that his elaborate and ultimately expensive route to the restoration of democracy offered some hope that whatever mistakes the Murtala/Obasanjo administration might have made in its transition programme that brought a civilian regime that lasted all of four years and three months, would have been sufficiently taken care of by the time it had run its course. His principal objection to the Nasser model was this:

> In the sixties or right from 1952, up to the sixties, seventies and even the eighties, the coup d'état was the in-thing. Before Nigeria's, there had been coups and counter-coups in other countries. But the situation has changed. I know the problems which brought in the military remain but over the years, people have matured and are now saying they want to do things by themselves. They want

to participate actively in politics and decide who should rule them. This feeling has become the in-thing and will make military rule unattractive. So, from now on, I believe we will witness a period of democratisation and economic liberalisation in many parts of the world.

Unlike some of his military colleagues, Babangida believed that the civilian politicians would be properly equipped to do a better job of leading the country this time around. He reasoned that there was no way they would have gone through the 'learning process'of his transition programme and not give the country good leadership. He did not think the military should arrogate to itself the right to rule in succession in mufti. Let the transition programme go on. And so it did.

However, some of those close to him say that despite his professed determination to go on with the drawn-out transition programme, his body language was increasingly showing that he was giving some serious thoughts to the Nasser model. He probably would have caved in to the pressures from his kitchen cabinet but, to use a local idiom, a big housefly flew into his soup.

On April 22, 1990, the nation was jolted by an early morning martial music and a coup broadcast on FRCN, Lagos. Early that morning some young military officers assaulted the president's official residence in Dodan Barracks, Lagos, with heavy armour in attempt to overthrow Babangida. Major Gideon Gwaza Orkar announced the coup against the president. The Orkar group, like the Chukwuma Nzeogwu group in 1966, were mostly young and middle-ranking officers. The coup failed but left a hole in Babangida's psyche. (See chapter 17).

The failed coup affected the course of events on the political front as well. Orkar and his group had accused Babangida of planning to perpetuate himself in power. Babangida's immediate response to this allegation was to convince the public he had no such plan. On August 27, 1990, the fifth anniversary of his assumption of power, Babangida unveiled the new shape of his administration with his announcement of a progressive 'civilianisation' of his regime as part of the "demilitarisation process ... in the sincere belief that a gradual adaptation of the requirement of the new institution would enhance the philosophy and logic of the transition to civil rule programme."[1]

Some of the changes he made in this regard looked like an edited script of the Nasser model. He abolished the office of the Chief of General Staff and retired Aikhomu who held that office. But now out of uniform, Aikhomu was named vice-president to Babangida. He effected the same structure at the state level. He appointed civilians as deputy governors to the military governors. More than 100 senior military officers from the three arms of the armed forces were retired. Some of them were promptly appointed supervisors of new organs of the transition programme.

He dissolved the Armed Forces Ruling Council and reconstituted it with fewer members. The public expected him to lift the ban on former public office holders. He refused to oblige and insisted:

> For the avoidance of doubt, I wish to reaffirm that the provisions of decree 25 of 1987 and as further amended by decree number 9 of 1989, are still in force.

Whether or not the demilitarisation process was dictated by the allegations of Orkar and co. remains a debatable point. From this point on, however, the transition programme took on a new life with a new dance step of one step forward, one step backward. Before the local government election of December 8, 1990, a new debate arose over the open ballot system used in the ward congresses of the parties. This system required voters to queue behind candidates of their choice. No ballot papers would be used.

Nigerians were divided over this option. Some supported it but others stoutly opposed it. Hardly unusual in a nation given to debates. The chairman of NEC, Humphrey Nwosu, initially opposed the open ballot system. He denigrated it as "a step into the dark abyss of time." The two political parties pitched their camps differently too. While the SDP supported it, the NRC opposed it. The Sultan of Sokoto, Alhaji Ibrahim Dasuki, weighed in on the side of those opposed to it. He argued that "queuing behind a candidate of your choice will make an opponent regard you as an enemy."[2] That was the fear of most people too.

Still, the SDP was persuaded that the open ballot system would ensure mass participation and reduce rigging. What decided it for the country was the AFRC support for this new voting system. That support converted Nwosu and instantly turned the chief electoral umpire into an apostle of the open ballot system. He had no problems rationalising his *volte face*: "Shall we continue to try a system that has failed us? Shall we not try another one as we did in the choice of political parties?" Nwosu wondered aloud.

On September 21, Nwosu formally announced the adoption of the open ballot system as the "...system most appropriate in our circumstances at this stage of our national development; something indigenous, simple, uncomplicated, cost-effective and credible..."[3]

There was a minor legal problem. The electoral act provided for the secret ballot in all the elections. The new open ballot system violated the act. When the opponents of the system pointed this out, government said no problem. It simply amended the relevant section of the laws. Case closed.

Babangida canvassed support for the system but to mollify those who felt that it was retrogressive, indeed for a nation that had used the secret ballot system before and since independence, he promised that it would be limited to the local government election originally scheduled for 1989 but eventually conducted in 1990, because it was more suitable to the grassroots than the secret ballot. It was a promise not kept.

But before the elections the politicians clearly demonstrated that it would take more than decrees or bans and disqualifications to create a new political culture in the country. Inter- and intra-party disputes over allegations and counter-allegations of plans by the parties to rig the election became rife, obviously to the amusement of those elements in the armed forces who gave the civilians little or no credit for their democratic temperament. Babangida was sufficiently worried about what he considered a threat to his transition programme that he summoned the party leaders to a meeting with him in Aso Rock, Abuja. After the meeting, the party leaders posed for the camera, beaming with smiles. They promised to end inter and intra-party disputes.

Early that year, the political parties received a shocker. In his budget speech, Babangida announced the withdrawal of government funding for them. "They are now on their own and must fend for themselves,"[4] he said. It remains unclear what led to the sudden change. Was it to assuage those who argued that the dependence of the parties on government for all their financial needs was antithetical to the democratic norm? The party executives protested the government decision. They reminded the government that the moneybags were lurking in the shadows. Government later went back on its words and continued the funding of the parties without further explanations as to why the government or Babangida changed their mind. It was simply a shuffle – back and forth.

Then it was back to the debate on the open ballot system, to the relatively successful conduct of the local government elections. Despite voter apathy and the consequent low voter turnout, the successful conduct of the election was attributed to the use of the open ballot system. Its critics saw it differently. They argued that the use of the open ballot system caused the low turnout and proved that the open ballot system would only induce further voter apathy and disenfranchise mostly the elites who would hate to openly queue behind candidates of their choice. They insisted on the secret ballot system to protect voters and also because they did not believe the secret ballot *per se* was responsible for election rigging and other malpractices in the conduct of elections in the country.

It would appear that the government saw some merits in the argument. However, it was not prepared to ditch the open ballot system entirely. Somehow, a middle ground was canvassed to protect voters from possible reprisals from candidates who lose at elections. The middle ground was *the modified open ballot system*. This was considered a fair meeting point between those who supported and those who opposed the open ballot system. This new system, the argument went, would allow voters to mark their ballot papers in secret but cast their vote in the open – and thus combine and reap the benefit of both worlds. The military administration must have patted itself on the back. These inventions truly modified the age-old ballot paper and how it could be used in Nigeria to prevent rigging.

The matter went back to the Armed Forces Ruling Council for a final decision. The council met on March 27, 1991. Again, the council shifted its position in its decision announced by Babangida. He said that based on the country's historical experience and the level of socio-political development, the AFRC decided that the open ballot system would be used for the remaining elections during the transition programme.

Babangida had reversed himself once more – and for what he believed was a good reason and thus defended his position:

> The whole process of election is about political choices, and whatever will make Nigerians to choose the right people to represent them, we will go for that. Our problems in the past have been the (secret) ballot and ballot papers and we want to make sure that this problem does not persist in our national life.[5].

Again, that decision would soon be changed.

The AFRC having voted for it, the electoral commission had no option but to vote for it too. The commission too felt that the middle ground had some merit. The commission re-examined the arguments for the modified open ballot system and accepted it at its meeting of May 22, 1992. According to Nwosu, this "unique voting procedure…combined the element of secrecy and open casting of vote."[6]

The AFRC legalised the modified open ballot system in decree 13 (*Presidential Election – Basic Constitutional and Transitional Decree*) of 1993. In his memoir published several years later, Nwosu credited the modified open ballot system with the "success of the 1993 presidential election in terms of its transparency, openness, fairness and peacefulness."[7]

Before the presidential election, Babangida delivered another jolt to the transition programme. On the sixth anniversary of his administration in 1991, he announced the creation of nine new states and 136 new local government areas. When he created Katsina and Akwa Ibom states in 1987, he promised they would be the last states to be created, possibly in the political history of Nigeria. Why did he reverse himself? He had no problem rationalising his policy reversal. This is how he explained his action:

> Because the demands were endless and the more you look at what people were demanding, the more convinced you are that they are genuine cases for this exercise to be revisited. And coupled with the fact that the Nigerian believes, quite rightly that it would only be done under a military administration. So, we felt we had this obligation to do what we thought was in the interest of the people and save them the problem later.

The new federal structure of 30 states and 589 local government areas brought with it new political problems that NEC and the political parties had not anticipated. They were thus suddenly confronted with newproblems they had no choice but to grapple with. Some adjustments once again had to be made in the transition timetable to accommodate the latest development. New dates for the primaries and the elections were fixed and changed in quick succession. The political parties were embroiled in a new power tussle. Members of the parties rejected the decision of the party executives to set up caretaker committees in the 290 local government areas affected by the creation of new local government areas.

There is no disputing this: Many Nigerians welcomed the creation of the new states and the new local government areas. However, not everyone took Babangida at his word that in creating the new states and local governments areas, he did no more than respond to the yearnings of the people. They saw ominous signs in his action, however popular or necessary it was. The late Alao Aka-Bashorun, former president of the Nigerian Bar Association, suspected that Babangida had a hidden agenda in going back on his words on the creation of more states and local government areas. "I have my very strong reservation of this government leaving in 1992,"[8] he said.

Babangida handily dismissed such suspicions. He insisted he was committed to the transition programme and intended to pursue it to its logical end. The primaries for the nomination of the governorship candidates of the two political parties were eventually held on October 19, 1991. The results were greeted in most of the states with ringing allegations of rigging and other electoral malpractices. Party members accused their leaders of abetting the malpractices to favour some candidates, particularly those of them who were said to be surrogates of the banned politicians.

With only three weeks to the governorship election, the parties were still unable to sort out themselves. The government refused to intervene because according to the vice-president, the government did not "...want to create a bad precedence to be inherited by a succeeding civilian government where a party in government in a state would intervene in the primaries of the other political party."[9]

However, when it became clear that the programme was heading for the rocks, government told NEC what to do. The commission stepped in and disqualified twelve men in both parties in nine states from contesting the governorship primaries rescheduled for December 3. SDP, the more fractious party, lost nine of its front-runners and the NRC three. Government appeared to hold some banned politicians responsible for the intra-party crises. A day before the rescheduled primaries, the late Major-General Shehu Musa Yar'Adua and twelve other banned politicians were arrested and detained by the government. They were taken before the transition to civil rule tribunal on charges of engaging in politics contrary to decree 25 of 1987.

The governorship and state assembly elections were held on December 14, 1991. They produced surprises. Despite the bad blood the primaries had generated in the parties, the elections were comparatively peaceful. NRC won the governorship election in 16 states to the SDP's 14. The intra-party feud in the SDP exacted its price. It lost two states considered to be safe for it - Katsina and Lagos. Still, it enjoyed a very comfortable majority in the legislatures of both states.

The results of the elections created two impressions that could not have been lost on Nigerians. Firstly, the elections were generally accepted as fair. Babangida himself attributed this to the open ballot system. He felt vindicated because, "given our past experiences in conducting elections which, in most cases, had been accompanied by violence, this new experiment has so far proved to be the most peaceful, most orderly and most widely accepted."[10]

Secondly, the relative peace that attended the elections convinced the government that the political "godfathers" were, indeed, responsible for the chaos in the conduct of the primaries. That conclusion was simplistic but government had good reasons to hold on to it like the holy writ.

Four days after the elections, the "godfathers" were released from detention on December 18. They had spent sixteen days in detention. The charges against them were also dropped. Then Babangida took another step backward – to the surprise of everyone. He lifted the ban on former public office holders. In political terms, this reversal carried the shock of an earthquake. Certainly, it brought joy to those left off the hook but the rest of the country was utterly confused by Babangida's latest reversal of himself.

Was Babangida paving the way to succeed himself? The allegation had become rife. Government tried to debunk it, assuring the nation, to borrow an expression from the space industry, that *all systems were go*. A government statement after a joint meeting of the AFRC and the National Council of State, said the president "shall remain disqualified for now and from succeeding himself."[11]

Government went on to explain that it lifted the ban, except for those who had been found guilty of abuse of office, because it was now convinced that the new breed politicians, in whose interest the ban was imposed to protect them from "the corrupting or unwholesome influence" of the older politicians, had come of age. They had matured within the framework of the two-party system to "hold their ground in an association or in competition with the old class."[12] The rate at which the new-breed politicians matured was not a stuff of biological enquiry. Government no longer feared the corrupting influence of old politicians and magisterially declared them free "to make their services available to the party of their choice and to government if they are so called upon to serve."[13]

To use a rather trite phrase, there was more than met the eye in the decision to lift the ban. For the almost five and half years that the ban lasted, the president and his lieutenants used every available public forum to defend it. Those who felt the ban was unjust and undemocratic did not relent in their pressures on Babangida and other top government functionaries to lift it. Aikhomu admitted that pressure on the government to lift the ban was truly heavy.

Babangida tried to play down the pressures on him but he did feel the weight. At least on three occasions, he raised the matter informally at council meetings. Each time, the other members of the council told him "the matter was closed." They wanted the ban to stay. The younger members of the council were strongly opposed to any attempts to reverse the decision. It would seem that in the end the pressure had the desired effect – and the military men relented.

Babangida must have thought the public would applaud him for bringing back the old brigade. There was no such applause. The public took a rather dim view of it. The president was disappointed by the generally cool public reactions to his latest "pragmatic, political decision." His critics sneered at it. The transition programme was beginning to groan under frequent surprise packages. And many feared it was being pushed towards the precipice by its internal contradictions and policy reversals. The president was now openly accused of playing the script of his alleged "hidden agenda." Interestingly and ironically, Babangida caved in to the pressures to convince his critics he had no hidden agenda.

Here is his explanation:

> The whole atmosphere was inundated with the feeling of unfairness, the feeling of a hidden agenda. People were saying we did not want credible people to

come in; that we did not want tough people to succeed us because we did not want to be exposed after leaving office. So, we just let go so that people with the needed experience and credibility could come and we could get out of all the talk about a hidden agenda because if we allowed them to persist, they would become a nuisance capable of making the people hate the government.

The Guardian newspaper spoke for many when it said the ban was "doomed from the very beginning because it attempted to achieve an impossibility."[14]

Babangida refused to admit this was so, insisting:

We lifted the ban, not because it had failed but because we were convinced that the new leaders had adequately adapted to the political setting, and the parties had been adequately institutionalised to permit entrance into the political arena by the banned groups. This administration believes that a new set of leaders has been allowed into the political arena who would not have had the opportunity to be there if there had been no ban on certain persons. We believe that these leaders can now hold their own in the arena and therefore, do not need to be overly protected.[15]

Babangida knew, at this point, that the ban was no longer popular with Nigerians. When he placed the ban, he knew that the "climate was conducive (and) everybody was happy when we took that decision" but as time went on, "the environment changed." He also admitted that "as time went on and political parties came up, people then began to shout, saying we were depriving the country of the much-needed experience, the much-needed tested leaders." Thus, he was persuaded to reverse himself. It would not be the last time.

II

Whatever happened on the political front did not stop Babangida from tackling two national issues. One was the movement of the federal capital from Lagos to Abuja; the other was the national census.

Babangida did not make the choice of a new federal capital. Murtala Muhammed did. The president was a member of the SMC in the Murtala Muhammed administration, which approved the choice of a virgin land in the middle part of the country as the country's new capital in place of Lagos. The Obasanjo administration opted for a phased development of the new capital over a fifteen-year period. The Shagari administration decided to make it much faster than that. Babangida continued the development of Abuja from where Shagari and Buhari left off. He spared no expenses on Abuja. From about 1986, some major political and national events such as the annual independence anniversary parades were held in Abuja. He inaugurated the political bureau, the constitution review committee and the constituent assembly, among others, there.

Abuja became a presidential retreat. Babangida went there often to escape what he called "the politically-charged atmosphere" in Lagos. Each time he headed for Abuja, the mood of the nation changed to one of heightened expectation of a major national policy decision. Very often, Babangida did not disappoint Nigerians.

On December 12, 1991, Babangida formally signed the legal instrument, *Federal Capital Territory, Abuja*, Decree 51 of December 12, 1991. Lagos ceased, as of that date, to be the capital of the Federal Republic. Babangida moved to Abuja the same day. Aso Rock, the presidential palace in Abuja, replaced Dodan Barracks.

On the face of it, there was nothing particularly significant about this. But Abuja, like most things in Nigeria, had become a source of a needless controversy. The development of Abuja was condemned by some vocal people from the south as a needless "rush" to move the capital out of Lagos. Obasanjo accused Shagari of spending more than one billion Naira on Abuja because he wanted to complete in one year what should take fifteen years. Money spent on Abuja was seen as a waste.

But more ominous was the religious herring dragged across the path. Some newspapers published stories alleging that there was a plan to "islamise" the new federal capital because road and other signs in public places in Abuja were written in Arabic. These things would be laughable elsewhere but not in Nigeria. The country was being polarised over Abuja along the well-known fault lines of Christian/Muslim and north and south. The debate on the status of Abuja became so acrimonious in the constituent assembly that the government declared it a "no-go" area.

Between 1863 when the first census was conducted in the Lagos area and 1953 when the last countrywide one was done before independence on October 1, 1960, the British colonial authorities conducted ten censuses in Nigeria. Not many people noticed at the time; nor did it matter to most Nigerians, not many of whom even knew what it was all about. Whatever resistance the colonialists encountered was dictated by the culture and traditions of the various ethnic groups in the country. Traditions do not approve of counting human beings.

Soon after the country became independent, however, census assumed a new political significance. What is ordinarily a technical exercise for purposes of gathering reliable demographic data and other vital information for planning and development purposes became a new turf for political contentions in the country.

Nigeria's first post-independence census was conducted on May 13, 1962. The politicians did not see it as a technical exercise but as essentially a political one. Politics is a game of numbers. Those who win are those who enjoy the advantage of numbers. No one knew this better than Nigerian politicians. The 1962 census became a contest in the numbers game. It says something of the ingenuity, if not the desperation of the politicians that, a new village was even "discovered" in the Eastern Region just before the 1962 census. It is thus easy to see why Nigerians have never quite known since independence how many they are in their own country.

The 1962 census kicked up a political dust that still swirls in the country. According to the results, the Northern Region had about 31 million people - some six million more than the Eastern and Western regions combined. The East and the West found this unacceptable. They refused to accept "that the scattered north could outnumber the crowded remainder...." of the country. [16]

The political heat generated by the disputed census figures threatened peace in the country. Something had to give if there must be peace. The census figures did. They were cancelled. The census was repeated from November 5 to 8, 1963. The political leaders did not trust one another. Census inspectors were exchanged among the regions to prevent the alleged falsification of figures. Again, the results gave the north more people than the southern regions combined. This time, however, the difference was less outrageous. Two million people were shaved off the 1962 figures in the north. The entire population of the country was put at 55 million, 29 million of whom were in the north.

Despite further protests over the new figures, they were accepted. Demographers were aghast. The new population figures represented a 74 per cent increase in the country's population in only ten years - an alarming annual growth rate of five and half per cent - making Nigeria the ninth most populous, and arguably, the most fecund in the world.

General Yakubu Gowon made census a priority in his nine-point political programme. On July 27, 1973, he inaugurated the National Census Board headed by the late Sir Adetokunboh Ademola, former Chief Justice of Nigeria. The board conducted Nigeria's third post-independence census from November 25 to December 1, that year.

The provisional figures put the country's population at 79.76 million, a modest increase, by the 1963 level, of 43.3 per cent in ten years. The six northern states turned in 51 million; the six southern states, 28 million. A press war along the old regional lines for and against the provisional figures shocked Gowon:

> I was really surprised that people were politicising the whole exercise. And I

told Chief Awolowo that I was displeased with his politicking with the exercise. All I wanted were accurate figures to help with economic planning.[17]

Gowon set up a census data review committee to review the provisional figures. He hoped the committee would make some realistic adjustments in line with demographic rules and turn in less outrageous and, therefore, more acceptable figures. The committee was still at work when he was overthrown. His successor, Muhammed cancelled the 1973 results and the country reverted to the out-dated figures of the 1963 census for planning purposes. Muhammed made no plans in his transition programme for another census. His successor, Obasanjo, adhered to Muhammed's political programme, which did not include a new national population census. The civilian administration in the Second Republic steered clear of it. Economic planning suffered because planners were forced to rely on out-dated figures and demographic conjectures.

The political bureau recommended the conduct of a new census to Babangida because "the unavailability of an acceptable census figure is a major embarrassment and an impediment to meaningful planning for the development of the country." It felt that "despite its sensitivity, a national census is necessary, unavoidable and is better conducted when the military is in power."[18]

Babangida readily accepted the challenge. Actually, Babangida decided, long before the bureau submitted its report to conduct a new census. He scheduled the census for the first three quarters of 1991 because "we cannot run away from counting ourselves simply because the exercise easily gets politicised."[19]

He inaugurated the National Population Commission with the late Shehu Musa, a mathematician and secretary to the federal government in the Shagari administration, as chairman on April 22, 1988. The commission was given three years to prepare and conduct the census nationwide.

Babangida was actively involved in the work of the commission. His ambition to succeed where others before him had failed, worked up his adrenaline. He launched a public enlightenment programme in May 1990, to educate the public on the meaning, uses and importance of a reliable national population census. This campaign was crucial to the work of the commission, if only to wean the populace from the popular conception of census in Nigeria, to wit: *the more we are, the more political and economic resources we will be entitled to from government.* To de-politicise census, routine demographic enquiries into tribe, language and religion were omitted from the questionnaire.

The commission approached its assignment with a measure of seriousness. It conducted three census pre-tests in selected enumeration areas in various parts of the country between November 1989 and December 1990, to test its own work plan, logistics, questionnaire and other field activities of the enumerators. A full dress rehearsal on March 12 and 13, 1991 followed. The census was finally conducted from November 27 to 29, 1991.

Babangida released the new population figures on March 19, 1992. Again, surprise. Demographers were wrong about Nigeria. Using the United Nations projected 3.5 per cent growth rate per annum and based on the 1963 figure of 55.6 million, population experts had estimated Nigeria's population at between 100 and 120 million.

They were wide off the mark. There were only 88,514,501 Nigerians. "For a nation whose enormous ego is linked to its enormous size," wrote *The Economist*, "the 1991 census figures ... came as a shock. If the numbers are correct, and UN observers say they are, then there are only 88.5 million Nigerians - at least 20 million fewer than expected."[20]

The census figures had moved from the outrageous to the disappointing. As usual, a potent mixture of politics, emotional and plain narrow-mindedness, greeted the new figures. Although the northern states still proved to be more populous (46,883,288) than the southern states (41,252,542), the difference was more credible than in the previous censuses.

Babangida tried to mollify those who would be inclined to dispute these figures:

> As a people who share a common nationhood, we need to constantly remind ourselves that census is yet another effort in nation building. It is not a contest in ethnic or religious strength nor is it a contest between regional, communal and cultural groups.[21]

The president might as well have saved himself the bother. Not everyone was satisfied with the figures as they affected their state or even gender. Disputes centred on three points, namely, that the country's population ought to be much higher than the provisional figures indicated; that there should be more people in the south than in the north and men should outnumber women in the country.

It was the measure of the success of the census that no serious, scientific or fundamental objections were raised against the figures. People were unhappy merely because the figures disappointed their assumptions. Sir Adetokunboh Ademola, whose own work in 1973 ended in grief, approved of the new figures. So did the United Nations, which monitored the conduct of the census. Sam Aluko, a well-known professor of economics, said the new figures had vindicated "those of us who had always believed that the 1963 census figures were highly inflated and that the various population projects based on them were equally unrealistic."[22]

Babangida refused to "join issues on those things that were based on uninformed logic."[23] But he took steps to offer the public a channel for the outpouring of their grievances. He set up a census tribunal under decree 31 of 1991 to deal with complaints over the conduct and the results of the census. Objections from states, local governments and individuals - some 104 cases - flooded the tribunal.

No one can deny the fact that Babangida had pulled off a "generally peaceful and successful enumeration exercise."[24] He had good reasons to feel good about it too.

The new census figures created some problems for the political parties. Party membership figures appeared to have followed demographic projections –and were clearly inflated. Differences between the projections and the provisional figures, made some adjustments in the membership of the parties inevitable. NEC ordered the parties to review their membership registers in line with the new population figures. The parties duly went back to the drawing board to produce new membership figures. This was an interesting development with serious implications for the transition programme. But at least, for Babangida, it was a song of victory.

Chapter Fifteen

Hands across the Heart

We shall redress development between rural and urban centres
–President Ibrahim Babangida

Ibrahim Babangida made no secret of his ambition to make his administration *the* watershed in the social, political and economic development of Nigeria. To put it another way, he envisaged a country neatly divided into two phases - Nigeria before Babangida and Nigeria after Babangida. It was a tall ambition. He knew it. But he was an ambitious president.

First on his agenda, of course, were the structural adjustment of the national economy and the emergence of a new ethos in national politics through the deliberate encouragement and cultivation of new breed politicians. The second major approach consisted of social development programmes directed at the various demographic segments in the country. These programmes are best appreciated in the larger context of the main thrust of his economic policy embodied in the philosophy of his controversial structural adjustment programme. His own summary of the philosophy of that programme was this:

> The main objective of SAP is to make the Nigerian economy self-sustaining and less dependent on imports (and channel the consumption pattern of Nigerians) away from the high demand for foreign goods including food items which inflate the foreign debts of the nation, to locally produced goods.[1]

Perhaps, the most important of these social and economic development programmes, from the point of view of what they set out to address in the social and economic repositioning of Nigeria, were the Directorate of Food, Roads and Rural Infrastructure, best known by its acronym, DFRRI, the Peoples Bank, Urban Mass Transit and the National Directorate of Employment, NDE.

Taken together, these programmes were primarily intended to awaken in the nation a new spirit of private enterprise towards a focused national development. They were innovative. More importantly, they touched ordinary Nigerians in ways that government policies and programmes never did before. They were programmes of the people, for the people.

These programmes and the privatisation of government-owned companies and parastatals, certainly reflected Babangida's views on what should be done and how it should be done to make Nigeria "a) a self-reliant nation and b) a great and dynamic economy."[2]

The volatile rise and dip in the fortunes of the nation's crude oil-dependent economy from the early eighties led to the collapse of several industries in the country that in turn threw hundreds of their former employees into the labour market. They joined a steady stream of new graduates and fresh school leavers and a growing army of unskilled labour that drifted in from the rural areas. The result was a general rise in unemployment in Nigeria. In the sixties, the unemployment rate was below two per cent. Nigeria had a working population of 18.3 million people with about five per cent in the public services of the federal and regional governments. However, by 1985, the unemployment figure had risen to about ten per cent – and growing.

Unemployment is always a major threat to economic and social development. Dr. Chu Okongwu, Babangida's minister of budget and planning, rightly noted that "mass unemployment remains the burning issue of our time and demands urgent, resolute action (because) it constitutes a waste of resources, represents the most visible evidence of social injustice, promotes crime and social instability and cannot be tolerated in a civilised society."[3]

Babangida knew that if he did nothing about this growing national problem, it would effectively sabotage his economic policies and undermine his social development programmes. In his 1987 budget speech, he admitted that unemployment had become one of the greatest problems his government had to contend with. He promised to tackle it. He wasted little time on this. He had earlier appointed a committee on unemployment with a presidential brief to provide him with strategies on how best to deal with it. The recommendations of the committee, approved by the federal executive council, led to the birth of the National Directorate of Employment, NDE.

The committee set up by Babangida must have certainly benefited from the work of the National Committee on the Creation of Gainful Employment set up by the Buhari administration. That committee suggested that one way to tackle unemployment in the country was for the government to encourage people to go into agriculture. Buhari did not act on the recommendations of the committee before Babangida overthrew him in a palace coup.

In his 1987 budget speech, Babangida said that the directorate would "concentrate its efforts on the reactivation of public works, promotion of direct labour, promotion of self-employment, organisation of artisans into co-operatives, and (the) encouragement of a culture of maintenance and repairs."

The Chief of General Staff, Vice-Admiral Augustus Aikhomu, formally launched the directorate on January 30, 1987. It had four core programmes, namely, special public works, agricultural sector employment, youth employment and vocational skills development and small-scale industries and graduate employment. Government initially voted N35 million for the take-off of the directorate. But by May that year, this was increased to N55 million. This, according to Babangida, was to enable the directorate facilitate job creation by guaranteeing "loan fund with the commercial banks to facilitate the granting of loans to persons seeking self-employment under its programmes."

Part of the reasons for this generous allocation was Babangida's belief that the directorate offered as good an opportunity as any for the country to enjoy the fruits of mass employment. As he put it in a broadcast marking his third anniversary in office on August 27, 1988, "the mobilisation of labour for productivity is an important factor in rebuilding the national economy." He believed the directorate could effect this mass mobilisation through "recruiting youths for training in the acquisition of new skills and providing opportunities for them to engage thereafter in self-employment." The president also banned mass retrenchment of workers in the private sector, arguing for effect, "after all, it is those in employment who constitute the market for the products of industry." The ban was clearly a public relations gimmick. Hiring and firing in the private sector is not subject to government approval.

The directorate conducted apprenticeship training in specific areas of individual choice for graduates and school leavers, hundreds of whom were daily wearing out their shoes chasing after unavailable jobs. The initial primary areas of apprenticeship training were in fashion design, catering, hairdressing, carpentry, vulcanising, auto mechanics, welding, blacksmithing and bicycle repairing. Emphasis was on the dignity of labour and self-employment. Apprenticeship trainees were paid a monthly allowance of N250.00; later increased to N500.00. Graduates of the training programme were then given soft loans of between N5, 000.00 and N35, 000.00 as seed money to set up their businesses, thus turning them into self-employed young men and women – in the true spirit of the structural adjustment programme directed at making the nation self-reliant with self-reliant individuals.

Within the first year of the programme, the directorate claimed that it succeeded in creating some 330,165 jobs throughout the country. Five years later, it put it at more than 1.5 million jobs. By that time, government had also spent N1.2 billion on the directorate. That was not a 'chicken change' in those days by any standards.

If one discounts the exaggeration that necessarily attends successes claimed for programmes of this nature, one would still be left with the fact that the NDE proved to be a reasonable interventionist agency in addressing unemployment in the country. Four years after its establishment, the *New Nigerian* believed that the directorate "has made an impact going by the number of public programmes it had initiated and implemented. The *New Nigerian* is convinced that the NDE is worth the money spent in setting it up."[4]

Not many people would totally disagree with that view. It is, perhaps, a measure of its relevance that successive governments have retained the NDE. But it had several problems, one of which was that most of the beneficiaries of its loans generally saw them as their own share of the so-called national cake. They refused to repay the loans. Poor rate of loan recovery still bedevils the directorate. This explains its rather poor impact on employment generation in the country. If adequate measures had been taken from the inception of the directorate to ascertain an elementary fact like the correct addresses of the beneficiaries (some of them gave fake, non-existent addresses) it would have helped in loan recovery. The directorate is still functioning, even if it may have deviated from its original brief in the Babangida administration.

II

The first two or three years of the Babangida administration were years of intensive activities on all fronts in his ambition to effect changes or set in motion a process for changing various aspects of the life of the nation. Thus one other area that engaged Babangida's attention less than three years after becoming president was the country's transport system, which was rudimentary and chaotic. Road transport was largely in the hands of private transporters. They could not meet up with public demands for lack of adequate capital and managerial know-how. The rail system and the inland waterway transportation system were in progressive decay. An attempt by the Obasanjo military administration to reinvigorate the railways by contracting out its management to an Indian railway company, RITES, in the seventies failed to do the magic. So, the Nigerian Railway Corporation, which once provided the country's most reliable means of transportation, found itself progressively abandoned.

It must be said, however, that the Gowon administration addressed itself to this national problem. The period witnessed massive public sector intervention in road transportation and haulage. No one needed to be told that transportation is critical to a nation's social, commercial and economic progress and development. Each of the then twelve state governments set up its own transport service. Private sector participation was either lacking or inadequate in most of the states of the federation. By the middle eighties it became clear that a co-ordinated national approach to the problem was both urgent and necessary.

Babangida decided to search for this approach. Early in 1988, he set up a taskforce on urban transit to advise him on what should be done to fundamentally change the situation. The taskforce began its work in March that year and turned in its report a few months later. It recommended a three step approach – short term, medium and long terms on land-based urban mass transit. Government subsequently set up a mass transit implementation committee to work out the modalities for implementing the recommendations of the committee.

Dr. Kalu Idika Kalu, the then minister of transport, chaired the committee. From this came the Federal Mass Transit Programme, with Air-Vice-Marshall Mohammed Yahaya as its sole administrator. It was renamed Federal Urban Mass Transit Agency in 1993, backed up by decree 67 of that year. The decree spelt out elaborate functions of the Federal Urban Mass Transit Agency, worth quoting in full. These were to:

a) plan and advise the federal government on policy issues affecting urban transit planning, operation and management in Nigeria;
b) formulate the overall national policy on urban mass transit to include the regulation of fare structure, safety standards and passenger comfort;
c) set federal government's objectives and priorities on urban mass transit on continuous basis and also convey to the public, the federal government's policy on urban mass transit development;
d) implement federal government's directives on mass transit;
e) monitor and supervise the operational activities of the state mass transit agencies and promote urban transport operators in relation to technical assistance projects received from the agency;
f) conduct or commission studies on all aspects of urban mass transit delivery system in Nigeria;
g) organise training workshops, seminars and conferences as it deems fit to enhance the performance of its role and those of mass transit delivery system in Nigeria and
h) perform such other functions, which may be assigned to it from time to time by the president, commander-in-chief of the armed forces.

Brigadier-General Stephen Ikya later succeeded Yahaya as sole administrator of the agency. Babangida invested much hope and financial resources in the agency. Details of what the Babangida administration spent on the agency are sketchy but by 1996 when he was no longer in office, government had pumped in as much as N5 billion into it from when he set it up. The bulk of that amount was spent during the Babangida administration. With the fund, the agency tried to carry out its statutory functions. It gave out 5,500 buses to the states that in turn sold them at subsidised rates to established or new transporters in their respective areas. It also gave buses to trade unions.

The Punch pointed out in its editorial of June 25, 1997, that the agency "was a deliberate effort by the government to ease the excruciating transportation problems afflicting most of Nigeria's urban centres." Babangida wanted the agency to do much more than that. He wanted a dramatic and sustained improvement in urban-rural transportation throughout the country. He expected transporters and potential transporters to take advantage of the opening up of the rural areas through the work of DFRRI to effect dramatic changes in urban-rural transportation as well as transportation within the rural areas.

Nigerians, to be sure, enthusiastically responded to this initiative. Hundreds of them became transporters overnight, courtesy of the agency. Buses with the inscription, Federal Mass Transit Assisted, became common sights on Nigerian roads. The attractive loan conditions offered by the agency attracted all takers, particularly those who had no experience in transportation. It charged three per cent interest a year initially. It was later increased to six per cent. Even at that, it was a generous term. It supplied buses with all the necessary spare parts to state governments, private transport owners and the trade unions.

On the face of it, Babangida's mass transit system looked successful. But even before he left office, some rot had set in. The agency faced some financial difficulties because some of the beneficiaries of its subsidised loans for the buses defaulted in loan repayments. By 1995, the agency was owed N450 million. The fault did not lie with the beneficiaries of the facility in the private sector but with the state governments. Loan repayment by the states averaged ten per cent; it was an impressive 70 per cent in the private sector. The agency operated a revolving loan. Loan default gradually but effectively crippled it. The Obasanjo administration scrapped it. FUMTA joined a long list of wonderful national developmental efforts that died, taking the dreams of millions of people down with them.

III

The Peoples Bank eventually suffered the same fate too. The idea for the Peoples Bank was borrowed from the runaway success story of a similar scheme initiated in Bangladesh by a Bangladeshi economist, Professor Muhammad Yunus. His experiment of trying to save the poorest of the poor in that country from merciless money lenders by giving them loans of about the equivalent of one United States dollar, led Yunus to found what he calls Grameen Bank, the poor people's bank, in 1983.

The bank gives loans without collateral to the poor in Bangladesh. It was a unique experiment in tackling poverty. The loans averaged less than one United States dollar per person at the inception of the bank. A pittance may be, but the poor rural dwellers at the mercy of moneylenders did not need much more than that to turn their lives around. The bank, now worth more than six billion US dollars, has taken millions of Bangladeshi out of poverty. The non-collaterised loans are part of the beauty of this innovative loan scheme. The poor had no collaterals any way. The only collateral Yunus banks on is their word of honour to repay the loan as and when due. Honour means a lot to the poor villagers. They keep their word of honour. The result is an impressive repayment rate of between 97 and 100 per cent.

Yunus had hit on a winning formula for tackling poverty. He and the bank were jointly awarded the Nobel Peace Prize in 2006. Yunus sees Grameen Bank as "...a message of hope, a programme for putting homelessness and destitution in a museum so that one day our children will visit it and ask how we could have allowed such a terrible thing to go on for so long."

His very successful experiment has never been quite replicated anywhere else in the world but it has inspired several efforts in several countries. Babangida was clearly inspired by what Yunus did and believed he could successfully replicate it in Nigeria. Nigeria is not as poor as Bangladesh. It is an oil rich country ironically battling with poverty, especially in the rural areas, which account for about 78 per cent of the population. He believed that the country needed a bank that would take care of the financial needs of the poor in the urban and rural areas.

Babangida's own answer to the problem was The Peoples Bank of Nigeria that he set up with a hundred per cent government funding in 1989, four years after he came to power and six years after Yunus showed that a non-traditional banking system tailored to the peculiar needs of the poor could be a catalyst in the fight against poverty. Its enabling law was decree 22 of 1990. Babangida calculatedly dramatised The Peoples Bank as the poor man's own bank by choosing Ajegunle, a poor ghetto in the Lagos metropolis and home to millions of poor people, as the venue for the formal launch of the bank on October 4, 1989. He went further in his dramatisation by appointing the late Tai Solarin, a well-known educationist, social critic and a champion of the poor and the down trodden, chairman of the implementation task force for the bank.

The bank had an initial take-off grant of ₦150, 000.00. Babangida was its first cashier at its launch. The happy loan beneficiaries walked on air as they received the money directly from the president. The loans ranged from ₦35.00 to ₦1, 500.00. Among the first fifty beneficiaries of the bank loan were shoe-repairers, tailors, food sellers and artisans. The very first beneficiary was a dressmaker, Mrs Hannah Ilodibe, who received a ₦1, 500.00 loan from the president. ₦2, 000.00 was the maximum loan to a beneficiary.

Within the first few weeks of its launch, the bank opened branches in eight states. By 1993, according to its first national co-ordinator and later, managing director, the late Mrs. Maria Sokenu, the bank had 250 branches and 508 satellite centres nationwide. It had also disbursed ₦300 million loans to about 1.6 million people. Sokenu claimed the bank achieved a loan repayment rate of 93 per cent, a figure that should be taken with a pinch of salt.

Sokenu painted a success story of the bank but its affairs were not that rosy. Within its first year of operation the bank was faced with operational contradictions and in fighting among members of the implementation task force. In a memo written sometime in 1990, Mohammed Haruna, a member of the implementation taskforce and the co-ordinator for Kaduna zone, identified the problems as a) "an increasing divergence from the original concept" of the bank b) "serious disunity of purpose within the Implementation Task Force under the chairmanship of Tai Solarin" and c) the inability of "the national co-ordinator, Mrs. (Maria) Sokenu (to give) a sound and consistent leadership to management."

Newswatch magazine assessed the first two years of the operation of the bank in 1991 and, on the basis of the information made available to it, came to the conclusion that "the Peoples Bank of Nigeria has developed all the symptoms of the complex Nigerian disease: ethnicity, the north-south syndrome, profligacy, inefficiency, maladministration, fraud and greed."[5]

Things were falling apart in the poor people's bank. The ministry of finance and economic planning that supervised the bank was so worried that it decided to investigate what was going on. The panel made some shock findings, one of which was that the members of the taskforce were at one another's throat. The report said: "The national co-ordinator and the zonal co-ordinators now operate as local tetrarchs in their small empires, pulling the head office and the zones in opposing directions and owing allegiance to no one but themselves. The implementation taskforce has become incoherent, unwieldy, unwilling and unable to work as a team."[6]

The investigative panel also reported that "complaints were rife of the insensitivity and high-handedness with which the national co-ordinator handled the affairs of the zones, especially in the release of funds and her stubborn refusal to carry out the decisions of the ITF, even when the supervisory ministry intervened."[7]

Government was eventually forced to take action. It dissolved the implementation taskforce but re-appointed Solarin as chairman of the board of the directors and Sokenu as managing director. But it would appear that the real problems of the bank had to do with its ill-defined operational guidelines. Sokenu and Solarin simply interpreted the mission of the bank entirely as they wished. Again, what the investigative panel established here is interesting. It said: "Riding on the wings of sentiment and emotion, the national co-ordinator manipulated the chairman to approve programmes which were never placed before the ITF for their consideration and approval." It cited several cases to buttress its conclusion, namely, the purchase of 15 buses for ₦7.055 million, ₦12,126,900.20 as loans to some beneficiaries under the umbrella of Mrs. Maryam Babangida's Better Life Programme and military officers' wives and the ₦4,502,800 given to some persons displaced from Maroko by the Lagos State Government.

These expenditures were clearly outside the operational guideline of the bank. But Solarin refused to accept that Sokenu clearly acted outside her mandate. He strongly defended her, arguing, "if you say the wives of junior army officers or the Maroko people are not in our programme, I would ask you, what then is in our programme? The programme offers opportunity to be innovative in trying to meet the needs of the poor. Or you think there are no poor and jobless women in the army barracks? The Maroko people you are talking about are low-income people who work as messengers, cooks, etc."[8]

Solarin, of course, got it all mixed up. Section 2 of the bank's enabling law stipulated the target group intended to benefit from the loans given by the bank. The law also provided that beneficiaries be given the loans as co-operatives. It provided no room for loans to transport owners or for the purchase of buses to be given to them, which the bank funded with a total of ₦40 million. And because each co-ordinator more or less did as he pleased without regard to accounting procedures, the investigative panel noted that "nobody can say now with any degree of certainty how exactly the bank spent ₦130, 920,102.54 since it went into operation in October 1989."[9]

The bank survived the Babangida administration but it was eventually scrapped. Nigeria thus failed to replicate the success story of the Grameen Bank in Bangladesh. Two possible reasons can be offered for the failure of the Nigerian experiment. Firstly, the Peoples Bank of Nigeria was a very good idea borrowed from a country with which Nigeria has nothing in common in terms of culture and social outlook. A loan of about the equivalent of one US dollar does not have the same value in Nigeria as it does in Bangladesh. What works for Bangladesh cannot, on that account, necessarily work for Nigeria.

Secondly, Grameen Bank is entirely a private sector experiment. Its Nigerian counterpart was a government experiment. Yunus had very little money to give. He required no elaborate bureaucratic set up to run his experiment. More importantly, he began the experiment from one small corner of the country, not nationwide. It spread only when it had succeeded. Everything about the Peoples Bank of Nigeria was the opposite of Grameen Bank.

No one knows for sure how much money was actually sunk into the bank by the federal government. According to *Newswatch* magazine, the federal government gave a take-off grant of ₦30 million to the bank in 1989. The bank subsequently received ₦200 million in 1990 and ₦290 million in 1991.[10] Sokenu claimed in 1993 that the bank 'mobilised' not less than ₦409 million.

Was the Peoples Bank of Nigeria a drainpipe? The late Gani Fawehinmi believed it was worse than that, arguing that "the so-called establishment of the Peoples Bank (was) a ruse to hoodwink and mislead the unwary, the innocent, the aggrieved, the cheated, the persecuted and the oppressed in our society."[11]

IV

Perhaps, the most controversial of Babangida's social development programmes was the Directorate of Food, Roads and Rural Infrastructure, DFRRI. It is worth looking at the directorate at some length for at least one good reason: it represented an original but ambitious attempt at transforming the rural areas of the country. Nothing of that magnitude had been attempted in the country before. It was almost unique in its ambition and comprehensiveness.

Babangida first dropped the hint about the programme in his 1986 budget broadcast in which he spoke of his government's decision to partially withdraw subsidies on petroleum products. This, he said, would "yield a total of about ₦900 million (savings)."[12]

This money, he said, would be used

> ...for education and for the purpose of rehabilitating various categories of roads in the country and especially for the development of a national network of rural and feeder roads in order to strengthen the massive effort for food and agricultural self-sufficiency in the shortest possible period. In that pursuit,

government will establish a Directorate of Food, Roads and Rural Infrastructure in the office of the president. The directorate will work closely with the state governments in order to reach the various communities in each of the 304 local government areas throughout the country.[13]

Babangida wasted little time in giving effect to this proposal. He constituted an eight-man board of the directorate, headed by Commodore Larry Koinyan, a member of the Armed Forces Ruling Council. Commodore Ebitu Ukiwe, the Chief of General Staff, inaugurated the board on February 7, 1986. Its enabling law was decree number 4 of 1987. The directorate was put under the presidency to ensure effective monitoring by Babangida himself.

According to Babangida,

> The motivation to give primacy to rural development in the country was not simply a response to an exigent national crisis, however grave that crisis was. Rather, it was a recognition that no nation can hope to be truly developed unless it starts by mobilising the vast majority of its population and strives assiduously to improve and transform the circumstances in which they live and earn their livelihood, and within these improved and transformed circumstances to motivate the citizenry and the nation to attempt to attain the possible highest goals and objectives. This task must start from our grassroots, namely, our rural areas where the majority of the citizenry of this country reside. From there, it should encompass the entire nation. Rural development is indeed the true and lasting foundation for national development. Rural development is therefore not for the benefit of the rural people alone. It is for the benefit of the entire citizenry of the country.[14]

This then was the basic philosophy of the programme. To appreciate Babangida's decision to initiate DFRRI, one must look at the place of rural Nigeria in the social and economic development of the country; or perhaps, its under-development. It is a fairly well known fact that Nigeria was an agrarian economy before crude oil, found in commercial quantities in the delta region of the country in 1956, began the slow but steady process of turning Nigeria into an oil rich country. Before then, its main cash crops, cotton, groundnuts, cocoa and palm produce, were the mainstay of the economy.

Agriculture was, and still is, in the hands of peasant farmers in the rural communities. A survey conducted by the board of DFRRI confirmed there were between 90,000 and 100,000 communities in the country. The neglect of the rural areas means in effect the neglect of these communities whose combined population was 75 per cent of the national population.

Governments, pre-and *post*-independence, concentrated development in the urban areas, the centres of political and economic power. The rural communities were comprehensively denied those things that have come to be known famously in Nigeria as basic social amenities - roads, water, light, educational and health facilities. The absence of these basic social amenities meant life was, and is, hard and even brutish for the rural dwellers. Life was comparatively easier in the towns and the cities where these facilities were available, even if inadequately. No one needed to be persuaded that the towns and the cities were where things were happening.

The rural-urban drift began as a trickle shortly after independence in 1960. As petro-Naira fuelled gigantic development projects in the towns and cities in the seventies, the rural-urban drift turned into a steady stream. An enormous human traffic poured into the towns and cities. The urban centres were soon choked with those that Brigadier-General Mobolaji Johnson, former military governor of Lagos State, once referred to, rather contemptuously, as the Dick Whittingtons. Lagos received the brunt of this rural-urban drift. It was the federal capital. Those who flocked into the city saw it as the El Dorado. They were happy to make their homes under overhead bridges, broken down vehicles and other unlikely places - to await the arrival of the good times they believed they saw in the horizon. For them, life under the bridges and broken down vehicles was much better than life back home in their rural communities.

By the early seventies, the rural-urban drift had become a serious national problem. Federal and state governments were increasingly worried. And rightly so. It was imperative for the governments to take steps to dam the flood of human traffic. The most obvious remedy was to revive agriculture in the rural communities - and keep the farmers and the young school leavers there.

This was the approach adopted by the Obasanjo military administration with its Operation Feed the Nation, OFN, a clarion call directed at the elite in the country to take up farming on a large commercial scale. Government hoped that if the elite took to farming, it would, a) dignify agriculture and make it attractive to young school leavers who thought of it as a lowly enterprise unworthy of their education and b) lead to large-scale, mechanised farming and ultimately change the face, if not the character, of agriculture in the country.

And there was the carrot. Financial assistance was available to potential farmers. The Nigerian Agricultural and Co-operative Bank Limited and the Agricultural Credit Guarantee Scheme, for instance, were primarily set up to give financial assistance to farmers, elite or non-elite. The Agricultural Credit Guarantee Scheme was set up in April 1978,

...to provide guarantee, in respect of loans granted by commercial and merchant banks for agricultural purposes, with the aim of increasing the level of bank credit to the agricultural sector. Between April 1978 and August 1979, over 1,000 loans amounting to ₦28.6 million were guaranteed.[15]

"One immediate result of the establishment of the agricultural credit guarantee scheme (was) the emergence of a new class of educated urban farmers."[16] Their emergence was something of a disappointment. It did not herald the anticipated dawn in the country's agricultural development and production. And as Shagari noted, it even threatened the peasant farmers, the authentic backbone of agriculture in the country.

Nigeria was still dependent on imports for much of its food needs such as rice, wheat as well as beef and poultry. The food importation peaked by 1981 when the country spent one billion Naira or $2.5 billion on it. That would be about ₦297.5 billion in today's value of the national currency.

OFN was short-lived. Shagari dumped it less than six months after he succeeded Obasanjo in October 1979. He initiated his own new agricultural development programme, the Green Revolution,

...to move this country rapidly towards self-sufficiency in food and agricultural raw materials (because) the future of this country is inextricably linked with the future of its agriculture.[17]

Green Revolution emphasised co-operative farming. Shagari spoke at some length about the place of co-operative farming in modern agricultural productivity at the grand opening of the head office building of the Nigerian Agricultural and Co-operative Bank Limited in Kaduna in December, 1979. He promised, and it would appear he was as good as his words, that his administration would give "the highest possible level of financial support ....to make the Green Revolution a vivid reality in our time."[18]

The most visible face of the Green Revolution programme was the acquisition and clearing of large tracts of land in virtually all the then 19 states for distribution to rural co-operative farmers. Its core philosophy of co-operative farming was a new concept in most parts of the rural communities where peasant farmers preferred to hold on to individual family plots of land. In areas of the country where co-operative farming was a new concept, government made no attempts to educate the peasant farmers on its virtues before the programme was introduced. This, certainly, contributed to the apparent failure of the programme. In the majority of cases, the peasant farmers refused to take up the cleared farmlands. The contractors collected their money; the cleared farmlands were allowed to become bushes again.

Green Revolution too had a short shelf life. Buhari scrapped it. And that ended two serious attempts to revive agriculture in the country.

By the time Babangida came to power, therefore, there were no dramatic changes in the country's agricultural productivity or in life in the rural communities. Babangida was no stranger to the brutish and deprived life in the rural communities. He was born in Wushishi, a typical rural area with a typical rural life in what is now Niger State. Babangida's father, Malam Ibrahim, was a victim of what could be attributed to rural neglect. When he took ill with jaundice, he had to be taken to the nearest hospital at Kontagora, 120 km away. The road was in such poor shape that the drive took more about three hours. Malam Ibrahim died a few days after his admission into the hospital. Perhaps, he might have lived if there was a hospital in Wushishi and he was treated early. Babangida was not one to forget that experience.

As he plotted his way to power, one of the things that worried Babangida was the condition of the rural communities and the country's near total dependence on importation to meet its food needs. About four months after he came to power, he pledged to give top priority to agricultural production, so we can "feed ourselves and the production should be such that we should be able to export and make sure that our industries are alive so that we can provide employment to the teeming masses of the population."[19]

Babangida, therefore, promised to "redress the imbalance in development between rural and urban areas and ensure a better standard of living for the majority of our citizens who live in rural areas."[20] His ambition was to end the "low production capacity, low income, poverty and its cultural manifestations, lack of basic infrastructures, poor housing, widespread illiteracy and ignorance"[21] in the rural areas if only to end or de-accelerate "unhealthy and dangerous drift of able young men and women from the rural areas to turn our cities into over-crowded centres of filth and crime."[22]

He came to power with a rudimentary blueprint for rural development. He had worked on the blueprint with the assistance of his close friend, Professor Isawa Elaigwu. They did a comparative study of how other countries, particularly India and Bangladesh, tackled their rural under-development. That rural development blueprint became DFRRI.

DFRRI differed fundamentally from OFN and Green Revolution in one important respect. It went way beyond food production. It represented, in so far as one could see, a major step in redressing rural neglect. In contrast, OFN and Green Revolution were narrow in their concept. Both primarily targeted accelerated food production.

Babangida, who prided himself on being a good student of social events, must have been guided in his programme by the failure of the two earlier major post-independence attempts at increased food production. The first lesson he applied to DFRRI was to broaden its concept. Increased food production was central to its philosophy but the basic thrust of DFRRI was to effect a dramatic physical change in the rural communities through infrastructural development. Emphasis was on rural roads and infrastructure throughout the 100,000 communities in the country. Anyone could see that this was as tall an ambition as they come.

The public received the programme enthusiastically. Some eight months after the programme took off, Babangida knew he had a winning formula for rural development. He barely resisted shouting Eureka! He enthused:

> The establishment of the DFRRI is based on our belief that the people in the rural society possess the knowledge that can be tapped by collective labour. It is based on the need to back such efforts with new techniques so as to boost the local knowledge and to upgrade their level of production.[23]

Or, to put it another way, according to *The African Guardian* weekly newsmagazine in its editorial of February 20, 1989:

> DFRRI was specifically designed to help ensure that the country achieves self-sufficiency in food production and that the rural-urban drift is curtailed by stimulating and sustaining productive activities in the rural areas.

DFRRI jolted everyone with its common sense approach to a fundamental national problem. Even the Nigerian press, easily the most sceptical institution in the country, went gaga over the programme. It continued to rhapsodise it even six years later. This was truly remarkable. To cite a few instances, the *Daily Sketch,* in its editorial of February 19, 1992, described DFRRI as "perhaps the best and first meaningful step to open up, develop and integrate the rural areas in the country." The paper said that although "the people did not think much of it" at the beginning, "today we are celebrating the sixth year of DFRRI's notable presence in Nigeria's rural recesses."

Another national newspaper, *New Agenda,* in its editorial of February 22-28, 1992, saw DFRRI as "a systematic attack on the underdevelopment which had been the bane of our rural communities all over the country" by the Babangida administration. The newspaper went on to say that the achievements of the directorate had, "for the first time in Nigerian history started to make Nigerians in the rural communities ... begin to feel that they belong to the same national family as those who reside in the urban areas, which had been the sole beneficiaries of national development efforts."

In its editorial of February 24, 1992, *The Guardian* described DFRRI as "one of the more successful programmes of the Babangida administration. To the administration," it said, "belongs the credit for discovering, as it were, the rural areas after decades of official neglect and making them the target of programmes designed to improve the quality of rural life..."

The Mail spoke in a similar vein in its editorial of February 9, 1991, on the fifth anniversary of the directorate. It said that "the establishment of DFRRI is, doubtless, one of the most imaginative initiatives of the Babangida administration. Though the majority of Nigerian people live, move and have their being in the rural areas, successive governments have rarely paid more than lip service to their wellbeing."

Babangida relished these encomiums. Who would not? If the Nigerian press said he was right, then he was. After all, according to Koinyan, "never before has the country witnessed the kind of concerted and comprehensive war which the Babangida administration has relentlessly waged against rural poverty, deprivation and powerlessness..."[24]

Opening up the rural areas through a network of all season roads was seen as the key to the success of DFRRI. In its first year of operation, therefore, Babangida gave the directorate a target of "rehabilitating some 60,000 km of rural feeder roads"[25] at an estimated cost of ₦500 million. This was clearly ambitious but Babangida could not resist the urge to have the directorate do more in less time, if only to re-assure himself that the programme was more than an informed gamble. Interestingly, the total budget for the directorate in 1986, the first year of its operation, was ₦433 million. This was less than what it voted for roads alone.

Babangida was thoroughly committed to the programme. The first two years of its operation showed how far the president was prepared to go to make it a success, if, that is, money was all it needed. The directorate was not starved of fund. Half a billion naira went to it in the two consecutive fiscal years of 1987 and 1988. In 18 months, the directorate received a total of ₦800, 591,533. It was enough money to do much but certainly, as it turned out, not nearly enough to do everything under the sun.

By the account of the directorate, the rural revolution was in full bloom. And then something happened to DFRRI. In their anxiety to meet public expectations, officials of the directorate began to make wild and exaggerated claims of performance. Figures were thrown at the public as evidence of achievements: ₦174 million spent on rural feeder roads; ₦100 million on rural water and sanitation projects; ₦37.1 million on the cultivation of fruit trees, etc, in 1987 alone.

It is difficult to understand, let alone explain, why the press was so thoroughly mesmerised by the success story of the directorate when, by its second year, doubts were already being raised about its actual performances. By 1988, the claims of performance by the directorate at the state and local government levels had become subjects of dispute in the press. Some publications began to take a more serious look at these disputes. Perhaps, the disputes also forced the public to take more than a casual interest in the activities of the directorate. *Hotline,* a bi-weekly magazine published in Kaduna, appeared to have set the tone when it commented in an editorial:

> We believe that a billion naira is a lot of money. We believe that when something slightly less than ten per cent of the national budget is committed to one directorate alone, we ought to see something for our money. We are aware of many rural areas that are still in darkness, that are still without potable water. Has a billion naira worth of impact been made this year in any of these areas?[26]

The *New Nigerian*, a federal government-owned newspaper, in its editorial of December 14, 1987, said, as if in answer to *Hotline* that "…. it is very much open to question if these fiscal blessings on DFRRI can be seen in physical projects."

But the questions raised by *Hotline* magazine were the same questions that other people had begun to raise about the programme. It was becoming increasingly clear that DFRRI was not delivering on its promise. Nigerians wanted "permanent, concrete, decent evidence of government presence and performance, not slogans"[27] but slogans were more easily available.

Exaggerated claims and, in very many cases, outright falsehood put out by officials of the directorate showed just how desperate they were to mollify growing public disenchantment with a programme which promised so much but was giving the public disappointingly very little. Government found it necessary to send in groups of inspectors to some of the states to independently assess the performances of the directorate. Most of the verification teams turned in reports that did not support the reported claims of the directorate. In 1987, for instance, Professor Akin Mabogunje, a member of the national directorate of DFRRI, visited Niger State on an inspection tour. He was so disappointed with what he saw that he told the then state governor, Col Garba Mohammed, that he scored the state directorate "zero for poor performances."[28]

The desire on the part of the DFRRI board to prove that the directorate was the revolution the country had been waiting for stretched their ambition to the point of naivety. DFRRI plunged headlong into all areas of human development, expecting, against the odds, to bring revolution to the rural areas in one fell swoop. In addition to roads, water and electricity, it took on rural sanitation, horticulture, agriculture, education, fishery, the production of goat and sheep weanlings, rabbitry, fruit seedlings, engineering and technology, rural industrialisation and whatever else caught the fancy of its board. There was no stopping the directorate.

Babangida's faith in the programme remained unshaken two years after he introduced it because "rural development is, indeed, the true and lasting foundation for national development."[29] Everyone agreed with him but it had become clear that his rural transformation programme was in trouble. Much of this was kept away from him. Instead, he was fed with an appetizing diet of success stories of the programme. By late 1992, however, Babangida knew that something had gone wrong with the programme. He confessed to being "worried about the assessment of DFRRI." Still, the bureaucrats shielded him from the truth. According to Babangida,

> .... unknown to me, the cabinet office sponsored verification teams of private people and some experts in the universities to go round and look at the rural areas and come out with statistics. We wanted figures; we did not want stories. I was pleasantly surprised by these reports because they were able to show that the lot of the communities in the villages had improved since the inception of the programme. I was convinced it was one of the most successful programmes that we have undertaken. I think they have reasonably met the objectives that we set for them.[30]

If he had been given the correct picture when things were going wrong, he could have brought it back on course. Once the president had articulated his vision of the new rural Nigeria, he left the logistics to the board of the directorate.

There were, at least, three problems with the execution of the rural development programme under DFRRI. Firstly, the directorate took on just too much. Its chairman, Koinyan, issued a fourteen-page press statement in November, 1987, giving a full list of the extent of its ambition - community listing, authentication, codification, publication, organisation of the territorial space (regional planning) and the organisation of people for socio-cultural, political and economic development, community development plans, community and social mobilisation, community self-help projects, adult education and rural manpower development, private sector relations, rural health education, home economics, information services, conferences, seminars, workshops and rural development data collection and analysis - are examples of the rather bizarre ambitions of the directorate.

Why did it take on so much when its officials ought to know that even with all the money in the world, DFRRI did not possess the managerial capacity or the logistics to solve every developmental problem in the country? It is difficult to understand why government allowed the directorate to go beyond its basic brief of increased agricultural production, opening up the rural feeder roads to improve movement and interaction between the rural and urban areas, providing water through the simple application of the borehole technology and assisting in the setting up and maintenance of rural health facilities.

Chief Olu Falae, secretary to the government of the federation at the time, correctly blamed the problems of the directorate on what he called its over-involvement. "It is in charge of roads and rural infrastructure, but going into agriculture, in my view, should not be one of the mainstream activities of DFRRI."[31]

Secondly, the funding formula adopted in the second year of the programme with the federal government contributing 75%; the states and local governments 15% and 7% respectively and the rural communities, three per cent amounted to an attempt by the federal government not to shoulder the full responsibilities of the directorate.

Thirdly, and perhaps most seriously, DFRRI like almost all government projects and programmes, was riddled with corruption. DFRRI officials passed off projects handled by other agencies of government as theirs. The quality of work executed by DFRRI contractors could hardly be poorer. Boreholes did not function the day after commissioning. Roads were washed out by rain. Culverts collapsed under their own weight. Various projects were abandoned in various stages of incompletion – monuments to the failure of the country's first articulated programme to confront the problems of rural under-development.

By 1992, the country had spent ₦1.9 billion on the programme. The amount of money reflected Babangida's belief in his rural transformation programme. But DFRRI required more than money to make the dreams of a transformed rural Nigeria come true. Perhaps, Professor Sam Aluko got it right. In a letter to the national directorate, he warned:

> Unless the problems of rural development are more effectively co-ordinated and the location of the main actors and catalysts of the various programmes and projects is firmly in the rural areas, particularly at the local government headquarters in the various autonomous communities, we will assess the effectiveness of the directorate mainly in terms of the huge sums of money spent, and less in the actual physical output arising therefrom.[32]

Criticisms of the directorate came fast and furious. Local government chairmen felt excluded from the affairs of the directorate. They met in

Kaduna in February, 1988, and issued a communiqué asking the federal government to disband DFRRI and hand over its functions and finances to them. Others called for its decentralisation, failing which, the federal government should convert it into a ministry. This, Koinyan strongly disagreed with, arguing that "the quickest way to kill the efforts of the directorate is to convert it into a ministry."

Babangida did not convert it into a ministry. Instead, he scrapped DFRRI as an autonomous agency and merged it with the ministry of water resources and rural development in 1992. Its failure was a sad, baleful end to a wonderful, hopeful beginning. Ironically, Koinyan unintentionally provided what turned out to be its apt epitaph. In his progress report in 1988, he said that

> ...experience has shown that government always comes out with a good policy to help its citizens but the operators, either out of naivety or inaction, always ruin the execution of such projects.[33]

It was a fitting epitaph too for the Peoples Bank of Nigeria and the Urban Mass Transit system.

The failure of these projects does not take away from Babangida the fact that he and his wife made separate but genuine efforts to make rural Nigeria a place of life and living and not one of deprivation and punishment.

The First Lady, Maryam, initiated a programme that complemented DFRRI and the Peoples Bank. Her Better Life for the Rural African Woman programme, initiated in September 1986, was formally launched sometime in 1987. Although rural women were its primary focus, the programme was an ambitious attempt to change the educational and economic lot of Nigerian women in general by opening them up to the peculiar challenges they face as women and as a critical element in the development process. The first three of its seven-point objectives were:

- To raise the social consciousness of women about their rights and roles, as well as their social, political and economic responsibilities.
- To sensitise, motivate and mobilise women for a more positive and fulfilling life.
- To encourage women to work together for better understanding and the resolution of their problems.

Aikhomu described the Better Life programme as "a forum for critical political consciousness (and) an institutional complement to many other government projects and programmes such as MAMSER, the

Peoples Bank…. targeted at the eradication of poverty among rural womenfolk."

Mrs Babangida received several international awards for her Better Life initiative. Perhaps, the most important to her was the Africa Prize for Leadership for Sustainable End to Hunger, given to her in 1991. The *Daily Champion* noted in its editorial comment of October 3, 1992: "Mrs Babangida has brought glamour to the office of First Lady. Her initiative raised the level of socio-political and economic consciousness of womenfolk in the country."

And thanks to her, the office of First Lady in Nigeria would never be the same again. First ladies who came after her initiated their own programmes. Imitation is still the best form of flattery, if not envy.

Chapter Sixteen

Bridges across Nations

It must be a sound and meaningful foreign policy
–Ibrahim Babangida

All countries are wary of a change of government in other countries largely because of the possibility of dramatic foreign policy reversals that might turn friends into enemies and enemies into friends. There is a greater anxiety with a change of government through a coup d'état. Military regimes generally tend to be inclined towards confused foreign policies in the name of radicalism. A new government usually finds it necessary, therefore, to quickly re-assure friends of its continued friendship and good neighbourliness.

Babangida followed this traditional script. He said nothing on assumption of office to raise the anxiety of the international community. He assured African countries they had no reasons to fear the direction of his foreign policy because "African problems and their solutions shall constitute the premise of our foreign policy."

Babangida dropped the hint it might not be business as usual on the foreign front by taking a swipe at Buhari's foreign policy. He said it was "... characterised by inconsistency and incoherency (and, therefore) lacked the clarity to make us know where we stand on matters of international concern to enable other countries relate to us with seriousness." He also accused Buhari of conducting vengeful diplomacy and lack of initiative. "Vengeful considerations," he said, "must not be the basis of our diplomacy."

In his twenty months in office, Buhari made no waves on the international scene. He was pre-occupied with more pressing domestic problems. He stuck to the traditional path of the country's foreign policy and remained true to the Afro-centric foreign policy objectives of successive Nigerian leaders. One major step he took was the recognition of the Polisario Front that for years fought Morocco for the independence of the Western Sahara. The Polisario Front, frustrated by the inability of the OAU to resolve the conflict, declared independence and renamed the territory the Saharawi Arab Democratic Republic, SADR. Some African leaders recognised the republic but Shagari vacillated. Buhari ended the country's foot dragging by recognising SADR. Evidence, perhaps, that

Buhari did nothing to undermine Nigeria's prestige as an African leader as far as his foreign policy was concerned.

Buhari's external affairs minister, Professor Ibrahim Gambari, who criticised the ousted Shagari administration's foreign policy as "bureaucratic, vague, and possibly out of tune with the aspirations for our country held by the informed public," argues that Buhari's foreign policy "remained Afro-centric, but with a greater shift to the centre which was in Nigeria's national interest." In general, he contended:

> The Buhari administration decided that the defence of Nigeria's national security and the welfare of her citizens would be the axis around which foreign policy would revolve. We thus projected the country's national interest along the lines of concentric circles of policy priorities, an orientation of foreign policy that was conceptually sound and consistent with the recognition of reduced national financial resources and power.[1]

Buhari's number two, the Chief of Staff, Supreme Headquarters, the late Major General Tunde Idiagbon, underlined this point at a meeting with the country's new ambassadors on May 25, 1984. He said that Africa being the centrepiece of the administration's foreign policy, the administration was committed to:

a) the eradication of all vestiges of colonialism from the continent and the liberation of Namibia;
b) the destruction of apartheid in racist South Africa;
c) the peaceful resolution of the conflicts in the continent; and
d) the development of the continent through regional co-operation such as ECOWAS.

Nearly one year after he assumed office, Buhari let the nation into his thoughts on his foreign policy and why, perhaps, he did not appear to be active on that front. At the annual patron's dinner of Nigeria's foreign policy think tank, the Nigerian Institute of International Affairs, in December 1984, he said:

> Nigeria is passing through a most difficult period characterized by the worldwide economic recession, drought and starvation and internally by the battle for national survival through the revival of its battered economy and a creation of a leadership imbued with discipline, public accountability and integrity. No country in the world can command the respect and admiration of the international community without a dedicated and purposeful leadership. Indeed, no country can conduct a successful foreign policy without first putting its house in order. A nation's foreign policy is derivative of its perception of its national

interests from various perspectives.

To lay a solid foundation for the successful pursuit of Nigeria's foreign policy, this administration has from its inception, laid strong emphasis on the adoption of realistic objectives, policies and programmes. We have taken tough but necessary measures to revamp the economy, rid this country of waste and extravagance, and inculcate discipline in our body politic. This has been complemented by other domestic policy measures for the well-being of our people, the revitalization of agriculture and agro-based industries, revival of factories in the manufacturing sector and a programme for the rapid but orderly development of our petro-chemical and liquefied natural gas industries...[2]

One of these "tough measures" was his purge of the Foreign Service. The Shagari administration, whatever might have been its failings elsewhere, is credited with making 1980-83 "the golden years of the Nigerian Foreign Service. (He) dealt effectively with sagging morale of the foreign service officers (by introducing) better conditions of service."[3] He opened eleven new diplomatic missions.

There was a downside to it. The foreign service was bloated with the appointment of more politicians than career foreign service officers as ambassadors. Even the lower cadre of the service witnessed the influx of political godsons. "People were recruited into the service on the basis of political constituencies and not on need" and the number of external affairs officers bloomed from fewer than 350 to more than 500 between 1980 and 1983.[4]

The influx of political appointees bred indiscipline. Some junior and senior officers who had godfathers among politicians in the ruling party became untouchables. Buhari's purge, unfortunately, threw out the baby with the bath water. Good and experienced career Foreign Service officers were thrown out of office. The purge affected more than 120 senior career Foreign Service officers and "sent a shock wave throughout the ministry of external affairs and Nigerian diplomatic missions abroad."[5] The Foreign Service was severely demoralised. A demoralised foreign service did nothing to enhance the foreign policy initiatives of the Buhari administration or the popularity of the general among serving and retired officers.

Despite his commitment to an Afro-centric foreign policy, Buhari ordered the expulsion of hundreds of illegal aliens from the West African sub-region to their home countries in May 1985. The difficult economic situation in those countries had forced their nationals to seek greener pastures in Nigeria. But they were blamed for the rising crime wave in Nigeria. Shagari too expelled thousands of them in 1983. The fault was less in the decision but more in the manner of its execution. Other African countries accused Nigeria of abdicating its Big Brother responsibilities towards them.

Nigeria's relationship with Britain became frosty in the wake of the abortive attempt to kidnap and crate home the regime's most vocal critic and Shagari's former powerful minister of transport, Alhaji Umaru Dikko, in 1984. He was abducted in broad daylight in front of his residence at Porchester in the Bayswater area of London. The British police later found Dikko in a crate at Stansted Airport. There was a diplomatic uproar.

Britain accused the Nigerian government of the crime. Government denied complicity in the kidnap attempt. Britain was unconvinced. Both countries recalled their high commissioners home.

Babangida was privy to the kidnap attempt. He says the government had to bring Dikko home to face trial because he "was a pain in the neck." He recalls that an Israeli sold the kidnap idea to a retired general. The retired general then talked to Babangida about it. He and the retired general, according to Babangida, talked to Buhari about it. The head of state allegedly approved it. The Israeli demanded $10 million for the job. Babangida however, subsequently played no role in the execution of the kidnap plan. Major Mohammed Yusuf, who was arrested by the British police when Dikko was rescued, was alleged to have co-ordinated the kidnap, reportedly with the full knowledge of senior officials of the Nigerian High Commission in Britain.

Nigeria and Britain were anxious to restore diplomatic relations between them. Only fourteen days after Babangida took over, Sir Geoffrey Howe, the British foreign secretary, visited him. He was the first high-ranking foreign official to visit Nigeria since the change of government in the country.

Babangida did have quite a bit on his plate on the foreign policy front. He had no problems saying the right things at the right places. On his fourth day in office, he followed the customary route of addressing members of the diplomatic corps. He gave the traditional assurance that his government remained committed to all bi-lateral and multi-lateral agreements entered into by the previous administrations. Foreign creditors had nothing to fear, he said, because he would pay their debts but "at a pace calculated to relieve the present pressure on the economy." Nigeria's borders with its neighbours would also be re-opened to human and vehicular traffic, he assured.

II

In foreign affairs, Babangida hastened a little more slowly than on the domestic front but he left no one in any doubts that he had a fairly good idea of where he wanted to go on that front too. He approached his foreign policy initiative with a measure of populism. He opened up its direction to a public debate. He had walked the populist path before by subjecting the pending decision on an IMF bridging loan for Nigeria to a similar national debate. He followed the same script in his search for a new political order for the country. He relished the mileage that debates earned him because they provided convincing evidence that he meant it when he said that his administration did not "lay claim to exclusive wisdom and knowledge." He found the concept of a participatory military democracy, a contradiction in terms, no doubt, to be his magic wand.

Now, he brought the same concept to bear on his foreign policy direction. Babangida kicked off a national foreign policy debate with a week-long All-Nigeria Foreign Policy Conference at the National Institute for Policy and Strategic Studies, Kuru, organised by the Ministry of External Affairs from April 7 to 13, 1986. Its theme was: "Nigeria and the world: Foreign policy options up till the year 2000." A colourful crowd of politicians, foreign policy experts, university teachers, representatives of labour and students unions, traditional rulers and military personnel attended the conference.

In his opening speech at the conference, Babangida played up his populist approach to issues of national importance. He said the

> conference fits into the style of this administration in which issues of our national life are subjected to popular participation. More importantly, this conference should provide an opportunity to evolve a new national consciousness on the goals and objectives of our foreign policy and thereby forge national cohesiveness and support for our foreign policy programmes.

He openly relished the fact that it was the first time that a Nigerian government "assembled such distinguished personalities from every facet of our national life to deliberate on our external relations. Indeed," he went on, "it is the first time they have all been brought together in any forum to share their experiences as well as their hopes for the future course of our nation's foreign policy."

Babangida tasked the conference with finding "an aggressive, virile and well thought-out foreign policy for the country." He provided the clue to how his mind was working on this by raising some fundamental questions about the goals of Nigeria's foreign policy. He asked:

What were Nigeria's goals at independence and have these goals remained static? If no, what are our goals today and what should they be in the next quarter of a century? Have we related these goals to the instruments for implementation? Have these goals been clearly defined to meet Nigeria's place and position in the world today?

He wanted a foreign policy that would ensure that the "words and actions" of Nigeria could "no longer be ignored in the world scene." It must be "a sound and meaningful foreign policy which can mobilize its entire people for the greater benefit of mankind. I implore you," he went on, "to move away from the traditional terrain by breaking away from the static conception of foreign policy analysis; you should be able to disaggregate our national interests into a quest for national survival as distinct from 'national aggrandisement' and 'national self-extension.'"

It was no longer enough, Babangida argued, for the country to bind itself to its Afro-centric foreign policy without clarifying and spelling "out in more specific terms, its parameters and indicators."

Yusuf Maitama Sule, Nigeria's former Permanent Representative at the United Nations, believed Babangida was right to convene the conference. He argued that:

A good foreign policy is one, which truly serves the people's interest, which reflects their will, and is therefore, not merely a reflection of the whim and caprices of a single leader. For it must be admitted that because of its very visible nature, foreign policy is something which a leader may wish to corner, so as to project his personal, (as distinctly opposed to national) image. It is, however, to the credit of General Babangida, that he has not just in an academic sense, borne the Nigerian people in mind in fashioning his foreign policy, but has indeed directly and actively involved them in the process. In this way, not only did people acquire a sense of commitment, but also the president himself got the inner satisfaction in all his policies [that] he is truly acting in accordance with the will of the people.[6]

Nigeria was 25 years old as an independent nation when Babangida shot his way into power in 1985. Within so short a period, it had had seven rulers, two civilians and five military dictators. Babangida was the eighth ruler and the sixth military dictator. This rapid turnover in its leadership and, in some cases, consequent political turmoil, left their marks on the country's internal problems and its foreign policy. Its foreign policy had generally oscillated between the conservative and the progressive.

Babangida noted three phases in Nigeria's foreign policy since independence in 1960. The first phase was the first five years of independence that lasted from October 1, 1960 and ended with the bloody overthrow of the Tafawa Balewa administration on January 15, 1966. The political crises in the wake of that coup and the counter-coup of July that year witnessed shifting loyalties among Nigeria's traditional foreign friends. One year and seven months after the military intervention, Nigeria fought a 30-month civil war with dramatic consequences for the shape and the direction of its foreign policy.

The second period lasted from the constitutional crisis in the wake of the January 15, 1966 coup to the end of the civil war in January 1970. The third phase lasted from the end of the civil war to the country's return to civil rule on October 1, 1979. Each of these phases witnessed events and changes at the international level that could not but have affected the direction of the country's foreign policy and its relations with other countries.

The third phase was thus far the most radical in Nigeria's foreign policy. That phase saw Nigeria shed its conservative Mr. Nice Guy image. General Murtala Muhammed's famous "Africa has come of age" speech at the OAU conference in Addis Ababa, Ethiopia, in 1975, set the tone for the radical posture. To show that he meant business, Muhammed, against all the odds, recognised MPLA led by the late Agostino Neto as the only genuine national liberation movement in Angola. He thus told off the United States and its Western allies that backed UNITA led by the late Jonas Savimbi.

The regime went even further. It nationalised BP and Barclays Bank and took punitive measures against other multinationals known to be aiding apartheid in South Africa. The sleeping giant of Africa was no longer afraid of taking on its enemies and the enemies of its friends. Nigeria would no longer be anyone's good boy. The world duly took notice.

Nostalgic as Nigerians were about that dynamic foreign policy period, Babangida did not want to merely reconnect to it. What he wanted to see was a new phase of the country's foreign policy defined as much by his vision of the country as a medium economic and military power as by definite national goals or interests it must pursue in its relations with other nations. As he put it at the Kuru conference,

> ...the goals we want to pursue in foreign policy must be justified in terms of the higher values which they are meant to serve. Thus money for or spent on foreign policy goals defined in national security terms, must be justified not on the grounds that it will protect national security but that by enhancing such security, it will serve to protect ultimate values such as individual liberty and human welfare.

He urged the conference to

>...address itself to how Nigeria can pursue her goals of national survival within (the) complex international power configuration. We should also identify the international entities that are relevant to our national survival and objective."

What was clearly dear to his heart was a foreign policy that would unambiguously show that Nigeria, to borrow from Muhammed, had come of age and become a "country whose words and actions (could) no longer be ignored in the world scene."

Foreign policy experts, political scientists and former diplomats presented a total of forty papers at the conference – a veritable fountain of analyses, facts and opinions. The radicals, led by the late historian, Dr. Yusuf Bala Usman, tried to turn the conference into a critique of Babangida's foreign policy so far. Citing the US-Libya confrontation in the Gulf of Sitre that year as evidence that the administration was failing in its duty to other African countries in their times of need, Usman accused the external affairs minister, Professor Bolaji Akinyemi, of reducing "our foreign policy to a mere diplomatic exhibition." Usman and the others were riled by the fact that after the bombing of Libya by the United States, Nigeria did not even issue what Professor Gabriel Olusanya called "the typically harmless statement urging both sides to find a mutual way to resolve their differences."[7]

III

Babangida did not make the report or the recommendations of that conference public. It is difficult to say for sure in what way or ways the conference influenced his foreign policy. But for all his populist approach to the direction of his foreign policy, the real architect of Babangida's foreign policy, such as it was in the early years of his regime, was Akinyemi, then 43 years old. Akinyemi is a professor of political science. He was, for eight years, the director-general of the Nigerian Institute of International Affairs. In that position, he was involved in the formulation of Nigeria's foreign policy for several years before he became its executor as external affairs minister in 1985.

He came into office, therefore, prepared for his assignment. He knew the weaknesses and the strengths of the country's foreign policy initiatives over the years. He knew the roads travelled and not travelled and what new paths the nation needed to cut through the dense foliage of international relations. As he saw it, "the general parameters of Nigeria's foreign policy hinge on the perception of the status of Nigeria as being that of an activist in the international system, an activist that is seeking respect rather than love."[8]

Akinyemi found a kindred spirit in the president. He adopted a hands-on shuttle diplomatic style popularised by Henry Kissinger, United States Secretary of State under presidents Richard Nixon and Gerald Ford. That style suited a world on the cusp of fundamental changes marked later in the life of the Babangida administration by the sudden disintegration of the USSR and the end of the Cold War between the Western and the Eastern bloc countries. More importantly, the style suited Babangida's temperament.

Akinyemi seemed like a good student and a great admirer of Kissinger but the man he admired most was General George Catlett Marshall, President Harry S. Truman's Secretary of State and later of defence, and the architect of the European recovery programme after World War II, now known and admired famously as the Marshall Plan.

Buoyed by Babangida's support and encouragement, Akinyemi brought excitement, style and panache to the conduct of Nigeria's foreign policy. Together, he and Babangida broke new grounds with new foreign policy tools that boosted Nigeria's credentials as an emerging important Third World country.

Akinyemi loved Babangida's disposition towards his foreign policy initiatives. He virtually rhapsodised the president when he told *Newswatch* magazine:

> President Babangida may, perhaps, be the first Nigerian George Marshall that we have as head of state; the intellectual soldier. Over the past eight years, before becoming head of state, he has made several speeches with foreign policy implications. He is a man who has his own image of the world and where Nigeria fits in. What he thinks Nigeria should be doing is very well articulated too. To that extent, having a discussion on foreign policy with the president is almost a constant intellectual debate because he has a systematic mind, and doesn't see things in isolation. What has made it easier being his foreign minister, which may explain why I was appointed, is that we do share a similar dream of what we think Nigeria should be internationally and where we think that Nigeria should be headed internationally.[9]

Eleven months after Babangida came to power, a rare opportunity for foreign policy activism literally dropped on Akinyemi's laps. The quadrennial sports competition among the 58 former British colonies and territories known as the Commonwealth Games, were scheduled for Edinburgh, Scotland, in July 1986. Akinyemi instantly saw a great opportunity for Nigeria to express its anger over British Prime Minister Margaret Thatcher's refusal to impose sanctions on apartheid South Africa. The sanctions were recommended by the Commonwealth Eminent Persons Group as a basket of measures to force the racists to end apartheid and embrace majority rule in that country. Black South African leaders, including Archbishop Desmond Tutu, welcomed and supported the sanctions but Thatcher argued that they would hurt the black people more than the whites.

Akinyemi was no lover of the Commonwealth. He had pushed for Nigeria to get out of it long before he became external affairs minister. Now, he had an opportunity to perhaps achieve that objective. He seized it with both hands. He pushed for the boycott of the games by Nigeria and persuaded Babangida that it was the right thing to do. On July 8, he presented a memo on it to the president. Babangida approved it. Nigeria's campaign for the boycott of the games was so successful that 30 countries boycotted the Edinburgh games. It was a diplomatic triumph for Babangida so early in the life of his administration. The foreign policy activism was a wonderful beginning for the new regime.

In his eight years in office, Babangida was a loud voice and a visible presence in virtually all the theatres of international politics. In many ways, he redefined and refocused Nigeria's foreign policy. Under him Nigeria cultivated and nursed a new image as an emerging economic power. He was a strong and persistent advocate of changes in the United Nations Security Council to reflect current global political realities. He wanted the council enlarged because in his view, limiting its membership to the five permanent members had "become both anachronistic and unrepresentative." Nigeria presented a formal proposal for an enlarged security council in the twilight of the Babangida regime early in 1993. It recommended that Africa and Asia be given two each of the additional seats in the council while one seat each is given to Latin America, Western Europe and Eastern Europe. "It is our considered view," Nigeria argued,

> that to continue with the status quo with respect to the security council not only perpetuates the council's representational inequality, but also negates the principle of democracy and universality which the charter of the UN speaks of in several of its articles.[10]

Nigeria was, of course, pursuing a vested interest. Babangida very much wanted Nigeria to be one of the two countries to represent the Africa region as a permanent member of the Security Council. Nigeria presented formidable credentials as the most likely candidate. Babangida's foreign affairs secretary, as the position was later known in the many changes for which the Babangida regime was notorious, Matthew Mbu, made Nigeria's ambition clear at his first meeting with envoys in Lagos in February 1993.

In his foreign policy posture, Babangida was clearly a pan-Africanist. One of his pet dreams was to put an African in the driving seat of the United Nations as its secretary general, at least, as an acknowledgement by the world body of "the deep commitment of African states" to it. He carried that campaign to the 46th session of the United Nations in October 1991in his capacity as chairman of the OAU. Nigeria put up a candidate, General Olusegun Obasanjo, former head of state. He did not get the job but in November that year, the first African, Boutrous Boutrous-Ghali of Egypt, did. He spent one term in office and was succeeded by another African, Kofi Annan, a Ghanaian. Nigeria also moved up the scale in another direction. Emeka Anyaoku, a Nigerian, became the secretary general of the Commonwealth. He was the first African to hold that position. Babangida, certainly, derived a sense of personal fulfilment from these developments that saw Africans in such exalted positions.

Part of Babangida's piece of good luck consisted of some momentous international developments in Africa and Eastern Europe that affected super power configurations and dramatically affected the direction of Nigeria's foreign policy initiatives. About three years after he came to power, the cold war between the West and the East ended rather suddenly with the disintegration of the Union of Soviet Socialist Republics, USSR. The former satellite states of the USSR in Eastern Europe went their separate ways as independent countries.

In Africa, the liberation struggle in Southern Africa was rapidly winding down. Namibia became independent in 1990, nearly five years after Babangida became president. The same year saw the release of the great Nelson Mandela from prison after 27 years. His freedom served notice that the end of apartheid was at hand. By the time that end came and Mandela became the first president of a multi-racial South Africa, Babangida was no longer in power but no one would deny him the positive role he played in Nigeria's historic anti-apartheid struggle going all the way back to the Gowon era.

The unravelling of the USSR might have been good news for the West but it was bad news for Africa. Eastern Europe became the new centre of international attention. Western nations and companies scrambled for a piece of the action in the newly independent former Soviet satellite states. Babangida was, perhaps, one of the few African leaders who saw that Africa was in trouble. He quickly drew attention of his fellow African leaders to the fact that "the picture that is evolving (following the rapprochement between the super powers) is one of a rapid disengagement from Africa. It appears the events occurring in other parts of the world have rapidly upstaged the problems and crises in Africa."

His fear that Africa was in for isolation probably set the stage for his commitment to a new face of Africa by Africans. The continent was still poor and under-developed. As Babangida saw it, things were bound to get worse unless African leaders recognised what was happening in Eastern Europe and elsewhere as a challenge they must face. He believed that Africa had become too important to allow itself to continue to be treated as "an object of pity and charity. A continent that has produced Nobel Prize winners in literature and peace should be a lion with a jewelled crown."[11]

Babangida, like everyone else, knew only too well that Africa had a long way to go to become "a lion with a jewelled crown." As he very aptly put it, the continent remained "the most vulnerable to adversity because of its relatively weak technological base, low level industrial capacity and the often self-inflicted fragility of its socio-political institutions."

The problems of African countries were compounded by poverty and conflicts in many parts of the continent that were, according to Babangida, "causing enormous destruction to lives and property, untold human misery and generating large-scale refugee problems." Yet African leaders felt helpless in addressing those problems.

The OAU charter provided for mediation, conciliation and arbitration in conflicts among member states but quite often, African leaders were reluctant to use this mechanism to resolve conflicts in and between member nations, their excuse being that the charter forbade interference in the internal affairs of member nations. The result was the do-nothing posture that compounded the despair of the African peoples and the desperation of the continent.

Babangida said that this was no longer acceptable. He argued that "the stipulation in the OAU charter on the avoidance of interference in the internal affairs of member countries was not designed to inhibit us from coming to assist in solving each other's problems. It was designed to discourage adventurism." The time had come, he said, for

> Africa to take its destiny in its own hands (because) we can no longer abandon the management of crisis in Africa to external actors. The time has come for Africans to assume full responsibility for the security of Africa. While the spirit of non-intervention remains sacrosanct, this should not be at the expense of humanity.

One of these theatres of internal conflicts was Liberia, a tiny West African country founded in 1822 for the resettlement of freed African slaves from the United States of America. The former slaves, known as Americo-Liberians, became the successive rulers of Liberia until 1980 when a sergeant in the Liberian Army, Samuel Kanyon Doe, toppled President William R. Tolbert in a very bloody coup. The president and thirteen of his political associates and almost the entire members of his family were wiped out.

Doe was from the Krahn indigenous ethnic group and probably held the highest military rank among the indigenous ethnic groups in the army. He became president and set up the People's Redemption Council as the highest ruling organ in the country. He later promoted himself to the hitherto unknown rank of commander-general. He transformed himself into a civilian president after he won a disputed presidential election in 1985. Doe was widely accused of corruption and brutality. The disputed 1985 election triggered a sustained armed opposition to his rule. By April 1990, Liberia was convulsed in a civil war.

Opposition to Doe was factionalised along ethnic lines. Charles Ghankay Taylor, an Americo-Liberian and a former official in the Doe government, led the strongest faction, the National Patriotic Front of Liberia, NPFL. This was the Americo-Liberian faction. Roosevelt Johnson and Alhaji Kromah led the Krahn and the Mandingo ethnic factions respectively. Doe held on to power but it was rapidly slipping away from his hands.

The leaders of the 16-member nation of the Economic Community of West African States, ECOWAS, watched the deteriorating situation in Liberia with obvious alarm. There was a "complete breakdown of law and order" in that country and yet, according to Babangida, the international community ignored

> the killings, the starvation, the general suffering of Liberians. Even those countries that have direct interest in Liberia and were deeply involved in the past, more or less decided to be spectators and concentrated their efforts on events in the Middle East where the level of human suffering is far lower (than in Liberia).

IV

The Liberian tragedy gave Babangida the opportunity to practise what he preached to his fellow African leaders. Babangida was first elected chairman of ECOWAS in 1987 and re-elected twice, an unprecedented expression of confidence in his leadership by the leaders of the community. He earned it by the sheer energy he invested in the affairs of the organisation. At the summit of the organisation in July 1987, Babangida launched a two-year economic recovery programme for the sub-region. The recovery programme consisted of 316 projects spread throughout the member-nations of ECOWAS. It was valued at $926 million US dollars.

It was an ambitious programme targeted at quickening the pace of economic and social development and improved economic management through public sector reforms in the sub-region. Babangida was rather fond of arguing that African countries had nothing to gain from feeling helpless. "Rather than sit down and bemoan the situation concrete actions (must) be taken to find solutions" to the problems that faced the continent. He hoped that the economic recovery programme would "serve as a guidepost and checklist for the formulation of individual structural adjustment programmes and national development plans."[12]

The leaders of ECOWAS faced hard choices. Should they do nothing on the grounds that the OAU forbade interference in the internal affairs of a member-nation or should they act to save the country and put an end to the horrendous human tragedy that it had become?

Babangida decided, without hesitation, that Nigeria could not and would not be indifferent to what was happening in Liberia. It must bear the Liberian burden as it did the burden of the liberation struggle in southern Africa. And lest anyone thought Nigeria was poking its nose into other nations' problems, Babangida said: "Nigeria has no apology to make when we take it upon ourselves as our bounden duty and solemn responsibility to help resolve the cases of instability in Africa (and in the case of Liberia) no sacrifice is too great in the cause of peace and greater political and economic integration of (the West African sub-region)."[13]

At the 13th summit of ECOWAS in Banjul, The Gambia, May 28-30, 1990, Babangida proposed the setting up of a standing mediation committee of four members to intervene in conflicts within and between member nations of the economic community. The proposal rested on Babangida's belief that a strong ECOWAS was "beacon of hope" for the sub-region. The members endorsed the proposal. They went a radical step further to back up the mediatory mechanism with a military force known as Economic Community Monitoring Group, better known by its acronym, ECOMOG. It was a novelty in Africa.

Liberia became the litmus test for this fundamental novelty. Every member-nation of ECOWAS contributed troops to ECOMOG. At its initial take-off, the members agreed that each country should bear the expenses such as salaries, allowances and welfare of its own contingent.

A Ghanaian army general initially commanded ECOMOG. Its command was later given to Nigeria and a succession of Nigerian generals proved their mettle there. Its operations lasted until the conduct of a presidential election won by Mrs. Ellen Johnson Sirleaf in 2005. She became the first female president in Africa.

Some pundits criticised the decision of the mediation committee to send ECOMOG forces to enforce the cease-fire as an attempt by the ECOWAS leaders to save Doe. This criticism missed the point. Doe had virtually lost his grip on power and the country. Babangida had no doubt that Doe had "been temporarily put out of action and without any legitimate constituted authority." But Doe could not be ignored as a factor in the crisis. Any arrangements for peace must still take him into consideration. After all, he was still the president. The mediation committee decided that the most viable option open to it was to persuade Doe to leave the country.

According to Babangida:

> We were in contact with him and sent a lot of messages to him and told him that in the interest of the country, he should leave and allow other people to come in so that peace would reign. We were not there to protect him.[14]

Doe refused to leave. It was a costly mistake - and one he did not live to regret. Yomi Johnson's troops captured and killed him in a most gruesome manner in September 1990. His killing exacerbated the crisis in the country.

And Liberia became, in Babangida's apt description of the situation, an "appalling human catastrophe." Babangida decided that there was no way that "Nigeria and other responsible countries in the sub-region (would) stand by and watch the whole of Liberia turn(ed) into one mass grave." Its potential for a disastrous ripple effect in the sub-region stared everyone in the face and prompted Babangida to argue that a Nigerian government did not need to be persuaded that it was in Nigeria's interest to "relentlessly strive towards the prevention or avoidance of the deterioration of any crisis which threatens to jeopardise or compromise the stability, prosperity and security of the sub-region."

He strongly believed that the decision to send ECOMOG forces to Liberia was "timely and bold" because "the entire world (was) watching and judging our collective capability in mounting an effective policy response to the critical economic, political and security challenges to our sub-region."

Given his conviction, Babangida spared no expenses to try to save Liberia. At the patron's dinner of the Nigerian Institute of International Affairs on December 15, 1990, he announced his decision to launch a Liberian rehabilitation and reconstruction fund for the reconstruction of the war-ravaged country. Unfortunately, for Babangida the Charles Taylor faction "arrogantly and intransigently assumed a hostile posture in spite of all efforts by the ECOWAS authorities and appeal to reason, political sanity and peace and security of the sub-region" and thus denied him the right to be acknowledged as the architect of the return of peace and a legitimate government in Liberia.

By the time Babangida left office in 1993, the guns were still booming in that country. However, all of Nigerian rulers after him maintained his policy on Liberia. It was an endorsement of his commitment to the resolution of the Liberian crisis because it was of strategic importance to Nigeria and the West African sub-region and, indeed, the continued relevance of ECOWAS. But no one should ignore the fact that Liberia was also costly to Nigeria in financial and human resources. Government has never given the official figure of Nigerian soldiers who died that peace may return to that country but unofficial estimate put the figure at between 200 and 500. The financial cost is put at between five and six billion Naira.

V

Africa was Babangida's springboard to a larger world, the Third World. One thing was paramount in his mind – how to address the deteriorating economic situation in Third World countries. Many of them were weighed down by a myriad of domestic political, economic and external problems that hobbled their rapid movement up the ladder of economic development and social progress. Babangida identified "the perpetuation of a discriminatory trading system, protectionism, a skewed international financial system (all of which) contrived to frustrate our efforts and deprive our hard-working population, particularly our peasant farmers of their just rewards on their efforts" among the external problems facing Third World countries.[15]

At the 46th session of the United Nations, he called for a Marshall Plan for Africa. He campaigned for the cancellation of Third World debts and the institution of a new international economic order to free Third World countries from their "heavy dependence on imports of consumable items and industrial raw materials, and most importantly (free) our industrial infrastructures from merely assembling semi-finished consumer goods...."

Babangida was not saying anything particularly new here. He was addressing an old problem that refused to go away. He was right to do so because as he saw it, the terms of trade of developed countries "continued to worsen; our balance of payments faced very challenging crises, and our combined share in the supply of processed and semi-processed industrial and consumer goods continued to dwindle, amounting to only ten per cent of global manufactures value-added."

Some genuine attempts were made by the so-called Third World leaders before Babangida to change the economic fortunes of Third World countries, the most significant being the formal coming together of these countries as Group 77 in 1964 to harmonise their economic policies vis-à-vis the dominant industrialised countries. Progress was slow. The action committee on raw materials of the Group 77 held its first meeting twenty-five years later in Abuja on April 3, 1989 and was addressed by Babangida.

However, some Third World countries raised the hope of economic and industrial progress. Within a decade, 1970-1980, four developing - countries, Singapore, South Korea, Brazil and India - broke through the international economic cordon and were rechristened newly 'Industrialised Developing Countries.' They had succeeded in "converting their resources and imported raw materials into industrial goods..." But the overall picture of the economy of Third World countries was still discouraging because they accounted for only ten per cent of the world's supply of semi-processed industrial and consumer goods. The four newly industrialised developing countries together took a larger proportion of this overall miserable share.

Some urgent and radical approach needed to be taken to increase the Third World's share of semi-processed industrial and consumer goods. Given the disparities in industrial and economic development among the Group 77, Babangida believed that the road to collective success lay in active co-operation "to promote collective self-reliance and self-sufficiency by pooling our resources, by eliminating duplication of efforts, and by harmonizing our economic and trade policies."

The Non-aligned Movement knew this only too well. At its summit in Zimbabwe in 1986, it recommended the setting up of a South Commission to assist developing countries, also known as South-South, formulate development strategies to tackle their crippling economic problems. It set up a 28-member commission, headed by the late Dr. Julius Nyerere, former president of Tanzania and a champion of South-South co-operation, the following year. Nigeria's renowned economist, the late Dr. Pius Okigbo, was a member of the commission. The commission submitted its report in 1990. Babangida launched the Africa version of the commission's report in Abuja in November that year. The Latin American version was launched in Caracas, Venezuela, in August the same year.

In his keynote address at the launch, Babangida once more drew attention to the "economic weakness" among Third World nations. He argued that the developed nations must share the blame for this because their own experts were involved in the formulation of the failed economic policies in the developing nations. His argument, certainly, echoed the failure of his own homegrown structural adjustment programme that was no different from the IMF cure-all drug administered to all ailing Third World economies with equally disastrous results. It must have troubled him that what he touted as a homegrown model of structural adjustment became the millstone that dragged his popularity down into the depths. Had it succeeded, it would have perhaps been an alternative model for Third World countries.

Babangida took a swipe at the developed nations, accusing them of perpetuating "a discriminatory trading system, protectionism, a skewed international financial system (that had) contrived to frustrate our efforts and deprive our hard-working population, particularly our peasant farmers, of the just rewards for their efforts."

At the ninth summit of the non-aligned nations in Belgrade, Yugoslavia in 1989, Babangida proposed what he called "a three-pronged approach for an enduring solution" to the debt burden, namely, outright cancellation of official debts to creditor-nations; 50 per cent of the resources under the structural adjustment fund of the IMF/World Bank and the sub-Saharan African facility of the World Bank be made available to countries with overdue debt service obligations to the two institutions which could then be re-purchased by the affected countries to their considerable relief.

He also proposed the setting up of an "international debt purchasing institution or agency under the aegis of the IMF and the World Bank to purchase the existing debts of developing countries at substantial discounts of up to 80 per cent." He wanted trade restrictions lifted so that Third World countries could compete with the developed economies so that "our people (may) enjoy our potential wealth which has largely been exploited over the years to the benefit of developed countries."[16]

A Third World leader seeking to champion its cause has an existing platform to do so in the Non-aligned Movement formed in Belgrade, Yugoslavia, in 1961, by leaders of independent states who wanted to promote what may be loosely called a third force, independent of the Western and Eastern bloc nations. Its founding fathers, all of whom are deceased, were Jawaharlal Nehru, prime minister of India, President Sukarno of Indonesia, Dr. Kwame Nkrumah, president of Ghana, Ahmad Sekou Toure, president of Guinea, President Gamal Abdel Nasser of Egypt and President Josip Broz Tito of Yugoslavia, its chief promoter.

Twenty-five countries joined the movement soon after its founding. By 2003, the movement had 116 member-nations – evidence, perhaps not only of its popularity but also of its acceptance as an authentic umbrella for the struggling nations of the South-South in the shifting sands of international politics. Third World leaders routinely pledge their support for and co-operation with the movement, their own version of the Western and Eastern blocs.

Babangida followed this traditional script on his taking over the government and urged "the non-aligned Movement to regroup and re-invigorate its determination to restructure the global economic system." In September 1986, Babangida addressed a full session of the movement in Harare, Zimbabwe, at which he made it clear he wanted the movement to do more in the de-colonisation of Africa than it was doing. He tasked it with a five-point strategy it must adopt to free Namibia and dismantle apartheid in South Africa: the non-aligned movement within the UN Security Council must demand the imposition of comprehensive and mandatory sanctions on South Africa; it must demand the immediate and unconditional implementation of Security Council resolution 435 for the independence of Namibia; it must resolve to strengthen the liberation movements through increased political and material support; greater financial and other assistance to SWAPO, the main liberation movement in Namibia and the movement must strengthen the capacity of frontline states to ward off South African aggression. His suggestion for a Non-Aligned Fund to assist frontline states that might be affected by sanctions on South Africa was adopted.

Non-alignment was an attractive proposition to Third World leaders. In theory it freed them from the apron strings of the East or the West. But its founding fathers knew only too well that it faced considerable difficulties, given the varied colonial experiences of the member-nations and their economic weaknesses. Despite their independence, therefore, these countries still depended on or sought the assistance of their former colonial masters in dealing with their economic and other pressing national problems. This situation was, certainly, anathema to non-alignment and contributed to the perceived weaknesses of the Non-Aligned Movement.

VI

Early in 1987, Babangida did what many thought both unrealistic and a stab in the back of the Non-aligned Movement. He promoted a new international organisation that came to be known as the Lagos Forum. His foreign minister, Akinyemi, initiated the Lagos Forum also known as Concert of Medium Powers, "as a new approach, designed to restore confidence in the international peace process, and to complement on-going efforts at international co-operation."[17]

The original name suggested it was a gathering of countries that have left the bottom league and were now somewhere in the middle of international power configuration and, therefore, deserved the right to be so recognised. Perhaps that was why it raised eyebrows around the world. Nigeria, an oil rich country and the most populous black nation in the world, was beginning to see itself as a medium economic and perhaps, just perhaps, military power. It was impossible for the rest of the world not to sit up and watch the new movement.

The first meeting of the Lagos Forum was held in Lagos from March 16 to 18, 1987. It was attended by delegates from Algeria, Argentina, Austria, Brazil, Egypt, India, Nigeria, Indonesia, Malaysia, Mexico, Senegal, Sweden, Venezuela, Switzerland, Yugoslavia and Zimbabwe. Nigeria was elected chairman of the Forum. The delegates decided the forum would be informal and consultative. The meeting generated some international interest, if not curiosity. Indeed, when the second meeting was held six months later, September 1-3, five more countries, Australia, Peru, Pakistan, Canada and Hungary, attended it.

Babangida actively promoted the Forum because he fully subscribed to Akinyemi's argument that "while Nigeria must and should be seen as an African actor, it must be visible and active in the world arena." He also believed the forum would revitalise the multi-lateral process and "fill gaps which characterise the present international system."[18]

Still the Forum ran into a storm of criticisms. Some people saw it as an attempt to destroy the Non-Aligned Movement; others believed that Nigeria was trying to bite more than it could chew. Professor Adebayo Adedeji, former executive secretary of the Economic Commission for Africa, ECA, pointedly said Akinyemi was "joking" in initiating the forum because

> The world will not accept us as a small, medium or big power except by our performance and that performance will be measured partly by the strength of our influence in the world, by the extent to which other countries listen to us, want our advice, guidance, accept and trust our leadership. Placing 142nd in the world economic league table is hardly flattering. A country, which is classified among the poorest, if it says it is a medium or whatever power, is living in a fool's paradise.[19]

Akinyemi remained unshaken in his wisdom in initiating the Lagos Forum and went ahead to stoutly defend it. "The Nigerian initiative on a Concert of Medium Powers," he argued was

> motivated by a deep concern at the lack of progress in the resolution of pressing global economic and political issues. What we perceive is a deteriorating

international environment in which concerted and sustained multilateral cooperation and action have been largely stalemated and paralysed, even as many of the major problems of our time have been coming to a head.

The idea is certainly not to create another United Nations. Indeed, one of our main objectives is actually to strengthen the United Nations system, which we cherish. The idea, therefore, is to create a forum comprising a number of countries small enough to be cohesive, yet large enough to be representative of the major stands and charts of international option.[20]

The Lagos Forum was not without some supporters who argued that it did Nigeria no harm to aspire to be a medium power in the emerging global power configurations. But it seemed ill fated. Despite Babangida's spirited defence, the Lagos Forum did not quite get off the drawing board as a new club of newly-arrived nations with sufficient medium economic and military powers to call the shots in international affairs in their own right. Part of its bad luck was that Akinyemi, its chief proponent, was removed as minister of foreign affairs. His successors, who probably did not believe in it, were happy to let the Forum drift down stream on the current of insouciance. By the time Babangida himself left office in 1993, the Forum was as good as dead. It was buried after his departure.

VII

It may be argued, with some justification, that Babangida wanted to be seen and accepted as an authentic Third World champion, committed to the promotion of Third World interests and development. This ambition coloured much of his foreign policy initiatives. He gave some indication of where his heart lay when he began to preach the gospel of dialogue and co-operation among Third World countries early in the life of his administration:

We support greater and more active contacts among Third World nations. This administration is convinced that dialogue with other Third World countries is necessary. We believe that such dialogues, if they could be systematically pursued, will lead to effective, useful and lasting co-operation in the long run.[21]

For him, important though it might be, dialogue was not enough. What he believed the Third World needed was, if you like, a homegrown initiative for mutual aid and assistance. At about the same time that he began to promote the concept of a new club of medium powers, he did what no leader anywhere in the world had done since the late President

John F. Kennedy established the American Peace Corps on March 1, 1961. He established the Nigerian version called Technical Aid Corps with similar objectives to those of the Peace Corps.

The Peace Corps had three well-defined objectives, namely, "helping the people of interested countries in meeting their need for trained men and women; helping [to] promote a better understanding of Americans on the part of the peoples served (and) helping [to] promote a better understanding of other peoples on the part of Americans." At inception, it was the most visible but the least intrusive tool of American foreign policy.

As often happens with unorthodox ideas, the Technical Aid Corps idea came about by accident from a request made to Akinyemi by the late President Thomas Sankara of Burkina Faso. According to Akinyemi, Sankara requested Nigeria to send him teachers of English because he wanted not only the members of his cabinet but all Burkinabe to speak English.

The minister relayed the message to Babangida. It then hit both men they could do even more. Babangida could do for Third World countries what Kennedy did for them through the Peace Corps. The president and the minister were excited by the prospects of sending young Nigerian professionals to serve Third World countries. After their discussion, Babangida asked Akinyemi to prepare a memo on an aid corps to the Federal Executive Council for approval.

Akinyemi duly prepared and presented his memo to the council for discussion and approval. Neither Babangida nor Akinyemi was prepared for the reaction of the council. The idea received a cool reception from all but two members of the council. The Chief of General Staff, Commodore Ebitu Ukiwe, dismissed it, according to Akinyemi, as "a scatter-brain idea...no merit, no value." Babangida saved the idea from ending up in the trash bin. He told Akinyemi to fine-tune his paper for his approval.[22]

And the Technical Aid Corps, TAC, was born. Babangida rightly saw it as a vital foreign policy tool with unimaginable dividends for Nigeria. At the formal launch of TAC on October 7, 1987, Babangida said its primary objective was "to assist black African, Caribbean and Pacific countries which regularly request for Nigerian technical assistance (and) was in furtherance of our commitment to our foreign policy which makes Africa its centre piece. This administration," he went on,

> believes that it is in Nigeria's national interest, and ....sacred duty to enhance the status of blacks all over the world...not by interfering in other people's affairs, or by playing Father Christmas, but by bringing a new realism to our aid policy of giving assistance on the basis of the assessed and perceived needs of the beneficiaries, and our national interest.

TAC was an ambitious foreign policy tool. Its relevance does not just lie in its novelty but by the breadth of its five objectives, namely:

> sharing Nigeria's know-how and expertise with other ACP countries; giving assistance on the basis of assessed and perceived needs of recipient countries; promoting cooperation and understanding between Nigeria and recipient countries; facilitating meaningful contact between youths of Nigeria and those of recipient countries; complementing other forms of assistance to ACP countries; ensuring a streamlined programme of assistance to other developing countries; acting as a channel through which South-South collaboration is enhanced; establishing a presence in countries which, for economic reasons, Nigeria has no resident diplomatic mission.

Curiously, the legal backing for this innovative scheme, decree 27, was signed into law only in January 1993. But Babangida got it right with this policy, the first of its type in the history of Nigeria. It is, to use a local analogy, the external equivalent of the National Youth Service Corps established by Gowon in 1973. Between its inception in 1987 and 2004, Nigeria sent 1,677 TAC volunteers to 33 African, Caribbean and Pacific countries.

As Nigerians like to say of policies that survive their initiators, *TAC has come to stay*. Babangida calls it "our demonstrable concern for the developmental aspirations of Third World." His successors in government and others agree. In 2003, the Commonwealth signed a memorandum of understanding with the federal government so that Nigeria, through the directorate of TAC, would provide Nigerian expertise to needy member states under the Commonwealth Assistance Programme. Both the United Nations Volunteer Service and the Japanese Agency for International Cooperation also wanted to tap into the success of TAC.

TAC today represents a viable instrument in Nigeria's foreign policy initiatives. Its acceptance by African, Caribbean and Pacific Countries is a tribute to Babangida's vision. Like the US Peace Corps before it, TAC is a non-intrusive foreign policy initiative. It is a Third World assistance scheme from oneThird World country to other Third World countries.

VIII

How would Babangida's foreign policy be assessed or labelled? Was it conservative or radical? It is difficult to pin one label or the other on it. In any case, conservatism and radicalism are out of fashion in contemporary international discourse. It would seem that the end of the Cold War also ended attempts to divide the world into extremes of conservative and radical camps. Events and circumstances determine the appropriate response of a country in its dealings with other nations. No country is ever entirely conservative or reactionary or entirely radical in its relations with other countries. This was why radicalism did not entirely define the so-called radical phase of Nigeria's foreign policy.

What Akinyemi tried to inject into the administration's foreign policy was the policy of consultation. He spelt it out at the Kuru conference thus:

> If we owe a responsibility to stand up for and respond to Africa, we are owed an obligation to be consulted when the situation allows for consultation. Nigeria must not and cannot allow states, which on their own free will adopt policies that lead to crisis to assume that Nigeria will automatically be dragged into the crisis.[23]

He did have a point but his critics dubbed it the "Akinyemi doctrine." It was not a flattering view of his thoughts. Professor Gabriel Olusanya, who, like Akinyemi, was director-general of NIIA, in his assessment of Babangida's foreign policy in its first year in office, observed: "We seem to have a very simplistic approach to foreign policy. There is a confused picture that is presented to the outside world which needs to be straightened out."[24]

The Babangida era raises two fundamental questions about his foreign policy. The first is what goals did he pursue? The second is, did he achieve them?

There are no neat answers to these questions. A foreign policy goal is at best a process by which a country defines or redefines its relations with other countries as circumstances arise. Changes in international politics are not within the competence of any one country or its leader. Foreign policy goals are, therefore, quite often at the mercy of the wind of change in domestic and international scenes. It may be possible for a country to assess the success or failure of its foreign policy goals by the number of friends or enemies it earns for itself by its stand on particular international issues or controversies. This, in itself, may not even tell the whole story. After all, there are no permanent friends or enemies; only permanent interests.

Babangida would, certainly, not be pleased to know that his foreign policy was also generally criticised as "lacking in clarity." The high turnover of his foreign ministers was partly to blame. However his foreign policy is assessed, it would be uncharitable to deny Babangida two things.

One, he did not hesitate to use Nigeria's military and economic muscle to pursue the goals of the country's foreign policy. In his time, Nigeria was visible in all the theatres of wars and conflicts through the UN peacekeeping force – from Namibia to the former Yugoslavia.

Two, he was not afraid of using the country's wealth to fund its foreign policy interests. Nigeria might not have reaped all the dividends it expected from these initiatives but the country was not the worse for them.

Chapter Seventeen

Crises of Power

(Trade unions are) a vital part of the nation's socio-economic structure.
–Ibrahim Babangida

Anyone who watched Babangida's charm offensive in the early months of his administration would be surprised that his regime earned Nobel Laureate Professor Wole Soyinka's unflattering description as a "government by proscription."[1] Babangida's capacity for dialogue was unprecedented in the history of military rule in Nigeria. No military ruler before him or after him approached governance the way he did. He was open to anyone who had anything to say to help him make Nigeria a better country. He felt free with the public and the public responded to him with genuine affection.

Yet, his eight years in power witnessed turbulent times in his relationship with individuals and organised groups. By the time he 'stepped aside' in 1993, Babangida had had a spat with the press, individuals, trade unions and professional groups. Bruises became cruel reminders that the man, who warmed himself into public adulation with his pyrotechnic style of administration, was a typical military dictator with a typical zero tolerance for opposition or even contrary opinions.

Babangida freely used the sledgehammer to swat whichever flies perched on his presidential nose. Yet, he did so in a rather innocent way that suggested he was loath to drawing blood. It is part of the Babangida mystique - that near-indefinable characteristic that makes it almost impossible for anyone to admire him or hate him all of the time. He had a rapid turnover of friends who turned into enemies and enemies who turned into friends and back again. His strategy is his disarming charm and his near infantile craving to be loved by all men and be friends to all men – and women.

This was both his weakness and his strength. In the view of some of his close associates, Babangida's problem was that he had too many friends. He was often forced by loyalty to friends to change policies to please his friends. That partly explains Babangida's strange capacity for self-subversion. Ironical as may seem, his inclination to please friends or people was also his strength. It was the source of his courage to dare and travel along roads less travelled.

Babangida came into office wooing the nation with promises of human rights and individual freedom, promises that do not come easily for military rulers. But within his first four years in office, his relationship with the press, labour and professional groups went unbelievably sour.

That led to a heap of ironies. The man who abrogated decree four and threw his arms around the Nigerian press, banned newspapers and magazines, beginning with the six month ban on Newswatch, Nigeria's pioneer newsmagazine, in April, 1987. The man who courted labour, dissolved the central labour union, NLC; the man who lifted the ban on the National Association of Nigerian Students, NANS, banned it; the man who gathered top university professors around him as members of the Presidential Advisory Committee, banned the central labour union of Nigerian university teachers, ASUU. And he had a running battle with the Nigerian Bar Association, NBA.

What went wrong? There are no easy answers but there are possible explanations. Nigerians did not read Babangida's lips from the beginning. At his first meeting with vice-chancellors of all the universities in the country on November 16, 1985, Babangida pledged to uphold academic freedom because his government regarded "academic freedom as an indispensable ingredient of all freedoms."

It was a winning pledge. There had been a steady erosion of academic freedom in Nigerian universities over the years through government actions expressly directed at the interests of the university community. Did he really promise unfettered academic freedom at the meeting with the vice-chancellors? No chance. In the euphoria of the times, not many people saw that his pledge for academic freedom came with a condition. He said:

> When the emphasis shifts away from the conception of academic calling, and moves to the idea of self-defined and self-determined mission to change society as a primary objective and to make this central focus of activity without proper and due regard to the will, wishes and beliefs of the society, then the academic has changed into something completely new and problematic for himself and for the society which supports his activity.

He was, of course, reminding the university community that academic freedom was not absolute. Or, to put it another way, it was his considered opinion that academic freedom, like all other freedoms, has a logical boundary beyond which he would not allow the university teachers to do as they wished - in the name of academic freedom. He understood the concept of academic differently from the way the university community did. These apparent divergent positions proved fatal to academic freedom under Babangida's watch as president.

In May 1986, Babangida amended the State Security (Detention of Persons) Decree 1984, better known as decree two. Under the original decree, the Chief of General Staff was empowered to detain anyone who, in his opinion, was a security risk for an initial period of three months without charging him to court. Babangida extended this to six months with the amended decree. But he tried to allay public fears by explaining that the amendments were not "a signal that the present administration is about to re-enact the reign of terror." He said they were meant to provide legal cover for the detention of certain persons arrested by the previous regime and had been in detention for more than three months. The amendment would tidy up the legal position of the detainees and facilitate the review of their cases.

Even now, it is difficult to accept that that was the only motive behind the amendment to the decree. By the time Babangida made that statement, he was fully aware that people were already questioning his human rights policy. Was he committed to it or was he merely paying lip service to it? He answered that question in his first anniversary broadcast on August 27, 1986. He insisted that nothing had changed.

But:

> Our human rights policy must not be mistaken for weakness or lack of clear direction. We shall endeavour to respect individual rights as long as they do not endanger the collective and greater rights of the nation.
>
> In fact, in his maiden broadcast a year before, he had unambiguously stated that the "Fundamental rights and civil liberties will be respected, but their exercise must not degenerate into irrational expressions or border on subversion."

Fifteen weeks later at the National Institute for Policy and Strategic Studies, NIPSS, Kuru, Babangida found it necessary to remind the country that his ideal society was one "which guarantees the individual freedom of thought, speech and action" but that the individual must still seek his "self-fulfilment within the limits of the law while at the same time voluntarily subsuming self to the wider and greater claims of the overall good."

These references clearly showed Babangida's mind-set right from the inception of his administration. In later years, however, he blamed the enemies of his government for the apparent derailment of his human rights policy. At the inauguration of the Armed Forces Consultative Assembly in 1989, he told the officers and men of the Armed Forces and the police that the enemies of the government were everywhere for reasons that should be obvious to them:

> The giant strides, which we have taken since the inception of this administration, have won us several enemies. We offended the business community and professional commission agents by removing import licensing and plugging other avenues for making quick money. We have offended the political class whose members squandered the savings which the military left in the government coffers in 1979 and also plunged the nation into heavy indebtedness abroad. We have also offended the professional politicians who want to hold this nation to ransom forever. We certainly must have offended those whom we have prevented from exploiting religion or ethnic sentiments to further their selfish interests.

II

The crises of power were not all generated by those the administration had offended directly or indirectly through its policies. Babangida could not escape the blame for some of the crises that bedevilled his administration as early as his first year in office. He courted controversies and, in certain circumstances, sabotaged what he stood for in the eyes of the public.

Early in January 1986, Babangida stepped on the slippery slope and brought the country close to a religious war. He 'smuggled' Nigeria into the Organisation of Islamic Countries, OIC. The French news agency, Agence France Press, better known by its acronym of AFP, broke the story. *The Guardian* newspaper picked it up. It shook a nation suspicious of inter-religious advantages.

The pressure by Nigerian Muslims for the admission of the country into the OIC began in September 1969, with the meeting of Arab countries in Rabat, Morocco. The late Alhaji Abubakar Gumi, grand khadi of northern Nigeria, headed a delegation to the meeting. General Gowon, the then head of state, sensed the danger in what the Muslims were trying to do and promptly wrote to King Hassan of Morocco to say that the delegation was on its own and did not represent Nigeria. On the strength of that letter, Gumi and his group were not admitted into the conference but were allowed in as observers. Nigeria had put the toe in the door. All federal governments after Gowon, including Shagari's, resisted the pressure to take the country through the door.

Babangida's close friends like Moshood Abiola, pressurised him to take Nigeria through the door. In December 1985, OIC invited Nigeria to its ministerial conference in Fez, Morocco, January 6 -10, 1986. This was a routine invitation and merited only an instruction from the ministry of external affairs to the Nigerian ambassador to Morocco to attend the meeting as an observer. However, Ahmadu Hamza, permanent secretary, ministry of external affairs, took a copy of the invitation to Babangida. Babangida approved that a Nigerian delegation led by Rilwanu Lukman, minister of mines and power, be given a diplomatic cover as an official delegation to the conference.

The Minister of External Affairs gives such diplomatic covers. But Bolaji Akinyemi, the minister, was kept out of the decision and no one asked him to issue the diplomatic cover. No matter. Lukman's delegation made up of Alhaji Abubakar Alhaji, permanent secretary, ministry of economic planning, Gumi, Abdulkadir Ahmed, governor of the Central Bank of Nigeria, and Ibrahim Dasuki, secretary-general of the Supreme Council for Islamic Affairs, had the necessary diplomatic cover.

The delegation formally tendered Nigeria's application to join the OIC to the conference. This was what the organisation had been waiting for. Nigeria was promptly admitted into the OIC. In its eagerness to admit Nigeria, the OIC waived its constitutional requirement that stipulates that a country applying for membership must wait for one year to know its fate.

Under the procedure and protocol, Babangida was required to bring the issue of Nigeria's desire to join the OIC before the council of ministers. The Armed Forces Ruling Council would then have the final say on the matter. It did not happen that way. And so when the story broke, all those who should have known but did not know, denied it happened.

Commodore Okoh Ebitu Ukiwe, the Chief of General Staff and the number two man to Babangida, knew nothing about it and said so when reporters confronted him with the AFP report. He said the matter was never discussed at any level of government. Prince Tony Momoh, the minister of information, corroborated Ukiwe.

What the press dubbed the OIC affair pitted Christians against Muslims – and divided the country along one of its biggest fault lines - religion. Christian leaders demanded immediate withdrawal of the country from the organisation. Muslim leaders insisted Nigeria must remain a member. The polity was heated. If Babangida expected this to be a storm in a teacup, he was wrong – and he knew it. Buffeted and fazed by the storm enitrely of his creation, he was forced to do some damage control to mollify the country.

Babangida said he was saddened because his intention was either misunderstood or misinterpreted for political purposes. He also felt let down by those he believed would support him. He claimed, against all the available evidence to the contrary that "OIC was more of a political and economic organisation than a religious one."[2] He could not have been ignorant of the objectives of the OIC spelt out in its charter, principal among which is "to promote Islamic solidarity among member states."

Babangida was flustered. Ray Ekpu, in his column in *Newswatch*, magazine of July 7, 1986, noted:

> The cumulative pain that the president felt from all these happenings was easily noticeable. His public appearances had shrunk considerably and when he did appear, his smile, which many had noticed as luxurious and velvety, had changed to something ashy, short and plastic, the kind of smile that originates from the teeth not from the bowels of the stomach.

Babangida referred the resolution of the crisis to a committee headed by Col John Shagaya, the Minister of Internal Affairs. The committee was to examine what Babangida described as "the implications of Nigeria's full membership" of the organisation. Christians and Muslims had equal representation on the committee, a recipe for virtually going nowhere. The walls now had a crack. The report of the committee was never made public. Babangida's luck held and he survived the storm with a visible limp into the future of his administration.

Babangida removed Ukiwe as Chief of General Staff and retired him from the navy on October 6 that year in rather shabby circumstances. An official explanation that Ukiwe had to go because of the so-called Abuja incident regarding the order of protocol in that year's independence anniversary celebration did not quite wash. Ukiwe was most likely a victim of power tussles in the AFRC but given the circumstances, he was regarded as the first high profile victim of the OIC imbroglio.

Thirteen days after he sacked Ukiwe and with the dust still swirling around him, a new dust storm circled about Babangida. On October 19, Dele Giwa, Editor-in-Chief/Chief Executive Officer of *Newswatch* magazine, was about to have breakfast with the London bureau chief of the magazine, Kayode Soyinka, in his house on Talabi Street, Ikeja, Lagos, when his son, Billy, delivered a parcel to him. Two men who stopped by in a Peugeot saloon car gave the parcel to Giwa's security man, Malam Musa Zibo, to give to Giwa. It bore the inscription, 'From the office of C-in-C.'

As Giwa attempted to open what he thought was a letter from Babangida, the parcel blew up in his face. It killed him. The murder shocked and horrified the nation both by the novelty of the murder instrument and by its cruelty. It was the first profile killing of a Nigerian journalist in Nigeria. The nation was aghast.

Who did it? That question dogged Babangida throughout his years in office. It still dogs him and may, indeed, do so for the rest of his life because a) the murder remains unresolved and b) nothing has yet ended the suspicion that his administration was to blame for it.

In his first public reaction to the murder Babangida spoke of his pain at the killing of one of the country's most popular journalists. He had known Giwa closely since he came to power. At The First Earth Run of UNICEF to mark the International Year of Peace at the National Stadium, Surulere, Lagos, on October 21, 1986, Babangida, referring to Giwa's murder, said:

> Only in the last 48 hours, this nation was saddened and affronted by the senseless murder of a promising young Nigerian professional – Dele Giwa – who was cut down in the prime of life through the most wicked and heinous means. As we mourn the untimely death of this young Nigerian, let us rededicate ourselves to the promotion of peace and harmony in this great nation of ours.[3]

Giwa made his name through his columns in the *Daily Times* and *Sunday Concord* (he was the pioneer editor of the latter) before he co-founded *Newswatch* magazine with Ray Ekpu, Yakubu Mohammed and Dan Agbese. He poured his passion for journalism into the magazine that blazed the trail in newsmagazine journalism in Nigeria. *Newswatch* was an instant success and was very popular. Its brand of journalism to quote Christopher Kolade, confronted "the society with the truth."

The circumstances leading to Giwa's murder, according to details pieced together by *Newswatch* magazine, were clumsily choreographed in a way that put some elements in the security services on the spot and led to speculations that the federal government did it. Three days before he received the lethal parcel, Giwa was invited by the deputy director of the State Security Services, SSS, Col A.K. Togun, and confronted with four allegations that were both frivolous and serious at the same time. He was alleged to be planning to publish "the other side" of the Ukiwe story.

Was this something to worry the government? If there were jitters in government over the way and manner the former number two man lost his job, it should be understood in the peculiar characteristic of Nigeria's national politics.

Ukiwe was the highest-ranking Igbo man in the government. The loss of his high-profile job as the number two citizen would be seen as the loss of the Igbo in the power configuration in the country. No trifling matter in a country in which public appointments are regarded as ethnic shares of the national cake. If there was "the other side" to the story, it probably meant that the magazine had facts that might make the government, to say the least, uncomfortable. There was no knowing how far and for how long the anger of the Igbo might burn – and the political consequences it might unleash on the country.

Newswatch had published a story, *The Sacking of Ukiwe*, in its issue of October 20, 1986, in which it told the story of the circumstances leading to his sack. If the editors of the magazine had new facts on the incident, of course, they would publish them but at the time the allegations were made, no such publication was contemplated by the magazine.

The second allegation was that Giwa planned to employ Alozie Ogugbuaja, a superintendent of police and the public relations officer of the Lagos State police command, if the police fired him. Ogugbuaja, a radical in his own right, testified before the Justice Akanbi panel set up by the government to probe the students' riots of May that year at which he made the telling statement that Nigerian soldiers pre-occupied themselves with eating pepper soup and planning coups. The government felt scandalised. He was suspended from his job. Dele and Ekpu had spoken to Ogugbuaja on phone and told him that if the police fired him, *Newswatch* would hire him. It was not known how this private conversation found its way into security circles. It was either Giwa's phone was bugged or Ogugbuaja's was.

The other two allegations were more serious – and Giwa rightly took a serious and worried view of them. He was alleged to be meeting with the leadership of the NLC, ASUU and the students union for purposes of destabilising the government and birthing a socialist revolution in the country. The fourth and perhaps the most serious allegation was that Giwa was holding discussion with some people to import arms into the country.

Giwa did not need to be told these allegations and the decision of the SSS to invite him went way beyond the routine harassment of the Nigerian press by security personnel. He told Ekpu, his close friend and deputy: "If they can think this of me, then I am not safe. They are only trying to give a dog a bad name in order to hang it."

Giwa took immediate precautions to protect himself. He complained to Tony Momoh, the minister of information, and the director of Military Intelligence, Lt-Col Haliru Akilu. Momoh told Giwa not to worry because "they just want to rattle you." Giwa immediately wrote his lawyer, Chief Gani Fawehinmi, and urged him to "take up the concern expressed with the SSS and the IG."

On the morning he was killed, Giwa returned Akilu's phone he made to his house the previous night. Akilu told Giwa he called to tell him that he should not worry about the allegations made by the SSS and that the matter had been settled. Giwa told him he was right to worry because it was an attempt to ruin his life and that he had reported the matter to his lawyer. Akilu told him it was "not a matter for lawyers. Don't bother yourself; the matter is now settled."

When Akilu phoned Giwa's home the night before, he spoke to Giwa's wife, Funmi. Akilu, according to Mrs Giwa, asked her for the direction to their house. As Funmi recalled it, Akilu told her that "the ADC has something for him, an invitation or something like that." Akilu later said that he wanted the address because he hoped to stop "over at the place on my way to Kano."

Fawehinmi put up a strenuous fight to compel the attorney general and the director of prosecutions of Lagos State to bring Akilu and Togun to trial for the murder. The Supreme Court to which he took the case ruled that he was free to institute private prosecution if the attorney general and the DPP failed to do so. Both of them stalled the case and never took it up.

If the sequence of events leading to Giwa's murder was bizarre, government attitude towards investigating the murder that shook the world was even more so. Momoh promised the government would fully investigate it. On October 20, Aikhomu assembled the security chiefs, each to explain to the press what he knew about the murder. Reporters were not allowed to question the security chiefs. Aikhomu then promised that "Government has no alternative than to carry out investigation into such a matter. We shall leave no stone unturned in our effort to find the truth."

As it turned out, no stone was turned and the truth was never found. Babangida was hopeful that the murder would be solved before he left office. He told the *Financial Times* of London that "like other cases of assassination, the Nigeria Police are working round the clock to get this unfortunate episode concluded. The police have, so far, been doing fairly well. I expect that in due course the police will come up with some useful results." The police came up with no such results known to the public.

The executive directors of Newswatch Communications Ltd as well as Fawehinmi separately took the matter to the Oputa panel set up by President Olusegun Obasanjo to look into all cases of human rights abuses in the country. The panel recommended that the federal government should reopen investigations into the murder. And there the matter rests.

Ironically, years after he left office, Babangida blamed the press for the failure of the police to "come up with some useful results." At an interview with *Newswatch,* in June 2000, he told the magazine: "I will rather accuse you the media of not doing more about it... The press and individuals should help the police, but I am not sure that you are helping them. You are not helping them to do their job."

III

Within his first year of assumption of power, almost everything that needed to go wrong with the Babangida administration did. Only four months after he assumed office, Babangida uncovered a plot to topple him. Vatsa and nine other senior and middle-ranking military officers from the army, the navy and the air force, were arrested, tried, convicted and executed in March 1986 for their part in the coup plot.

The dust had hardly settled on that when a bloody crisis involving students and the authorities erupted in Ahmadu Bello University, Zaria. By the time he inaugurated the Armed Forces Consultative Assembly some three years later, there had been a series of other social and political crises, including the SAP riots that were not particularly pleasant for the administration. Naturally, Babangida put two and two together and came to the conclusion that these were calculated plans to subvert his administration. In such a climate of disquiet, the first casualty would be human rights because, according to Babangida, "the military had a duty to ensure that it does not allow its detractors to deflect it from fulfilling its obligation to the fatherland."

IV

Crises are inevitable in all forms of government. They arise either as reactions to the actions and the decisions of government or as a consequence of disappointed expectations. How a government handles the crises of power or emerges from them provides history with the major means by which it is judged. The crises that attended his administration almost to the very end also showed that Babangida did not always get it right. His first series of crises came from the one constituency whose friendship he set out to cultivate right from the beginning – labour.

Nigeria boasts of vibrant trade unionism. The country had as many as 1,000 trade unions up to the late seventies. It did not have a central labour union until the Murtala/Obasanjo administration created one, the Nigeria Labour Congress, NLC, with 42 affiliates through decree 22 of February 1978. The first attempt by the union leaders to create a central labour union with the same name in 1975 to be led by the veteran trade unionist, the late Wahab Goodluck, failed for reasons we need not go into here.

Trade unions serve vital purposes in relations between employers and employees in both the public and the private sectors. Without them, the lot of employees in the hands of their employers would be 'brutish.'

Perhaps because of this, neither the public nor the private sector anywhere in the world is particularly fond of trade unions and their activist leaders. At the best of times, relationship between employers and labour unions is characterised by mutual suspicion and distrust. But all governments try to be in good terms with labour unions. No one can pretend not to know that labour unions have inherent capacity through sits-in and strike actions to undermine government and paralyse a country's economy.

Babangida did not need to be persuaded that the co-operation of the NLC and its affiliated unions was critical to industrial peace without which it would be impossible for him to execute his programmes. He was aware of the lingering issues between the Buhari administration and labour. Some of the unresolved issues between labour and government, such as the austerity measures and the wage freeze, brought the NLC into a series of confrontations with government dating back to the Shagari administration in the Second Republic. The congress planned to go on strike in August 1985 to force the Buhari administration to stop the widespread retrenchment of workers in the public sector with ripple effects in the private sector. It shelved its plan when Babangida emerged as president.

Twenty-eight days after he assumed office, Babangida launched his charm offensive to bring labour into his orbit when he formally met with the leadership of the NLC. The NLC chairman, Ali Chiroma, led the six-man labour team to the meeting with the president. The labour leaders went to the meeting with a shopping basket of workers' demands that included the rejection of the IMF bridging loan, the de-freezing of wages, a return to collective bargaining and an end to retrenchment that had affected about 300,000 people in the public and the private sectors.

It is not unusual for labour to expect a new administration to be sympathetic to its cause. Babangida did not disappoint the labour leaders. He too, he said, was worried about the rising unemployment in the country. He said his government did not intend to let Nigerians suffer and was, therefore, "looking into the practical details of mobilising unemployed persons who have no immediate prospects of employment to engage in public works or other activities of communal and social value until such a time (that) they (could) secure suitable jobs." He promised, for the umpteenth time, that his administration would "not force any decision on the people of this country; rather, before arriving at decisions, it will take cognisance of the yearnings and aspirations of the Nigerian people."[4] He invited labour to join hands with his government "to build a new society based on co-operation, social justice and self-reliance; and to evolve a new attitude in the labour movement for the benefit of our country."

Babangida wanted the labour leaders to go beyond their customary struggle for the welfare of the workers, important though that might be, and help him to revamp the economy and enthrone new political and social orders in the country. The times were hard, the president said. It was important for the congress to appreciate what the country was going through and resist the temptation of asking for more pay, including a new national minimum wage.

After all, he told the labour leaders, Nigerian workers were much better paid than their counterparts in Egypt, a developing country like Nigeria. International Labour Organisation, ILO, statistics showed that Nigerian workers put in a 40-hour week compared to a 56-hour week in Egypt. But the Egyptian worker earned the weekly equivalent of ₦9.00 in the manufacturing sector and ₦15.00 in the mining sector. His Nigerian counterpart earned ₦30.00 and ₦17.60 per week in the manufacturing and mining sectors respectively.

Babangida tasked the labour leaders with helping the government find answers to five critical national questions: how can the government curb unemployment? How can demands for more pay be checked? How can productivity be raised? How can government interference in the economy be reduced? How can imports be curbed and efforts in non-oil sectors promoted?

In raising these questions with the labour leaders, Babangida intended to achieve one fundamental objective – to convince them that he treasured their inputs and that he regarded them as partners with his administration. The labour leaders must have found this apparent inclusiveness by, of all things, a military administration, both surprising and irresistible. They probably left the meeting virtually walking on air.

On Labour Day on May 1, 1986, Babangida played up the importance of trade unions "as a vital part of the nation's socio-economic structure," and invited the workers to join hands with his government "to build a new society based on cooperation, social justice and self-reliance."[5]

He left Nigerian workers in no doubt that he was their true friend. He extended compensation for injury to all workers in regular employment throughout the country; introduced compulsory insurance cover to all employees by employers and set up a national productivity centre "to promote productivity consciousness." He topped these with a generous donation of money, vehicles and office equipment to OATUU, the central African labour body, "to guarantee its independence from undue influence of international trade union organisations."[6]

Babangida's most dramatic action was the unbanning of Nigeria's eleven leading trade unionists. Under the *Trade Union (Disqualification of Certain Persons)* decree 15 of 1977, the Murtala/Obasanjo military regime banned them from participating in trade union activities for 'various improprieties and endless leadership tussle.' The government acted on the recommendations of the Justice Duro Adebiyi tribunal set up early in 1976 to probe the labour unions and their leaders.

Two of the affected men, both of whom are now deceased, were synonymous with trade unionism in Nigeria. One was the late Chief Michael Imoudu, fondly known as Nigeria's labour leader number one. The other equally famous trade unionist was Wahab Goodluck. These men, the best-known faces in trade unionism in the country dating back to the colonial days, were put out in the cold for about ten years. They were almost forgotten in that gulag.

Babangida understood the public sentiment over the fate of the ageing labour leaders whose fire of union activism had been effectively smothered by the ashes of time and circumstances. He knew that he stood to reap a bounty harvest of public and labour goodwill by unbanning them. It was the smart thing to do. Babangida said he took the action in the true spirit of his regime's "principles of fundamental human rights and compassion."

But in less than a year, Babangida's carefully cultivated relationship with labour began to show signs of strain. The economy must accept part of the blame. One of the measures, among others adopted by the Babangida administration to help shore up the economy, was to reduce the salary of workers in the public sector. The labour leaders felt betrayed. They objected to the government decision. They also objected to the privatisation and commercialisation of government-owned companies and parastatals. Government stood its ground. Labour stood its ground. Its honeymoon with the new administration was about to end.

The rupture came in June 1986 - much sooner than either party probably expected – and through no fault of either party. On May 22 and 23 that year, a bloody clash between the police and the students of Ahmadu Bello University, Zaria, left twenty students dead. The nation was shocked. Professor Ango Abdullahi, the vice-chancellor of the university, invited the police into the campus to disperse the students from the front of the senate building where they had gathered to protest the expulsion of their union leader from the university.

The university authorities clearly mishandled a simple matter. For reasons that still remain baffling, the university authorities were irked by the decision of the students union to mark the eighth anniversary of the nation-wide student crisis in 1978, better known as Ali Must Go, a reference to demands by the national body of the students' union for the sacking of the then federal commissioner for education in the Murtala/Obasanjo administration, Col Ahmadu Ali, over the increase in tuition fees paid in the universities. In that protest, several university students lost their lives in the hands of the police.

The offence of the ABU students this time around, according to the authorities, was that they marched to Amina Hall, the female hostel, in an alleged contravention of a regulation that banned male students from the female hostel. The students apologised but the authorities were determined to exact their pound of flesh. They expelled the student union leader, suspended one student for the rest of the academic session and formally warned several others to be of good behaviour. The students thought the decision was high-handed and unjust. They decided to protest it to force the authorities to rescind it. It was at this point that the police entered the picture.

The killing of the students kicked up a national storm and was roundly condemned by all segments in the society. The senate of the University of Ibadan took the unusual step of issuing a formal condemnation of the killing and the mishandling of the crisis by the authorities of ABU. Students in all the universities, colleges of education and polytechnics throughout the country protested the killing. Some of those protests were violent, leading to the destruction of government and private property. The official response was to close down all these institutions.

The Babangida administration was not in any way involved directly or indirectly in the crisis in the university. But ABU being a federal university and the police being a federal civil force, the administration could not escape moral responsibility for the unprecedented brutal action of the police against unarmed university students. As a *Newswatch* columnist, Adebayo Williams put it, "...the ABU tragedy demonstrates that a human rights policy is a sham without a humanised police force."[7]

Babangida did his best to cool the national temper. He apologised for what happened in Zaria on Children's Day on May 27. He also set up a commission of enquiry headed by Major General Emmanuel Abisoye to investigate it. The NLC felt that the ABU tragedy was an indication that student unionism, and by extension, labour unions, were under threat once again in the country. The congress held an emergency meeting shortly after the incident and decided to register its sympathy for the students with a massive public demonstration on June 4. It was not to be. The federal government aborted the planned demonstration by arresting and detaining Chiroma and five other executive members of the congress. Government also locked up the national headquarters of the NLC. This was bad news for labour and the human rights community.

Chiroma and his colleagues were detained for ten days. They sued the government, arguing that its action against the NLC was intended to "cow the Nigerian people into submission, contrary to the declared policy of President Babangida to respect the fundamental rights of all Nigerian citizens."[8]

The government action chilled its relations with labour. Nothing would be quite the same again between the two parties although Chiroma tried to take it in his stride by arguing that their problem with the government was "to be expected because there are always problems between a capitalist government and trade unions..."[9]

Government action against the NLC had only one interpretation in the press and the court of public opinion – the regime had deviated from its human rights posture. Indeed, by the time of the ABU tragedy, labour had cause to feel that weeds were beginning to cover the full length of the regime's human rights path. The weeds first appeared when the government tried to use the NLC to achieve its objectives in the 1986 federal budget. Government took the novel step of inviting labour to make its inputs into the budget. Although the government later claimed that labour accepted the invitation and made its own input, the labour leaders denied this. What is not in dispute is that the NLC refused to support government's plan to withdraw subsidy on petroleum products as part of cost-cutting measures in the 1986 budget. The decision of the congress did not please the administration. The two parties began to warily watch each other. A growing flood of mutual suspicion threatened the bridge of understanding and co-operation.

Babangida continued to cultivate labour in the hope that its leaders would form a credible band of loyal preachers of his new economic gospel of lean and difficult times today, fatter and easier times tomorrow. Babangida still hoped that he would be able to convince the NLC to support the withdrawal of subsidy on petroleum products. He had made up his mind to withdraw the subsidy, partially or fully, in 1988. During the preparation of the 1988 budget, therefore, "the government initiated a meeting with top NLC leaders (in November 1987) at which both sides agreed to do some trade-offs."[10]

Under this agreement, government agreed to "substantially review" fringe benefits paid to civil servants and end the wage freeze in the private sector. The NLC agreed not to oppose the government measures. It also agreed to moderate its criticism of the structural adjustment programme, the plank of the Babangida administration's economic reform programme.

The ink had hardly dried on the agreement when the labour leaders probably realised that they had shot themselves in the foot. They immediately and unilaterally broke the agreement. Government was shocked by this and even more shocked to see the labour leaders "intensif(y) their campaign to discredit government rationale for withdrawing the subsidy. (They provided) facts and figures on the comparative differences in per capita income and take home pay between Nigeria and some countries whose petroleum prices the government had used to show the level of oil subsidy in the country."[11]

The NLC leaders knew that they "had tapped a groundswell of popular opposition to the proposed measure. (They would) not let go such a golden opportunity to burnish their image dented by the public resentment of their vacillation, indecision and lack of leadership at a time workers were facing unprecedented economic hardship."[12] Their anti-subsidy withdrawal campaign was so successful that it forced the government to shelve the plan.

The labour leaders savoured their victory but they needed no one to tell them that they had crossed the line. Government smarted from this 'betrayal.' It waited "for the NLC leaders to falter or make the wrong move." They did. The quadrennial delegates' conference of the NLC was held in Benin City, Edo State, from February 23 to 26, 1988. Chiroma was re-elected president for another term. His re-election was challenged by another faction of the congress led by Takai Shamang, Kano State chairman of the NLC. The congress was then factionalised into the so-called Marxists (Chiroma faction) and democrats (Shamang faction).

All available evidence showed that government caused and fuelled the NLC crisis for its own purpose. It funded the Shamang faction in an effort to get rid of Chiroma and his "difficult executive." But Shamang was no match for the wily Chiroma who had become popular for trumping government argument on fuel subsidy. The factionalisation was more cosmetic than substantial but it gave government the opportunity to put its anti-labour plans into immediate effect. It declared the congress "illegal" and "unlawful" and dissolved the executives of both factions.

For the first time in its history, the NLC was banned under the *National Economic Emergency Decree 22 of 1985*. Chiroma and the members of his executive were arrested and detained for four days and charged with sedition. Government later dropped the charge. Alao Aka-Bashorun, national president of the Nigerian Bar Association, NBA, at the time said the ban was "a dangerous precedent." No one needed telling.

Government then appointed a sole administrator, Michael Ogunkoya, for the NLC. He was instructed to probe the fund and the property of the congress and those of its affiliate labour unions. Babangida was obviously bent on nailing the leaders. The minister of labour and productivity, Abubakar Umar, accused the labour leaders of "ideological intolerance and narrow selfish interests." He said it had "become increasingly clear that the leaders of both factions had already sealed up their minds and had decided to relentlessly pursue definite and pre-planned courses of action with the aim of either remaining in office or getting into office by all means, fair or foul." But government was determined "that never again will the central labour organisation be permitted to break up and revert into inconsequential little unions which are ready tools of manipulation and subversion of industrial peace, harmony and security of the nation."[13]

V

Caging the NLC did not bring industrial peace for Babangida and his administration. Trouble came from other trade or professional unions. The most prominent, and certainly in the view of the government, the most troublesome of these, was the Academic Staff Union of Universities, ASUU, the umbrella union of university teachers. The union gave Babangida a cautious reception at the inception of his administration. Early in September 1985, the ABU branch of ASUU sent a fifteen-page letter to the president in which it advised him to ignore pressures from the private sector and other vested interests to ditch some "positive decisions" of the Buhari administration. ASUU urged Babangida to reject the IMF loan under the terms and conditions stipulated by the IMF because it would lead to a drastic fall in the value of the Naira and open the economy to foreign interference and exploitation.[14]

ASUU was a very strong and vocal union. It fought for academic freedom and university autonomy consistent with university culture and tradition in the free world; better pay and conditions of service for its members and a revamping of the university system. It was also a strong voice in national affairs. Successive military dictators in Nigeria tended to treat ASUU leaders as tolerable nuisance.

Babangida's initial attitude towards the university teachers gave no indication that he too would treat their union the same way. He set out as the most intellectual-hugging ruler that the country, up to that point, had ever had. He drew the bulk of the members of his Presidential Advisory Committee from the universities. The renowned economist, the late Professor Ojetunji Aboyade, headed the committee.

The first indication that he too wanted to relate with ASUU on his own terms came from the University of Benin in 1987. The university had some internal problems with the members of the executive of the academic staff union. The university authorities took no prisoners. It sacked five lecturers, one of whom was the popular national president of ASUU, Dr. Festus Iyayi. ASUU fought back. It took the matter to a Benin high court and asked the court to over turn the sack. In its preliminary ruling, the court restrained the university authorities from sacking the five lecturers. The federal government threw its weight behind the university authorities and rendered the judgement of the court a nullity.

ASUU had, in fact, extracted a pledge from Aikhomu that government would not interfere in the matter between it and the authorities of the University of Benin. Perhaps, encouraged by this pledge, ASUU challenged the composition of the council of the university at another Benin high court. The matter was yet to be heard by the court when the government reneged on its pledge and issued decree 36 of 1987. The decree re-affirmed the sacking of the teachers. It stipulated they were not to be reinstated. They never were. ASUU rightly described decree 36 as "a disrespect for the rule of law."

Decree 36 was issued, ostensibly, to reconstitute the university council. Its intention was less honourable. Its real intention was to quash both the legal challenge to the constitution of the council and nullify the court decision that the sacked teachers be given back their job. Relations between the teachers and the government entered an openly sour phase. It could only get worse. It did.

On January 18, 1988, ASUU requested Idris Abdulkadir, the executive secretary of the National Universities Commission, NUC, for a meeting to conclude an agreement with the commission on the implementation of the new salary structure and fringe benefits for university staff. Somehow, Abdulkadir denied their request for a meeting and instead directed the universities to either adjust their salaries to a maximum of ₦27,000.00 for professors and being able to enjoy the pension and gratuity specified in the unified grades salary structure or adopt a structure not related to the unified grades salary structure and lose pensions and gratuities. Even now, it is difficult to explain the reaction of the executive secretary to the routine request by the union. It would appear that both sides had reached a breaking point.

After months of exchange of correspondences between the union and the NUC on the one hand and between the union and the federal ministry of education on the other hand, the teachers gave the government a one month ultimatum within which to pay the elongated salary scale with twenty per cent differential along with the revised fringe benefits with effect from January 1, 1988. It also demanded that government should respect the right of the senate of all the universities to close or re-open universities. The federal government had usurped this function in all the universities and closed down or re-opened universities as it suited it. The ultimatum expired June 30. The federal government did not budge.

ASUU called out the teachers on strike. Government apparently knew this would happen. It was ready with the sledgehammer. The minister of education, Professor Jibril Aminu, former vice-chancellor of the University of Maiduguri as well as a former executive secretary of NUC, gave his former colleagues forty-eight hours to return to work. The teachers ignored him. On July 7, Aminu delivered the killer punch. He announced an indefinite ban of ASUU. Babangida attributed his decision to ban the union to what he vaguely described as "unreasonable demands" on the part of the university teachers.

The ban lasted for twenty-five months and was lifted on August 27, 1990, the fifth anniversary of the Babangida administration. Babangida couched his decision to lift the ban in benevolent terms. He said he did it to allow the "organised members of the university community (to) make positive contributions to the emergence of a new socio-political order."

The ban effectively crushed whatever was left of university autonomy and academic freedom in Nigerian universities. It also marked the beginning of government's systematic crackdown on university teachers. The government had simply convinced itself that ASUU was a pain in the neck. It refused to understand where the union was coming from. Nigerian universities were already faced with a progressive deteriorating condition. Under funding led to poor and decaying infrastructures and a drastic fall in the standard of teaching and research in all the universities, nearly all of which at the time were owned by the federal government. The first wave of brain drain began at this point. Many lecturers, faced with a bleak future at home, sought greener pastures elsewhere.

In a series of petitions to the government, ASUU suggested ways of halting the deteriorating condition and the brain drain to save the university system. But what it received in return from the government were the constant harassment of university teachers and "constant breach(es) of university autonomy, laws and statutes by government as well as the suppression of academic freedom."

The government usurped the statutory right of the governing council of all the universities to appoint and discipline university staff and then proceeded to purge the universities of "leftist" or "radical" teachers "for teaching what they were not paid to teach." They were either summarily sacked or forcibly retired in full contravention of university laws and regulations.

In the first wave of these actions in 1988, the government retired or sacked several of such radical or leftist university teachers, among whom were the late well-known radical and a thorn in the flesh of the northern establishment, Dr. Yusuf Bala Usman, an historian at the Ahmadu Bello University, Zaria; Professor Obaro Ikime, another well-known historian at the University of Ibadan, Professor Omotoye Olorede and Dr Idowu Awopetu, both of Obafemi Awolowo University, Ile-Ife, and Dr. Festus Iyayi of the University of Benin. Only Usman got his job back. He contested his forced retirement in the court and the court ruled in his favour. Somehow, the government obeyed the judgment.

But the sudden and clumsy deportation of Dr. Patrick Wilmot of Ahmadu Bello University, Zaria, was perhaps the most naked attempt by the government to bring the university teachers into 'line.' Wilmot, a Jamaican, had lived in Nigeria for many years and was a well-known and informed critic of apartheid South Africa. But in a twist of irony, the government accused him of being a "double agent" who "had persistently and conscientiously worked against the interest of Nigeria."

The university teachers returned to the trenches early in 1992 over their rejection of the recommendations of the Longe Commission for a 45 per cent increase in the salary of university teachers. They contended that it fell short of the "African average" and was unrealistic considering the depreciation of the Naira. The national president of ASUU, Dr. Attahiru Jega, contended that the white paper did not address their other demands such as gross under-funding of the universities and enhanced university autonomy. The union again called out its members on strike on July 20.

Two days later, the government proscribed the union for the second time. This time, the government went much further – to virtually bury the union. It prohibited the teachers from unionising and backed up its decision with decree 24 of 1992. The decree ousted the right of the courts to question anything done by the government under the decree.

Aikhomu accused the leadership of ASUU of being "provocative, uninformed and insensitive to the economic realities of the country." Government, he said, acted to save "the nation's children and their parents, including those of us in government from suffering because the silent majority of university teachers were being led by the nose by a group of so-called radicals who would not listen."[15]

Babangida saw nothing wrong with what the administration did. As far as he was concerned, it was in the interest and furtherance of university autonomy. He justified his decision to outlaw unionisation in universities with his surprisingly cynical view of university autonomy:

> Every university should be recognised for what it is and everybody is talking of autonomy. They say universities must be given autonomy, and we are trying to do so and nobody is prepared to accept that autonomy which means less dependence on an apex organisation. So, what we are saying as far as this is concerned is let each university evolve, let each university run its own affairs, let each university be run the way it wants to be run.[16]

VI

Did Babangida see labour unions and professional associations as a threat to his administration? He refused to be drawn to a categorical answer but merely acknowledged that problems between government and labour were not unusual:

> Well, any country that believes in democracy has to accept that at any given time, there is always the problem between organised labour movement and the government and these have always been resolved through continuing dialogue between the labour unions and the government and we have been doing precisely that.[17]

In his dealings with trade and student unions and professional bodies Babangida proved to be the grand master of his shuffle dance step. For every one step he took forward, he took two backwards. He offered the carrot and he used the whip in equal measure to achieve his purpose. He banned and unbanned unions and professional associations as it suited not just his fancy but perhaps more importantly to show who was boss and the extent to which he was willing to let anyone or a group of persons push him and his government around.

But he continued to face challenges in the social, economic and political fronts. His great economic reform programme, SAP, faced intense public criticisms because of some difficulties blamed on the programme. These difficulties became the famous pains of SAP that led to riots in May 1989, led by university and polytechnic students nation-wide. Babangida did not need to be told that the riots were direct threats to his transition to civil rule programme. He interpreted them as attempts "to destroy the credibility of the military as a group" and because the enemies of the administration were exploiting the "biased and erroneous" image of the military as a privileged class insulated from the sufferings of the generality of the people, "individual soldiers and their properties (were) made target of attacks by vandals supposedly protesting against the policies of government."

Babangida decided it was time for him to unite the armed forces and the police behind him and his policies. The armed forces were his primary constituency. He reached to this constituency by setting up the Armed Forces Consultative Assembly as "a consultative body that will liaise between the Armed Forces Ruling Council and the government on the one hand and the generality of the Armed Forces on the other."

The assembly, made up of selected commanders in the army, the navy and the air force, senior staff officers, very senior warrant officers and equivalent in the navy and the air force and the police, was inaugurated not long after the SAP riots on June 5, 1989. The assembly had three primary and five secondary objectives that, taken together, underlined Babangida's worry that the enemies might have penetrated his primary constituency and his desire to monitor the pulse of the armed forces to keep its men and officers in check or, at least, prevent them from doing anything funny. It was also a desperate move by Babangida to sensitise the armed forces to the "crucial and potentially destructive challenge" they faced "as a group" and thus unite them to confront the 'several enemies' that he said the administration had unwittingly won for itself, thanks to its 'giant strides.'

The primary objectives of the assembly were:

a) to constitute an information management system for the Armed Forces as a channel of communication, whereby essential information about governmental matters, directions and thinking flows down the ranks, and reactions to these filter back right up to the apex
b) to nurture, sustain and promote, through informal discussions, esprit de corps, within the Armed Forces;
c) to explore ways and means of ensuring that in the transitional period and beyond, our professional ethic is supportive of democratic norms and values,

The secondary functions of the assembly were the:

a) provision of critical advice to the Presidency and the Armed Forces Ruling Council over general policies, programmes and decisions of government;
b) provision of critical information and suggestions about the performance of the military in government;
c) provision of political awareness and information base for members of the Armed Forces;
d) provision of a sense of belonging and participation of officers and men of the Armed Forces in government; and
e) to bring up any other pertinent matters for discussion and clarification.

SAP was the most criticised of Babangida's programmes. He was clearly rankled by these criticisms and knew they were like termites eating into the wood on which he was carving the new nation. He was pained by the fact that the programme had "been used as the excuse for waging war against the government in some parts of the country." The problem, as he saw it, was that "the average Nigerian (had not) fully grasped the philosophy behind SAP partly because of the misinterpretations which some mischief-makers (gave) some elements of the programme."

He devoted the major part of his address to the assembly to the rationale for the programme and to solicit their total support for it, not only because there was "no viable alternative" to it but more importantly because if the programme was abandoned mid-way, "the pains of trying to reintroduce it at a later stage will be worse than the current pains and we may perish in the process."

Babangida's primary objective in setting up the consultative assembly was, to use a military expression, to rally the troops behind him. He told the officers and men that they were in it together and therefore, "my appeal to you is that the military must not allow itself to fall prey to the divisive antics of our detractors. We must not let the military as an institution be humiliated or be disgraced out of office as was the case in some countries which are now back to square one or even worse. We, by our collective action hold the key to the stability of this country..."

Did Babangida act too late in trying to rally the troops? A little over ten months later on April 20, 1990, he had a rude answer to that question during the fasting period in the holy month of *Ramadan*. Babangida saw off his last visitors to Dodan Barracks late on the night of April 19. He then went up to his bedroom upstairs in the family quarters. As was his habit, he started "fiddling with television; tried BBC, Sky, CNN and all that and it went on until about 2 a.m. I fell off."

A couple of hours or so later, his wife, Maryam, woke him up. She had heard some shootings. She told her husband she was sure "something was happening." Babangida tried to re-assure her. "I told her nothing was happening." He was mistaken. A bloody coup attempt to topple him was under way with a heavy armour bombardment of his residential quarters in Dodan Barracks. He and his family narrowly escaped death.

The coup plotters wanted to wipe out Babangida and his family outright, hence the heavy armour assault on the family wing of his official residence. To borrow a popular Nigerian saying, Babangida and his family escaped unhurt *by the grace of the almighty God*. But the heavy armour assault on Dodan Barracks claimed a major victim, the ADC to the president, Lt-Col U.K. Bello. Bello, described by his former course mates and senior officers as a fearless officer, had attempted to confront the coup plotters using an armoured vehicle stationed in Dodan Barracks. He got into the vehicle. He did not know that it had been sabotaged and put out of service, possibly by collaborators in the presidency. As he climbed down from the vehicle in apparent confusion and disappointment, he was killed instantly in a hail of bullets.

Most of the young officers involved in the failed coup were Babangida's students when he was an instructor in the Nigerian Defence

Academy, Kaduna. Even as president, Babangida maintained close contact with some of them. Orkar, he says, was "very close to me." Babangida met Orkar sometime in November 1989 when the major, then stationed at Shaki, Oyo State, complained of a broken bridge. He told the president that a soldier who attempted to cross it with his child lost the child in the process. Babangida felt touched. He ordered Major General Mamman Kontagora, the Minister of Works, to repair the bridge immediately.

Lt-Col Tony Nyiam, perhaps the most senior officer among the coup plotters, was also "very, very well-known" to Babangida. He wrote regularly to the president on political and other issues he felt strongly about. The president counted him among his ardent supporters in the military. To see that all these officers plotted to kill or outst him was too much for Babangida.

Babangida's confidence in his primary constituency was badly shaken and his ego sorely bruised by the coup attempt. Orkar was from Benue State. The leader of the coup was said to be Major Saliba Mukoro. He, like most of the coup plotters, is from the Niger Delta. Brigadier-General Fred Chijuka, director of defence information, described Orkar as "a very intelligent and brilliant officer."

Orkar accused the Babangida administration of being "...dictatorial, corrupt, drug baronish, evil men, sadistic, deceitful, prodigalistic (and) unpatriotic." The coup script read like a minority revolt. Orkar announced the coup "on behalf of the patriotic and well-meaning people of the Middle-Belt and the southern parts of the country." He gave three main reasons for their decision to oust Babangida. The first was to prevent him from installing himself as life president. He gave a catalogue of what he and his colleagues regarded as credible evidence in support of their suspicion, among which were "his appointment of himself as a minister of defence, his putting under his direct control the SSS, his deliberate manipulation of the transition programme...(and) his recent fraternisation with other African leaders that have installed themselves as life presidents."

Their second reason he gave for the coup was to free

> the marginalised, oppressed and enslaved peoples of the Middle-Belt and the South (and their) children yet unborn from eternal slavery and colonisation by a clique of this country (who thought it was) "their birth right to dominate till eternity the political and economic privileges of this great country to the exclusion of the people of the Middle-Belt and the South.

By 'clique,' Orkar meant people from Sokoto, Borno, Katsina, Kano and Bauchi states. He and his colleagues took the strange decision to excise the five states from the federation. They would be re-admitted into the country subject to their meeting certain conditions, one of which was "to install the rightful heir to the Sultanate, Alhaji Maccido, who is the people's choice."

Their third reason was "to lay a strong egalitarian foundation for the real take off of the Nigeria State or states as the circumstance may dictate." Ominous. Did the coup plotters intend to break up the Nigerian State into Nigerian States? The naivety of their intention showed all through Orkar's speech and served notice that the country faced a clear and obvious danger from factions within the military establishment lured by the lust for political power.

Babangida was the intended victim of the Orkar coup. He was neither killed nor toppled but he was still the greatest loser. The bloody attempt to remove him from office shattered the myth of his invincibility and popularity within and outside his primary constituency – the armed forces. He was confident enough to repeatedly assure the nation and the world that his regime would be the last military administration in the country. Now he knew better. His coup against Buhari did not, after all, shut the door in the face of all politically ambitious elements in the armed forces. He began to watch his own shadow. Babangida's door, always open to all comers until then, was now shut in the face of all but only a few trusted officers.

The young men, as it were, forced him to confront his mortality. Babangida very candidly admitted years after he left office:

> I tell you, it was something you never, ever expected. Suddenly it proved you wrong. Secondly, Orkar was one officer I knew very, very well. I saw him a couple of weeks before the abortive coup. We talked and he told me about the problem at his location in Shaki and asked me to tell Kotangora (minister of works and housing) to award a contract to resurface part of the road. It came as a shock that he should have been involved in this kind of thing. Thirdly, I have always been an advocate of bloodless coups. That they could go to the extent of violence also gave me a real shock.

His real shock was not that it happened but that he and the IBB boys let down their guard. He said he had always told the group that since they eased out someone else from office, they should not be naïve enough to discount the possibility of some other group easing them out too. He said he pointedly told them:

> I don't want anyone of you to sit down and think somebody may not attempt to ease us out. So, we had to be vigilant. We didn't suspect that Gideon and the rest of them were planning anything. You could see it was all against those

privileged few perceived as IBB boys so sometimes I had to protect them by making them less vulnerable.

The failed coup had a profound effect on Babangida in several ways. Perhaps what worried him most about the coup was the ethnic and sectional composition of the coup plotters:

> When I looked at the composition of people who were involved in this coup, quite frankly, they were in the minority groups of this country. It is the Rivers, the Ijaws, Itsekiris, Tivs, etc. So, something went into my head and I began to think there must be something that bound them together. And I began to get worried about the deployment of officers. Some of these officers were very bright. 'Plum' job, they were not getting it. So, they felt that may be they didn't belong to the famous caliphate or even religion. That disturbed me.
> I then began to get worried about the whole political direction of the country. I began to get worried that something must be amiss. One could have thought we had a highly knit organisation, which is devoid of either religion or ethnic sentiment. We got worried that we were not yet a nation and this feeling became prevalent in the armed forces.

His immediate reaction was to narrow the circle of his trusted friends in the military: "I really had to change my attitude in governance, even my perception about people and individuals." He could no longer take the loyalty of his officers and men for granted. There were implications here. It redefined the character of the Babangida administration for the rest of its life. Where Babangida was open and casual, he was now decidedly remote – and even cold. Something always gives when a man has to watch his own shadow. Babangida says he learnt a most valuable lesson from the failed coup:

> One of the things I learnt was that if everything is okay, then everybody would be with me. But in the event of a problem, you will be left alone till either you take a decision or die. So, I began to think, why don't I do things the way I perceive them and then leave everything to my conscience? I became more individualistic.

By being more individualistic, he meant that he withdrew more and more into himself. A small circle of the faithful formed around him and deemed it its profound duty to shield Babangida from possible harm from any and all directions. This shielding, however noble its objective might have been, also meant that Babangida was effectively shielded from keeping his fingers on the pulse of the nation. The secret of his survival so far had much to do with his capacity to open himself up to all manner of views. Now, he was forced to rely on the views of the small circle of the faithful.

Babangida's first major public comment on the failed coup came at the 12th graduation ceremony of students of Command and Staff College, Jaji, on June 29, 1990. He seemed to admit that he acted too late in constituting the Armed Forces Consultative Assembly. He told the graduating students that "the event of April brought home to us the fact that the internal mechanism of institutional coherence and survival in the Armed Forces appeared to have dramatically failed."

He put the blame on politics; or more correctly, the military involvement in politics since January 15, 1966. It was his view – and it is difficult to disagree with him on this point – that the military involvement in politics had eroded "our organisational ethos and much valued professionalism." Inevitably, therefore, Babangida argued, that "cohesion, discipline, hierarchical structure of command, nationalism, a sense of Puritanism and 'esprit-de-corps were being dangerously subverted."

It confronted the military with a new challenge, which, according to the president, was "how to pull back and rebuild what had been or was being systematically destroyed. The attraction of political power for young elements in the military put the future of the military in jeopardy."

He said:

> The aborted coup provided a dress rehearsal of the potential problems which your generation and of the social environment which you have cultivated in the barracks pose to the future development of the military and the nation. The naivety of the attitudes of this generation to the military and the nation was also exposed in the aborted coup. Those who hatched the coup and implemented it were apparently not part of the civil war and do not seem to know any lessons of that war. They assumed naively and wrongly that a coup of the dimension they planned could be contained and implemented as a purely military affair; they assumed that society and government were spoils that inevitably went to the victor in the battle between factions within the military. Had they been part of the experience of the civil war, they would have known that they were inevitably plunging the military into another civil war and with it the society within which they sought to harvest their efforts. This is why we must remain ever thankful that bloody as the April 1990 attempt was and painful as the losses incurred are, the success of that attempt would surely have precipitated a civil war.. Most frightening is that, we as a nation, are not yet immuned [sic] against threats of civil war.

Chapter Eighteen

June 12

You had the chance to make history but you blew it.
−An unnamed General to Ibrahim Babangida

1992 AD opened on a rather bright political note for the country. Babangida's transition programme was winding down. The Orkar coup and whatever suspicion it raised in the minds of the public about the transition programme had receded more or less into history. The electoral commission successfully conducted the governorship and state assembly elections in December 1991. Civilian state governors took office in January 1992 and inaugurated their various state assemblies shortly after.

In effect, full civil rule returned to the states early in the year with renewed optimism in Babangida's successful conclusion of his transition programme by the fourth quarter of the year. The schedule of elections did not name a specific date for the final hand over in the fourth quarter but it was generally assumed to be October 1, Nigeria's independence anniversary and also the day that the Murtala/Obasanjo regime returned the country to civil rule in 1979.

Perhaps, more importantly for Babangida, he had achieved one of the objectives of his drawn-out transition programme − his own version of the military/civilian cohabitation known as diarchy, once touted by the late Dr. Nnamdi Azikiwe, in 1974 as a possible antidote to military interventions in the political administration of the country. Nigerians did not generally buy Zik's formula but he might have been pleased to know that Babangida was one of his very important converts. Babangida promoted the uniqueness of his transition programme as a phased and flexible learning process to enable the government "use the lessons gleaned from the implementation of the programme at previous stage to achieve more effective results at the next."[1]

Some form of diarchy had been factored into the entire process. Babangida tested the diarchy waters with the conduct of local government elections on non-party and later on party basis in 1987 and 1990 respectively. Civilian chairmen and councillors under military governors then ran the local governments. The civilianization of the two tiers of government − state and local governments - by early 1992, was slightly delayed. Had decree 19 of 1987, known formally as *The Transition to Civil Rule*

(Political Programme) Decree 1987, been implemented according to the original disengagement schedule, diarchy would have been in full bloom in the states by 1992. Under the original schedule, local government elections would have been conducted in the fourth quarter of 1989; state governorship and state assembly elections in the first and second quarters of 1990. By the fourth quarter of that year the state executives and the legislatures would have taken office. Babangida would remain president and the AFRC would retain its powers as the highest legislative body in the country.

This was not exactly the Zikist model of diarchy but it would do just fine for Babangida's purposes. After all, he was conveniently following the script of the Political Bureau that had advised

> a broad-spaced transition in which democratic government can proceed with political learning, institutional adjustment and a reorientation of political culture at sequential levels of politics and governance, beginning with the local governments and ending at the federal level..[2]

The country was all but set for the two remaining critical elections – the national assembly and the presidential - scheduled for the third and fourth quarters respectively. And then to everyone's surprise, some shadowy groups emerged on the political scene to campaign for an extension of military rule beyond the fourth quarter of 1992. In their advertisements in local and overseas newspapers, the shadowy groups argued that the country was not yet ready for civil rule.

The most prominent and vociferous of the Babangida-must-stay campaigners called itself, rather tongue in the cheek, the Association for Better Nigeria, ABN. It unmasked itself in early March 1992 with its aggressive advertisements in local and foreign newspapers in which it specifically advocated for four more years for Babangida. ABN said that "the military must not hand over a poisoned chalice to a rag-tag civilian administration under the guise of a transition to democracy."[3]

Was Babangida behind these campaigns? His critics believed they felt the hands of Esau but heard the voice of Jacob. This was no rocket science. Orkar had accused Babangida of a hidden agenda to remain in office for life. It was not difficult to accept these campaigns as proof of that allegation.

Babangida denied he was behind them. He said that he too was embarrassed by the campaigns. But if the campaigns embarrassed him, why did he not stop them? The campaigns were not illegal but they clearly violated the spirit of the transition programme and cast serious doubts on Babangida's promise to return the country to civil rule according to the transition schedule drawn up by him and his colleagues in the AFRC.

Babangida defended his decision not to stop the campaigns or arrest the campaigners by arguing that:

> You must look at the whole scene. Just like people who write those things, I also listened to somebody who says if the military don't go by the time they say they will go, over my dead body, there will be bloodbath in the streets of Lagos and so on. You may as well, say why don't I go and get that man who is threatening government with bloodbath if I don't go? It is a free society.[4]

He shrugged off criticisms of his decision not to stop the campaigns. They did not "bother me at all. I knew right from the word go that I would not be trusted; I would not be believed; so I will just continue to do what I believe to be right."[5]

The leader and the chief financier of the association was the maverick politician, Arthur Nzeribe, Babangida's close friend. ABN played a more ignoble role about a year later when it went to court to stop the June 12, 1993, presidential election and later the release of the election results. Babangida believed Nzeribe's role in the entire transition saga, including the annulment of the presidential election, was essentially "mischievous." He admitted that during the period of the campaigns by ABN and other some other groups, he and Nzeribe

> .. had a lot of talks, arguments, letters, papers, but I did not tell him that this is a good idea, go ahead to do it. But then one of the attractions, quote and un-quote, was that the government needed another body that would counteract all the other democratic forces such as the committee on human rights, committee on democracy and everything that was wholly anti-government in their campaigns. We thought we needed such a body which in any case would counter; let it be seen that okay, they don't like you but another association also liked you. So, when I discussed with him I also made it quite clear to him that the whole idea for me to continue did not make sense. But it (ABN) was a platform to counter all the Ganis, the Ransome-Kutis, etc. I wasn't opposed to it. If we didn't stop them abusing me, why should we stop somebody who was praising us? Principally this is the way I looked it at the time.

In his eight years in power, Babangida courted controversy as if it was the fuel he needed to keep going. In the midst of the crisis of confidence in his transition programme generated by the campaigns for four more years for him, Babangida went ahead to "do what I believe to be right." He moved the goal post of the transition programme. Military rule would no longer terminate in the fourth quarter of 1992. The handover date was quite suddenly shifted from the fourth quarter of 1992 to January 2, 1993 – the third time in the series of shifts. The presidential election was rescheduled for December 5, 1992.

However, the national assembly elections retained the original date of July 4, 1992. No reasons were given for this latest change but it kept Babangida's critics quite busy trying to prove that the transition programme was heading nowhere. Despite his confidence in himself and his transition programme, almost everyone could see that "the country was experiencing a profound crisis of governance unanticipated by the transition programme."[6]

The campaigns by ABN and other shadowy groups were actually the tip of the enormous local and international pressure mounted on Babangida to renege on his handover pledge. On the seventh anniversary of his coup, he held a casual private meeting with the civilian state governors who came to share the moment with him. Discussions turned to the military disengagement. To his surprise, according to Babangida, the governors suggested the time was not ripe for him to go. They told Babangida, as he now recalls it, that if he went ahead with his handover date, he would be handing over "in chaos." Babangida heard them out and told them: "If you love me, pray that I hand over in peace as I have promised."

The campaigners piled pressure on the First Lady, Maryam, too. Some foreign countries did not explicitly tell Babangida to stay on but he believed their body language told him they would not mind if he did. Was he allowing himself to be 'persuaded' to stay on? Many people had no problems believing that the persuaders were actually trying to persuade the persuaded.

II

In the middle of May 1992, Babangida was jolted by "communal and industrial unrests; student crises; and the general unease and discomfort over the economy" in several parts of the country. Zangon-Kataf in Kaduna State, typified the communal violence in which scores of lives were lost and private and public property were also destroyed. The violence began on May 15 and soon spread to Kaduna and Zaria towns. In Lagos, violent student and civil society protests over the pains of the structural adjustment programme lasted from May 12 to14.

Had the country become transition-to-civil rule weary? Several people thought so. But the Armed Forces Ruling Council had only one interpretation for the violence: enemies of the government were at work, challenging its authority. The administration had to fight back in a way that left no one in any doubts that it would neither retreat nor surrender.

The council met and deliberated "on the communal and industrial unrests; the student crises; and the general unease and discomfort over the economy," for six hours on May 22. On May 25, Babangida spoke to the nation "with a heavy heart over the recent acts of violence that have beset our beloved country." He blamed the violence, as governments in Nigeria are wont to do, "on political snipers, fired and primarily motivated by selfish political interests, who are committed to discrediting the military out of office."

He said the administration was "faced with just two options:

> One is to throw in the towel and jettison our far-reaching reform programmes that are targeted at making our country a great nation.... The alternative is to battle on, fortified in the knowledge that all great nations in modern history have not emerged in a single leap...

The council decided, Babangida said, "to battle on, fortified by our belief in a greater and better tomorrow." In line with this, the council decided, among others "a) to continue to protect and defend the sovereignty and territorial integrity of Nigeria; b) to protect the lives and property of all Nigerians; c) to defend the integrity of the transition programme at all costs; d) to crackdown on all persons, associations and groups that seek to either derail the transition programme or destabilize the nation: e) to carry out appropriate changes in the machinery of government in order to overcome observed lapses."

His administration, the president said emphatically, would "not be hurried out of office, neither shall we be bullied, through illegal actions, to abandon the path of planned economic and political progress." He admitted there were problems but argued that those problems could not "be solved through unnecessary confrontation and mindless carnage..."

Babangida is a past master at conciliation. He talked tough but he knew he had to lower his voice, telling the people:

> We have travelled a long way; we are so near our destination that we must resist all temptations that seek to divert us from our objectives.
> The future is already part of our today. It is beckoning unto us. We have worked together carefully and the dawn of our tomorrow is just around the corner. We should not sit back and allow the promise of a great tomorrow to slip out of our hands.

Events soon showed that the "great tomorrow," riding home on the back of his transition programme, had become uncertain. The primaries for the election of candidates for the national assembly elections were held throughout the country on May 23, two days before the president read 'the riot act.' Nine days before the elections on July 4, NEC invoked the provisions of decree 48 of 1991 as amended by decree 6 of 1992, to disqualify 28 of the leading senatorial and House of Representatives candidates in both parties. Under the law, the commission was not obliged to give reasons for its action. It happily gave none.

The parties quickly found replacements for those disqualified by the commission. The low turnout in the July 4 elections was blamed on the open ballot system resented by the elite who felt it took the country back to primitive political basics. However, the elections were largely successful, if by default. This time, the SDP limped back into the lead nationwide. If its luck held, the party would win the presidential election. This possibility caused some disquiet in military circles. According to Babangida, the military felt that the ideal situation in the third republic would be for one party (SDP) to control the legislature and the other (NRC) to control the executive. This, he believed, would ensure stability in the Third Republic. Unfortunately for the military, this was a matter to be decided by the electorate, not by decree.

The conclusion of the national assembly elections threw up some untidiness in the transition programme. In the original timetable, the national assembly would be inaugurated on July 27, a little over two months before the president took office on October 1. The revised timetable shifted the presidential election to December 5 but left the inauguration of the assembly for July 27 as originally scheduled. This meant that the assembly would now function under the military. Babangida removed this crease in the transition programme by declaring that the inauguration of the assembly would have to wait for the new president to avoid "the constitutional anomaly of an unelected president inaugurating an elected legislature."

However, in the original schedule, this did not seem to be a problem because Babangida, an unelected president, would have inaugurated the assembly two months before his civilian successor took office. His sudden deference to the sanctity of the constitution was part of the manipulation of the transition programme to suit certain exigencies. On July 27, Babangida addressed the national assembly legislators-elect and urged them to spend the six months of their idle time touring and learning about the country and its numerous social and political problems.

A great piece of presidential advice. The legislators were going to make laws for the good of the country. They needed to be armed for their legislative duties by knowing the country and appreciating its many social, economic, political and even religious problems. Just great.

With the national assembly elections out of the way, the nation shifted its attention to the last and the most important in the series of elections - the presidential election. First step, the presidential primaries. NEC, not averse to experiments, introduced a new one into the presidential primaries by dividing the country into six zones. It then staggered the primaries over six weekends beginning from August 1. The commission believed this would make for better monitoring but the parties rejected this process. They feared a bandwagon effect. They wanted the primaries to be held the same day throughout the country. The commission had its way.

The presidential primaries attracted a motley crowd of aspirants, most of whom merely provided comic political relief. Some of them made a brief appearance in the news media and quickly dropped out of sight. Stiff monetary conditions imposed by the two political parties whittled the crowd of aspirants to a manageable number of some 23 'serious' men. With the ban lifted, the old brigade joined the presidential race in full force.

The first round of the election was greeted with the usual charges of rigging by the losers who went a step further in their protest to ask the electoral commission not to conduct the five remaining rounds because they had lost confidence in the party executives. NEC refused. It rightly insisted this was the responsibility of the political parties. The party executives cancelled the results of the first round of the primaries. The staggering of the primaries by NEC was a huge mistake. Still, the commission stuck to it but collapsed the six zones into three and staggered the primaries over three weekends.

The losers, some of whom were united in their grief and boycotted the third and final rounds of the primaries, again rejected the results of the first round. Major-General Shehu Musa Yar'Adua and Malam Adamu Ciroma were the leading candidates in the SDP and the NRC respectively. You needed not go further to see that the concept of the new breed politician, the initial anchor of Babangida's political re-engineering programme, blew in the wind.

The losers wanted the entire primaries cancelled for alleged irregularities. Their complaints were sweet music to the ears of the military men, some of whom watched what was going on among the politicians with barely concealed contempt for them. The AFRC, playing the role of a concerned arbiter, was only too pleased to step in and "sort out the politicians." On October 6, the council directed NEC to investigate the allegations of electoral malpractices in the conduct of the presidential primaries. An easy task for the commission, which now appeared to be dancing to the tune of the barely hidden drummer.

In its rather predictable report to the council, the commission claimed that virtually all the presidential aspirants and the party executives broke the electoral rules. It said it established that "the primary elections were characterised by rigging, electoral malpractices...multiple voting, manipulation of electoral results, arbitrary cancellation of results by returning officers to favour candidates."[7]

Armed with this comprehensive indictment, the AFRC nullified the entire primaries. It went one shocking step further by dissolving the executives of the two political parties at the national, state and local government levels. On its instruction, the electoral commission appointed caretaker committees for the two parties. The disturbing implication of this was that the government, as indeed the discerning feared from the beginning, was treating the two political parties as government parastatals. It could only be so, given the fact that the government founded and funded them. But even as part of the learning process, this was taking things rather too far for the good health of the putative Third Republic.

The losers in the presidential primaries could not have bargained for what the AFRC did to the entire process and the political parties. In its rather endless search for a purported perfect system, the AFRC asked NEC to drop the primaries and devise a new method for the selection of presidential candidates. The primaries rather than their conduct by the leaders of the two political parties, took the blame. Not for the first time in the political history of Nigeria, the baby was flushed down with the bath water.

The transition programme had clearly degenerated into a series of experiments. Its end had also become rather murky at best and uncertain at worst. Four weeks after the AFRC took the unprecedented step of dissolving the executives of the political parties it banned all the 23 presidential aspirants from contesting the nomination of their parties for being "incidentally and severally" responsible for bringing the primaries to grief. Babangida said the council took the decision because the "actions of the aspirants have had grave consequences of undermining, forestalling, distorting and prejudicing the realisation of the transition programme within the stipulated time."[8]

The January 2 handover date became apparently shaky. It required no expert to read what the hand wrote on the wall. Obasanjo could take it no more. On November 13, the former head of state released to the press the text of a speech he had intended to give at the meeting of the National Council of State that month and which was postponed. He sent a copy of the speech as a letter to Babangida. Obasanjo brutally attacked the transition programme, pointing out:

> In the name of political engineering, the country has been converted to a political laboratory for trying out all kinds of silly experiments and gimmicks. Principle has been abandoned for expediency. All kinds of booby-traps were

instituted into the transition process. The result is the crisis we now face.[9]

Obasanjo said what many Nigerians wanted to say but were afraid of doing so. Babangida pointedly ignored his former commander-in-chief. He carried on with further shocks to the system. In the midst of the furore generated by Obasanjo's letter, Babangida announced the decision by the AFRC to shift the hand over date from January 2 to August 27, 1993. That date would mark Babangida's eighth anniversary in office.

The council also approved a new method for electing the presidential candidates known as Option A4, one of the eight options submitted to it by the electoral commission, in place of the primaries. This option provided for a four-stage election process from the ward to the national level. The politicians, as they well might, took the blame for this new development in the transition programme. As Babangida noted:

> History will bear us out that the present political impasse....is caused by the inability of the two political parties to conduct successfully their internal selection process of producing presidential candidates acceptable to the generality of Nigerians... (because) the aspirants and the party executives at all levels could not play the game according to the rules that guide the democratic process.

Several people thought they saw it coming. A month before Babangida dropped the bombshell of the shift in the handover date, General T.Y. Danjuma said he doubted that Babangida was leaving because if indeed, he intended to leave on January 2, 1993, he would have "begun to say good-bye to the states."[10] The former Chief of Army Staff appeared to have said much less than he knew or suspected.

But as far as Babangida was concerned, the politicians were to blame. He gave the impression that he was willing to sacrifice his honour as an officer for the more important task of effecting positive and lasting changes in national politics and how the game must be played *post* his era. If the politicians had behaved themselves, he argued, the ruling council would not have had to do what it did:

> The (presidential) candidates gave us all indications, you know, that things might not go well. We were in contact with them. We talked with them because we know them and they didn't hesitate to express some misgivings about a number of things. And many of them felt so strongly that if we allowed the elections to proceed the way they were going, the primaries were going to be a child's play. Then there was the feeling about a particular part of the country always producing the president. At that time, the really credible or serious candidates were all from the North, both in the NRC and the SDP. If you read

some of the commentators in the newspapers, you find this feeling was widespread. We weighed it.

The regime was not unduly worried about its credibility. It could live with questions hanging over it. Aikhomu put it rather nicely: *"We should be realistic and forget about credibility problem. What we are thinking about is the unity and stability of the nation."*[11 (Emphasis added)].

Babangida took more surprise actions. The national assembly was inaugurated and given token legislative powers as more or less a junior legislative partner with the ruling council. Whatever happened to the "constitutional anomaly" that prevented Babangida from inaugurating it five months earlier? It evaporated, obviously.

Babangida made two other fundamental changes that took effect from January 2, 1993. He restructured his administration. The National Defence and Security Council, NDSC, replaced the Armed Forces Ruling Council, AFRC, as the highest legislative body in the country. Was this merely a change in nomenclature? Difficult to say. The NDSC retained and exercised all the powers of the AFRC. However, it was not difficult to see that even if the fundamental legislative functions of the new council were the same as those of the AFRC, the change represented Babangida's steady push towards a diarchy. His real intention was to reduce the over-arching power of the military and refocus it on its constitutional duty of national defence and security while leaving the military president freer hands to rule.

This was made quite clear by his decision to replace the council of ministers with the Transitional Council headed by a civilian who performed the role of a prime minister. Ministers were also re-designated secretaries, as in the United States. Again, the nation was never told the import of this last item. Babangida's new presidential model now replicated the republican model with a president as head of state and a prime minister as head of government that Nigeria had from 1963 to 1966. Babangida denies that was his intention. He does not believe in "the concept of president and prime minister. I believe in the concept of a president for the whole country."

Babangida handpicked Chief Ernest Shonekan, a well-known technocrat, and chairman of the United Africa Company Plc., as chairman of the Transitional Council. The AFRC devolved powers to the Transitional Council to enable it "see to the successful day-to-day running (of government)." Under its enabling law, decree 54 of 1992 (*Transition to Civil Rule Programme*) decree, the council exercised supervisory role over the transition programme but in a manner that gave it no executive control over it. That authority remained with the NDSC. According to Babangida, the ruling council decided, "to civilianize the federal cabinet to maintain the support and the goodwill of the people."

A progressive civilianization of the military administration, with fewer military faces and more civilian faces, was not, in his view, merely cosmetic:

> We thought the best thing was to make these changes because we also knew that what the Nigerian wanted at the time, I think, was just a change; anything was going to be accepted. People were getting tired of seeing our faces and so on. So, we thought that bringing in new people would also help to dampen this cynicism. We said, ok, since we have not been able to conduct elections, let's push it to another body that will pursue the process up to the end. They will look at the ministries, continue with the programme, and try to clean up whatever needs to be cleaned up in the preparation for the next programme. We see them as a sort of a transition council for the in-coming civilian administration.

The decision to set up the Transitional Council was actually taken in October 1992. Before Babangida submitted the proposal to the AFRC, he consulted some politicians, technocrats and senior military officers. There was a big storm at one of such meetings of officers from the rank of colonel and equivalent in the navy and the air force. The storm arose over a subtle campaign by some members of the president's kitchen cabinet for a full-blown diarchy with Babangida continuing as president for an unspecified period.

The proponents of this model of diarchy argued that the civilians showed no serious evidence that they would behave better than they did in the First and Second Republics and, therefore, the Third Republic was already in danger of coming to grief. Those who opposed this option were more concerned about the integrity of the military. They argued that the military must adhere to and complete the transition programme and leave the political stage.

Babangida found that the politicians were more amenable to his proposed diarchic arrangement than his military colleagues. According to him, the politicians felt "quite strongly" that the country was drifting into chaos and needed the military, for which read Babangida, to stay on.

Babangida knew where he was going. He had merely given others a chance to have their say. It was up to him to decide. He prepared council memo for the change in the handover date from January to August, the setting up of the NDSC and the Transitional Council. When he presented this to the AFRC, Babangida sailed into the storm. Members of the council were almost violently divided over the proposals. Babangida was quite surprised by the turn of events in the council:

It was a very, very tough meeting, one of the toughest I had handled in my seven years as president because we had the military to contend with, the society to contend with and so many other factors. And even at that meeting, initially, the opinions were divided. There were those, for example, who felt very strongly that we should forget about the election and stick to the second of January whether they have done elections or not. Let's just give it up and go. There were others who said no, that that would mean abdication; that we had failed. So, it was bloody tough; a real tough meeting, coupled with the fact we even asked the military to give us their own views on this. But after talking for 48 hours, we were able to accept a consensus. We stayed that long because I insisted that everyone must agree with what we were trying to do. I wanted the commitment of virtually every one of us.

The meeting was adjourned abruptly on the first day ostensibly to cool tempers. The real reason was to enable Babangida more time to sell his proposals on one-on-one basis to those of his colleagues opposed to them. Day two of the meeting was less stormy. Those who were opposed to the proposals had "seen reason." The council approved his proposals.

These changes necessitated a new schedule in the transition programme spanning first, second and third quarters of 1993. Its enabling law was decree 13, *Presidential Election (Basic Constitutional and transitional provision) decree 1993*. For the first time since 1987, a specific date, August 27, 1993, was chosen as the handover date. The presidential election was scheduled for June 12, 1993.

III

Babangida regarded the 23 presidential aspirants disqualified from participating in the presidential election as the first eleven among the politicians jostling for power. Their ban paved the way for the emergence of new political actors on the stage of the transition programme. With the first eleven put out in the cold, there were few runners in the field. Two men easily emerged from the thin crowd of presidential aspirants.

One was the billionaire philanthropist, Bashorun M.K.O. Abiola, who nursed a presidential ambition going back all the way to the Second Republic. Abiola was a leading national executive member and one of the major financiers of the National Party of Nigeria, NPN. He intended to contest the presidential election on the platform of the party in 1983. The party moguls erected obstacles in his way. He quit the party and partisan politics altogether in anger in 1982.

He was affected by the ban on former politicians and public office holders and unsuccessfully challenged his ban at the tribunal. With the ban lifted, he joined SDP in January 1993 and was elected the party's presidential flag bearer at its convention in Jos in March that year.

The other man was Alhaji Bashir Tofa, who, like Abiola, was a national executive member of NPN. He was the party's national financial secretary. He picked the presidential ticket of the NRC at its convention in Port Harcourt in March 1993.

Both men were Babangida's close friends. Babangida was not quite comfortable with this. He says he feared people would accuse him of manipulating the transition programme to favour his close friends. He even tried to discourage Tofa from contesting the election:

> I told him in the presence of about 13 of his colleagues. I advised him not to seek for that election. I didn't support him. He was not a winning candidate.

Babangida said he supported Abiola's presidential bid and helped him "a lot morally and financially in the campaign." He said he gave Abiola N35 million. Before Abiola entered the presidential race he and Babangida "talked of the pros and cons of" of Abiola's presidential ambition. And when Abiola "eventually decided that he wanted to go (for it) I supported the idea that he should get it."

Babangida had wanted to make Abiola the chairman of the Transitional Council because he believed his friend "enjoyed tremendous political goodwill. His name was a household name. He had the international contact and Nigeria too had a very good chance of having someone like him heading that organisation."

But some of Babangida's colleagues in the ruling council opposed it. They accepted though, that Abiola could be a member of the council. Babangida told Abiola he would bring him in as a member and ensure that the members of the Transitional Council elected him chairman. The AFRC had decided that the chairman of the Transitional Council should come from the Southwest where Abiola came from. But Abiola rather wanted Babangida to announce him as chairman "straight away." He told Babangida that that was how his family wanted it because they feared that the president might change his mind once he made him an ordinary member. "Left to me," says Babangida, "I wanted to make him the chairman. Then he dictated and blew it."

IV

The National Electoral Commission was more or less coasting home. Only the presidential election now remained to be conducted. The others had gone well so far. The chairman of the commission, Professor Humphrey Nwosu, needed no one to tell him that the conduct of the presidential election was critical to the entire transition programme. In his address at a workshop for electoral and assistant electoral officers as part of the preparations for the election, he said "the stakes are indeed very high. The eyes of the world are focused on Nigeria where an indigenous and, unique experiment in democratic governance based on two grassroots- oriented political party system is going on."[12]

But the clouds were gathering. The National Defence and Security Council did not openly object to the two presidential candidates – Abiola and Tofa – but some elements in the military in cahoots with some of the politicians wanted to stop them from contesting the election. Several times the council, pressurised by these elements, came close to disqualifying the two men. Some members of the council felt that neither Abiola nor Tofa was fit to be president. They assailed Abiola's character. Babangida recalls that "they never saw him as somebody who was morally upright or fit…"

They tried to blackmail him as a government contractor to whom the government owed a lot of money "and they didn't feel comfortable that this would be their commander-in-chief."

The luck of the presidential candidates held because, according to Babangida, the council feared that "if we stopped it (the election), we would be in trouble again. What was paramount in our mind then was we wouldn't like to be accused again of not wanting to leave office. So we said let the bloody thing go on."

The decision to "let the bloody thing go on," was actually a booby trap. The military men, according to Babangida, believed "that we would have an inconclusive election. We thought we should be fair to let it run and when it became inconclusive, then we would take whatever action that we deemed necessary over a re-run or a re-election or something like that."

Abiola proved to be a more astute and popular politician than the military gave him credit for. As soon as he hit the road in his campaigns, the people responded to him in a way that unsettled those elements in the military that did not like him. About a week or so before the June 12, 1993, presidential election, security reports indicated that Abiola would certainly trounce Tofa beyond dispute. He would win on the first ballot.

The election would not be inconclusive. The report caused some jitters in military circles. What to do?

Enter Nzeribe and his military-must-stay campaign outfit, the Association for Better Nigeria, ABN. Abimbola Davies, regarded as the number two man to Nzeribe in the association, went to an Abuja high court on June 10 to stop the presidential election for alleged irregularities and corruption in the conduct of the SDP primaries won by Abiola. ABN alleged that Abiola used money, as if others did not, to induce the majority of the delegates to vote for him. At 9.30 pm on the same day, the court, presided over by Justice Bassey Ita Ikpeme, now deceased, threw the spanner into the works. She "restrained (NEC) from conducting the presidential election on the 12th day of June, 1993."

Her ruling was a blow to the solar plexus of the transition programme. It clearly violated the sanctity of decree 13 of 1993. She was not ignorant of its Section 19 (1) that unambiguously provided that

> no interim or interlocutory order of ruling, judgment or decision made by any court or tribunal before or after the commencement of this decree in respect of any intra party or inter party dispute or any other matter before it shall affect the date or time of the holding of the election or the performance by the commission of any of its functions under this decree or any guidelines issued by it in pursuance of the election.

Nor was she unaware of a subsisting appeal court pronouncement on the provision of the decree. Her judgment was the first major indication that the transition programme was under serious threat. Nwosu tried to salvage it. He appeared before the NDSC on June 11 and put up a strong argument in favour of going ahead with the election. He argued, quite passionately, that if the election was postponed, the election materials already on site would be compromised.

NEC had enough protection under the decree to ignore Ikpeme's ruling. But the attorney general and minister of justice, Clement Akpamgbo, the nation's chief law officer, had a different take on the issue. He did not support Nwosu's position; instead he advised that the election be postponed in obedience to the court order. NEC could then appeal and have the order set aside by a superior court.

Babangida was torn between the two opposing views. In the end, he sided with NEC. He ordered the commission to go ahead with the election as scheduled. It turned out to be another booby trap – and the commission was soon caught in it.

The commission conducted the election as scheduled on June 12. Local and international observers adjudged to be the freest and the fairest in Nigeria's political history so far. Before NEC could formally release the results, ABN struck again. It went to another high court in Abuja to stop the commission from announcing the results and declaring the winner. ABN argued that NEC defied a subsisting court order restraining it from conducting the election. Justice Dahiru Saleh agreed with the association. On June 21, he ruled that NEC acted "in open violation of a court order, and as such I cannot but hold that the election is not legal…" He granted the prayers of ABN and duly ordered the commission not to announce the results "until the matter is finally settled."

NEC, rather than stick to its guns, appealed the judgment. All hell broke lose. There followed a flurry of court orders from Lagos and Benin on the commission to announce the results of the presidential election. Any hopes that Nwosu and his team would coast home with national honours for a job a well done evaporated eleven days after the election. Babangida struck again. He annulled the election on June 23. He dissolved NEC. And he repealed all the decrees pertaining to the transition programme.

June 12 came to grief. And the country was in grief. Babangida's elaborate and expensive transition programme had hit a coral reef. The annulment shocked the country and the world. A poisonous combination of military intrigues and high wire politics brought the programme to its knees. Nigeria was convulsed in a political crisis similar to what it faced when the young majors staged their bloody coup on January 15, 1966. The failure of the transition programme to deliver on its promise of a *new* Nigeria with a new democratic culture grounded on a restructured economic base drove the stake deep into the heart of the nation.

Still, June 12 also drew the line on the sand of Nigerian politics. It generated a heady current that forced concessions and compromises and in the end achieved what Abiola intended to achieve, even though others and not he, benefited from it – power shift.

Local and international protests over the annulment told Babangida in very clear terms that this time he had dribbled the country to a dead end. He did not expect his transition programme to end this way. Perhaps, Kismet had a different idea. June 12 became, and remains, Babangida's albatross; his cross.

V

One of the best military minds in the country had badly miscalculated. Babangida expected the politicians to make a right royal mess of the presidential election and thus give him the excuse to stretch the transition programme. His guess was that the election would either be inconclusive or Tofa would squeeze through with a thin margin over Abiola. Had Tofa squeezed through with a thin margin, as the president generally expected, his election would have been annulled on the pretext that the military wanted a southern president. This, according to Babangida, would have presented no problems for the government because "we also knew from our analysis that he (Tofa) was a much simpler person to be disqualified than Abiola. If Bashir (Tofa) had won that election, honestly, we would not have given it to him."

That statement suggests that the Babangida administration made up its mind not to respect the decision of the Nigerian electorate, no matter who won the election. Babangida believed that the south would have supported the administration if it prevented Tofa, a northerner, from succeeding him as president.

This was not entirely an idle calculation. *The Guardian* newspaper canvassed the nullification of the results of the presidential primaries in October 1992 mainly because the leading candidates in the two political parties, Shehu Yar'Adua (SDP) and Adamu Ciroma (NRC), were northerners. The possibility of a northerner succeeding Babangida loomed large. So did the possibility of power not shifting to the south. In its editorial of October 5, 1992, entitled *To Save Nigeria, The Guardian* was clearly unhappy about this possibility:

> The presidential primaries were so massively, cynically and shamelessly rigged that any government that is produced at the end of the process will be without legitimacy.
>
> The situation is worse. The two presidential candidates that will emerge at the end of the day are from the same part of the country – the Far North. This is disturbing given the national composition of the country. Even more so is the fact that the two political parties are today under [the] firm control of the political elite from the same part of the country. This is undesirable and unacceptable.

It is perhaps true that the newspaper did not speak for the south. It is also perhaps true that many southerners shared its views and sentiment on this matter. The clamour for power shift was no longer an isolated political battle cry. It had become a strong agitation critical to the political health of the country.

Attempts have been, and are still being made, to explain why the election was annulled. The easy pick in these attempts is that the military acted a northern script to prevent power shift to the south. Professor Omo Omoruyi, a close associate of Babangida and former director-general of the Centre for Democratic Studies, set up by Babangida as part of his political re-education of Nigerians, suggests there were "real reasons" and "formal reasons" for the annulment of the election. He contends that "the formal reason" was given by Babangida in his broadcast on June 26 in which he said, among other things that

> to proclaim and swear in a president who has encouraged a campaign of divide and rule amongst our various ethnic groups would have been detrimental to the survival of the Third Republic.

Omoruyi points out that Abacha's coup against Shonekan was the "real reason" for the annulment. He says that the decision to annul the election was taken after meetings in Minna and Abuja on June 18, 21, 22 and 23 and that Babangida "did not act alone on June 23 when the annulment was announced."[13]

The announcement of the annulment was as clumsy a piece of work as they come, indicating, in Omoruyi's view that "there was no visible person or clique in charge of the annulment, hence the annulment statement was unsigned, undated and carried no government letter head or seal."[14]

Perhaps Omoruyi is right in asserting that Babangida could not have acted alone in annulling the election. He may also be right in saying that the annulment was not even the president's idea. However, Babangida refuses to say whose idea it was and how or whether it was forced on him. He simply insists that it "was collective. But I only accept full responsibility though because I was the leader."

From what has been pieced together so far in researching for this book, the decision to annul the election was not 'collective,' if by 'collective' Babangida meant that the members of the National Defence and Security Council were privy to it. Admiral Augustus Aikhomu was the number two man in the hierarchy of the administration. He knew nothing about the decision to annul the election. Most members of the council were similarly in the dark about it. When Aikhomu heard the announcement of the annulment, he phoned a very senior officer in the security force and enquired: "What the hell is happening?" The officer said he too did not know and that he was shocked by the announcement.

The annulment, according to a former member of the council, "took some of us by surprise. Only a few people were happy with it. Many of us were very unhappy with the turn of events. Aikhomu was furious."

Chief Duro Onabule, chief press to the president, also knew nothing about the annulment. He too was said to have been angry when he heard the announcement.

At an emergency meeting of the National Defence and Security Council following the annulment, Babangida was shocked by how truly angry most members of the council were with him. There was, he admitted, virtually a shouting match in the council chambers. There were, obviously, quite a few red faces that morning over the fate that befell the June 12 presidential election just when everyone thought that the transition programme was destined for a glorious end.

One senior official of the administration who knew about the annulment was Chief Clement Akpamgbo, the attorney general and secretary of justice. Babangida went to Katsina on the morning of June 23, the day the annulment was announcement, for the funeral of the late Alhaji Musa Yar'Adua, Minister of Lagos Affairs in the Balewa administration in the First Republic. Just before he left Abuja, he instructed Akpamgbo to draft a statement annulling the election. Akpamgbo duly carried out the instruction. By the time the president returned to Abuja, the statement had been put out to the press by Nduka Irabor, press secretary to the vice-president.

The mystery of the annulment is, now perhaps, locked up in the murky waters of Nigerian politics. Babangida's personal role in what turned out to be his ultimate political defeat remains unclear at best. The best explanation he could offer is that they annulled the election because they simply felt uncomfortable with an Abiola presidency. He said:

> Nobody was (comfortable). The military wasn't; the politicians were not. I had meetings with a lot of them in groups and individually. There were some who jubilated that Abiola after all did not get it. From the west (south-west) to be specific. Even there they said thank God.

Yet, here is a curious contradiction. Babangida says he "would have been a happy man" if Abiola had succeeded him as president. "I could live well with Abiola as president." He is reasonably confident that if he had insisted Abiola would have "been at least sworn-in" as president. He chose not to insist because

> My sixth sense told me that I might lose at the end. But I had a strong belief that I might lose a friend. Therefore, I decided that the best thing was to err on the side of caution.

The possible loss of his friend was only one of his worries. Babangida was equally worried about his life and the lives and safety of his family. Given what was playing out around him, he had very genuine reasons to fear that he "might lose at the end." Omoruyi quotes Babangida as telling him in the heat of the crisis:

> They will kill me; they will kill the president-elect, Chief MKO Abiola if I went ahead with the election and announced the winner…, which we all know

to be Bashorun MKO Abiola. I know so; I am not daft. He won; he tried. I feel bad about the whole matter.[15]

Abiola even tried to persuade Babangida to let his election stand, telling him, as Babangida recalls it, "knowing you very well, you can walk through a mountain. I know you can help me to get to that seat."

Babangida could not walk through this mountain. He was no longer effectively in control of the situation. Too many interest groups, within and outside the military and among the politicians, had surfaced and effectively blocked June 12. Its revisit in any positive sense had become totally impossible for the president. In the military itself, there were three camps – those who supported the annulment, those opposed to it and those who were indifferent.

Babangida did not seem to have any immediate plans for the *post* annulment of the election. Maybe, if he did, circumstances did not quite permit him to put such plans into effect. He was forced to flow with the tide. And he had to carry the can. It was up to him to manage the crisis and pull the country out of the quagmire into which it had been driven by what was clearly an insensitive political decision.

His best hope was that the storm that greeted the annulment would sooner than later run its course and the sea would become pacific again. After all, he was dealing with a country with a demonstrable record of unsustainable anger at official wrongdoings. The only problem, and it was a big one at that, was that this time, he was sorely mistaken. Public anger burnt fiercely each day and no one could mistake the political heat in the country for the vagaries of the tropical weather. The politicians, of course, huddled with the military men quite busily working out self-serving compromises that would, and did eventually, sink Abiola's undeclared victory.

VI

Sometime in early July 1993, Babangida convened a meeting of the National Defence and Security Council to decide on the next line of action. He made it clear to the members that he wanted absolute unanimity on whatever decision the council arrived at on the way forward. He even threatened that "if there was any one voice of dissent, then I will get down." He was shocked to find the officers sharply divided over June 12 on political and professional grounds. "The political environment affected some of the senior officers," he recalls. Obviously.

Some of the officers "were die-hard SDP who felt that the party had won the day and, therefore, we should call SDP and go back to the barracks." Some other senior officers who were not SDP supporters supported that position, according to Babangida, because

> they had reached their peak and were almost at the end of their career and should the military decide to stay longer, they were not sure of what their future was going to be. So, they kept on insisting that the military had given its word and, therefore, it had to go. They argued passionately on that. But the brigadier-generals and colonels felt very strongly that the annulment should stand. They were vehemently opposed to the two candidates – both Moshood Abiola and Bashir Tofa. They were viciously against both of them. They didn't like to see any one of them as president of the country.

The situation was much tougher than Babangida had expected. Positions had hardened on both sides of June 12. The meeting lasted for three days. By the third and last day of the meeting, the heat of passion cooled down somewhat, positions softened and shifted and a roadmap began to emerge. The council "toyed with many ideas" and eventually settled on a new presidential election. It tried to sell this idea to the political parties to bring them "on board." And that, recalls Babangida, "was how we came about trying to involve the political parties, especially the party leaders on how we could move the nation forward. We also tried to intimate the state governors. They were more or less supportive."

The council added what it believed was a sweetener to its decision to conduct a fresh presidential election before August 27. The two presidential candidates of the two political parties would come from the south. According to Babangida, Obasanjo and some other southern leaders were allegedly "very excited about this." They might have been but if the idea was to give it to a southerner, then it just did not make sense for the administration to annul the election of one southerner in order to give power to another southerner. The odds for a new presidential election were heavily stacked against Babangida and his administration. Still, he and Aikhomu, his vice-president, set to work to win over the party leaders

> to get them to provide southern candidates for us. We divided the job between ourselves. The vice-president was more disposed to NRC. I felt free talking with the SDP than NRC. So we tried to tell them what we wanted. Then we compared notes and then tried to see what we could do. But we had gone far in making them present two presidential candidates all from the south. Then we began to talk to the north to convince them that it was in their interest to have a southerner as president.

Babangida thought this was going on well but then quite suddenly, the state governors, who had given the impression initially that they would support a new presidential election, balked. Babangida recalls that

> the governors, especially the SDP governors, said they could not go back to their states and constituencies to sell the idea of a new presidential election to them because people were tired of elections. When we found that their argument destroyed ours, we dropped that idea and opted for a transitional government. Firstly to allow tempers to cool down and secondly, to allow the masses time to reflect and so on. We decided on February or March 1994. We thought that was enough time to get Humphrey Nwosu and the rest of them to prepare for another election.

The transitional government was the most viable option open to the NDSC in the circumstances. The council appointed a tripartite committee chaired by Aikhomu to work out the details and the modalities for what became the Interim National Government, ING. Its enabling law was decree 61 of 1993, jointly drafted by Professor Ben Nwabueze, secretary for education in the Transitional Council and his counterpart in justice, Clement Akpamgbo.

The country heard about the Interim National Government for the first time on August 17 1993 when Babangida addressed a joint sitting of the National Assembly. This was the occasion at which he made the famous declaration that he had "offered....to voluntarily step aside as president and commander-in-chief..." as his personal sacrifice. It was a curious choice of phrase and a pointer to the circumstances of his leaving office. His colleagues in the armed forces chose to give their beleaguered commander-in-chief a soft landing and ease him out of power.

Babangida says he made up his mind not to stay beyond August 27, 1993. He contends that he had "a very, very strong feeling that" if he had wanted to continue in office beyond that date "the boys would have supported me." He thought better of it. Given the circumstances he faced before and after the presidential election, he knew it would be unwise for him to hang on. As he puts it: "I probably would be stretching my luck too far." It did not take rocket science to appreciate that.

The Interim National Government was hammered out of compromises between the Abacha and the Babangida factions in the armed forces in and outside the ruling council. In his address to the legislators, Babangida played down this aspect and chose, instead, to make it sound as if the military and the politicians were on opposite sides of the divide. He said:

> We arrived at the point of an Interim National Government by a spirit of give and take. We have made tremendous progress in moderating hitherto rigid po-

sitions on the current political impasse through dialogue. The administration has, on its part, shifted ground from its initial insistence on the holding of fresh presidential election before August 27. The two political parties have equally moderated their extreme positions on the solution to the political impasse. By bending over backwards, the parties to the political impasse demonstrated their commitment to moving our country forward.

Babangida noted what he called "the significant properties of the Interim National Government." There were four of them, the two most important being:

a) The Interim Government is the heir-apparent to the present Military Government at the federal level in lieu of a democratically elected federal executive;
b) The Interim Government is not and cannot be a Transitional Government. It is not an EXTENSION by a REPLACEMENT of the present Transitional Government.

It is still not easy to appreciate the difference or why he found it necessary to emphasise that point. The same man, Shonekan, headed the ING and the Transitional Council before it.

Babangida spelt out the six functions of the Interim National Government. We need not to go into them here except to note that Babangida expected this contraption made up of his appointees to do what his own military administration could not do, namely, "to bring to conclusion the long march to democracy by overseeing the election of the President of the Federal Republic of Nigeria."

Babangida defends the decision to annul the election as wise in the circumstances:

The decision, which this administration took in respect of the June 12 presidential election, remains in my judgment, the best for our country. The decision obviously hurt my friends but I, for this purpose and on this occasion, wanted to be counted on the side of the nation – my country.

It was his way of reacting to insinuations that he betrayed his good friend, Abiola. At an interview with the author several years after he left office, Babangida said that that charge would hold water only if he had "promised I would give it to him and then did not."

The Interim National Government was a compromise between the two factions - Babangida and Abacha - in the council. As part of that compromise, two other options came up for consideration. These were:

a) that Babangida and Aikhomu should retire and leave office by the terminal date of August 27. This meant that the Chief of Defence Staff and the service chiefs, including the Inspector-General of police, would all remain in office. Or b) the Chief of Defence Staff and the service chiefs, including the Inspector-General of police would all retire with Babangida and Aikhomu. The council accepted the first option.

However, Babangida over-turned this decision after he and Abacha met in his office just before the council met sometime towards the end his administration. Before this meeting, he inserted a clause in decree 61 specifically stipulating that in the event of a crisis that made it impossible for the ING to function, the secretary of defence, being the most senior among the secretaries, should take over.

This clause pleased Abacha. It was what he wanted. He was the secretary of defence in the Transitional Council. He would be the only military face in it – and thus effectively the power behind the throne. Babangida appointed him to the same position in the Interim National Government. Babangida specifically provided for his friend in the enabling law of the Interim National Government because he wanted him "to back this character (Shonekan)." He explains:

> So, two of us left the office. We went into the meeting where all the service chiefs were waiting. So, I told them. I think it was a short meeting. I told them we have taken a decision that I was going, Aikhomu was going, the deputy chief of defence staff was going and other service chiefs were going with me. I think it jolted some of them. I said the minister of defence was going to stay because he was the most senior officer. In the event of anything happening, Nigerians would wake up one morning to say we have heard that before. We don't want another Gideon Orka. I thought the Interim National Government needed a very, very strong muscle so as to punch effectively.

Abacha's favoured treatment by Babangida lent some credence to the widely circulated story that one of the conditions he gave Babangida for supporting his coup against Buhari was that he too would take his turn at ruling Nigeria. Although no one is willing to admit it, it also lent credence to the suspicion, hardly muted at that, that the presidential election was annulled as Abacha's condition for not overthrowing Babangida in the twilight of his administration. As it turned out, the man who would give the ING "a very, very strong muscle" shove it aside within three months and put the crown on his own head as head of state and Commander-in-Chief of the Armed Forces. If that was his ambition, then he realised it at Babangida's expense.

Abacha, according to Babangida, "remained fiercely loyal" to him from the inception of his administration. However, "towards the dying days of the transition," Babangida noticed that the famously goggled one was beginning to chart his political future at his expense. What happened, according to Babangida, was that

> there emerged a group of other forces who felt there had to be a change. And they rallied around him. They thought he probably was the only one who could get this dictator to see things. So, may be he began to be aware of the feelings of the military and may be the feelings of the larger society outside the military. The Abiolas of this world, the human rights groups and some sorts of other activists in the military were trying to convince him to take over or talking of a coup d'etat against me. But he knew and I knew that a coup at that time was the most undesirable thing to do. I think he also told them. May be there were other undercurrents because governance, especially military rule, is full of intrigues. But fortunately for me, at least, I was not detached from the military. So, I knew everything that was going on.

Both men kept wary eyes on each other. It said something about the degree of their mutual loyalty that Babangida more or less ran the ring around Abacha in the ING set up. He conceded the political turf to Abacha and held on to the military turf. Babangida knew that Abacha had more than his leg in the door but the president tried to play a smart one on his good friend. His appointment of new service chiefs before he stepped aside made it clear that Babangida intended to hold on to the military turf by planting his trusted loyalists in those strategic offices. He needed to 'balance the forces' in both camps. He appointed Lt-General Joshua Dogonyaro Chief of Defence Staff, Lt-General Mohammed Aliyu Gusau, Chief of Army Staff, Rear-Admiral Suleiman Saidu, Chief of Naval Staff and Air Commodore Nsikan Eduak, Chief of the Air Staff. These men would keep an eagle eye on Abacha and possibly checkmate him should he venture into the military turf.

Abacha, of course, knew what this meant. He knew the game. He needed no one to tell him what he must do to consolidate his power and achieve his ultimate political ambition of becoming head of state. All he had to do was wait for his good friend to step aside and he would step in with his own men and grab the military turf as well.

VII

On the morning of August 27, 1993, President Ibrahim Badamasi Babangida signed decree 61 into law. With that stroke of the pen, Nigeria had a new government. It was neither elected nor did it come to power through the barrel of the gun. It was a political contraption without precedent in the country but one intended to soothe the frayed nerves of the nation and, as Nigerians like to say, move the nation forward; or at least, prevent it from toppling over the precipice to which June 12 was pushing it. Babangida had shown once more and perhaps for the last time, that he was truly the master at rescuing himself from sticky ends. He had brought the curtain down on the Ibrahim Badamasi Babangida era in Nigerian politics.

Later that morning, Babangida left Aso Rock, Abuja, for his hilltop country home in Minna, Niger State. His eight years in power had ended in a whimper, not with the big bang of glory and public applause for which he so much craved from that first day he came into office on August 27, 1985. Such a promising beginning, such a disappointing ending. Fate does have a cruel sense of humour.

Epilogue

Selected speeches of President Ibrahim Babangida from 1985 to 1988 were published in a book with the arresting title of *Portrait of a New Nigeria,* sometime in 1988. Its title reflected Babangida's ambition as Nigeria's eighth ruler in its 25 years of independence. In his foreword to the book, Tunji Olagunju, one of the president's closest friends and his Minister of National Planning, noted that "a new political and economic thinking, based on a recognition of the realities of our times, runs through the book."[1]

New thinking. An apt phrase. Babangida used every opportunity to demonstrate his love for new thinking on the myriads of political, economic and social problems that hobbled the country since independence. He openly shopped for them. He encouraged dialogues between his administration and the people - as could be seen in the IMF and the foreign policy debates - to mine new thinking on some of the critical problems that faced the country. After all, he made it clear from his very first day in office that his administration laid no claims to 'a monopoly of wisdom.'

Babangida made no pretences about his ambition to be different and to be seen to be different – in style and substance – from the two civilians and the five military men who ruled the country before him. Within the first few weeks of his takeover, Babangida was on a roll as a man with a sense of historical mission. The sheer breadth of his innovative steps left few, if any, in any doubts that he came into office with the firm belief that by the time he was through with his political, economic and social transformation programmes, Nigeria would be a transformed new nation sporting a portrait pretty close to what the redoubtable founding fathers of the nation dreamt of at independence on October 1, 1960.

It is difficult not to give Babangida due credits for his dreams and his ambitions, even if he did not quite realise them and eventually became a victim of the unintended consequences of his most costly mistake, the annulment of the June 12, 1993 presidential election. The early months of his administration raised a lot of hope in his capacity to make the nation rise from the ashes of its past failures. He came into office with a blueprint for some radical and dramatic changes he believed the country needed to turn its fortunes around. It was a tall ambition but the man had the courage of his own conviction and an eye on his place in the political history of a potentially great nation flapping about in the murk of its own failures. He came that he might make a difference. In his inaugural broadcast justifying his coup, Babangida invited Nigerians to note that

...this country has had since independence a history mixed with turbulence and fortune. We have witnessed our rise to greatness, followed by a decline to the state of a bewildered nation. Our human potentials have been neglected, our natural resources put to waste.

He was not short of new thinking; he was not afraid of experimenting with them and he did not fear to tread where the angels could only tiptoe. With his bulging basket of new thinking, Babangida sought to show that if anyone could remake Nigeria and put it on a steady course of greatness, he was the man thrust on the nation's political stage by providence. He took the road not yet travelled in the economic, political and social re-engineering of the country. For him, it would not be, to use the current politically correct parlance, *business as usual*. He did not want to merely patch up the cracks on the country's political walls or cosmetically tinker with its economic and social problems. He was bent on a radical transformation of the nation on all fronts - to primarily salvage "our battered economy (and) bring about a new political culture" but more fundamentally, to make Nigeria the country of everyone's fervent dreams of what a great and in the words of the Second National Development Plan, a just and egalitarian country should be.

The changes came fast and even furious, as if he was trying to make up for the nation's lost time. He conceived each dramatic change as a new pillar in his urgent task of constructing his new Nigeria. All Nigerian leaders before him shared a poor reputation for economic management. Babangida brought a new thinking into the management of the economy by tackling its defective structural base. His structural adjustment programme, SAP, was the main plank of his economic transformation programme. SAP was primarily intended "to restructure and diversify the productive base of the economy in order to reduce dependence on the oil sector and imports." Although its template belonged to the IMF and the World Bank, Babangida believed he could use it to transform the Nigerian economy. In the end, the programme sunk his hope and the accolades attesting to his economic husbandry did not follow.

Nigeria is cursed with complex political problems complicated by the colonial structure of its federation and the nature of its federalism. These are no mean problems. The country had been searching through its many constitutions for the ideal political system for its socio-political peculiarities long before independence from British colonial rule. Babangida continued with the search through his Political Bureau because "our task is to bring about a new political culture which, like a veritable fountain head, would bring forth a stable, strong and dynamic economy."

The search for that new political culture led Babangida to do what no one before him had done on the political front. He founded, funded and imposed a two-party system on the country. The National Republican Convention, NRC, was "a little to the right;" and the Social Democratic Party, SDP, was "a little to the left" of the political spectrum. The leftists had a platform in one and the rightists in the other. Neat and simple.

Babangida had a perfectly good explanation for this novelty in the political history of Nigeria. He wanted to wrest the control of political parties from the rich, also known less endearingly as 'Moneybags' and thus make all Nigerians "equal founders and equal joiners" of each party. The two-party system initially caused some disquiet for fear that it would polarise the country along its well-known fault line of religious divide with Christians flocking into one party and Muslims into the other. Events later proved Babangida right. The two-party system was a sensible solution to the centrifugal tendencies inherent in the politics of the country. It failed, of course, to make the Moneybags irrelevant voices in our national politics. It did no more than romanticise political equality at a great expense to the nature and the philosophy of party politics.

In his eight years in power, Babangida, like the hurricane, tried to pull down every tree that stood in his path. He left almost nothing untouched. His 1988 civil service reform, the first such major reform since independence, took the axe to the trunk of the civil service. Under that reform, with which top technocrats vehemently disagreed, permanent secretaries were re-designated director-generals and denied their professional status as accounting officers of their ministries. That responsibility was given to ministers and commissioners. Its implication was the politicisation of the civil service.

Babangida did, or attempted to do, titanic things to create the Babangida Era that would be the veritable watershed in the history of Nigeria. It did not quite work out that way for him. He left office eight years later not in a blaze of glory but in circumstances that put the Babangida mystique through the shredder. Fate left him holding the short end of the stick and has problems with assigning him an honoured place he sought and worked for in the nation's political history.

His former colleagues as well as his friends and political associates in the armed forces generally spoke well of him. Some of them believed that Babangida, more than anyone else, was personally equipped to succeed as the best leader Nigeria had at least up to that point in its political history. He was a meticulous planner and was always one step ahead of others. He was reputedly the only man who knew where he would be over a given period of time. He was a tough military man who was not afraid of taking decisions and acting on them, even if, as the saying goes, the heavens would fall. He had all he needed to succeed and become the permanent giant on the nation's political stage - something he craved for. But he blew it – with serious consequences for all he stood for, all that he sought to accomplish, his new portrait of the country and the country itself. His failure to rise up to the higher and critical dynamics of a country in transition hobbled the country itself and unravelled his contributions to its development.

What went wrong? Why did the man who showed so much promise as a ruler end his days in power as a villain and the cruel victim of his own sense of mission in government? There can be no easy answers. If man is the architect of his fortune or misfortune, Babangida was the architect of his. If all men are fettered by the cruel twist of fate, Babangida was too. Indeed, in his case, the cruel twist of ironies is truly cruel. He loved new thinking and welcomed radical departures from old mores. He was ever willing to put new ideas to work. But no new thinking served him for long. His prosecution of new thinking was patchy and he showed remarkable capacity not to finish what he started. He dribbled the country with his endless and abrupt changes in the transition programme. He was not nicknamed Maradona for nothing. Indeed, it is said today that he dribbled himself into political irrelevance.

Part of the problem was that he craved public applause and approval so much that he was always willing to reverse himself if that would guarantee him the sound of even an isolated hand clapping. His major policies became victims of this attitude of mind, hence the frequent shuffles that became the destabilising hallmark of his administration.

A leader is often a lonely man; alone with his thoughts and alone in his decisions and alone with the consequences of his actions and decisions. In his loneliness, a leader must hold on tightly to his principles. They are his lifebuoy in the choppy seas of competing political and other interests. Babangida often failed to appreciate this elementary fact of power. He willingly sacrificed principles for expedience.

He loved motion and movement and made governance a series of shock treatments. The problem was that he saw these as ends in themselves rather than as means to some well-defined ends.

The very things he cherished – his courage, his ambition, his capacity for friendship – and his willingness to gamble, even when a gamble was patently an inadvisable choice, humbled Babangida. His courage failed him when he needed it most – to walk out on power.

The economy and politics were the two critical pillars on which Babangida sought to erect the portrait of a new Nigeria. Both pillars failed to sustain his dreams. By the time the structural adjustment programme ran its course in about two years, its unfortunate acronym of SAP had acquired a different and sinister meaning as a new definition of an economic management policy that sapped the nation and left its people in a worse economic situation. The structural adjustment programme is today remembered for one thing: the pains it visited on the country and its people. His two-party system did not survive him and the country reverted to the multiplicity of mushroom parties in the name of democratic pluralism.

The failure of the structural adjustment programme, the very fundamental plank of his economic development programme, might have been the triumph of politics but the fault must be laid squarely at Babangida's door. The so-called SAP riots of 1989 frightened him. But more importantly, he failed to treat the programme as a process without a limit rather than as a shock treatment with a limited end. He needed to stick to the core of the programme but reserved the right and the liberty to tinker with the means based on his experience in prosecuting it. Given its philosophy, the success of the structural adjustment programme would have had a lasting salutary effect on the development of the economy as well as its management by successive administrations.

Babangida regarded political power, the most intoxicating and the most dangerous aphrodisiac on earth, as a game. He derived a near-infantile joy from playing this very deceptive game. The game got the better of him and robbed him of the hardheaded determination he needed for the prosecution of his programmes. In the end, none of his many truly innovative programmes was prosecuted to a logical conclusion. He more or less sabotaged them with his constant reversals. He dismantled many of them before he left office - SAP, DFRRI and MAMSER, among others.

Babangida made some fundamental mistakes of the head and of the heart. Everyone born of a woman does, if that is a good excuse for human foibles and failures. All fundamental mistakes exact some stiff prices from those who make them. Babangida's most fundamental political mistake was, of course, June 12. The annulment of the presidential election threw pails of black paint on his portrait of a new Nigeria. The ship of his greatness foundered on the rocks of June 12. June 12 sabotaged him and erected a permanent wall between him and greatness. And because of June 12, history is compelled to take an unkindly view of Babangida's place in the political history of Nigeria.

Is it fair to judge Babangida, what he did and what he stood for, by this one admittedly heavy political miscalculation? The least that can be said is that however fair the writers of Nigerian history may wish to be to Babangida, only the truly naïve would fail to recognise that June 12 was more a careless mistake by a man who failed to recognise that with that election, that finest hour he craved for had come. June 12 was a spectacular culmination of Babangida's own incredible capacity for self-sabotage.

June 12 was larger than the late Moshood Abiola who won the election but lost the chance to become president. June 12 was the watershed in the politics of Nigeria. Yet the man who brought the country to that desirable end failed to see it for what it was – his and the nation's date with history. June 12 was the watershed whose time had come. The genie was out of the bag. Nothing could put it back.

Had Babangida recognised this, his courage would have sustained him – and the June 12, 1993 presidential election, acknowledged locally and internationally as the freest and the fairest election ever conducted in the country so far would remain his one true legacy and ultimate triumph. But, and this is another cruel irony, June 12 achieved what it set out to achieve without Babangida. Six years after the election was annulled, June 12 became the sole determinant of power configuration in the country. It shifted political power from the north to the south in 1999.

Abiola did not become president. His loss has become his greatest gain. He made June 12 possible. He made power shift possible. Few men have gained so much from their losses.

The real loser in the June 12 debacle was Babangida. His sabotage of June 12 made June 12 possible. He lost the right to claim it as the triumph of his political engineering. It was not part of his political calculation. It was a triumph of the accident of politics.

References

Chapter Four

1. Interview with Newswatch magazine, published September 28, 1992.
2. Muffett, D.J.M, *Let the Truth Be Told,* Page 168
3. Obasanjo, Olusegun, *Nzeogwu*, Page 83
4. *Nzeogwu* Page 83
5. *Ibid.,* page 83
6. *Interview with Newswatch* magazine.
7. *Ibid,* Interview with Newswatch magazine published November 2, 1992.
8. *Ibid*, Page
9. Obasanjo, Olusegun, *Ibid*, Page
10. *ibid* Page 79
11. *ibid* Page...
12. *The Nigerian Civil War* by John de St Jorre (Hodder and Stoughton, 1972) Page 44
13. *ibid*
14. Ibid, Page 42
15. Elaigwu, Isawa J., *Gowon*, page 52
16. Danjuma: Interview with Newswatch, November 2, 1992
17. Danjuma: Interview with Newswatch.
18. *Newswatch,*
19. *Gowon,* Page 65

Chapter Five

1. *Gowon*, Page 65

2. *Gowon,* Page 69

3. Babangida, Maryam: *The Home Front,* Fountain Publications, 1988, Page 22.

Chapter Six

1. Special issue of *The Nigeria Standard* newspaper published by Benue-Plateau State Printing and Publishing Corporation, Jos

2. *The Nigeria Standard,* October 20, 1974

3. ibid

4. ibid

5. Lindsay Barrett: *Danjuma, The Making of a General,* Page 81

6. *Gowon*, Page 228

Chapter Seven

1. Hausa for *Is that you?*

2. Nka yi wasa, Hausa for *If you play Wayo* is pidgin for trick

3. *Newswatch*, January 8, 1990. Page 20

4. *Newswatch,* August 22, 1988 Page 9

5. *Suya* is Hausa for shish kebab

6. *Gowon*, Page 257

7. *Gowon*, Pp 262-263

8. *Newswatch,* January 87, 1990, page 20

9. *Ibid*

10. Babangida's address at the graduation ceremony of the institute, October 26, 1985

11. Babangida's address at the graduation ceremony of the institute, October 22, 1988

12. *Newswatch,* November 27, 1989, Page 17

Chapter Eight

1. Shagari's inaugural broadcast, October 1, 1979

2. *West Africa* magazine, November 21, 1983

3. *Rise and Fall of the Second Republic,* Page 221

4. Shagari: World Press Conference, January 8, 1980

5. *The Rise and Fall of the Second Republic,* Page 154

6. Brigadier Sani Abacha's coup broadcast, December 31, 1983

7. ibid

8. Shagari's budget speech to the National Assembly, January, 1981.

9. *The Rise and Fall of the Second Republic,* Page 113

10. Ray Ekpu, *The Last Days of Shagari, Newswatch,* May 20, 1985

11. Shagari, Shehu, *Beckoned to Serve*, Heinemann Educational Books Plc., 2001, page 457

12. *Newswatch*

13. Shagari, Shehu, *Beckoned to Serve*, Heinemann Educational Books (Nigeria) Plc., 2001 pages 457-458

Chapter Nine

1. S.G. Ikoku: *Nigeria's Fourth Coup D'etat, Options for Nationhood,* (Fourth Dimension Publishers), 1985, Page 1.

2. *Ibid* Page 4

3   See below

4   See below

5   See below

6   All quotes here taken from Buhari's first broadcast reproduced in *Major-General Muhammadu Buhari, Nigeria's Seventh Head of State,* published by the Federal Ministry of Information, May, 1984.

7   *Ibid,* Page 11

8   *Ibid,* Page 6

9   Edwin Madunagu: *The Buhari administration in history, The Guardian,* Nov. 28, 1985

10 *Daily Times* editorial, January 11, 1984

11 Interview with *Guardian*, January 22, 1984

12 Buhari's address to the Diplomatic Corps, January 4, 1984

13 Major-General Muhammdu Buhari: World Press Conference, January 5, 1984

14 Buhari: Interview with FRCN, Kaduna, in *The Punch,* July 25, 1985

15 Buhari: New Year broadcast, January 1, 1984

16 Quoted by Taiwo Obe, *The Guardian*, September 1, 1985

17 Federal Republic of Nigeria Official Gazette, No. 15, Vol 71, March 19, 1984, Page A33

18 *Ibid,* Page A35

19 *The Nigerian Journal of Contemporary Law,* Vol. 1 No. 2 of December, 1970, Page 287

20 *The Federal Military Government (Supremacy and Enforcement of Powers) Decree 1984,* in Supplement to Official Gazette Extraordinary No.30, Vol. 71, 18th April, 1984

References

21 *Supplement to Official Gazette Extraordinary No. 18, Vol. 71, 4th April, 1984 - Part A*

22 *Sunday Tribune*, February 24, 1985

23 T.O. Elias: *Nigerian Press Law* (University of Lagos/Evans Brothers), 1969, Page 6.

24 *Ibid*, Page 7

25 Supplement to Official Gazette No. 13, Vol.63, 11th March, 1976, Page A-53

26 Gen. Olusegun Obasanjo: Address to representatives of the mass media, September 18, 1978, pp 4, 5 and 6

27 *The Guardian*, Sunday, May 5, 1985; Page 4

28 *Ibid*

29 Buhari's interview with VOA, *The Guardian,* Sunday, May 5, 1985

30 *The Nigerian Tribune,* August 30, 1985

31 *Newswatch*, September 9, 1985

Chapter Ten

1 *Time*, September 9, 1985, page 33

2 Abacha, Coup Broadcast

3 Babangida, budget speech, December 31, 1985

4 Buhari, Muhammadu, *Moments of Truth*, Federal Ministry of Information, page 36

5 Babangida, maiden broadcast, August 27, 1985

6 *Ibid*

7 Babangida, Independence Broadcast, October 1, 1985

8 *Business Week,* September 9, 1985, Page 33

9   Babangida, Ibrahim, October 1 broadcast, 1985

10 Babangida, October 1, 1985

11 Babangida: October 1, 1985 broadcast

12 *Daily Times,* December 4, 1985, page 5

13 Toyin Falola and Julius Ihonvbere: *The Rise and Fall of Nigeria's Second Republic, 1979-84,* Page 83

14 *Muhammadu Buhari, Nigeria's Seventh Head of State,* Federal Department of Information, Lagos, P. 34

15 Falola and Ihonvbere, *Ibid,* Page 84

16 Babangida: Address at a seminar Economic Recovery, Eko Hotel, Lagos; September 24, 1985

17 Babangida: Address at swearing in of ministers, September 12, 1985

18 *Business Concord* editorial, September 13, 1985

19 *The Triumph,* October 13, 1985

20 *New Nigerian,* October 15, 1985

21 *National Concord,* October 7, 1985

22 *The Washington Post*

23 Babangida: 1986 budget speech

24 *Ibid*

25 Babangida: Speech at NIIA Patron's Dinner; *Sunday Times,* December 13, 1987

26 *New Nigerian,* October 15, 1985

27 Babangida, 1986 budget speech

28 *Newswatch,* August 8, 1988

References

29 Buhari: interview with FRCN, Kaduna, July 25, 1985; quoted in *Newswatch* of August 8, 1988

30 Babangida: 3rd anniversary broadcast, August 27, 1988

31 Babangida: 1986 budget speech

32 *Newswatch,* August 8, 1988

33 *Ibid*

34 Babangida: Broadcast, June 26, 1986

35 *Ibid*

36 Gen. Olusegun Obasanjo, *Newswatch,* December 4, 1987

37 *Adjustment in Africa,* Husain & Faruqee,

38 *International Herald Tribune,* quoted by *National Concord,* March 25, 1987

39 *The Punch,* July 23, 1987

40 *National Concord,* March 25, 1987

41 Isaac Aluko-Olokun, Philip, et al

42 *Ibid*

43 *Ibid*

44 *Newswatch,* September 5, 1988

45 *National Concord* editorial, July 2, 1986

46 *Lagos News* July 3-10, front page comment

47 *The Nigerian Tribune* editorial, July 8, 1986

48 *The Lagos News, ibid*

49 Ishrat, et al, pp 225-6

50 *National Concord,* August 27, 1987

51 *Newswatch,* October 5, 1987, page 63

52 *Newswatch,* September 4, 1987, Page 47

53 Babangida, Oxbridge annual spring lecture, March 16, 1989

54 Adedotun Philips & Eddy Ndekwu, editors: *Structural Adjustment Programme in a Developing Economy: The Case of Nigeria,* NISER, Ibadan, Page 239

55 *Newswatch,* December 4, 1987, Pages 18 and 19

56 *Newswatch,* September 5, 1988

57 Babangida, speech at NIIA annual patron's dinner, *Sunday Times,* December 13, 1987

58 *Newswatch,* September 5, 1988

59 *Newswatch,* August 29, 1988, Page 19

60 Babangida, Oxbridge lectures, *ibid*

61 Babangida: Address to the inaugural meeting of the Armed Forces Consultative Assembly, June 6, 1989

62 *Ibid*

63 *Ibid*

64 *The African Guardian,* September 4, 1989

65 *The Guardian,* Editorial, August 27, 1990

66 *Adjustment in Africa,* Husain & Faruqee, page 245

67 *Ibid* page 248

68 *Ibid,* Page 246

Chapter Thirteen

[1] *Sunday Times*, January 29, 1984, page 11

[2] Babangida: Inauguration of Political Bureau, January 13, 1986

[3] *Ibid*

[4] *Ibid*

[5] *Ibid*

[6] *Ibid*

[7] *Newswatch*

[8] *Ibid*

[9] CDC report

[10] Political bureau report

[11] Political bureau report

[12] Babangida: Broadcast, July 1, 1987

[13] Babangida: Nation-wide broadcast, July 1, 1987

[14] *Ibid*

[15] Babangida: broadcast to the nation, July 1, 1987

[16] Bureau report

[17] *Newswatch*, April 13, 1987, page 21

[18] Babangida: Address to the Constitution Review Committee, September 7, 1987

[19] *Newswatch,* September 15, 1988

[20] IBB: Inaugural address to the CRC, September 7, 1987.

[21] *Ibid*

[22] Babangida: Nation-wide broadcast, September 23, 1987

[23] *Newswatch*, August 29, 1988

[24] Text of the summary of the CRC report

[25] Babangida: Address at the inauguration of CA, Abuja, May 11, 1988

[26] *The Nigerian Tribune,* August 8, 1989 (Editorial).

[27] *Newswatch,* April 17, 1989, page 18

[28] *Ibid*

[29] Babangida: Broadcast to the nation, May 3, 1989

[30] *Ibid*

[31] *Ibid*

[32] Babangida: address to the nation, May 3, 1989

[33] *Newswatch,* March 27, 1989, page 10

[34] Babangida: Speech at the acceptance ceremony of the draft constitution, April 5, 1989

[35] *Newswatch,* March 13, 1989, page 21

[36] *Ibid*

[37] *Newswatch,* March 20, 1989, page 24

[38] *Newswatch,* October 23, 1989, page 17

[39] *Ibid*

[40] *Ibid*

[41] *Ibid*

[42] *Ibid*

43. Ray Ekpu, *Newswatch,* August 13, 1990

Chapter Fourteen

1. *Newswatch,* September 17, 1990, page 19

2. *Newswatch,* September 22, 1990

3. *The Guardian,* October 3, 1990

4. Babangida, budget speech, January 1, 1991

5. *The Guardian,* March 28, 1991, page 1

6. Nwosu, Henry, *Laying the Foundation for Nigeria's Democracy*, Macmillan, 2008, page 123

7. Nwosu, Henry, *ibid,* page 124

8. *Newswatch,* September 16, 1991, page 18

9. *Newswatch,* November 25, 1991, page 25

10. Babangida: 1992 budget broadcast

11. *The Punch,* December 21, 1991, pages 20-21

12. *Ibid*

13. *Ibid*

14. *The Guardian,* Editorial, December 30, 1991, page 14

15. Babangida: 1992 budget broadcast

16. Trevor Clark: *A Right Honourable Gentleman: The life and Times of Alhaji Sir Abubakar Tafawa Balewa,* page 610

17. J. Isawa Elaigwu: *Gowon: The Biography of a Soldier-Statesman,* Ibadan, 1985, page 176

18. Political bureau report

19 Babangida: broadcast to the nation, July 1, 1987

20 *The Economist,* March 28, 1992, page 57

21 Babangida: text of speech announcing the acceptance of the provisional population figures by the AFRC, March 19, 1992

22 *The Guardian,* April 5, 1992, page A7

23 *Daily Times,* April 1, 1992

24 Babangida: 1992 budget speech

Chapter Fifteen

1   Ibrahim Babangida, address to Armed Forces Consultative Assembly, June 5, 1989

2   Ibrahim Babangida, Address to the Nation on the Transition Programme to civil Rule, July 1, 1987

3   *The Guardian*, March 1, 1991, pages 1-2

4   *New Nigerian* (editorial) May 7, 1991

5   *Newswatch*, April 22, 1991, pages 13-22

6   *Newswatch, ibid*

7   *Newswatch, ibid*

8   *Newswatch, ibid*

9   *Newswatch, ibid*

10 *Newswatch*, October 5, 1992, pages 29-30

11 *Newswatch, ibid*

12 Ibrahim Babangida's budget speech, December 31, 1985

13 Ibrahim Babangida, *ibid*

References

14 Ibrahim Babangida, Goodwill message on the second anniversary of DFRRI, February 7, 1988

15 Tijjani, Aminu & Williams, David, *Shehu Shagari: My Vision of Nigeria*, Frank Cass, 1981, page 221

16 Tijjani, Aminu & Williams, David, *ibid.*, page 221

17 Tijjani, Aminu & Williams, David, *ibid.*, page 222

18 Tijjani, Aminu & Williams, David, *ibid.*, page 220

19 *National Concord*, December 4, 1985

20 Babangida: Speech at NIPSS, October 26, 1985

21 Babangida: Speech at a seminar on integrated rural development, *Citizen*, Oct. 15, 1990

22 Babangida: Speech at NIPSS, October 28, 1986

24 Koinyan, Larry, *National Policy on Integrated Rural Development, National Concord*, September 5, 1991, page 11

25 Babangida, Ibrahim, 1986 budget speech

26 *Hotline,* December 14-27, 1987

27 Ezekiel Akiga, quoted in *Newswatch*, March 28, 1988, page 20

28 *Ibid,* page 17

29 *Newswatch,* March 28, 1988, page 20

30 *Ibid*

31 *Newswatch*, September 4, 1989, page 49

32 *Newswatch*, March 28, 1988, page 20

33 *West Africa*, September 12-18, 1988, page 1664

Chapter Sixteen

1. Gambari, Ibrahim A., *Nigeria at Home and Abroad, Selected Speeches*, edited by Thomas Okpaku, Chaneta International Publisher, 2007, page 137

2. Oyelakin, Oladejo L.O., *The Nigerian Foreign Service Administration*, ICI (Directory Publishers) Ltd, 1989, pages 231-232

3. Oyelakin, Oladejo, L.O., *ibid.*, page 228

4. Oyelakin, Oladejo L.O., *ibid.*, page 228

5. Oyelakin, Oladejo L.O. *ibid.*, page 230

6. Odi Chukwuma, E., *Ibrahim Babangida's Foreign Policy Triumphs*, Bissau Investment Ventures Ltd., 1991, page 15

7. *Newswatch*, August 4, 1986, page 21

8. *Newswatch, ibid.*, page 21

9. *Newswatch*, August 4, 1986, page 20

10. *Daily Times*, August 4, 1993, page 1

11. *Daily Times*, December 12, 1986, page 13

12. *Vanguard*, July 9, 1987, pages 1 & 8

13. *Daily Champion*, December 24, 1990, page 17

14. *Sunday Times*, October 7, 1990, pages 13-14

15. *New Nigerian*, November 9, 1990, page 6

16. *New Nigerian*, July 6, 1987, page 6

17. Oyelakin Oladejo, L.O. *ibid.*, page 238

18. *Daily Champion*, December 15, 1988, page 9

19. *The Nigerian Economist*, August 16, 1993

20. Oyelakin, Oladejo L.O., *ibid.*, page 238

21. *Daily Times,* December 5, 1985, page 5

22. *Newswatch,* August 4, 1986, pp 19-21

23. *Newswatch, ibid.,* page 19

Chapter Seventeen

1. Wole Soyinka quoted by *African Concord*, August 22, 1988, page 24

2. *Newswatch,* February 24, 1986, page 15

3. *The Guardian,* October 22, 1986, pages 1&5

4. *The Guardian*, September 24, 1985, pages 1 & 2

5. *New Nigerian*, May 9, 1986, page 2

6. *Ibid*

7. *Newswatch*, June 16, 1986, page 33

8. *National Concord*, December 19, 1987, page 1

9. *Sunday Times*, June 23, 1986, page 4

10. *Newswatch*, March 14, 1988, page 15

11. *Newswatch, ibid.*, page 15

12. *Newswatch, ibid.*, page 14

13. *Newswatch, ibid.*, page 14

14. *New Nigerian*, September 13, 1985, page 9

15. *Daily Sketch,* August 11, 1992, page 1

16. *Citizen,* August 24, 1992, page 21

17. *The Nigerian Herald*, August 30, 1988, page 2

Chapter Eighteen

1. Nwosu, H.N., *Laying the Foundation for Nigeria's Democracy,* Macmillan, 2008, page 74

2. Political Bureau Report, page 225

3. *Newswatch,* March 23, 1992, page 54

4. *Daily Times,* April 1, 1992, page 1

5. *Citizen,* August 24, 1992

6. Olagunju, Tunji, *et al, Transition to Democracy in Nigeria,* Safari Books, 1993, page 245

7. Nwosu, H.N., *Laying the Foundation for Nigeria's Democracy,* Macmillan, 2008, page 210

8. Babangida, broadcast to the nation, November 17, 1992

9. *Newswatch,* November 23, 1992

10. *Newswatch,* November 2, 1991

11. *Newswatch,* November 23, 1992

12. Nwosu, H.N. *op cit.,* page 248

13. Omoruyi, Omo, *The Tale of June 12,* Press Alliance Network Ltd., 1999, page 26

14. Omoruyi, Omo, *ibid,* page 155

15. Omoruyi, Omo, *ibid.,* page 163

Epilogue

1. *Portrait of A New Nigeria,* Precision Press, 1988, page 1

Index

A

Abacha, Sani, 46, 84, 173, 400, 401, 413
Abdullahi, Ango, 167, 361
Abiola, Moshood, 122, 165, 196, 352, 388, 389, 390, 391, 392, 393, 395, 396, 397, 399, 407, 408
Abisoye, Abisoye, 43, 137, 218, 362
Abubakar, Abdulsalami, xii, 13, 14, 15, 17, 19, 20, 21, 25, 30, 35, 38, 42, 43, 79, 103, 122, 138, 188, 204, 213, 221, 224, 235, 352, 353, 364, 419
Abuja, ii, xi, 20, 27, 31, 125, 161, 169, 170, 171, 216, 273, 275, 294, 295, 339, 354, 391, 392, 394, 395, 418
Aburi, Ghana, 93
Academic Staff Union of Universities, ASUU, 231, 365
accord concordiale, 158, 159
Adedeji, Adebayo, 342
Ademola, Adetokunbo, 296, 298
Ademoyega, Adewale, 78, 80
Adibe, Jideofor, xii
Adonis & Abbey Publishers, x, xii
Africa Prize for Leadership for Sustainable End to Hunger, 321
Agbese, Dan, ii, iii, vii, viii, x, 355
Agricultural Credit Guarantee Scheme, 312
Aguda, Akinola, 120, 125, 167, 170, 171, 202
Aguiyi-Ironsi, J.T.U., 20, 42, 74, 77, 79, 80, 81, 82, 84, 85, 87, 89, 90, 91, 93, 130, 174

Ahmadu Bello University, Zaria, 83, 358, 361, 367, 368
Aikhomu, Augustus, 175, 235, 267, 279, 284, 287, 293, 303, 320, 357, 366, 368, 386, 394, 397, 398, 400
Akilu, Haliru, x, 104, 190, 195, 204, 357
Akinjide, Richard, 157, 159
Akinrinade, Alani, 3, 43, 143
Akintola, Samuel Ladoke, 62, 79
Akinyemi, Bolaji, 237, 330, 341, 343, 344, 346, 353
Akpamgbo, Clement, 391, 395, 398
Aku, Aper, 112
Alele-Williams, Grace, 211
Ali, Ahmadu, 361
Aluko, Sam, 239, 241, 298, 319, 415
American Peace Corps, 344
Aminu, Jibril, 22, 107, 158, 366, 367, 421
Ankrah, Joseph, 92, 93
Anti-SAP riots, 242, 244
Anyaoku, Emeka, 333
Armed Forces Consultative Assembly, 242, 351, 358, 369, 375, 416, 420
Armed Forces of the Federal Republic of Nigeria, 79
Asika, Asika, 94
Aso Rock Villa, Abuja, 27
Aso Rock, Abuja, xi, 289, 402
Association for Better Nigeria, ABN, 378, 391
Australia, 23, 46, 342
Awolowo, Obafemi, 58, 61, 92, 120, 145, 146, 157, 158, 159, 161, 165, 210, 221, 228, 265, 266, 267, 297, 367
Ayuba, Tanko, 1, 188, 196, 198

Azikiwe, Nnamdi, 160, 278, 377

B

Badamasi, Muhammadu, xi, 5, 11, 19, 43, 193, 198, 213, 401, 402
Balewa, Tafawa, 42, 62, 77, 79, 82, 158, 209, 221, 329, 395, 419
Bali, Domkat, 73, 86, 134, 167, 216, 218
Bamali, Nuhu, xii
Barewa Old Boys Association, 39
Bayero, Ado, 211
Benue Province, 20, 58
Better Life for Rural Women Programme,, 103
Better Life for the Rural African Woman programme, 320
Bitiyong, Musa, 215, 216
Block Buster, 21, 23
Bonny Camp, 4, 127, 128, 129, 130, 131, 133, 143, 188, 196, 197, 198
Boutrous-Ghali, Boutros, 333
Bretton Woods institutions, 238
Brigade of Guards, 115, 117, 118, 133, 134
Broadcasting Corporation of Northern Nigeria, 58
Buhari, Mohammadu, 5, 175, 188, 208, 210, 213, 263

C

Captain Cruickshank,, 46
Chijuka, Fred, 372
Ciroma, Adamu, 165, 383, 393
Citizen newsmagazine, 139
Code of Conduct Bureau, National, 276
Coker Commission, 266
Cokshine, Martin, 46
Command and Staff College, Jaji, 104, 145, 149, 273, 375

Commonwealth Eminent Persons Group, 332
Commonwealth Games in Canada, 1954, 78
Concert of Medium Powers, 341, 342
Constituent Assembly, 266, 272, 274, 277, 278
Constitution Drafting Committee, CDC, 265, 267

D

Daboh, Godwin, 112
Dada, Garba, 29, 35, 44, 86
Danjuma, Theophilus Yakubu, 2, 4, 42, 77, 82, 84, 86, 94, 97, 103, 116, 121, 124, 125, 128, 129, 130, 131, 133, 134, 135, 136, 141, 143, 145, 150, 177, 385, 409, 410
Dasuki, Ibrahim, 288, 353
Decree Number 4., 182
Defence Intelligence Agency, 206
Degedege, x
Dikko, Umaru, 174, 326
Dimka, Buka Suwa, 3, 4, 124, 126, 127, 128, 130, 131, 132, 133, 134, 135, 136, 137, 138, 139, 140, 141, 142, 143, 147, 200, 216, 218
Directorate of Food, Roads and Rural Infrastructure, DFRRI, 310
Directorate of Foods, Roads and Rural Infrastructure, DFRRI, 232, 246
Dodan Barracks, 27, 105, 107, 118, 134, 135, 136, 137, 147, 183, 210, 219, 287, 295, 371
Doe, Samuel Kanyon, 335, 337
Dogonyaro, Joshua, xii, 5, 77, 78, 102, 117, 124, 127, 128, 132, 134, 140, 141, 143, 144, 145, 146, 147, 176, 194, 195, 196, 197, 198, 199, 200, 401

Duba, Garba, xii, 14, 21, 22, 30, 33, 36, 38, 45, 47, 49, 50, 52, 55, 56, 59, 62, 82, 84, 100, 102, 103, 104, 108, 138, 217, 218
Dutch auction, 240

E

East-Central State., 94
Eastern Region, 10, 92, 93, 94, 95, 107, 296
Economic Commission for Africa, ECA,, 342
Economic Community Monitoring Group, 336
Economic Community of West African States, ECOWAS, 335
Eid El-Kabir, 193
Ejoor, Ejoor, 91
Ekpu, Ray, 181, 209, 283, 354, 355, 356, 411, 419
Elaigwu, Isawa J, x, 81, 282, 314, 409, 419
Etsu Nupe, 19, 39

F

Falae, Olu, 319
Fawehinmi, Gani, 310, 356, 357
FEDECO, 157, 273
Federal Executive Council, 121, 145, 175, 344
Field Marshall Montgomery, 99
Fifth National Development Plan, 223
First Division of the Nigerian Army, Kaduna., 42
Foreign Exchange Market, 238, 240
FRCN, 16, 118, 173, 178, 194, 287, 412, 415

G

Gambo, xii, 11, 193, 195
Gang of Five, 21, 22, 23, 29

Gbulie, Ben, 42, 96
General Rommel,, 99
Giwa, Dele, 181, 207, 354, 357
GNPP, 158, 160, 161, 270
Gomwalk, Joseph, 112, 126
Gowon, Gowon, x, 84, 89, 92, 94, 105, 109, 119, 135, 141, 143, 263
Green Revolution Programme, 162, 313
Gusau, Aliyu Mohammed, 189, 401

H

Haruna, Mohammed, x, 4, 139, 308
Hausa/Fulani, 10
Howe, Geoffrey, 210, 326

I

IBB Library, 39
Ichoghol, David, 97
Idiagbon, Tunde, 167, 170, 175, 177, 190, 199, 206, 208, 213, 222, 324
Idi-Araba, 102
Idoko, Jerome, xii, 23
Ifeajuna, Emmanuel, 78, 79
Igbos, 10, 85
Ige, Bola, 180, 181
Ikime, Obaro, 367
IMF debate, 219, 225, 226, 227
Imoudu, Michael, 361
Inienger, John Mark, xii, 97, 98, 99, 100, 101, 103, 104, 105, 139
Interim National Government, 46, 398, 399, 400
Inuwa Wushishi, Muhammadu, 9, 35, 39, 44, 96, 170
Irabo, Nduka, 395
Iyayi, Festus, 365

J

Jega, Attahiru, 368
Johnson, Mobolaji, 74, 89, 125, 312, 335, 337

Jos, ix, x, 87, 112, 125, 137, 142, 167, 169, 241, 282, 389, 410
Justice Irikefe panel, 123

K

Kano, 10, 22, 74, 81, 100, 123, 126, 149, 152, 157, 158, 161, 163, 165, 191, 211, 230, 357, 364, 372
Kennedy, John F, 165, 344
Kingibe, Baba Gana, 122, 284
Kissinger, Henry, 331
Kolade, Christopher, 131, 132, 133, 355
Kontagora, Mamman, 9, 10, 12, 16, 20, 21, 36, 102, 123, 314, 372
Kyari, Abba, 59, 84, 86, 87

L

Lagos Forum, 341, 342, 343
Lagos University Teaching Hospital, 102
Lar, Solomon, 169

M

Mabogunje, Akin, 317
Madiebo, Alex, 73, 74, 85
Madunagu, Edwin, 176, 412
Magoro, Mohammed, xii, 20, 21, 23, 34, 35, 38, 39, 43, 47, 48, 86, 131, 137, 138, 167
Maimalari, Zakari, 59, 79, 80
MAMSER, 229, 269, 276, 320, 407
Mandara, Zanna Bukar, 169
Manufacturers Association of Nigeria, 236, 242, 245
Maradona, Diego, 27, 406
Marshall Plan for Africa, 338
Maryam Babangida Drive, 9
Mass Movement for Economic Reconstruction, Social Justice and Self-Reliance,, 229

Mbadiwe, KIngsley Ozurumba, 158, 273
Mbu, Matthew, 333
Middle East, 335
Mid-West, 79, 91
Minna, xi, xvi, 6, 9, 11, 12, 13, 15, 16, 19, 22, 23, 38, 44, 56, 123, 193, 194, 195, 196, 198, 208, 394, 402
Momoh, Tony, 353, 356, 357
Muhammed, Murtala Ramat, 1, 38, 52, 84, 89, 105, 116, 117, 118, 119, 120, 121, 122, 123, 124, 125, 126, 127, 131, 132, 133, 137, 140, 141, 142, 143, 170, 186, 216, 218, 263, 265, 285, 294, 297, 329, 330

N

Naguib, Muhammed, 285
Namibia, 324, 333, 341, 347
Nasarawa State, 14, 171
Nasko, Gado, xii, 5, 20, 21, 22, 26, 30, 31, 35, 36, 37, 38, 43, 45, 50, 53, 73, 85, 87, 101, 138, 144, 167, 168, 189, 190, 191, 194, 195, 204, 213, 214, 215
Nasser, Gamal Abdel, 285, 286, 287, 340
National Advanced Party, 161
National Association of Nigerian Students, NANS,, 211, 350
National Census Board, 296
National Committee on the Creation of Gainful Employment, 302
National Council of State, 119, 120, 175, 293, 384
National Defence and Security Council, 386, 390, 394, 396
National Defence and Security Council, NDSC, 386
National Directorate of Employment, NDE, 246, 301, 302

National Economic Reconstruction Fund, 246
National Institute for Policy and Strategic Studies, Kuru, 327
National Institute for Policy and Strategic Studies, NIPSS, Kuru, 351
National Intelligence Agency, 206
National Population Commission, 276, 297
National Republican Convention, NRC,, 281, 405
National Security Organisation, 179, 190
National Universities Commission, 366
National Youth Service Corps, 345
Ndagi, Jonathan, xii, 23
Ndiomu, Charles, 218
NEPU, 22, 24, 270
Neto, Agostino, 329
New Nigerian Development Company Ltd, 23
New Political Order, 223, 263, 264
Newbreed, 184
Newswatch magazine, 201, 207, 209, 242, 283, 308, 310, 331, 354, 355, 409
Niger Province, 11, 15, 20, 123
Nigerian Agricultural and Co-operative Bank Limited, 312, 313
Nigerian Bar Association, NBA, 179, 209, 350, 364
Nigerian Defence Academy, 47, 71, 80, 107, 150, 188, 190, 372
Nigerian Military Training College, Kaduna, 38, 45
Nigerian Security Organisation, 144, 206
Nigerian-American Chamber of Commerce, 229
Non-aligned Movement, 339, 340, 341

Northern Group of Provinces, 60
Northern Peoples Congress, 34, 58
Northern Region, 10, 33, 34, 42, 57, 58, 61, 71, 74, 81, 296
NPP, 158, 159, 160, 161, 270
Nsukka, 94, 95
Nwosu, Humphrey, 279, 281, 288, 290, 390, 391, 392, 398, 419, 424
Nyako, Murtala, xii, 28, 167, 204
Nyerere, Julius, 339
Nzeogwu, Chukwuma, Kaduna, xvi, 72, 73, 74, 75, 76, 77, 78, 79, 130, 140, 287, 409
Nzeribe, Arthur, 379, 391

O

Obasanjo, Olusegun, 105, 162, 241
Ochefu, Anthony, 115, 120
Odumegwu-Ojukwu, Chukwuemeka, 74, 77, 79, 91, 142, 241
Ogaba, Pita, x
Ogbeha, Tunde, 170
Ogugbuaja, Alozie, 356
Ojokojo, Jimmy, 127
Okezie, J.O.J, 106, 107
Okigbo, Pius, 339
Okongwu, Chu, 302
Okotie-Eboh, Festus, 79
Olusanya, Olusanya, 330, 346
Olutoye, Olufemi, 116
Omoruyi, Omo, 393, 424
Onabule, Duro, 279, 394
Onitsha, 104
Onosode, Gamaliel, 233, 234
Operation Cockscrow, 61
Operation Damisa, 73
Operation Feed the Nation, 162, 312
Organisation of Islamic Countries, OIC, 271, 352
Organisation of Petroleum Exporting Countries, 164

Orkar, Gideon Gwaza, 287, 288, 372, 373, 377, 378

P

People's Liberation Party, 276
Peoples Bank of Nigeria, 246, 307, 308, 309, 310, 320
Peoples Bank of Nigeria, PBN, 246
Plateau State, 14, 112, 125, 135, 141, 148, 167, 169, 410
Progressive Parties Alliance, 160
Provincial Secondary School, Bida, xvi, 14, 19, 20, 24, 34, 115, 213
PRP, 158, 160, 161, 165, 270

Q

Queen Elizabeth II, 19, 41

R

Rawlings, Jerry, 176, 218
Reagan, Ronald, 237
Regular Officers' Special Training School, 41
Remawa, Mamman, 124
Republic of Biafra, 94
Republic of Botswana, 202
Republic of Cameroun., 136
Revenue Mobilisation Commission, 276
Revolutionary Council of the Nigerian Armed Forces, 75
Ribadu, Mohammed, 35, 46, 71
Royal Niger Company, 41
Royal Niger Constabulary, 41
Royal Nigerian Army, 38, 48, 49
Royal Nigerian Navy, 34
Royal West African Frontier Force, 41

S

Sadat, Anwar, 285

Saharawi Arab Democratic Republic, SADR, 323
Sami, Sani, xii, 21, 22, 28, 35, 38, 43, 116, 133, 134, 135, 136
Sardauna, 33, 34, 79, 82
Sardaunan Sokoto, 71
Second National Development Plan (1970-1974),, 228
Shagari, Shehu, 5, 9, 20, 142, 152, 157, 158, 159, 160, 161, 162, 164, 165, 166, 167, 168, 169, 170, 171, 174, 175, 176, 177, 179, 186, 188, 189, 203, 217, 221, 222, 226, 230, 233, 234, 238, 276, 294, 295, 297, 313, 323, 324, 325, 326, 352, 359, 411, 421
Shagaya, John, xii, 55, 56, 59, 129, 130, 131, 132, 133, 134, 136, 150, 151, 176, 196, 198, 217, 354
Shelleng, Abdullahi, 97
Shodeinde, R., 76, 77, 79
Shonekan, Ernest, 386, 394, 399, 400
Sijuade, Oba Okunade, 211
Sir Willink Commission, 58
Social Democratic Party, 122, 281, 405
Solarin, Tai, 186, 210, 307, 308, 309
South Africa, 324, 329, 332, 333, 341, 368
Southern Cadets Regiment, 41
South-South co-operation, 339
Soyinka, Wole, 210, 219, 349, 423
Sule, Yusuf Maitama, 43, 127, 166, 328
Supreme Court of Nigeria, 120, 157, 202, 274
Supreme Military Council, 1, 5, 79, 90, 93, 114, 119, 120, 124, 140, 151, 175, 195, 208, 263, 278, 284
Switzerland, 342

T

Tafida, Dalhatu Sarki, 170
Taiwo, Ibrahim A, 35, 108, 115, 116, 120, 121, 137, 412
Tanzania, 59, 339
Taylor, Charles, 335, 337
Technical Aid Corps, TAC, 344
Technical Committee on Privatisation and Commercialisation, 235
Tofa, Bashir, 389, 390, 393, 397
Togun, A.K., 127, 130, 355, 357
Tolbert, William R, 335

U

Udoji, Jerome, 111
Ugokwe, Christopher, 55, 62, 71, 72, 133
Ukiwe, Okoh Ebitu, 208, 311, 344, 353, 354, 355, 356
Umar, Dangiwa, xii, 20, 124, 188, 204, 235, 364
Umezeoke, Edwin, 159
Umuahia, 99, 101, 103, 106, 107, 138
Union of Soviet Socialist Republics, USSR, 333
United Africa Company Plc, 386
United Middle Belt Congress, 58
Unity Party of Nigeria, 145, 157, 180
University of Ibadan, 25, 78, 151, 362, 367
UPN, 145, 157, 158, 159, 160, 161, 180, 270

Urban Mass Transit, 301, 305, 320
Uzala, 98

V

Vatsa, Mamman, 21, 22, 35, 36, 38, 98, 138, 152, 213, 214, 215, 216, 217, 218, 358
Victoria Island, Lagos, 4, 127, 128
Voice of America, 186

W

Wayas, Joseph, 159
West African Frontier Force, 41
Western Sahara, 323
Wey, Akinwale, 79, 89, 91
Wilmot, Patrick, 368
World Bank, 224, 232, 237, 238, 240, 245, 340, 404
Wya, Abdul, 1, 2, 73, 105, 140

Y

Yar'Adua, Shehu Musa, 95, 109, 115, 116, 120, 121, 123, 124, 137, 174, 292, 383, 393, 395
Yugoslavia, 340, 342, 347

Z

Zimbabwe., 342
Zungeru, 9

To borrow a hackneyed phrase, Nigeria has had a *chequered political history* before and since independence from British colonial rule on October 1, 1960. Two sets of actors – the civilian politicians and the military politicians - have been on the national political stage since January 15, 1966. General Ibrahim Badamasi Babangida was one of them. In his eight years in power as president, or perhaps more correctly as *military president*, he affected the course of Nigeria's events, for better or for worse, in a way that few, if any, before him did. It is not possible to tell Nigeria's story without Babangida's part in it.

The book is the story of **IBB**, the little orphan from Minna, Niger State and his meticulous rise to the top of his profession and the leadership of his country. Perhaps, more importantly, it is the story of Nigeria, its post-independence politics and power, told from the perspective of the actions and decisions of one of the main actors on the country's political stage. The events that shaped the Babangida era did not begin on August 27, 1985, the day he staged a palace coup against General Muhammadu Buhari. They began long before that. This book is the definitive story of the military, politics and power in Nigeria.

Dan Agbese holds degrees in mass communications and journalism from the University of Lagos and Columbia University, New York, respectively. He is a former editor of *The Nigeria Standard*, the *New Nigerian* as well as former general manager of *Radio Benue*. Agbese was one of the founders of the trail-blazing weekly newsmagazine in Nigeria, *Newswatch*. He was until April 2010 the Editor-in-Chief of the magazine. He is the author of several acclaimed books, including *Nigeria their Nigeria, Fellow Nigerians, The Reporter's Companion, Style: A Guide to Good Writing* and *The Columnist's Companion: The Art and Craft of Column Writing*.

Agbese is also a highly-regarded newspaper columnist.

www.ingramcontent.com/pod-product-compliance
Lightning Source LLC
Chambersburg PA
CBHW070057020526
44112CB00034B/1418